CONTEMPORARY PERENNIALS

THE MACMILLAN COMPANY
NEW YORK • CHICAGO
DALLAS • ATLANTA • SAN FRANCISCO
LONDON • MANILA

IN CANADA
BRETT-MACMILLAN LTD.
GALT, ONTARIO

CONTEMPORARY PERENNIALS

RODERICK W. CUMMING
AND
ROBERT E. LEE

With Drawings by
Allianora Rosse

NEW YORK
THE MACMILLAN COMPANY

The Macmillan Company, New York
Brett-Macmillan Ltd., Galt, Ontario

Printed in the United States of America

To E. O.

which stands for Each One who has in any way contributed to the successful completion of this book

Contents

Part 1

PLANNING, PLANTING, AND CARE OF THE GARDEN

The Role of Perennials in the Garden

Perennials, long hailed as the backbone of the garden, seemingly should not require further championing. Nevertheless, an account here of their numerous virtues may arouse a renewed enthusiasm in the experienced gardener, while it serves to introduce this valuable group of plants to the novice.

Horticulturally, a perennial plant is defined as one that normally lives at least three years *under local conditions.* Many perennials last for the lifetime of a man; some longer. On the other hand, a biennial lives only two years; an annual, one year. The same species of plant—a perennial, for example—may behave differently (that is, as a biennial or annual) in a situation in which it is not at home.

A herbaceous perennial is one with stems that usually die to the ground each winter. Plants that arise from bulbs, such as daffodils and tulips, are also perennials, and herbaceous ones, but because of their different manner of growth they are placed, in horticultural parlance, in a separate group.

A woody perennial maintains a persistent stem (a trunk) or stems (as in shrubs) above ground. All trees and shrubs and some of the vines are woody perennials. A few plants seem to fall between two categories, in that they have semi-persistent woody stems. These often serve in the same capacity as the herbaceous plants in a garden. Some of them are included here, but this book concerns mainly herbaceous perennials for the garden, in contrast to woody plants and bulbs. These perennials are the mainstay of almost any successful planting during the greater part of the year.

Thus the very definition of perennial connotes a degree of permanence not achieved by other herbaceous plants. Annuals cannot be set out in much of this country before the end of May, and the first frosts of autumn nip their growth and end their decorative cycle. Spring-flowering bulbs are indispensable for early color, but their brief period of bloom is followed by gradually browning foliage and, in midsummer, bare spaces of ground.

Even if perennials never flowered, their spring resurgence of varied shoots and leaves still could not be overlooked. The returning life they bring to the garden is as much a part of the shaking loose of winter's shackles as are bird songs, greening lawns, and trees breaking into leaf.

When John Ruskin wrote that "Contrast increases the splendour of beauty," he might well have been thinking of perennials, for there is infinite diversity among them and each seems to enhance its neighbor. Few personal tastes cannot be satisfied; few garden areas cannot be improved by their use. With perennials there is no scope for monotony.

Leaf variation alone is boundless, in texture and hue as well as in shape. Individual flower forms offer wide opportunity for choice, from many-rayed asters to the cups and bells of campanulas; and from the little flat-topped flowers of tunica to deep tubes, ranged one above the other, as in foxglove. Types of inflorescence—the forms of the clusters in which flowers are borne—also provide a great array, with summer phlox in dome-shaped panicles, delphinium and loosestrife in slender spires, beebalms and scabiosas in compact heads of intricate design, and the modern chrysanthemums alone in an astounding diversity of forms.

Color can almost outdo the rainbow, for there are indescribable blends as well as relatively pure hues. Columbines, irises, primroses, and these same present-day chrysanthemums well illustrate the rich palette of perennials. Gaillardias are brilliant, with their rich reds contrasting with bright yellow; platycodons (balloon-flowers) leave a cool impression with their open bowls of blue-purple; peonies and phloxes give diverse effects according to their hues, from white and pastel pink to intense depths of color. White lilies are the purest of all white, and thereby offer the supreme contrast in any planting. Yellow, a bright and useful color, helpful alike to blend and to set off other colors, is at times almost in surfeit.

Height and habits of perennials range widely, too, from restricted mounds of candytuft to towering panicles of plume poppy. Low edging plants, such as teucrium (germander), can create precise borders, but a sprawling one like creeping myrtle spreads without restraint. Liatris (blazing star) is rigidly erect; baptisia, gracefully arching; babys-breath is lax and airy. Echinops (globe-thistle), yucca, and a few other large perennials are so dominant in stature that they serve best as lone accent specimens. Some designers use them for what they call sculptural effects in the garden.

More credit should be given perennials for their season-long appearance. The swordlike leaves of iris, the majestic growth of peonies, and the slender grace of penstemon branches are decorative throughout the season. Today's superb daylilies, never unkempt or dowdy, can also be attractive as foliage plants when their flowers are spent.

Fragrance is by no means lacking in perennials, yet it is not universal. Dianthus blooms are generally spicy in scent; chrysanthemums pungent. Phlox is redolent of old-fashioned gardens. The fragrance of violets and of lavender, too, often arouses nostalgic associations.

Differences among perennials in their adaptability to soils and exposures can be to the gardener's advantage where his conditions stray from the average. Hostas (plantain-lilies), for example, thrive in partial shade and heavy soils, while echinaceas (purple coneflowers) prefer light sandy positions in the sun. Epimedium will increase in gratifying manner in the shade. For a comparable foliage effect to follow spring bloom, doronicum (leopards-bane) requires sun. Cardinal-flower will tolerate, even respond with favor to constant moisture about the roots. Artemisias, on the other hand, generally demand the dry, porous, alkaline soil in which most species grow in nature. Lythrums, spiderworts, and many other kinds, however, do well almost anywhere.

From spring's initial burst of activity, perennials create a season-to-season panorama in the border. In any given period there are flowers to provide showy displays. It is possible to devise a color scheme for spring, then repeat the colors with new flowers in succeeding months, with perhaps three peaks of bloom. However, many gardeners prefer the more casual sense of continuity provided by a steady succession of ever-changing bloom. In such a sequence, the first Christmas rose may follow the last chrysanthemum by a scant few weeks.

The cut-flower value of perennials is extraordinary, with peonies, delphiniums, pyrethrums, and chrysanthemums often raised in quantity to this end alone. At the other extreme of usefulness is the semi-wild or naturalized planting, which will almost invariably be the better for such delicate, yet showy and distinctive, plants as thalictrum (meadow-rue) and filipendula (dropwort).

Convincing proof of the popularity of such plants as irises, phloxes, and daylilies is the vast number of new varieties introduced over the years. Yet favorite old forms, with their sentimental attachments bound in the literature and in gardens of the past few centuries, may be more appropriate in certain situations than their more spectacular modern counterparts.

All told, the perennial in any form or any situation is an amply rewarding garden subject.

Planning the Flower Garden

Because a garden should express the personal taste of its creator (who, ideally, is the owner), few specific rules for its plan will be given here. Rather than dogmatic precepts, only certain guiding principles will be suggested.

Before embarking on a plan, the gardener should understand the nature of a perennial garden. He should appreciate its essential character as "a thing of beauty" to be enjoyed—and worked in—half the year or more. To achieve this basic aim, he must give some thought to the types of plants to be selected. Consideration for their placement, habit, size, color, form, and cultural requirements is essential if each one he chooses is to become an effective element in the planting.

Contemporary gardens of perennials need no longer be restricted to herbaceous perennials alone, as in England where a border of perennials used to be an integral part of every landscape design. In fact, on present-day properties the word "border" only occasionally fits the flower garden. Nevertheless this term, a carry-over from our English heritage, is still used for convenience to indicate the area where flowers are being or are to be grown.

In England many gardens still have separate areas set aside for annuals, perennials, tender bedding plants, and alpines. In the United States the tendency is to combine these and other types of plants to create an over-all effect of long-lasting color and beauty. A garden or border usually contains spring flowering **bulbs**, from the crocus in March, hyacinths and daffodils in April, to tulips in May, that give a much needed splash of color before even early perennials come into bloom. Bulbs can well be planted around such perennials as Japanese anemones and dictamnus, which are retarded in making early growth. Then, as these expand, they can cover the area left when the bulb foliage dies. If large spaces are left for bulbs, annuals can be set directly over the bulbs without harm to either.

Annuals distributed in a border can be invaluable for filling in around early-blooming perennials, to give color later in the season. They are especially useful to hide the bedraggled foliage of Oriental poppies in midsummer, and many are good sources of cut flowers. In new gardens where spacing has been ample to allow for eventual increase in size of perennial plants, annuals can give the area a comfortably filled effect. Moreover, a well filled border tends to restrict weeds by shutting off their light source.

Dwarf shrubs are also incorporated by some gardeners. *Daphne cneorum, Hypericum patulum* 'Hidcote,' or *Spiræa bumalda* 'Anthony Waterer' can serve this purpose. A new globe arborvitae called 'Hetz Midget' matures slowly to a maximum height of one foot, to offer whimsical rounded accents near corners or rocks.

Larger shrubs, such as forms of *Deutzia gracilis* or *D. lemoinei*, can also be used among perennials. *Cotoneaster horizontalis* or *C. apiculata* can cover rocky crevices or sudden slopes, where they will sparkle with red fruit each autumn. Some gardeners treasure a tall forsythia just off the edge of a border to replace a tall background perennial, but dwarf forms such as *Forsythia viridissima* var. *bronxensis* seem more appropriate. This one provides a gnarled novelty only two feet high, well covered with small yellow flowers in early spring. In cold climates, *Buddleia davidii*, vitex, caryopteris, and some lespedezas die to the ground each winter, thus behaving like perennials, and equally worthy of a place in the border.

Roses are usually more effective if kept in a separate area by themselves. The beauty of a rose in foliage, bud, or flower is often lost when surrounded by annuals or perennials. However, floribunda roses are floriferous for the major part of the growing season, and one sometimes sees them spotted in borders.

Tuberous or tender bulbous material such as dahlias, tigridias, acidantheras or montbretias can be strategically placed through a planting to add interest. Tuberous begonias can well supplement primroses in shaded areas in mid and late summer, to provide accents of color. A selection of lilies which will provide a succession of bloom from June to October will add a note of distinction to any garden.

In brief, the gardener of restricted space but catholic tastes can count on a fine mixed border based on perennial mainstays.

In contrast to such diversity, the one-genus border containing, for example, only irises or peonies is for the specialist or fancier.

For the average gardener, perhaps only daylilies and hostas have a sufficient range of types and blooming seasons to be tailored to such a venture. On the other hand, those who are away all summer may find a garden composed of spring-flowering bulbs and chrysanthemums will best suit their purpose.

LOCATION OF THE GARDEN

The area where flowers are to be grown should be located where it blends with and complements the design of the entire property. A circular bed of flowering plants in the middle of a large lawn panel is rarely appropriate. Contours of the property, indicating natural boundaries, may very well determine the ideal spot for the garden area. Some thought should also be given to views from windows or from a terrace, with groupings of spectacular specimens so situated that they may be enjoyed without going into the garden.

While the conventional border is often placed across the back of the property, or along one or both sides, it may be that a triangular area in one corner is adequate. For the beginner, a small dooryard garden may be sufficient. A space between the house and garage or car port, or an area formed by an ell or wing of the house might also be utilized. The important consideration is that the garden should fit into and enhance the over-all design.

Perennials have many uses and need not be restricted to a border. Low-growing ground covers such as ajuga (bugle) may be effective under shrubs, while some taller, more rugged specimens such as echinops (globe-thistle) may add needed midsummer color when planted among shrubs.

Where there is an abrupt change in grade, a rock garden can often solve the problem by eliminating the need for mowing a difficult spot. Gravel or chipped slate can be incorporated into the top few inches of soil to make an appropriate setting for most perennial rock garden plants. These same plants can also be effective in a dry rock wall, a type of planting somewhat neglected in this country.

While some perennials fit into a formalized type of planting, others are well suited for naturalizing. Their persistence and continued beauty without benefit of care gives them unsurpassed value where cultivation is not practical. At the other extreme are the perennials that are adapted to use in tubs, planters, or boxes for terrace, patio or penthouse.

The ideal exposure for any group of flowering plants is one mostly sunny, with a small segment in partial shade; a situation that allows the widest selection of desirable plant material. Obviously, an open strip of land that runs north to south gains the optimum of the shifting sun's rays. If the whole area is lightly shaded for only two or three hours daily, no harm will result, but it is the planting in constant dense shade which becomes somewhat of a problem to maintain in steady color. The individual restricted to a northern exposure because of nearby hedges, trees or buildings has the most serious problem. However, although only a limited amount of sunlight is likely, there is no need to despair; usually some perennial can be found to solve the problem.

Windswept areas are far from desirable because the taller plants, as well as the more fragile types, will require staking, while many others will not be able to stand up against strong gusts. If possible, occasional shrubs or evergreens should be set nearby to act as windbreaks.

A fence, hedge, wall, or building may make a most effective background, but should be at least three feet from the border's edge. Then one can readily walk along both sides, and a free circulation of air will be possible to help keep plant diseases at a minimum. Moreover, walls often have unseen rubble at the base, buried by builders, and this can hamper adjacent plants. Hedges may have strong, penetrating roots which will prey on the perennial's source of food and water if too close. Metal sheets are sometimes sunk near the rear of the border to prevent further encroachment of tree roots or those of large shrubs.

While the site need not be of tabletop flatness, a fair degree of levelness is ideal. Deep slopes wash badly in rains and over winter, with messy accumulations of mud and debris the aftermath. In addition, plant roots may be dangerously exposed, and fertilizers quickly leached.

Not to be overlooked in locating a garden is the proximity to a water outlet. Especially in areas subject to prolonged drought this is imperative.

If perennials are to be grown in a border, the actual outline of the border usually needs to be adjusted to the terrain. Some feel that gentle curves, not too geometrically precise, best carry the informality desired. Others are partial to a straighter line, or have only such space that this treatment becomes practical.

The dimensions of the garden are governed largely by the owner's space, ambition and purse. By no means should anyone plan a garden larger than he can maintain. Better to start with a small area, and later increase the plantings in successive years according to the dictates of time and energy than to begin with a large garden and always have to apologize for its unkempt appearance.

Widths may vary according to preference and space available. The narrow border hardly allows large groups of any given plant for spectacular effect. However, the small-property owner can enjoy a perennial garden of slender proportions if he selects a variety of showy specimens, especially those with a long blooming period. The more spacious garden of five feet or more in width can absorb and should have groups of three to five similar subjects for due emphasis and appreciation. It is also the wide border that can make effective use of perennials planted in drifts.

DESIGNING THE GARDEN

Perhaps an acceptable garden can come into being without any formal planning, but it is far wiser, before planting, to make an actual diagram of the garden-to-be. This is an interesting task for a winter's evening, but the size of the area to be cultivated might better have been estimated some hot day in August when the weather would limit ambitions to what is practical, as far as maintenance is concerned; otherwise, the energy and hopes of

December may exceed the interests and capabilities of August.

For the diagram, a sheet of graph paper is recommended, each square scaled to represent one foot of ground space. The proposed garden is roughly outlined. Then several bays or groups of plants definitely desired are marked in at certain points. Gradually, other blocks of material are dovetailed in until a temporary plan is achieved.

Crayons can depict the colors of each group, and notes can be made as to time of bloom and heights. Now, individual skill and knowledge begin to play an important role, as the border's balance, the plants' cultural requirements, and their height, color, season of bloom, and habit all enter the picture.

Placement according to height

Perennials encompass a range in height from about three inches to somewhat over eight feet. Usually in the front rank one finds the low-growing types, not over fifteen inches tall. These plants should be kinds that look well all season, with good foliage as well as attractive blossoms. Dwarf hardy asters, lavender, cushion-type chrysanthemums, and dianthus are but a few examples. Low rock garden favorites such as perennial candytuft, arabis and alyssum may spill over the front edge to soften a harsh straight line. A more formal edging can be created by using teucrium or sweet woodruff if the plants are frequently clipped. Annuals such as dwarf marigolds or sweet alyssum may fill the summer breach.

The middle portion holds the subjects of medium height, roughly two to three feet. Here are the compact, steadily blooming plants that have become garden favorites. Small faults are often overlooked if effective color is produced. Daylilies, Shasta daisies, summer phlox, campanulas, and platycodons are popular choices. In some species there are cultivars of varying heights. For example, *Phlox paniculata* 'World Peace' may attain four feet while 'Mia Ruys' is a white counterpart only twenty inches tall.

Consigned to the background are the taller plants. Wide gardens can utilize hollyhocks, plume poppies or delphiniums that tower to seven feet or more, but in smaller areas, lythrum, aconitum, and the taller cultivars of phlox may be more appropriate.

Placement by color

A constant succession of color in the garden is ideal. Therefore, one should not find an excess of any given color at any one time, while other colors are conspicuously absent, nor should a certain color be unwittingly restricted to just one portion of the border. Gardens have been created all in white, all in blue, or yellow. This may be acceptable in small specialized areas, but the general border so designed would lack the interest derived from color combination or contrast, and would limit the material available.

Color precepts are more likely to be abused in the small garden crammed with a startling variety of favorites. Here color for harmony is perhaps best sought; the larger borders can use color confidently for accent or emphasis.

Color combinations can arouse considerable controversy among gardeners. Some feel that a good balance of color throughout the season is more important than actual composition. Others are emphatically sensitive to clashing colors in juxtaposition. Actually, Nature can be accused of being audacious in some blendings, as in multicolored fuchsia flowers, but seldom are the three primary colors, red, blue and yellow, found in the same genus. This may be a hint to omit one of them in any adjacent planting.

In the garden, red may be called warm, blue termed cool, yellow considered brassy, pink described as delicate, and magenta avoided as undesirable, but white is championed by all garden designers. White flowers growing between those colors which would otherwise clash will be a harmonizing influence. White, so luminous in the evening hours, will brighten dark spots of the garden and become increasingly important in any planting to be seen during twilight or evening hours, such as in a patio, on a terrace or where gardens are used as outdoor living rooms.

Repetition of a color can be overdone, too. For instance, a showy group of red phlox may be outstanding in one area; however, if repeated elsewhere in the garden, it might lose its effectiveness by overexploitation. Pink phlox in the second spot would possibly be more suitable.

Foliage color is not to be disregarded. Silvery-leaved artemisias and veronicas contrast with the very dark green of aconitum foliage. Gray-green bearded iris foliage is well set off against the shiny dark leaves of dictamnus. The almost white effect of the leaves of *Stachys olympica* or *Lychnis coronaria* increases interest by the contrast it makes with most other plants.

Placement by season of bloom

Here the goal is to have a good measure of bloom distributed throughout the garden during the entire growing season. Few gardeners relish isolated spots of color alongside stretches completely devoid of flowers. The wider the area, the easier it is to plan a sequence of bloom from early spring to autumn frosts.

The smallest garden can utilize narcissus (April), tulips (May), iris (May–June), peonies (June), delphiniums (July), summer phlox (July–August) and chrysanthemums (August–October), and thereby achieve a colorful display over most of the season. Naturally all the tulips or all the phlox would not be planted in a group together, but should be repeated at various spots so that there would be color throughout the border at any one time. Larger gardens would include greater variety of plant material, but with the same purpose in mind.

The smaller the garden, the greater use will be made of plants having a long blooming season, simply because there is not space for those of short duration. Coreopsis, heuchera, anthemis, gaura, *Campanula carpatica,* and *Viola cornuta* are just a few with extended flowering periods.

Placement by habit, form, and texture

A thorough knowledge of plant habit is profitable in the planning stage. Realization of the amount of growth likely after two or three

PLAN OF A BORDER 6 FEET WIDE IN THE SUN

Scale: 1 inch = 5 feet

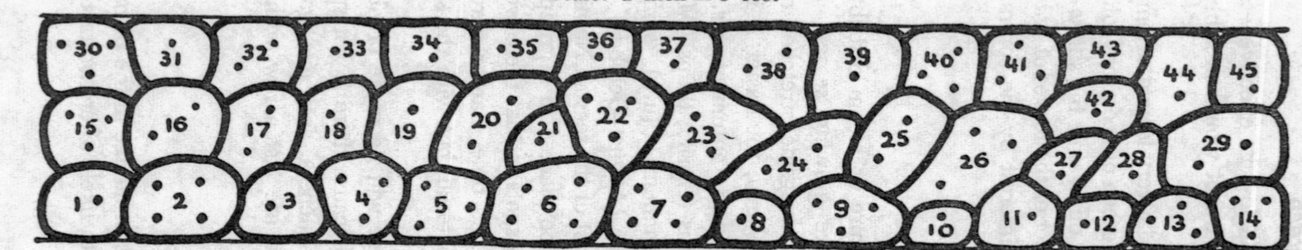

This planting plan assumes a garden six feet wide and approximately thirty feet long, in a sunny location, with soil of average fertility. Here, as in the two plans to follow, the small dots indicate the actual placement of the plants. Modern cultivars are used in each plan wherever feasible.

PLANTING KEY

(Number of plants needed in parentheses)

1 *Daphne cneorum* (1)
2 *Heuchera* 'Snowflakes' (4)
3 Spring: yellow daffodils (3)
Summer: dwarf yellow marigolds (4)
Fall: *Chrysanthemum morifolium* 'Bowl of Gold' (1)
4 *Veronica* 'Minuet' (3)
5 *Phlox subulata* 'Alexander's Giant' (pink) (3)
6 *Platycodon grandiflorum* var *mariesii* 'New Alpine' (4)
7 *Dianthus* 'Spotlight' (4)
8 *Aster* 'Pink Bouquet' (1)
9 *Arabis caucasica* 'Flore-pleno' (3)
10 *Lavandula officinalis* 'Hidcote Variety' (1)
11 Spring: *Tulipa præstans* 'Fusilier' (red) (6)
Summer: Petunias (red) (3)
Fall: *Chrysanthemum morifolium* 'Lipstick' (1)
12 *Cerastium tomentosum* (1)
13 *Campanula carpatica* 'Blue Carpet' (3)
14 *Alyssum saxatile* 'Luteum' (3)
15 *Veronica* 'Sunny Border Blue' (3)
16 Spring: Yellow Darwin tulips interspersed (7)
Summer: Yellow dwarf marigolds interspersed (8)
Fall: *Chrysanthemum morifolium* 'King's Ransom' (yellow) (3)
17 *Lythrum* 'Morden Pink' (2)
18 *Hemerocallis* 'Painted Lady' (1)

19 *Papaver orientale* 'Helen Elizabeth' (pink) (1)
20 *Aster* × *frikartii* 'Wonder of Staffa' (2)
21 *Artemisia schmidtiana* 'Silver Mound' (1)
22 *Phlox paniculata* 'Elizabeth Arden' (3)
Spring: Red single early tulips in foreground (6)
23 *Anthemis tinctoria* 'Grallagh Gold' (2)
24 *Pæonia tenuifolia* 'Flore-pleno' (2)
25 *Hemerocallis* 'Painted Lady' (2)
26 *Chrysanthemum maximum* 'Mark Riegel' (3)
27 *Lilium*, Mid-Century Hybrid 'Joan Evans' (yellow) (1)
28 *Gypsophila* 'Bodgeri' (1)
29 *Monarda* 'Granite Pink' (2)
30 *Iris sibirica* 'Eric the Red' (3)
31 *Aster novi-belgii* 'Eventide' (1)
32 *Chrysanthemum coccineum* 'Crimson Giant' (2)
33 *Thalictrum rugosum* (1)
34 *Aster novæ-angliæ* 'Harrington's Pink' (1)
Spring: White Darwin tulips interspersed (6)
35 *Pæonia lactiflora* 'Karl Rosenfeld' (1)
36 *Echinops* 'Taplow Blue' (1)
37 *Gypsophila paniculata* 'Bristol Fairy' (1)
38 *Lilium speciosum* 'Rubrum' (2)
39 *Potentilla fruticosa* 'Moonlight' (shrub) (1)
40 *Liatris* 'White Spire' (3)
41 *Delphinium*, Pacific Hybrid 'Black Knight' (3)
42 *Dicentra spectabilis* (1)
43 *Boltonia asteroides* (1)
44 *Thermopsis caroliniana* (1)
45 *Thalictrum rochebrunianum* (1)

PLAN OF A BORDER 6 FEET WIDE IN PARTIAL SHADE

Scale: 1 inch = 5 feet

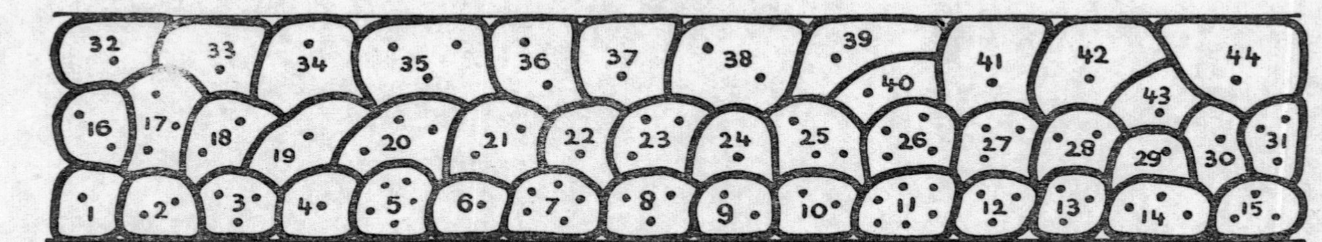

Here the plan is an example of a border of the same dimensions as the previous one, but situated in partial shade. If a part of the garden to be planned is in the full sun and the rest shaded during most of the day, portions of the previous planting plan could be appropriately combined with a section of this one.

PLANTING KEY

(Number of plants needed in parentheses)

1 *Aster* 'Little Red Boy' (dwarf) (1)
Yellow crocus in foreground (6)
2 *Polemonium cæruleum* 'Blue Pearl' (2)
3 *Dicentra eximia* (3)
4 *Helleborus niger* (1)
5 *Phlox divaricata* var. *laphamii* (5)
Yellow bedding violas interplanted (3)
6 *Aster* 'Pink Bouquet' (dwarf) (1)
White daffodils in foreground (3)
7 *Epimedium* × *rubrum* (5)
8 *Asarum europæum* (3)
Blue crocus interspersed (8)
9 *Eupatorium cœlestinum* (2)
10 *Lamium maculatum* (2)
11 *Primula* × *polyantha* mixed (6)
12 *Heuchera* 'Rhapsody' (3)
13 *Dicentra formosa* 'Sweetheart' (3)
14 *Brunnera macrophylla* (3)
Yellow daffodils interspersed (3)
15 *Asarum europæum* (3)
16 *Monarda didyma* 'Cambridge Scarlet' (2)
17 *Chrysanthemum maximum* 'Mark Riegel' (3)
18 *Anemone* × *hybrida* 'September Charm' (2)
19 *Hosta decorata* (1)
20 *Trollius ledebouri* (3)
21 *Alchemilla vulgaris* (2)
22 *Dicentra spectabilis* (1)
23 *Campanula persicifolia* 'Blue Gardenia' (3)
24 *Lysimachia clethroides* (1)
25 *Doronicum* 'Madam Mason' (3)

26 *Aquilegia,* McKana's Long Spurred Hybrids (4)
27 *Chrysanthemum maximum* 'Jennifer Read' (3)
28 *Clematis heracleifolia* var. *davidiana* (2)
29 *Papaver orientale* 'Cavalier' (1)
30 *Hosta plantaginea* (1)
31 *Astilbe* × *arendsii* 'Red Sentinel' (3)
32 *Boltonia asteroides* (1)
33 *Thalictrum rugosum* (1)
34 *Aconitum bicolor* (1)
35 *Iris kaempferi* 'Margaret S. Hendricksen' (blue) (3)
36 *Cimicifuga simplex* (2)
37 *Filipendula rubra* var. *venusta* (1)
38 *Aster novi-belgii* 'Marie Ballard' (soft blue) (2)
39 *Cephalaria tatarica* (1)
40 *Hosta glauca* (1)
41 *Lilium henryi* (1)
42 *Thalictrum rochebrunianum* (1)
43 *Hemerocallis* 'Dauntless' (yellow) (1)
44 *Forsythia intermedia* 'Linwood Gold' (1)

Undercarpeted by:
Pulmonaria saccharata (3)
Convallaria majalis 'Fortin's Giant' (6)
Mertensia virginica (2)
Muscari botryoides (12)
Phlox divaricata 'Snowflakes' (3)

PLAN OF A BORDER 3 FEET WIDE IN THE SUN

Scale: 1 inch = 4 feet

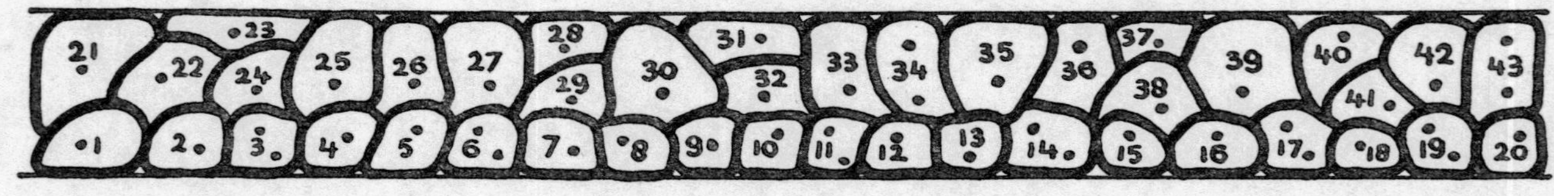

Many new homes today are on small properties that do not accommodate expansive plantings. The gardener with limited space could adapt this plan to a sunny area only three feet wide. Fewer plants of any one kind are used, and the choice of material is more restricted to types with restrained growth habit.

PLANTING KEY

(Number of plants needed in parentheses)

1 *Daphne cneorum* (1)
2 *Chrysanthemum morifolium* 'Powder Puff' (white) (1)
Scilla sibirica interplanted (5)
3 *Dianthus* 'Spotlight' (2)
4 *Aster* 'Pink Bouquet' (dwarf) (1)
5 *Veronica* 'Minuet' (1)
6 *Trollius europæus* (2)
7 *Polemonium cæruleum* 'Blue Pearl' (1)
8 *Sedum spectabile* 'Brilliant' (1)
9 *Alyssum saxatile* 'Luteum' (1)
10 *Platycodon grandiflorum* var. *mariesii* 'New Alpine' (1)
11 *Heuchera* 'Rhapsody' (2)
12 *Euphorbia epithymoides* (1)
13 *Phlox subulata* 'Intensity' (1)
14 *Campanula carpatica* 'Blue Carpet' (2)
15 *Artemisia schmidtiana* 'Silver Mound' (1)
16 *Geum* × *borisii* (1)
17 *Salvia jurisicii* (2)
Crocus, yellow, interplanted (6)
18 *Iberis sempervirens* 'Purity' (1)
19 *Campanula carpatica* 'White Carpet' (2)
20 *Arabis* 'Pink Charm' (1)
21 *Hemerocallis* 'Dauntless' (yellow) (1)
22 *Lilium* 'Enchantment' (1)
23 *Sedum maximum* 'Atropurpureum' (1)
24 *Veronica* 'Icicle' (1)
25 *Baptisia australis* (1)
26 *Achillea* 'Coronation Gold' (1)
White Darwin tulips interspersed (3)
27 *Aster novi-belgii* 'Eventide' (1)
28 *Pæonia lactiflora* 'Mons. Jules Elie' (pink) (1)
Salvia splendens between 28 and 30 (red) (1)
29 *Phlox paniculata* 'Mia Ruys' (white) (1)

30 *Thalictrum rugosum* (1)
31 *Lilium speciosum* 'Rubrum' (1)
32 *Gypsophila* 'Rosy Veil' (1)
33 *Chrysanthemum maximum* 'Mark Riegel' (1)
34 *Chrysanthemum coccineum* 'Helen' (pink) (2)

35 *Platycodon grandiflorum* 'Bristol Bluebird' (1)
36 *Chrysanthemum morifolium* (1)
Red Darwin tulips interplanted (3)
37 *Lilium candidum* (1)
38 *Asclepias tuberosa* (1)
39 *Delphinium* Pacific Hybrid, 'Summer Skies' (blue) (1)

40 *Gypsophila paniculata* 'Bristol Fairy' (1)
41 *Doronicum* 'Madam Mason' (1)
42 *Iris* 'Ola Kala' (deep yellow) (1)
Tall yellow zinnias interspersed (4)
43 *Lythrum* 'Morden Pink' (2)
Yellow daffodils interspersed (3)

years governs the space allotted each subject. Rapidly spreading plants may quickly engulf less aggressive neighbors if not properly spaced or annually divided. Snow-in-summer, a typical offender in spite of its dwarf nature, needs at least two feet of space. Conversely, trollius will increase in size very slowly so that several plants may be set close together. A single echinops (globe-thistle) is picturesque, but a large group would seem grotesque. Even the peony and dictamnus (gas-plant), so rewarding as specimens, are not for thoughtless massing.

Individual plant character enters in as well. The seemingly small babys-breath or sea-lavender of April will swell into billowy masses by midsummer, and space must be allotted accordingly. The foliage of Oriental poppy, doronicum, and bleeding heart disappears during summer so these plants are best hidden by other plants at this time. Large masses of types with short blooming seasons, such as bearded iris and many biennials, should be avoided; planting on a modest scale avoids later stretches of dullness.

Garden plants classified as to form are vertical (delphinium, hollyhock), horizontal (*Phlox subulata,* candytuft), or intermediate, which includes the vast majority. Various forms are best interspersed to avoid monotony and to create interest. All the delphiniums, foxgloves, and aconitums restricted to one area, with all the horizontal forms kept to another section, would be monotonous and poorly balanced.

The good designer also looks for variety in foliage forms and textures. Coarse leaves, as on hosta, hollyhock, and hibiscus, are improved in appearance by association with those of finer texture, such as aquilegia and thalictrum. Plants of medium foliage size combine well with the fine leaves of blue flax. Swordlike leaves of iris and yucca can be contrasted with the succulent sedums. The beauty of the dark, scalloped leaf of heuchera is enhanced near peachbells' pale, smooth green.

The well-considered plan allows for each of these factors noted above: height, color, season of bloom, habit, form, and texture. When they are all given due attention the gardener's reward will be enjoyment from the earliest breath of spring to autumn's heavy frosts.

Yet a garden is a dynamic project, and its owner, ever alert to ways of improving his planting, will be making notes throughout the season for future alterations. Crowded plants will need more room; certain colors require more favorable vantage points. Fragrant plants may call for attention, with some to be added, others transplanted to spots near terraces or paths. Although a garden's first year is never a proper test, changes may be needed in time if individual plants vary from the standard or from expectations in behavior, growth, or time of flowering.

Outdated material eventually will be replaced with choice new plants from the breeders' offerings. Although the most promising of the latest selections are mentioned among the plants described in this book, the list will ever be changing as long as sincere plantsmen continue to seek more desirable forms.

Prelude to Planting

Plants in nature grow in soil, and most of them grow best in deep, porous soil that is well supplied with nutrients for them. Hard, compacted, shallow soil will make a puny garden. Sand and clay each have their drawbacks. Very seldom is the soil in any chosen location suitable for gardening without advance preparation. It is advantageous if this can be started in the fall.

What form this preparation takes will depend upon the type of soil, its depth, and the general sort of plants to be cultivated in it. Therefore it should first be tested for its needs and capabilities. Few gardeners can accurately judge untried ground, but most states have experiment stations, state colleges, or local extension agencies which offer soil testing services to residents. A cardboard container holding about a pint of dry soil should be sent to one of these agencies. To get a true evaluation, samples should be taken not from just one spot, but from the whole area concerned, and at depths varying from 2 to 18 inches. The samples should be mixed thoroughly, the container filled, and name, address, and a statement of the proposed use of the soil enclosed. In due time a report may be expected giving recommendations. These should be carefully followed.

Reports on soil tests usually stress the organic matter content of the soil; unfortunately it is frequently very low. Organic matter, or humus, is the material derived from partial decomposition of animal or vegetable matter by fungi and bacteria. Its value for the growth of plants can scarcely be overemphasized.

Humus lightens heavy, sticky clay soils by opening them up and thus providing better aeration. Paradoxically, it also improves light sandy soils by furnishing coarse particles which have greater water-holding capacity. Water is essential for utilization of the nutrient elements in the soil, for plants, unlike animals, cannot ordinarily absorb solid foods. Most nutrients enter a plant in solution through the roots. The better the root system, the more nutrients can be absorbed.

Growth of the roots is aided by good drainage and unrestricted air movement, and these are made possible by humus as well as the presence of water. These conditions also encourage the multiplication of useful soil bacteria, which further aid plants in their complicated nutritional process. Since such bacteria are only slightly active in very sandy soils, the addition of humus to them is almost a necessity.

In addition to its soil-conditioning properties, organic matter, as it slowly decomposes, may release growth stimulants and other chemical compounds needed by plants. Liberal amounts of organic matter can also help to keep the soil in better balance as to acidity or alkalinity.

The form of humus used is often governed by local availability. For example, animal manures are becoming increasingly scarce, particularly near large cities. If available, year-old cow manure is excellent. Other types, from poultry, sheep, swine, or horses, are best applied in the fall to allow decomposition over winter. These forms, if used immediately before planting, may cause fatal root injury.

Peatmoss, usually in a dry, brown, shredded state, is relatively slow to decompose and it provides long-lasting effects in the soil. It does not burn, it is not harmful near roots, and it does not bring in weed seeds, as manures may. It is easier to work with peatmoss if it is first moistened. Otherwise it is dusty, and if left on top of the soil in a dry state, it may blow away. Though the nutrient content is negligible, and the reaction acid, peatmoss is a valuable soil conditioner, especially in small urban gardens.

Leafmold is darker and of varying consistency, but when available, it is highly desirable. Even fallen leaves turned into the soil in late autumn will add a surprising humus content by the succeeding spring. Old sawdust, when available, is another valuable soil amendment. On properties where a compost pile can be screened from view, gardeners may find that this alone provides an adequate supply of organic matter.

Lime should be applied only if so advised by the soil tester. Its purpose is to make the soil reaction less acid, and to free some of the nutrient elements more rapidly. If used in excess, however, it may be detrimental.

Some gardeners are firm believers in purely organic gardening, and will employ no chemical fertilizers. Humus however, is not extremely rich in the elements essential for plant growth, and continued research has shown that supplementary nutrition is frequently desirable. In addition, a number of plants do not thrive in the moisture-retaining soil created by continued application of organic matter. Therefore, besides a certain amount of humus, some chemical fertilizers may also be needed. Which kind to select may be determined by the soil tester's report.

Every chemical fertilizer sold bears a numerical formula of three figures, such as 5-12-10. These figures indicate the percentage, in alphabetical order, of nitrogen, phosphorus, and potassium, which are the three essential elements in the mixture. The balance of the material in the bag is inert filler, without which the chemicals would damage the plants.

Some fertilizers are compounded for fast action; others release their elements gradually over a long period. Most are so made that part of the fertilizing value is made available immediately, the remainder at a slower rate. The specific needs of the soil and plants in question should be known, and the fertilizer should be selected accordingly. All the information needed should be found on the label.

In a 5-12-10 fertilizer, the first numeral, in this case 5, signifies 5 per cent nitrogen. This element is especially important for chlorophyll, the material that gives its green color to vegetation. Nitrogen in excess may cause weak, soft growth and an abundance of foliage at the expense of flowers. A lack results in gradual yellowing of the foliage, stunted growth, and undersized flowers.

The middle number, 12, represents 12 per cent phosphoric acid. Phosphorus is important in storage organs and in parts undergoing active growth. High phosphorus content increases root production; an excess may result in hard brittle stems, and a deficiency may cause dwarfed plants with improperly expanded leaves that may have red margins.

The last number, 10, refers to the potash content. Potassium plays an important role in photosynthesis, the process whereby a plant manufactures the sugars and starches which are its food. If excessive, it may burn the roots; when deficient, the margins of the lower leaves may turn yellow, then brown. If the deficiency is not corrected, this discoloration will be noted on successively higher leaves.

Plants also require small quantities of other elements, known as minor, or trace, elements. When a test shows that any of these (boron, for example) is lacking in the soil, it is important to select a fertilizer that contains the required minor chemical as well as the essential nitrogen, phosphorus, and potassium.

While humus is preferably worked in during autumn preparation of the garden site, fertilizers are better applied before planting in spring. If turf covers the selected location, in the autumn it should be turned over with a rotary cultivator or a spade so that it can decompose over winter. If time for this disintegration is not allowed, air pockets will later develop. These may cause nearby plants to die gradually because they are not firmly rooted. If sod must be removed in spring, it should be stripped off and added to the compost pile.

For best results, the ground should be broken up to a depth of 18 inches. A better garden can usually be achieved if this is done in the fall. For this purpose, rotary cultivators, which can often be rented by the day, will prove far less laborious than hand spading. Then in the spring, after raking and removal of stones and the largest undecomposed lumps, the border is ready for planting.

In locations of habitually poor drainage, where water stands for days after a heavy rain, additional measures may be in order. Soil should be removed to a depth of at least 18 inches, then the probable hardpan causing the condition broken up. Before the soil is returned, a bottom layer of 3 or 4 inches of stones or coarse gravel can be added to increase porosity. Agricultural drain tile may be a last resort if the problem remains serious.

The gardener must realize that plants vary in requirements of soil acidity, fertility, and texture. Nevertheless, a border prepared as advised will be fundamentally sound and adaptable to spot treatments for needs of specific plants.

Planting and Maintenance

After the soil is thoroughly conditioned, and a plan has been carefully prepared, the next step is the planting. If the soil has meanwhile become hardened or compacted, it should be loosened by spade or rotary cultivator; if it is muddy, it will be necessary to wait until it can be easily worked. The garden plan should be consulted, distances measured out, and exact locations for specific plants indicated with stakes or garden labels.

If the plants have been delivered and it is not convenient to set them out for several days, it is advisable to put them in pots of soil, water them well and place them in the shade until they can be planted. Even if they can be planted immediately, nonetheless, especially if the area is so large that a long time may be required to complete the job, it is important to see that the roots do not dry out. Excessive soaking of roots, however, even overnight, would create undesirable waterlogging. Therefore it may prove helpful to stir enough soil in a pail of water to create a thin soupy paste. Roots gently swirled in this mixture will be neither too dry nor too wet. Unless they should get baked dry, they will be well protected against desiccation by sun and wind.

Individual needs can best be taken care of at planting time. If more humus is needed for some plants, it is incorporated in the soil before the plant goes in. If lime is a requirement for others, the proper amount is worked in there where needed. Holes should be large enough to allow the roots to be arranged as they normally grow: broad holes for phlox, iris, and other shallow, fibrous-rooted material; deep ones for peonies, oriental poppies, and similar plants with large fleshy roots or long taproots. Each plant is set at its proper depth, as ascertained beforehand. Delphiniums, for example, rot if the crown is buried, but heucheras thrive if set 1½ inches below the soil line. As the soil is filled in, firm pressure in toward the plant crown settles the ground above and around the roots, eliminating dangerous air pockets. The top inch of soil is left loose.

After the plants are in, a thorough watering follows. Weak starter solutions of soluble fertilizers are sometimes added to the water to stimulate root growth. Finally, identification markers, if they are to be used can be inserted for each plant or group.

If plants with considerable foliage wilt after being set out, covering them with a peach basket for a few days during the hours of strong sunlight will provide shade until the roots can meet the moisture needs of the leaves.

Although most perennials are planted in spring, many can be successfully established in late summer or early fall if time is allowed for adequate growth before killing frosts. Materials set out late will usually do better the following year if given winter protection.

Pride in one's garden diminishes with the appearance of weeds. These unwelcome intruders take water, nutrients, and light from the cultivated plants. Frequently they also harbor and encourage insects and diseases. However, if never granted a head start, weeds present no insurmountable problem.

About a week after planting, the entire border may be lightly cultivated to loosen the surface inch of soil. Any form of hoe or scratcher is suitable for breaking the crust, thus making the soil more receptive to moisture and at the same time uprooting young weeds in their most defenseless state. Occasional cultivation throughout the season will normally suffice.

The use of chemical weed killers or herbicides that kill weed seeds in the ground are too much of a risk in an established planting. Frankly, for small plantings such treatments seem unnecessary since occasional cultivation should not be tedious for the gardener or dangerous for the plants.

When leaves increase and weather becomes warmer, it is well to be vigilant against insects and diseases. An all-purpose spray or dust applied every ten days or so is prudent, but spot infestations should be attacked without delay.

An increasing number of gardeners use summer mulches, such as an inch or two of peatmoss, buckwheat hulls, old sawdust, or grass clippings loosely spread over open spaces. These tend to conserve soil moisture and discourage weeds. They should be applied only after soils are well soaked, of course. Some mulches dry out and blow away, some are potential fire hazards, some may be locally expensive, and a few, if thickly spread, actually exclude rain from the ground. If a mulch is under consideration, one should check the materials available and decide which is best for his garden. Often the Agricultural Extension Service, generally located in the county seat can be of help.

Perennials cannot long survive without water. Not only is water needed for the intake of nutrients from the soil, but the water constantly lost by leaves through transpiration must be replaced. Because Nature cannot be depended upon to supply optimum amounts of rainfall throughout the growing season, consideration of the water requirements of a garden is imperative.

The type of plant and the soil structure determine the need for water. Shallow-rooted plants, such as monarda (beebalm), wilt more speedily than deep-rooted baptisia (false indigo). Wilting generally means dryness, but mole runs or air pockets of other kinds around the roots can also be the cause. Tight, heavy soils do not allow moisture to seep down to the root zone of the plants. If a handful of soil taken from 6 inches below the surface (since the surface always dries first it may not necessarily be indicative) can be compacted into a loose ball, it is not yet dangerously dry. If the particles do not hold together, water is needed.

Whatever the mechanism used, water should be applied so that it soaks in slowly until small puddles linger on the surface. Rotary sprinklers are effective and labor-saving, although a strong breeze may prevent thorough coverage. Porous soil soakers are practical on level ground, and have the advantage of not wetting the foliage. Watering cans are best for individual plants or very small areas. An ordinary hose with nozzle can be used, but of course requires the prolonged presence of the gardener. Few persons are willing to hold the hose in one area until the soil is moist to a depth of 6 inches.

Wet foliage is a haven for germinating disease spores; therefore water is best applied at a time during the day when the leaves will dry quickly. This usually means well before sunset, although wind as well as sun dries out plants. However, if watering is necessary and can be done only in the evening, it is better then than not at all.

Frequent light sprinklings foster the development of undesirable surface roots, rather than the deeply anchored, substantial growth that is preferable. Consequently, one thorough soaking each week is far more beneficial than nightly sprinkling. Naturally, overwatering may cause soggy soil and root damage, but unless a sprinkler is forgotten for a long period, this is unlikely to happen.

On a host of multiple-flowered plants, such as phlox and asters, superior flowers develop if stems are thinned to about four in each clump. Likewise, on peonies and chrysanthemums larger blossoms are obtained by disbudding, the practice of leaving but one bud to develop on each stem. This practice is often essential for exhibition blooms.

Plants with large, heavy flowers (peonies); tall, slender stems (delphinium, hollyhock); and those growing too laxly or tending to bend in strong winds, may require staking for both appearance and safety. Unobtrusive but sturdy bamboo canes, painted green, make ideal stakes. String or raffia is tied first to the stake, then loosely around the stems, never drawing the stems up to create a squeezed or choked appearance. Neither stake nor string should be obvious when the operation is completed.

Removal of old, faded flowers throughout the season serves several worthy purposes. Unsightly remnants are eliminated, plant energy is not squandered on the development of seeds, unwanted seedlings do not crop up, and most important of all, the blooming season of the plants is usually prolonged. Only the flower or flower cluster should be snipped off, because the foliage below will continue to manufacture food. Incidentally, if volunteer seedlings which have reverted to a common type do appear beside phlox, anthemis, or hollyhocks, they should be weeded out; otherwise the less desirable forms may choke the parent plant and eventually take over in its place.

In poor soils or in very rainy seasons, additional fertilizer may be needed in midsummer. A light application may be sprinkled around each clump, raked in, and immediately watered into the soil. Each spring it will be beneficial to work in shallow applications of compost, well rotted manure, or other organic matter, as well as slowly available chemical fertilizers.

Division must not be neglected when individual plants require it. There is no standard rule governing how often perennials should be divided. The performance of each clump determines whether or not it needs attention. If it is overgrown or choked, if a hard woody crown has developed in the center, if quality of bloom is deteriorating, then it is time for division. Rampant growers in good soil, such as many asters, helenium (sneezeweed), physostegia (obedient-plant), and even some chrysanthemums, can be divided annually; plants of aconitum (monkshood), asclepias (milkweed or butterfly-weed), dictamnus (gas-plant), peony, and platycodon can remain undisturbed for many years.

In general, spring-blooming plants should be divided in late August or early September; later-blooming perennials can be attended to in early spring, but this is by no means a hard and fast rule. Bearded iris and primroses, for example, are easily divided a few weeks after flowering. Individual plant requirements, climate, growing conditions, all have to be considered. Where winters are severe or where early frosts are likely, spring is perhaps the best time to tend to the task. Whenever done, attention to watering is essential until new roots have developed.

When the need arises for transplanting, perennials are customarily moved at the same time of year that they would be divided. Of course, potted material may be set out, with proper care, at practically any time of the growing season. Many plants, such as Canterbury bells and chrysanthemums, may be moved successfully even when in full bloom if, during the process, an undisturbed ball of soil is carefully retained about the roots.

As late fall arrives, winter preparations begin. When stalks wither beyond further value, they should be cut back to 3 or 4 inches. These stubs will aid in holding winter cover and will serve as identifying signs the next spring. Old stems and foliage should be burned to prevent their carrying over insects and diseases.

Since winter is so unpredictable in many areas, perennials, if not protected, are often at the mercy of changing temperatures. Unless the roots are deeply anchored, alternate freezing and thawing will result in heaving, which causes great damage by exposing the roots to extreme cold and drying. In other situations, low temperatures may kill the less hardy species, warm spells will encourage premature growth, and extended winter rains may induce rot. Therefore, unless there is a certainty of a steady snow cover, winter protection is often advisable in cold climates. However, with the wide range of perennials available, many present-day gardeners prefer to grow those that survive in their area without protection.

The prime object of a winter mulch is to maintain a solidly frozen, dry border all winter. For this purpose, where salt marsh hay is available, a protective layer 3 or 4 inches deep is recommended. It should be applied after the ground freezes hard—but only then. It does not pack, rot, or leave weed seed. Old sawdust is another acceptable material. Leaves, which are frequently used, have a tendency to mat and rot, preventing aeration in soggy weather. Evergreen boughs, as from old Christmas trees, are useful for cover and as weights to prevent wind loss of lighter mulches. Mounds of sand or ashes are sometimes placed over the crowns of delphiniums where rotting is a severe problem. If the border is left unprotected, plants should be checked during thaws and reset if heaved upwards. Gardeners possessing coldframes may use them for overwintering questionably hardy plants such as *Aster frikartii*, some of the salvias, and the shallow-rooted chrysanthemums.

Propagation of Perennials

Nearly all gardeners eventually try their hand at propagating their own perennials by means of seeds, divisions, or cuttings. For several reasons this is a desirable practice and human curiosity in the processes involved often leads to an intriguing hobby.

Stocks of favorite subjects can be increased by division or cuttings at little or no expense, for oneself or for exchange with other avid gardeners. Often vegetative propagation by the gardener himself offers the only means of acquiring additional plants from outstanding selections or mutations. Seeds offer engrossing possibilities of obtaining new and unusual forms, sometimes from distant lands.

Many nurserymen encourage plant propagation by the amateur. Rather than competing with their business, they feel that the care required, plus the occasional failures, will arouse a greater appreciation of good nursery stock and of what it takes to produce it.

SEEDS

By and large, seeds produce the greatest increase, for some perennials set tremendous quantities. Not all perennials can be expected to reproduce faithfully to type; plants of mixed parentage normally yield variable offspring, a fact that greatly interests those with experimental tendencies who enjoy the possibility of obtaining something different. Indeed, many amateurs take up hybridizing in later years, and a number of choice plants have been originated by such hobbyists.

It is desirable for economy's sake for gardeners to raise their own biennials, such as hollyhocks, foxgloves, and Canterbury bells. For convenience it is also wise to raise such common subjects as coreopsis, Iceland poppies, and thymes, for nurseries find these increasingly less profitable to grow. The same is true of numerous rock garden plants; therefore, propagating for one's own needs will save much fruitless searching in commercial outlets.

Seeds, either purchased or collected from the garden, should be stored in tight envelopes, bottles, or paper boxes, in definitely cool, dry places. If allowed to become moist, they may start to germinate or rot. Once sown, on the other hand, proper moisture is constantly required.

Some seeds germinate quickly, others only after a considerable delay. Hard-coated seeds of primroses, rock garden plants from alpine regions, and certain others are often treated by alternate freezing and thawing in an ice cube compartment for several days before sowing, as if to duplicate natural winter conditions. Lupine seeds may be soaked for one day in lukewarm water to soften their hard seed coats. Delphinium germinates best at cool temperatures, thermopsis at high temperatures. Envelopes in which seeds are purchased normally provide valuable tips on handling each kind, as well as giving the average time required for germination. Only general hints can be given in one chapter on the subject.

The proper time for sowing varies, but nearly all perennials are fairly successful in the still relatively cool ground of early spring. However, seedlings from spring germination do not always flower during the first year. In fact, seedlings of peonies, dictamnus, and some lilies may not develop into flowering plants until three to five years have passed.

Seeds of a number of plants that are mature by midsummer can be profitably sown as soon as they are ripe. Aquilegia, lychnis, and biennials are typical of these. Such seeds ordinarily germinate rapidly and the plants may become large enough to bloom the next spring. Germination of certain others, such as dictamnus or trollius, which may be sown at the same time, will be delayed until warmer days arrive the following spring. Primrose and penstemon seeds should be sown as early as the soil is workable, for with these, as with delphinium, cool temperatures will hasten germination. Seeds ripening late in the season, such as those of asters, cimicifugas, and chrysanthemums, are as a rule, held over for spring sowing.

The preferred site for a structure for a seedbed is a lightly shaded area. In the absence of a greenhouse, the next most desirable device is a coldframe, 3 to 5 feet wide, built of substantial planks or cement blocks to about 1 foot above the ground level. A board 12 inches wide may be placed across the top to allow the sower to sit comfortably, while another short board on the seedbed itself permits the feet to rest without harming the surface. Frames can be shaded or protected from downpours by glass sash or even storm windows, or, for temporary economy, frames covered with clear plastic.

Open areas in the garden are sometimes prepared for seeds. These can be protected from the elements by heavy cheesecloth, burlap, or kraft paper tacked onto a framework of sturdy stakes driven into the ground.

Wherever located, the seedbed needs careful preparation. A mixture of about one-third good loam, one-third peatmoss or leafmold, and one-third sand, all thoroughly worked together, will make a good medium for sowing. Peatmoss is less likely to pack or harden on the surface than is shredded leafmold. The bed should be 4 to 6 inches deep, raked free of all stones and lumps, and the top inch screened for really fine consistency. Then it is firmed lightly with a straight-edged board or metal tamper. Never tamp a seedbed heavily, for only a loose, aerated surface assures the roots the oxygen they need.

Some gardeners prefer to substitute vermiculite or ground sphagnum moss for sand in the planting mixture; others prefer to use only vermiculite, but in this case, dilute liquid fertilizers must be applied after the seeds begin to germinate. Still others are testing the use of a plastic covering for an entire seed flat, to conserve moisture.

In sowing seeds out of doors or in a frame, a narrow lath can be used as a straightedge to mark rows on the bed; one's finger or a pointed stick drawn alongside providing the shallow trench or drill to receive the seed. The depth necessary is only about twice that of a seed's diameter; excessively deep sowing is invariably fatal to success.

Thin sowing is recommended, with at least one seed's thickness as the interval between individuals. Thick sowing produces spindly, weak growth that requires quick transplanting. Also, the damping-off fungi may run wild in crowded rows, causing seedlings to curl, turn yellow, and die.

When a row has been sown, the soil mixture should be pressed lightly over the seeds and the next row marked about 3 inches distant. Each kind of seed should be designated by a label in its row or part row, with the plant name and date of sowing. Extremely fine seeds may be sown on the surface without covering, followed by a very gentle raking to work them into the soil.

When sowing is finished, a careful watering should be given. A can with fine nozzle attached is ideal; water spouting from large openings washes the surface badly. Seedbeds must remain moist, although never soggy enough to encourage rotting or damping-off. For a while, they require some shading from the hot sun. Burlap or double cheesecloth can be laid either on the soil itself or on the sash to provide such protection. In the open garden, with no glass, a structure of wooden strips with shading material tacked around and over its supports will suffice. Here, heavy kraft paper is the favored protection against rain damage.

The bed should be examined at least once daily. As soon as germination commences, all covering should be removed from the surface and placed on top of the sash, for shading is still vitally important. As growth continues, the seedlings should be gradually exposed to air and sunlight to harden them. The seedbed should still be kept moist, but the gardener must remember that fungi are encouraged by wet foliage during cool nights or dark days.

Small quantities of seed are often sown in flats, pots, or even cigar boxes, placed on window sills and elsewhere in the home. However, such locations often become too warm for best results. If the seeds are sown in early spring, the pots or flats should be moved outdoors, during warm days at least, as soon as signs of germination are noted so that the seedlings will be hardened by gradual exposure before being permanently planted. The flats or pots should be prepared by covering the drainage holes with pieces of broken crock or pebbles. The soil mixture should be about ½ inch from the top. The seeds are covered by screening some additional soil over them, then they are watered thoroughly.

When two or three sets of true leaves appear, it is time to plant the seedlings, placing them at least 1 inch apart in individual pots, shaded beds, or flats. A light application of fertilizer may be made at this time. It is wise to shade the plant for a few days after transplanting. In another three weeks or so, if weather permits, they are ready for the border.

Fall-sown seeds outdoors will winter over in position if lightly mulched with hay or straw. When spring growth has barely begun, and the seedlings are large enough to handle, they can be set in their permanent places in the garden. The cool days of early and mid spring are perfect for solid new root and top growth.

DIVISION

Although perennials blooming in spring are generally divided in August or September, some growers prefer to divide everything in spring, while growth is still dormant and the weather remains cool and moist. This is often more satisfactory in regions where winters may be severe or open; plants started early will establish secure root systems by autumn and will be less susceptible to heaving in winter.

No special equipment is essential beyond a digging tool and a strong, sharp knife. Clumps to be divided must be dug carefully to avoid undue root injury, and the soil should be shaken or washed free. If it is late summer, wilting will be reduced if the foliage is cut back half way. Strong, matted plants may have to be pried apart at the crown, with spade or fork, in order to get divisions of workable sizes. With the knife, cut the crown into sections of two or three eyes or shoots, and trim the roots to 4 or 6 inches, depending on individual vigor. Mangled roots should be removed with clean cuts to encourage quick new growth.

If severe cuts or bruises appear on the crowns, dusting with powdered charcoal or ferbam will ward off disease. Each division should be reset firmly in good soil and watered heavily. Plants reset after August should be given winter protection to prevent heaving.

Very small divisions, but with at least one shoot, are feasible if a large increase in plants is desired, but these may not flower until another season. Sections of normal size will probably bloom on schedule. For the most part, the older central portions of the clump can be discarded, since better results come from the vigorous young outer growths. Certain plants—hellebores and bleeding hearts are familiar examples—are relatively touchy about splitting and tolerate no abuse or rough handling.

A number of perennials—lysimachia, ajuga, and creeping phlox among them—normally provide rooted stolons or runners which may be severed from the mother plant and transplanted elsewhere. With dianthus, layering may be accomplished by bending the stems to the ground and pegging them down. When rooted, these new plants may similarly be removed and used elsewhere.

STEM AND LEAF CUTTINGS

The short sections of branches used in propagation by cuttage are technically softwood cuttings, in contrast to the hardwood cuttings derived from mature twigs of woody plants. Among housewives softwood cuttings are often called slips. Facilities for rooting cuttings vary greatly, from homemade devices for the small-scale amateur's garden to the sleekly mechanized equipment of a commercial establishment with its vast greenhouses, frames, bottom heat, hormones, automatic mist systems, and the like. However, most professional growers confess a grudging respect for the skilled amateur who often roots material which repeatedly defies the specialist.

In general, plants blooming in spring provide the best cutting stems in midsummer; later-flowering subjects are likely to root well when cuttings are taken in May or June. The average cutting should be 2 to 3 inches long, firmly limber (neither too hard nor too soft), and free of flower buds. Naturally, small rock garden plants, such as *Achillea lewisii,* that rarely produce shoots over an inch in length will provide shorter cuttings.

The medium in which the cuttings are placed must be clean, sterile, and practically devoid of fertilizers. Sharp, coarse sand still pleases most propagators of perennials; it is cheap, readily obtained, and easily watered or drained. Vermiculite, perlite, and shredded sphagnum moss are other media that may be used. Any material, before being used a second time, must be sterilized. Very easily rooted cuttings are often successful in water alone, but the resulting plants are not always sturdy enough for outdoor use.

A layer of clean new sand or other rooting medium, to a depth of at least 3 inches, is necessary. It may be spread in flats, pots, or frames. If only open ground is available, sufficient soil should be scraped off for the top of the sand layer to be level with the surrounding ground.

If sand is used, it is leveled, moistened heavily, tamped rather well, then watered again. Vermiculite needs only leveling and watering; it should not be tamped at all. Whatever the medium, dirt or foreign matter should always be carefully excluded as a potential source of fungi. Next, a clean, narrow board, not over 3 inches wide, is used to mark the rows in the flat or frame. A sterilized putty knife drawn alongside the board will cut slitlike trenches in which the cutting may be inserted.

Cuttings should be selected with attention to healthy foliage and firm stems. A razor-sharp knife is essential. The stem is cut evenly below a node. Bottom leaves are removed to allow easier sticking in the sand, and top leaves may be trimmed lightly to lessen the risk of wilting. Once removed from the parent plant, the cuttings should never be allowed to wilt. A hormone rooting-powder can be dusted on the cut stem ends, and the excess powder shaken off, as too much may be harmful.

The cuttings are then inserted in the opened rows at 1- or 2-inch intervals, to a depth of about half the stem length. When the row is completed, the board used for marking is placed about ¼ inch away, and tapped lightly with a hammer along its entire length. This firms the cuttings into close contact with the sand; a final watering further guarantees a tightly set row.

On sunny days cuttings will require shading to prevent excessive water loss. Newspaper or cheesecloth is suitable for shading but is best supported a few inches above the cuttings to allow air circulation. In a coldframe, whitewashed sash is often sufficient. The rooting medium must never dry out on hot days, so a misty overhead watering is advantageous. However, as evening approaches the foliage should be dry to lessen the danger of disease.

As rooting occurs, new top growth will appear and the cuttings will become well secured in the sand. Gradually all shading is removed to harden the foliage for transplanting. When roots are strong, the cuttings may be potted, flatted, or set in shaded soil for a few weeks; then they are ready to take their places in the border.

Cuttings rooted in the open can stay there all winter if the sand is shallow and if occasional liquid fertilizers have been applied during the growing season. Roots will then reach the soil itself, and with winter protection, will produce fine plants for early spring.

The periods required for rooting vary with the plants and the condition of the stem. Lythrums may take only a week, chrysanthemums three weeks, platycodons over a month. The ease of striking root also ranges widely, with delphiniums and lupines often troublesome. Hollow and milky stems can give much trouble; in fact, results improve if the cuttings of milky stems (such as platycodon) actually wilt until bleeding stops before their insertion in the rooting medium.

Cuttings of a few plants (dianthus and lavandula, for example) root well if branched side shoots are torn, not cut, from the main stem, with a heel of tissue still attached.

While leaf-bud cuttings are more often used in propagating woody plants, heuchera, hibiscus, and sedum, among herbaceous kinds, can be increased by this method. Each cutting consists of one mature leaf, a small portion of stem, and a bud where the petiole joins the stem. Much greater increase is possible this way than with longer stem cuttings, but the sand must never become even momentarily dry.

Recent experiments worthy of the amateur's notice, though of more practical use in commercial nurseries, concern rooting under mist irrigation. Here there is no need to trim the foliage or firm the cuttings in the medium, nor is there any need for shade. The intermittent overhead veil of moisture that is automatically misted over the cuttings during the daylight hours keeps them turgid at all times. As roots develop, the mist is gradually withheld, to condition the plants before transplanting. An ingenious home gardener can rig up a hose to provide an intermittent mist for the plants he wants to propagate.

ROOT CUTTINGS

Where an abundance of thick, fleshy roots exists, these can be effectively used in propagation. Root-cutting procedure is chiefly practiced with echinaceas, Japanese anemones, Oriental poppies, gaillardias, *Brunnera macrophylla,* and with summer phlox. Yet hostas, which have numerous heavy roots, will not respond to this method.

Plants to be increased may be dug in fall; the best fleshy roots, often whitened, are removed and cut into sections 1½ to 3 inches long. Recent tests indicate that greater success is probable if roots are set upright in rows instead of scattered horizontally. It then becomes important that the top (the point nearest the parent plant) be uppermost. Hence, the bottom is cut slantwise, the top squarely level, for easy identification. New shoots will seldom be produced if the root cuttings are upside down.

A mixture of soil, peat, and sand is placed in flats. Into this the root cuttings are inserted so that the top of each is about ½ inch below the surface. The flats are watered and stored in coldframes over winter. In late spring, growth should be sufficiently advanced to allow planting in the open. Bloom will often occur the same year. In the absence of frames, such cuttings can be set in prepared beds in the open in early spring, but transplanting is seldom possible before early summer. Heavy initial watering upon transplanting is desirable in either case.

Oriental poppies require special treatment because of the short dormant period during which they can be moved safely. In August the clump is dug and roots are sliced into 2- to 4-inch lengths with cuts designating the top and bottom ends. For about a week, the cuttings are stored in moist sand until bleeding stops and callousing begins. The roots are then potted one to a pot of light soil, at least 2½ inches deep, then plunged in frames or open ground to remain until spring. Protection over winter is essential. Fall moving would be risky with such small material, but the plants must go into the border very early in the spring, before long tap-roots develop.

An advantage of root cuttings lies in the fact that old woody plants can be used as source materials. When stem cuttings are impossible, this method generally presents a speedier means of reproduction than does division.

Insects and Diseases

Insects and diseases have always preyed upon man's plantings and probably always will, to some extent. They could inflict inestimable damage if unchecked, with the weak, poorly growing plants suffering the worst. Nevertheless, swift, intelligent use of the proper chemicals will preserve the beauty of a garden. The whole matter of what, when, and how to apply pesticides is simplified each year. Moreover, the pest problem is seldom as grim as idle talk suggests, and should deter no one from having an outstanding garden of perennials.

To begin with, a fungicide is a substance designed to combat diseases caused by fungi, while an insecticide is employed against insects. Because neither can normally be expected to fulfill the other's purpose, they are combined in many of the products marketed today.

At present, great attention is being focused upon the development of these reliable all-purpose sprays or dusts, which for the most part are quite satisfactory. Designed to control sucking insects, chewing insects, powdery mildew, and various other foliage diseases, these compounds accomplish in one operation what would otherwise require separate applications. Some dusts in this group are packed in inexpensive cardboard cylinders fitted with dispensers so that the chemicals can be used without transfer to regular garden dusters. The ready-to-use aerosol or spray bombs now available also are extremely handy for treating only a few plants or for spot infestations.

Whichever one decides to use, liquid or powder, it should be stored in a dry, cool spot out of children's reach. All packages or bottles should be plainly labeled and kept tightly sealed. If the container is not impervious to light, it must be placed where sunlight cannot strike it. Under such conditions, many insecticides and fungicides remain useful a second year.

Government regulations require all spray or dust containers to be precisely labeled as to contents and the degree of toxicity to humans, with suggested antidotes. While not all of the compounds packaged for home gardeners are necessarily fatal to humans, they are best respected and used only as directed. Regulations also require statements as to the amounts required and methods of preparation. Furthermore, proof of the material's effectiveness must be furnished the government agency. Thus, the amateur is quite well protected against fraudulent claims.

Various devices for spraying or dusting are offered for sale, with constantly improved models cropping up annually. Every purse and every size garden can be accommodated. These implements should be operated, cleaned, and stored as recommended in their instruction sheets, to assure long, fruitful service.

Spray materials are sold either as wettable powders to be mixed with water, or as emulsions (liquid concentrates that are diluted with water). Emulsions are easier to prepare and do not require the constant agitation needed with powders to insure complete dissolving. They leave less noticeable residue on plants and are more easily stored. However, if not applied exactly as directed, they are also more likely to burn foliage.

Fungicides applied as dusting powders are less active than the same substances in sprays, but are handier to use in small quantities for quick jobs. The purchaser should specify his method of application when buying pesticides, since a spraying compound is especially treated to dissolve thoroughly in water, and is not suitable for dusting.

Whether to spray or to dust is a question each gardener can decide for himself after weighing the advantages and disadvantages of each method.

Among the advantages of spraying are these:

1. It is more economical from the standpoint of coverage.
2. The dried residue is more resistant to changing weather than is dust, thus provides longer protection.
3. Weather conditions at the time of spraying are less important (dust clinging best if dew is present).
4. If one makes up his own all-purpose spray, it is easier and more satisfactory to combine all the ingredients in one solution than it is in a duster.

Advantages of dusting include:

1. Dusters are lighter and easier to carry.
2. Dusts require no mixing or measuring of contents.
3. Dusters are easily assembled, operated, and cleaned. In fact, unused dust may be left in the device until another application is necessary. In contrast, spray tanks must be cleaned after each treatment.

The new gardener, not addicted to either method, might well be advised to use a spray. Whichever method is decided upon, thorough coverage is imperative, especially on the underside of the leaves, so that no uncovered areas are left open to attack.

A few random notes from recent experiment station findings are worthy of mention. Nicotine sulfate, long a favored insecticide, disappears from foliage quite rapidly and is now secondary to malathion. Rotenone dust clings longer than pyrethrum; methoxychlor is effective against certain insects unharmed by DDT. Arsenate of lead, an old standby against chewing insects, is now chiefly favored for trees only; methoxychlor appears more efficient on perennials and is also less toxic to human beings.

Some researchers believe powdery mildew is best controlled if the spray or dust is applied during late afternoon as the new mass of disease spores emerges, rather than in the morning, when only a few old spores are active. At any rate, it is important to have leaf surfaces protected, regardless of the time the spores emerge. Karathane and Mildex are likely to supplant sulfur as mildew controls, since they are less likely to damage foliage.

One way of reducing infestations is to treat the soil instead of the plant. Oxyquinoline sulfate is a promising liquid soil drench that can be used against diseases right where plants are growing. Corrosive sublimate (bichloride of mercury) and other mercurials still have their followers, too. Soil fumigants, effective against insects, root nematodes, and weed seeds, are available, but when they are used some time must elapse before the ground is safe for planting.

Spraying or dusting will control pests, but neither is a substitute for clean culture in the garden. Eradication of weeds may eliminate alternate hosts of some diseases; burning old stems and foliage in the fall removes overwintering spores of diseases as well as the eggs or larvae of some insects.

If difficulty is encountered in identifying insect or disease troubles, assistance is usually available from trained personnel, county extension agents, state universities, or experiment stations.

It is beyond the scope of one chapter to provide detailed information on the amounts and methods of application of the various compounds. Each pesticide package gives exact instructions for the use of that particular formula; these should be followed exactly. With so many new pesticides introduced each year, some of the older ones are quickly outdated. Some experiment stations publish authoritative, up-to-date information exploring the relative effectiveness of the formulations available.

The following table mentions the insects and diseases most likely to be encountered in the perennial border and suggests materials for their control.

Insect	*Controls*
Ant	Chlordane (dust)
Aphid	Malathion, nicotine sulfate
Beetle, blister	Rotenone, DDT, methoxychlor, lindane
Beetle, Japanese	DDT, methoxychlor (chlordane in the soil to control grubs)
Borer, corn	DDT

Insect	*Controls*
Borer, iris	DDT, malathion, methoxychlor
Cutworm	DDT, chlordane
Cyclamen mite	Malathion, aramite
Foliar nematode (chrysanthemum)	Sodium selenate (in ground)
Four-lined plant bug	DDT, methoxychlor
Leafhopper	Malathion, DDT, methoxychlor, lindane
Leaf miner	Malathion, DDT, methoxychlor, lindane
Mite, red spider	Malathion, aramite
Scale	Malathion in summer, dormant oil sprays or lime sulfur when dormant
Slug	Metaldehyde dusted on soil
Spittlebug	Malathion
Tarnished plant bug	DDT, methoxychlor
Thrip	Malathion, DDT
Wireworm	DDT, chlordane

Disease	*Controls*
Damping-off (seed flats)	Captan, semesan
Leaf spot	Ferbam, zineb, maneb, captan
Powdery mildew	Karathane, mildex, sulfur
Rust	Zineb, maneb, captan
Botrytis	Zineb

Nomenclature

No one has yet devised an easier way to remember an object than to give it a definite name. The casual gardener sometimes grumbles that the scientific names of his favorite flowers seem puzzling, that they are awkward and tedious to learn, or even that they are laughable. However, without some degree of order in any field of endeavor, only confusion can result.

The business of raising and selling plants is now world-wide, and becomes ever more extensive and intensive. Speedy transportation of seeds and plants by land, sea, and air brings the gardeners of many nations closer than ever before. Seedsmen in particular dispatch their catalogs to many countries of varying languages. Unless some universal method of classification and naming is followed, no gardener can be certain that the plants he orders are the ones he desires.

Common or local names are in no way dependable for certain identification in all parts of the world, or even throughout this country. For example, three totally unrelated plants are known to American gardeners as cowslip. What might they be called in Asia or Europe? Thankfully, they would be recognized by horticulturists and botanists the world over by their scientific names, *Caltha palustris, Mertensia virginica,* and *Dodecatheon.* To add to the possible confusion, cowslip in England refers to *Primula veris.* Similarly, in this country, both *Lythrum* and *Lysimachia* are commonly known as loosestrife.

Although tentative efforts toward the same goal had previously been made, Carl Linnæus first formalized a consistent nomenclatural procedure in 1753 when he published a two-volume study called *Species Plantarum,* in which all known plants were identified by a binomial (two-name) system. Latin was selected because of its status as the universal language of scholars.

The first portion of Linnæus's binomial designated the name of a *genus.* For instance, he placed the yarrows in a genus he called *Achillea.* The second portion, allowing for special differences among the yarrows, was given to a particular *species.* Hence, the woolly yarrow is properly *Achillea tomentosa* to any botanist anywhere. The binomial *Achillea tomentosa* is the specific *name* of the plant, whereas the specific *epithet* in this example is *tomentosa.* Related species are grouped into genera (plural of genus), and genera into families. The family name usually ends in -eæ, often in -aceæ.

The world's taxonomists are constantly reviewing the literature of plant names and descriptions. Occasionally, it becomes necessary to change the name of a plant, priority of publication of a name often being the ruling factor in the decision. The rules for naming horticultural plants are contained in the "International Code of Nomenclature for Cultivated Plants," adopted in 1958, and available in the United States from the American Horticultural Council.* Plants, as well as people, should be called by their correct names. When a woman's name changes through marriage, she does not continue to be called by her maiden name.

The term "variety" has long been loosely employed to designate variation, botanical or horticultural, within a species. The 1958 Code suggests that all horticultural variants, those types which originated in, or are maintained in cultivation, be termed *cultivars.*

New cultivar names are not to be in Latin, are to be capitalized, and are to be set off by single quotation marks, as in *Achillea filipendulina* 'Gold Plate.' When the word *variety,* or the abbreviation *var.* is used, it indicates that the plant in question exists in the wild, and has been assigned the botanical rank of variety. Sometimes, however, a hybrid developed in cultivation has been given a Latin name. The multiplication sign "×" preceding such a name indicates that the plant is of hybrid origin; for any hybrid two parents may be indicated in parentheses, as in *Epimedium* × *rubrum* (*E. alpinum* × *E. grandiflorum*). This would mean that the epimediums given the specific epithet of *rubrum* are hybrids, of which the parents are *E. alpinum* and *E. grandiflorum.*

One of the aims of this book is to encourage the use of the latest and most authentic nomenclature of perennials. In general, the names of all plants mentioned follow the *Manual of Cultivated Plants* by L. H. Bailey (1949 edition). The exceptions are the result of changes made necessary since that edition was published. A name in parentheses immediately following the correct name (except when it gives the parentage of a hybrid) is a synonym by which the plant is sometimes listed in trade catalogs.

* Care of Arnold Arboretum, Jamaica Plain 30, Mass.

Part 2

PLANTS FOR THE GARDEN OF PERENNIALS

Observations on the 560 or more species of plants described on the following pages are based primarily on experience in the northeastern states. In regions where climate and soil are different, plant performance, date of flowering, hardiness, and height may therefore be at variance. Adjustment to one's own situation should, however, be no more than a simple exercise. The general comments about the plants will apply wherever they are grown.

ACHILLEA — Yarrow — Compositæ

The ability to survive in spite of neglect is an important attribute of this genus, the botanical name of which is traced to Achilles, who was believed to have used certain species as medicinal aids for his warriors. There are about 100 kinds native to Europe and the Orient, but not many are grown for ornament; more than a few are weeds.

Garden Value: The genus may be loosely divided into the small rock garden types and taller plants that merit a place in the border. The more rugged kinds, such as *A. filipendulina*, are better as specimens in a border or among shrubbery plantings than when massed, except in naturalizing schemes. Several are useful as cut flowers. Nearly all easily resist droughts. An abundance of flowers is produced in ideal locations, and the fernlike texture of the foliage is attractive throughout the season.

Soil and Exposure: Average to poor soil, somewhat on the dry side, is needed; heavily fertilized or rich soil and moist situations lead to weak growth and inferior bloom. Full sunlight is preferred, as in their native habitats.

Care: Planting is generally safe in either fall or spring. When blossoms wither, the stems should be cut back to focus attention on the attractive foliage. Most species can be left in place three or four years, but *A. ptarmica* and *A. tomentosa* often need annual division for best performance.

Propagation: Seeds may be sown in early spring, but they yield some inferior plants. Cuttings may be made in midsummer for choice forms or for swift commercial propagation. When revitalizing old clumps or increasing stock of cultivars, spring is the best time for division.

Species

A. *ageratifolia* var. *aizoon* (*Anthemis aizoon*). This form is superior to the type and carries small pure white flowers, one to a stem, mainly in June and July. A silvery-leaved prize for the rock garden, it seldom grows more than 6 inches high.

A. *filipendulina* (A. *eupatorium*), Fernleaf Yarrow. The botanical name refers to the dissected leaves, which resemble those of some filipendulas. Although a robust plant may grow to 4 feet, it will present a graceful appearance because of the deeply cut grayish foliage. Numerous small yellow flowers are grouped in corymbs, like flattened saucers, 4 inches or more across. From June to September they provide cut flowers which are especially attractive on the superior cultivars.

For example, the cultivar 'Gold Plate' bears huge 6-inch butter-yellow trusses atop imposing 4½-foot plants. With globular echinops or delicate babys-breath, the flowers are superb in bouquets; their life in water is prolonged if the lower leaves are thoroughly stripped. The flowers also dry well for use in winter arrangements or ming-tree gardens. 'Parker's Variety' is not quite as heavy as 'Gold Plate' but is equally useful and just as drought resistant.

'Coronation Gold,' a chance hybrid between A. *filipendulina* and A *clypeolata,* is a first-class newcomer from England, with the virtues of an intermediate height of 3 feet, pleasing gray-green foliage, and masses of 3-inch mustard-yellow clusters over a lengthy period of bloom—June through August if seed formation is prevented. It appears to be a promising acquisition, and is well suited to today's smaller gardens.

A. × *lewisii.* This hybrid between A. *tomentosa* and A. *argentea,* raised at England's famed Ingwersen nursery, may be better known by the name 'King Edward IV.' Small clusters of primrose-yellow flowers are carried on 8-inch stems above woolly, gray-green tufts from June to August. In fairly good soil and with watering during dry periods, it has been compared to "a dash of moonlight on a frosty mountainside."

A. millefolium var. *rosea.* The species *A. millefolium* is the common yarrow of American meadows, seldom seen in our gardens. In rural England it is encouraged in pastures to ease cattle's digestion, and in parts of Sweden it is valued as a hop substitute in brewing beer. The variety *rosea,* with pink or red flowers, is worth while as a garden subject. 'Crimson Beauty' is very dark in color and of value as a cut flower.

A. nana. The cushions of white flowers are most effective in rockeries and do not exceed 4 inches in height when grown in sandy soil.

A. ptarmica, Sneezewort. The common name stems from the bygone practice of drying the roots for homemade snuff: "wort" is the ancient Anglo-Saxon word for plant. Generous clusters of small globular white flower heads, usually quite double, are borne on wiry 2-foot stems in midsummer. Florists use them as bouquet fillers, but their rampant tendencies and less attractive foliage are drawbacks in the garden. Cultivars, easily propagated, usually outshine plants raised from seed.

Of these, 'The Pearl' was christened "the great cemetery plant" by seedsmen of the '90's because of its ease of culture and freedom of bloom; it is an old garden standby. 'Perry's White' is noted for much doubled flower heads. 'Snowball' ('Boule de Neige') is only 14 inches tall, with fine white double heads. 'Angel's Breath' is new and warmly approved for its profusion of pure white blooms; it grows to 24 inches tall.

A. taygetea. When true to type, this native of Greece is an 18-inch pyramid of soft primrose-yellow flower clusters. Neat habit, gray foliage, and splendid cut flowers from June to August are certain from the better strains of seed.

A. tomentosa, Woolly Yarrow. In rock gardens, between flagstones, or used as a ground cover in sunny areas, woolly yarrow may be walked upon occasionally with little damage. Brilliant canary-yellow heads on 10-inch stems are effective in June and July. The woolly gray leaf rosettes spread rapidly, unless growing in very poor soils. In the Alps these tufted carpets act as foils to show off blue gentians. 'Moonlight' is more subdued in coloring and less invasive in growth than the species.

Final Comment: Undoubtedly the additional species featured in European catalogs warrant trial in America.

ACONITUM Aconite, Monkshood, Wolfsbane Ranunculaceæ

The potent drug aconite is distilled from *A. napellus*, and another species from the Himalayas once provided the poison used for arrows in India. English records show that misguided persons have scraped aconite roots as they would horseradish, with dire results. Common sense dictates that these plants belong in the flower garden, far from the vegetable plot.

Medieval associations are indicated by the common names, to which helmet-flower and friarscap may be added. Theophrastus is said to have coined the name *Aconitum* from widespread colonies of plants found at Acona, Greece. Native habitats range through Europe, North America, and Asia.

Garden Value: Tall spikes of dark-colored, hooded flowers add dignity to the perennial border, as specimens or in small groups. They are especially striking with the white flowers of phlox, lilies, or Shasta daisies. In addition, the dark glossy foliage, never coarse in effect, is attractive throughout the season. Aconitums are often planted with delphiniums to continue the vertical background effect into the latter part of the season. When naturalized, they create pleasant effects around wooded outskirts. Most are commendable when cut.

Soil and Exposure: Performance is best in partial shade and in a moist, deep, rich soil, high in humus content, where light applications of superphosphate have been incorporated.

Care: In early autumn, preferably, the tuberous roots are set just below the soil line, at least 2 feet from other plants. They require winter protection the first year. Spring planting must be accomplished early before extensive foliage develops. Adequate water during summer droughts is important, but little other care is needed except, perhaps, staking the taller types. The plants increase so slowly they can remain undisturbed for many years.

Propagation: Sizable clumps may be divided in spring or early fall. It is imperative to avoid getting any root or leaf juices in the mouth. Seeds do not germinate readily or give uniform results.

Species

A. bicolor (*A. napellus* var. *bicolor*). In August, 3- to 4-foot plants bear rather showy flowers of cloudy white edged with China blue.

A. carmichaelii (*A. fischeri*). Slightly smaller stature, excellent foliage, and densely compacted spikes of lustrous blue all commend this patrician from China. Blooming in August and September, it combines well with *Aster* 'Harrington's Pink.' *A. carmichaelii* var. *wilsonii* (*A. wilsonii*) towers to 6 or 8 feet with violet-blue flowers in September, making an excellent combination with early chrysanthemums.

A. henryi (*A. autumnale*). This species differs from the others in that the dark blue flowers are borne in open-branched inflorescences. Plants are 4 feet or so in height, and bloom from late July until September. 'Spark's Variety' is a robust 6-foot specimen superior to the type, with flowers a deeper shade of blue.

A. napellus, English Monkshood. A variable species, it ranges from 4 to 6 feet in height, with blue to violet flowers in erect spikelike racemes from late July through August. The foliage is more finely divided than in the others.

A. vulparia (*A. lycoctonum*), Wolfsbane. Usually 3 feet or so high, with small yellow flowers in July, this is a novelty for the border.

Final Comment: Gardeners should note the changes in nomenclature for this genus and realize that some plants in commerce are incorrectly named. Also, many of the species are variable. With normal precautions, there is no need to be perturbed by the poisonous nature of the roots, seeds, and leaves.

Achillea filipendulina
Æthionema pulchellum

Aconitum napellus
Ajuga reptans

ÆTHIONEMA **Stonecress** **Cruciferæ**

"Stonecress" refers to the readiness of the genus to be at home in almost any rocky pocket of ground. The majority of the species are native on the parched limestone cliffs of the Mediterranean region. The name *Æthionema,* from two Greek words meaning scorched filaments, refers to the singed appearance of the stamens.

Garden Value: Most stonecresses are bushy little subshrubs, relatively evergreen, and seldom over a foot tall; in initial growth they tend to be prostrate. Crisp gray- to blue-green foliage competes in interest with terminal racemes of pink to rose-colored candytuft-like blooms. Flowering from May to July, they are useful in rock gardens, dry wall plantings, or along the front edge of a border.

Soil and Exposure: Stonecresses are accustomed to dry, alkaline, sandy loams. They will not tolerate poor drainage, and performance may be disappointing unless lime is added to acid soils. Full, open sunlight is recommended, to duplicate conditions where they are found growing wild.

Care: Small plants, preferably potted, transplant with ease in the spring; long roots make older specimens difficult to move. After blossoming, plants can be sparingly trimmed to encourage new shoots. Where winters are cold and open, a light covering of evergreen boughs prevents burning of the persistent foliage.

Propagation: Seeds of all species may be sown in spring, but the named cultivars seldom reproduce true to type. Cuttings are easily rooted in summer. Division in early spring or immediately after flowering is rewarding only in proportion to the number of outer shoots, for the center of the clump is woody.

Species

Æ. coridifolium (*Iberis jacunda*), Lebanon Stonecress. The height of the partially decumbent stems is usually restricted to 6 inches. Flowers are rose-pink with lilac veins. Some of the material in commerce listed as *Æ. pulchellum* actually belongs here.

Æ. grandiflorum, Persian Stonecress, Giant Stonecress. In view of the abbreviated 12-inch stature normally encountered, the latter common name seems a trifle facetious. On walls the slim branches trail, but in the open they stand erect. Soft pink flowers blend with silver-edged leaves of steely blue-green.

Æ. iberideum. This trim 6-inch cushion of gray foliage bursts into bloom during April and May. Snow-white flowers show infrequent tints of lilac. A rarity in gardens.

Æ. pulchellum. From Asia Minor, it attains a height of only 6 to 8 inches because of the primarily horizontal growth. The soft rose-pink clusters borne in June and July are mildly fragrant, and make a pleasant combination with the slender bluish leaves. 'Warley Rose' is the hybrid most often available. It forms excellent 6-inch mounds of steel-blue leaves and is so blanketed with vivid rose-carmine blooms that superficial resemblance to *Daphne cneorum* is suggested. It is said to have originated in the garden of Gertrude Jekyll, noted English plantswoman. 'Warley Ruber' and 'Borsch's Sport' are darker, approaching Tyrian rose tones.

Final Comment: It is significant to remember the stonecresses are Spartans toward drought but do not tolerate wetness.

AJUGA **Bugle, Bugleweed** **Labiatæ**

Ajugas solve many problems where ground covers are needed. The numerous species are widely distributed, but those of Europe are the finest; relatively few are commonly listed in catalogs of this country. Many plant sources are inexact in nomenclature, and natural variations have been frequent, so confusion is not uncommon.

Garden Value: There are few better carpeting plants, especially for adverse conditions. Small blue flowers in spikes that rarely exceed 10 inches in height are abundant in May and June. While most often used as a ground cover in shade, even at the base of trees where grass will not grow, ajuga is also satisfactory in rock gardens or as an edging for a border. The demand for frequent division may be an adverse factor.

Soil and Exposure: General tolerance of poor soils and either full sun or deep shade adds immeasurably to its value.

Care: Occasional division, governed mainly by space considerations, is all that is necessary.

Propagation: Division is practical in spring, after flowering. Seeds sown in early spring or autumn will provide many plants; they can usually be relied upon to produce variations.

Species

A. genevensis, Geneva Bugle. Lacking creeping stolons, it spreads less than the commoner *A. reptans*, yet frequent division may be necessary. The flowers, in erect 12-inch spikes, are a bright blue. The cultivar 'Pink Spires' is a handsome subject with pure pink flowers and foliage that tends to remain evergreen much of the winter. 'Brockbankii,' with rich deep blue flowers, is intermediate between *A. genevensis* and *A. reptans*, but does not spread as rapidly as the latter.

A. pyramidalis. Considered by some the finest bugle because the clumps increase slowly. Its tubular flowers of bright gentian blue are conspicuous on 9-inch stems. Performance is best in partial shade. 'Metallica-crispa' is widely distributed in the trade as the bronze ajuga. Its metallic leaves take on red tints in autumn. 'Tottenham Blue' is a fine British selection, with clear steel-blue blossoms.

A. reptans, Carpet Bugleweed. The most ubiquitous of the genus, it is exceedingly stoloniferous. Typical forms produce large clumps of shining green foliage and 8-inch spikes of deep blue flowers. Many variations are available, among them: 'Variegata,' with yellow mottling of the foliage; 'Purpurea,' with deep bronze-purple leaves; and 'Alba,' which has white flowers and light green foliage, and which increases more slowly than the species.

Final Comment: Careful search through catalogs will unearth numerous other forms of interest.

ALCHEMILLA — Lady's Mantle — Rosaceæ

This genus is of value to the gardener interested in the unusual for partially shaded areas, perhaps in border foregrounds or rock gardens. The few species are prized for their handsome, palmately lobed foliage as well as for the clusters of small chartreuse flowers in July. The delicate sprays can be used in small bouquets or successfully dried. Plants are easily grown in partial shade in any average soil that has enough organic matter to prevent summer baking.

A. *vulgaris,* the species most often grown, is commonly called Lady's mantle because, according to legend, it contributed to the adornment of the Virgin Mary. It is noted for its rounded grayish leaves, sometimes expanded to widths of 4 inches, the lobes creased like segments of a fan. When in full bloom the long stems arch, reducing the height to about 18 inches. *A. alpina* is about 6 inches shorter and is suited to small groupings. *A. speciosus,* a 9-inch rarity seen only in choice rock gardens, has interesting pitted leaves which are covered with silky hairs; flowers are cream-colored.

Propagation from seeds is simple, although divisions of large clumps can be made in early spring.

ALSTRŒMERIA **Peruvian-Lily** **Amaryllidaceæ**

Named by Linnæus for his friend, Claus Alstrœmer, this genus comprises several showy South American species that should be grown more extensively, and would be were it not for the misconception that they are not hardy. *A. aurantiaca* is the hardiest, surviving in Rhode Island, New Jersey, and in central New York to the shores of Lake Ontario. Granted, where winters are severe, these plants should be placed in sheltered areas or given winter protection. In warmer climates other species, as well as the Ligtu Hybrids, which have a wider color range, can be grown.

Garden Value: Bright orange-yellow flowers on 3-foot stems, good for cutting, are colorful in June and early July, adding a note of distinction to a border.

Soil and Exposure: The fleshy roots should be planted 6 inches deep, in partial shade where there is a light, well-drained soil with adequate humus.

Propagation: Seeds are sown as soon as ripe in August directly in the garden where the plants are to stand. Divisions can be made in the fall after the foliage has matured and turned yellow.

Final Comment: Alstrœmerias are valuable subjects for the gardener interested in trying the less common plants.

ALTHÆA Hollyhock Malvaceæ

Although the hollyhock is a biennial, it is included here because it self-sows so readily that, once established, it perpetuates itself year after year.

Althæa, from the Greek "to cure," reminds us of the healing qualities once credited to some members of the genus. *A. rosea,* the only species generally grown, first reached England in 1593, and has long been popular both there and in America.

Garden Value: Plants vary from 5 to 8 feet, with single or double flowers, and a wide color range; only blue is not represented. Tall and vertical in form, they are usually placed in the background, often serving to screen unsightly objects. The colorful spikes of flowers open in July and August.

Soil and Exposure: Of very easy culture in average soil and sunny areas, they require no special conditions.

Care: Staking is recommended in windswept regions. If, after several years, volunteer seedlings revert to single-flowered types with ordinary colors, it is wise to dig all plants and start with a new packet of seeds. Removal of faded flowers will help prevent seeding. Weekly spraying with a fungicide controls hollyhock rust, a disease evidenced by large orange spore cases on the foliage. An insecticide may also be needed where the Japanese beetle is a pest. Clean culture, consisting of elimination of cheeseweed (a member of the same family and an alternate host for the rust) and burning old foliage and stems each autumn, is advisable.

Propagation: Seedsmen offer several fine strains: Pompadour, ruffled doubles of ball-shaped form; Chater's, ordinary doubles of diverse colors; and Allegheny, semidouble flowers predominating, with fringed petals. There are also annual strains which bloom the current year if seeds are sown under glass in February.

ALYSSUM **Alyssum** **Cruciferæ**

The splash of brassy yellow provided by the common alyssum is well known and often over-exploited. More attention to the less common forms might be a step forward.

The name *Alyssum,* of Greek origin, connotes cures for madness; various species were once commonly known as madwort in England. Most of the species come from the Mediterranean region. The annual sweet alyssum, not a member of this genus, is *Lobularia maritima.*

Garden Value: Nearly every rock garden boasts at least one alyssum, with its yellow glitter in April and May and the fine gray foliage which may persist to some extent over winter. Agreeable contrasts are possible when used with spring-flowering bulbs, creeping phlox, arabis, dwarf columbines, and *Daphne cneorum.* Small groups add foliage color contrast in the border where they are often used as edging plants.

Soil and Exposure: Alyssums thrive in full sun and well-drained light soil which has not been heavily fertilized.

Care: Some species are short-lived unless sheared after bloom to promote new shoots. Division every third spring rejuvenates old clumps and curbs excessive spreading of some types.

Propagation: Seeds sown in spring or early fall yield variable results. Choice plants are best propagated from cuttings taken in midsummer. Although they do not always root easily, such cuttings form the principal commercial means of increase. Division and layering in the spring are also possible.

Species

A. montanum. Somewhat similar to the common *A. saxatile,* it is a neater plant, never over 8 inches in height, and with fragrant flowers. No doubt greater attention will be focused on this species in the future. *A. moellendorfianum* is a closely related species worthy of notice.

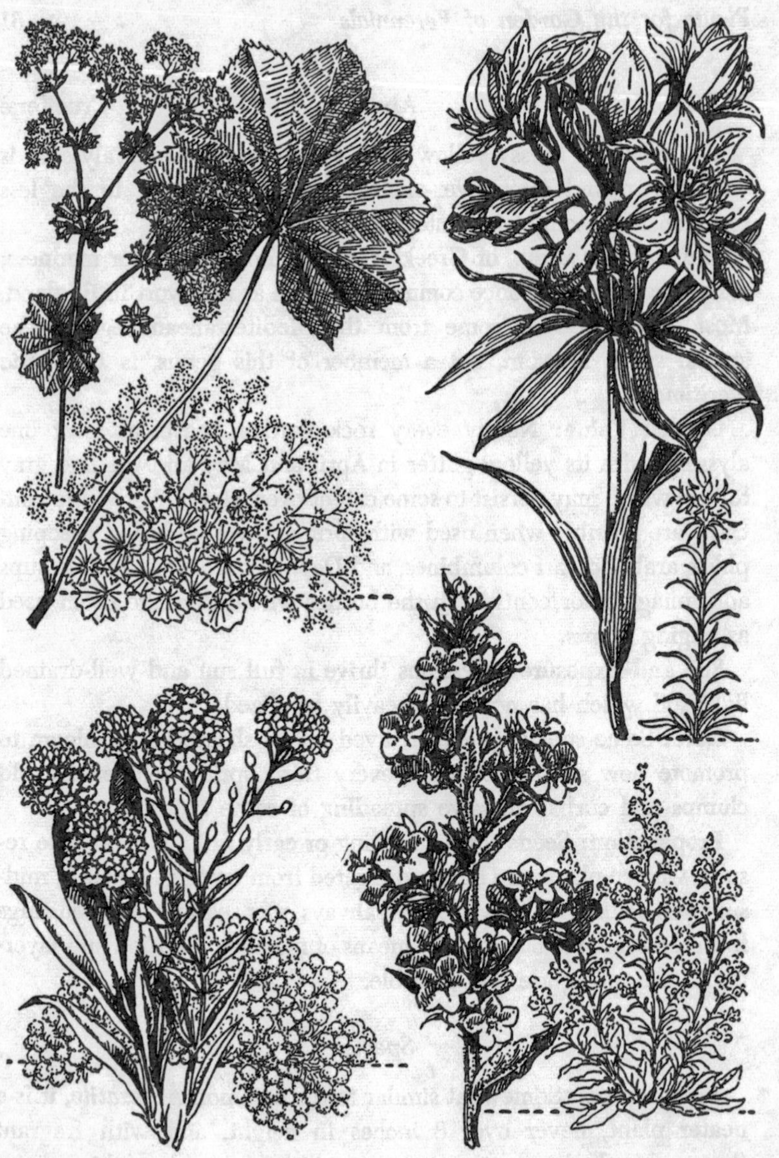

Alchemilla vulgaris
Alyssum saxatile

Alstrœmeria aurantiaca
Anchusa azurea

A. murale, Yellowtuft. Medium-yellow flowers on 18-inch stems appear in June and July, extending the effect of *A. saxatile.* Self-sowing is inevitable, but unwanted plants can easily be culled. Plants offered as *A. argenteum* usually turn out to be *A. murale.*

A. saxatile, Basket-of-Gold, Goldentuft. There is a tendency to overplant this species. It is apt to sprawl coarsely, and the clusters of tiny yellow flowers on 12-inch stems are a hue of which a little goes a long way. 'Dudley Neville,' blooming somewhat earlier, is an English selection with flowers shaded from peach-buff to chrome yellow; seedlings vary considerably. 'Compactum' is a much neater, more compact plant than the type. The double-flowered form of this cultivar is rare but most desirable, blooming well into June. It produces no seeds so must be propagated vegetatively. Forms listed as 'Luteum,' 'Citrinum,' and 'Sulphureum' are identical, and with 'Silver Queen' or 'Sulphur Queen' vary in having lemon-yellow flowers which are quite attractive with the gray leaves. Not as hardy as the species, they deserve a light winter cover of evergreen boughs.

A. serpyllifolium. A midget for the rock garden, it has tiny foliage and 2-inch stems of bright yellow flowers.

A. spinosum. Distinct from the others in the genus, this sub-shrub is a mass of white bloom from May to early July. The dense spiny growth forms a silvery 12-inch hummock. If unprotected, it may windburn during open winters, but will survive. 'Roseum' varies in flower color from deep rose to paler shades when grown from seed.

Final Comment: Still other species that are under test may prove worthy of merit.

AMSONIA Amsonia Apocynaceæ

The genus was named *Amsonia* in 1760 to honor a Virginia physician and botanist by the name of Charles Amson.

Garden Value: Plants are hardy, dependable, slow-growing, of the easiest culture in sun or partial shade, in moist or dry soils, with no insect or disease problems—yet they are not often planted. As specimens or in groups of three, they add an unusual note in borders. Wiry stems are tough and resistant to the high winds common along seasides. In spite of a milky sap, the unusual flowers are effective when cut.

Propagation: The simplest method of propagation is by spring-sown seeds. Cuttings are sometimes rooted in midsummer, and division of the deeply rooted clumps is possible in very early spring.

Species

A. tabernæmontana. Native from Pennsylvania to Kansas and southward, it is an appropriate garden plant, 3 feet tall, with terminal cymes of many steel-blue flowers in May and June. If the shoots are pinched at the tips in late April, a panicled habit results. The willow-like foliage is green all summer but turns golden in autumn.

A. montana. 15 inches high, with pale blue flowers, it is suitable for large rock gardens or the front of a border.

A. ciliata (*A. angustifolia* var. *tenuifolia*). A recent introduction by Mary F. Henry of Philadelphia, as yet untested but promising, it has feathery foliage and large aquamarine flowers. It spreads by underground runners, rare for the genus.

Final Comment: The neat, restricted growth of amsonias commends them to the attention of those with limited space.

ANCHUSA — Bugloss — Boraginaceæ

The common name is from the Greek, *bu-gloss,* meaning ox-tongue, a reference to the shape and roughness of the leaves. The botanical name, also from the Greek, denotes a pigment obtained from the roots of some species, and once used as a cosmetic. Most of the species are native to Europe and Asia Minor, but not more than a half dozen are grown in our gardens.

Garden Value: The true-blue flowers account for most of the limited popularity of the genus. *A. azurea* makes a showy background subject, while *A. cæspitosa* is small enough for the rock garden or border foreground.

Soil and Exposure: A light, well-drained soil is imperative. Plants thrive in full sun, but tolerate light shade.

Care: Spring-planting is suggested, and staking thereafter may be needed for the taller sorts. Watering is extremely beneficial during dry spells. To prevent overcrowding, volunteer seedlings should be thinned out each year. Division is normally needed each third spring.

Propagation: Cultivars are best propagated by division in spring. Seeds of ordinary types, sown in spring or fall, will give numerous plants from which the best should be selected for planting in the garden.

Species

A. azurea (*A. italica*), Italian Bugloss. Loose racemes of bright blue flowers along branching 3- to 5-foot stems are produced from June through August. Cultivars are superior to the type. 'Dropmore,' a onetime favorite, may reach 6 feet, with turquoise-blue flowers at their best in June and July. 'Opal' is virtually a lighter-toned duplicate. 'Morning Glory' is a notably sturdy and profusely blooming type with large gentian-blue flowers. 'Feltham Pride,' a bright blue English selection, is more compact than the type, with dense flower clusters. 'Loddon Royalist' is a recent introduction of neat habit, not over 3 feet tall.

A. barrelieri. Plants 2 feet in height produce panicles of small, cobalt-blue flowers with white or yellow throats in May and June. They combine well with doronicums and spring-flowering bulbs, in arrangements as well as in the garden. Mature plants do not always transplant safely.

A. cæspitosa. This species is represented in the trade by a mutant form named 'Blue Stars,' a well-branched plant 15 to 18 inches tall bearing electric-blue flowers from late April well into July. A dry location with perfect drainage is a prerequisite for success with this cultivar; otherwise it may be short-lived.

A. myosotidiflora. See *Brunnera macrophylla.*

Final Comment: Porous drainage is the prime factor for success with any member of the genus.

ANDROSACE **Rock-Jasmine** **Primulaceæ**

These tiny stoloniferous rock garden plants, not over 4 inches high when in bloom in May and June, resemble dwarf primulas, to which they are related. Leaves form basal rosettes at the ends of stolons, and these provide the principal means of propagation. The species most often grown are the pink-flowered *A. primuloides* and the rose-flowered *A. sarmentosa,* the second of which is faster growing. Lesser known species with white flowers are available.

Appropriate plants for scree or moraine soils, all members of the genus will colonize readily—but never become invasive—if given perfect drainage and partial shade. For those more interested in the restrained miniature than the spectacular, rock-jasmine will be a happy choice.

ANEMONE **Anemone, Windflower** **Ranunculaceæ**

Some anemones may be temperamental garden subjects, but the fresh wholesomeness of the spring-flowering ones, and the grace of the later Japanese types, well repay any attentions required for success.

Anemone, from *anemos* or wind in Greek, apparently derives its name from the open, windy reaches some species inhabit in nature. There are about 100 species ranging over North America, Europe, and Asia but only a quarter of them are cultivated. *A. coronaria* is one of the tender, tuberous group known to florists as St. Brigid anemone.

Garden Value: Some species can be readily naturalized. Dwarf species are effective in rock gardens, and the taller ones are valued in perennial borders, preferably in small groups. A few, notably the late-blooming Japanese types, provide good cut flowers if picked before the heat of midday and properly conditioned. The fall-blooming types are valued because the texture of the foliage and of the delicate flowers differs from that of most late season flowers, including asters, chrysanthemums, heleniums, and helianthus.

Soil and Exposure: With very few exceptions, as noted, anemones do best in a rich soil containing adequate humus, but provided with sharp drainage. Most species tolerate full sun if the soil is moist, but partial shade is recommended for superior performance.

Care: New plants should be set out in spring so they will become firmly established by winter. Thorough watering is necessary during dry summers. Once established, plants grow slowly and do not need to be disturbed for many years. When necessary, transplanting is done in early spring. The black, gray-striped blister beetle can strip Japanese anemones to skeletons in July or early August, so spraying with DDT or rotenone before one leaves on vacation may pay dividends later in the season.

Propagation: Seeds of dwarf species are sown in early spring or fall. If necessary, divisions of older plants can be made in early spring. Root cuttings provide the commercial means of increase for Japanese anemones. Two-inch pieces of roots are placed in sandy loam—outdoors in early spring, under glass in winter.

Species

A. blanda, Grecian Windflower, Sapphire Anemone. Very early in the season the 6-inch mounds of neat compound foliage display bright blue flowers, although variants of pink and other shades may occur. In ideal locations it will colonize readily.

A. hupehensis. Similar to Japanese anemone, but a much smaller plant, usually not over 2 feet in height, its rose-pink flowers begin in August. *A. hupehensis* var. *japonica* (*A. japonica*), taller, more varied in coloring and in number of flower parts, blooms in September. The white form generally listed as 'Alba' occurred spontaneously in a private French garden, and may be known to Europeans as 'Honorine Jobert.'

A. × *hybrida,* Japanese Anemone. The late Alex Cumming of

Bristol, Connecticut, and others have interbred selections of *A. hupehensis* var. *japonica* to develop taller strains, varying in color and flower type, which flower as early as mid-August. Almost all modern garden selections of the so-called Japanese anemone are now grouped under this name. These choice plants will not thrive in dry summers, soggy winters, or windy, unprotected sites.

Elegant though coarsely compound foliage and delicate blossoms are attractive features of the cultivars, most of which are 3 feet or more in height. Among them are: 'Kriemhilde,' semidouble, with creamy pearl-pink blooms on thick, bronzed stems; 'Queen Charlotte,' semidouble, pink; 'Mont Rose,' semidouble, large clear rose flowers; 'Marie Manchard,' semidouble, white, superior to 'Whirlwind,' the older cultivar which was found growing in a Rochester, New York garden in 1888; 'September Charm,' single, silvery pink shaded rose-mauve; 'September Sprite,' single, rosy pink, 12 to 15 inches high and often recommended for rock gardens.

A. × *lesseri.* A hybrid between *A. multifida* and *A. sylvestris*, 12 to 15 inches tall, it resembles the latter in habit but has bright cherry-crimson flowers in May and June.

A. nemorosa, European Wood Anemone. The type grows to 8 inches and is ordinarily white-flowered, but rose and purple forms exist, as well as doubles. 'Royal Blue' is a much showier selection, with deep blue flowers on 6-inch stems.

A. pulsatilla, Pasque-Flower. Brought to England by Roman invaders, it still flourishes in chalky downs where they made camp. The common name refers to a green dye used for Easter eggs. In early spring, flowers appear on gradually elongating 8-inch stems; silken, finely cut foliage appears next, then more blossoms, and finally plumy seed pods which have been characterized as tiny, feathery mops.

Attractive forms in blue, white, pink, and red are in cultivation; a yellow Caucasian newcomer is being tested in England. 'Mrs. Van der Elst' is an especially admirable rose-pink cultivar. Performance of all forms is best in dry pockets of a light-textured soil containing some humus and lime; rich ground spoils the compact habit.

A. sylvestris, Snowdrop Anemone. Aromatic, satiny white blossoms, 2 inches across, are generously borne in May and June on 15-inch stems. Colonies develop in favorable locations.

A. vitifolia. From Nepal, it was sent to England by Dr. Nathaniel Wallich, "the father of Indian Botany" before 1900. While generally considered half-hardy, it has wintered Connecticut conditions successfully, and should be successful farther south. In early August, large pale pink blooms appear on 2- to 3-foot stems.

ANTHEMIS Chamomile, Golden Marguerite Compositæ

Drought resistance makes this genus important to the week-end gardener with little time for maintenance.

Anthemis, the Greek name for the chamomile, is now applied to about 100 species indigenous to Asia and Europe, notably in the Mediterranean area. Some species have escaped in North America, and a great many can be classed as undesirable weeds.

Garden Value: Anthemis offers a providential answer for difficult, sandy soil in grueling heat. Some species fit into borders or can be massed in naturalized stretches, others are rock garden types, while a few have herbal value. They are acceptable as cut flowers although certain older forms of *A. tinctoria* temporarily "go to sleep" after being cut.

Soil and Exposure: Light porous ground is necessary since winter-killing results from poorly drained situations. Full sun is recommended, although creditable bloom may occur in partial shade.

Care: Spring-planting is normally best. The larger species require about 2 feet of space between plants. Removal of faded flowers prolongs the blooming season and limits self-sowing. If not divided each second year, *A. tinctoria* is likely to develop a dead area in the center of the clump. Aphids occasionally become troublesome, but are easily controlled with malathion or nicotine sprays.

Propagation: Seeds reproduce faithfully for most species, but give wide variation from cultivars. Spring-sowing is recommended. Divisions can be made in spring or early autumn; cuttings usually root best when the summer heat has passed.

Species

A. aizoon. See *Achillea ageratifolia* var. *aizoon.*

A. biebersteiniana. The 12-inch height, silvery leaves, and large yellow, daisy-like flowers, which appear chiefly in June, all contribute to make a fine rock garden subject.

A. cupaniana. Native to the Apennine Mountains of northern Italy. At a height of 12 inches, numerous white flowers glisten most of the summer, and the silvery leaves are attractive all season. While it is well suited for walls, rock gardens, or at the base of shrubbery, some spreading is to be expected. It will not tolerate wet ground.

A. nobilis, Chamomile. As an herb, it may be brewed into a strong but soothing tea; as a spreading ground cover, the ferny aromatic clumps blanket sandy soils. Inconspicuous white flowers occur on 8-inch stems. An old doubled form may still exist.

A. sancti-johannis. The name honors St. John, the patron saint of a Bulgarian monastery near the spot where the plant was first collected. About 2½ feet tall, it should produce bright orange flowers, but the color is extremely unreliable from modern seed sources. Because the habit is not as weedy as in other species, it has been crossed by English breeders to *A. tinctoria* on a limited scale.

A. tinctoria, Golden Marguerite. In Europe this plant often becomes a pestiferous weed, self-sowing on rubbish heaps; yet it is the source of today's cultivars, most of which originated in England. The late Amos Perry introduced several of note. 'Kelwayi' is 2 feet tall, with deep yellow flowers. 'Perry's Variety' has large pure yellow blossoms. 'Thora Perry' is a hybrid with orange tints of *A. sancti-johannis,* but the plant lacks vigor. 'Golden Dawn,' a double-flowered variant which first appeared in a Pennsylvania garden, requires annual division to insure survival. 'Moonlight' differs in having soft primrose-yellow blooms which blend well with anything blue. Perhaps 'Grallagh Gold,' from an amateur in northern Ireland, is best of all. Its gleaming butter-yellow flowers, borne on 2½-foot plants, are good for cutting. 'Beauty of Grallagh' comes from the

Anemone hybrida

Aquilegia hybrida

Anemone pulsatilla
Anthemis tinctoria
Arabis caucasica

same source, and is reported to be more compactly upright, with larger, even richer coloring.

Final Comment: Seedlings of all cultivars should be culled out, as they will revert to the common type, and possibly choke out the parent plant in time.

AQUILEGIA Columbine Ranunculaceæ

Columbines have long been popular garden plants, even since Elizabethan times. John Gerard, author of the famous *Herbal* (1597) commended them "for the beautie and variable color of their flowers."

The botanical name is of uncertain origin, but may come from the Latin *aquila*, meaning like an eagle, possibly a reference to the resemblance of the spurs to an eagle's beak. "Columbine" alludes to a dove, the spurred flowers supposedly resembling this bird.

The various species are native to Asia, Europe, and North America. Those indigenous to Siberia and similarly cold regions tend to be dull and small, but warmer zones produce greater flamboyance. Western United States perhaps offers the most colorful types, although nearly any species will please the fancier. Many of the cultivated types are hybrid races of indefinite parentage.

Garden Value: Numerous dwarfs are suitable for rock gardens, while the larger types enhance perennial borders, where they are most effective in groups, or as naturalized masses if informality is the keynote. Long-spurred races blend well with doronicums and bearded iris, but the plants function by virtue of foliage as well as of flowers. Their attractive compound leaves fill in early vacancies that are later taken over by poppies, lilies, phlox, and other summer flowers. As cut flowers, columbines are uniquely, if briefly, engaging. Aquilegias interhybridize and self-sow in the garden, the seedlings reverting in time to less desirable types; hence occasional renewal is suggested.

Soil and Exposure: Sharp drainage is mandatory; light soils with adequate humus for moisture retention are recommended. Plants tolerate full sun although light shade prolongs the flowering season and encourages naturalizing.

Care: Planting is permissible in early spring or late summer. Seed pods should be removed as soon as the flowers fade. Leaf miners and stem borers may be pests, but new plants easily grown from seeds solve the problem. The presence of leaf miners is indicated by unusually pale foliage in which the white winding trails of the miners are obvious. Infected leaves should be burned, and the remainder of the clump treated with DDT or malathion.

Propagation: The principal method is by seeds, which germinate easily. The plants from spring-sown seeds, however, do not flower until the next year. Sowings may also be made in August, or as soon as the seeds are ripe. Division may be carefully attempted in August or September for unusual types.

Species

A. *alpina*. Dwarf and enduring, it is a valuable asset for the rock garden. Flowers may be powdery blue, or blue and white. 'Hensol Harebell,' an improved selection, is deeper blue, but may grow to 2 feet in height.

A. *cærulea*, Rocky Mountain Columbine. Colorado's state flower has lavender-blue sepals, white petals, and 1½-inch spurs on plants 2½ feet in height. Completely white forms also appear. In hotter climates, it becomes short-lived and has been blamed for a like shortcoming in the long-spurred hybrids, to which it has contributed heavily. A hybrid between this species and A. *flabellata*, named 'Helenae,' is 15 inches tall with blue and white flowers. In spite of its hybrid nature, reproduction from seeds is remarkably true.

A. *canadensis*, American Columbine. Native from Nova Scotia to Georgia, it thrives on sunny gravelly ledges. Brilliant red sepals combine with yellow petals; the spurs are short and straight. When well grown, plants attain heights of 2 feet, but in rich soil lax growth results.

A. *chrysantha*. Native to the Rockies and Southwest, this long-spurred species of variable yellow shadings is one source of the garden hybrids. Plants 3 feet tall all have rich dark foliage. Of easy culture.

A. clematiflora. A name applied to spurless sports from the long-spurred hybrids known as the Mrs. Scott Elliot strain. The 3-inch blossoms in several colors somewhat resemble those of climbing clematis.

A. ecalcarata (*Semiaquilegia ecalcarata*). Reginald Farrer, renowned British plant collector, spurned this oddity from Western China as "an ugly, little quaint maroonish flower." Actually the tiny spurless blooms are nearly coppery chocolate, on 12- to 18-inch stems. It may need frequent renewal by seeds.

A. flabellata. Pale green foliage and waxy lavender-blue flowers are typical of this appealing 15-inch species from Japan. 'Nana,' only 6 inches tall, has white flowers in late April.

A. glandulosa (*A. jucunda*). Inconsistent in performance, it is beautiful when well established. Plants 18 inches high produce large nodding blooms of rich blue and white.

A. jonesii. This hard-to-grow collector's item from the Rockies is an exquisite dwarf of blue-gray foliage and relatively large blue flowers on 6-inch stems. Best in neutral to slightly alkaline soils, but it will not tolerate drought.

A. longissima. Because of the pale yellow coloring and the 4- to 6-inch spurs, this species has been incorporated in the parentage of the long-spurred hybrids. West Texas to New Mexico is the arid homeland.

A. oxysepala var. *yabeana.* This extremely hardy species from East China, producing vigorous 2½-foot plants with metallic blue flowers in early May, could well be bred into the long-spurred races to increase longevity.

A. vulgaris, European Columbine. Sturdy, long-lived plants 2 feet or so tall have flowers with short, hooked spurs, although some races are spurless. Other variants occur with double flowers. Colors are often uninspiring.

A. × hybrida. This name is often given to garden races of long-spurred flowers. Such species as *A. cærulea, A. longissima, A. chrysantha,* and *A. canadensis* have been interbred to create handsome but often transient strains. Heights of 3 feet are common. Flowers in a wide range of colors appear primarily in June and July, but scattered bloom appears throughout the season.

'Snow Queen,' 'Copper Queen,' 'Rose Queen,' and 'Crimson Star' are all self-descriptive names, and all grow surprisingly true from seeds. Of several outstanding strains, two are recommended: Mrs. Scott Elliot, an old standby; and McKana's Giant, an All-America Seed Trial winner in 1955, noted for its sturdy growth, superb color range, and exceedingly large flowers, many of which have spurs 4 or more inches long.

Final Comment: Most gardeners will find that the advantages of columbines far outweigh their transitory nature and other limitations.

ARABIS **Rock-Cress, Wall-Cress** **Cruciferæ**

If the name *Arabis* refers to Arabia, it may signify the preference of the genus for dry sites. Very few of the 100 or so species are frequently cultivated, but several recently introduced are still being evaluated as garden subjects. In the wild they range over a considerable part of the temperate regions.

Garden Value: Rarely more than 12 inches tall, the rock-cresses fit into rock gardens, dry walls, and even borders, where they are sometimes used as edging plants. The commoner types are apt to be rampant spreaders, but the profusion of bloom in the spring is a refreshing sight. The foliage of most is effective all season, and some have evergreen tendencies. A few are slightly fragrant. The small sprays are frequently helpful in short arrangements in spring.

Soil and Exposure: A loose porous soil with good drainage should be provided. Full sunlight is best even though shade results in more abundant foliage.

Care: Planting is advised for early spring, or when in full bloom if a ball of soil is kept around the roots. When flowering ceases, clumps should be sheared back about one-third for better aeration and increased branching. Early each third spring, division will prove beneficial.

Propagation: Seeds of the species may be sown in early spring or late summer. Cuttings are taken in summer for cultivars, superior selections, and double-flowered forms. Division of all is possible in early spring.

Species

A. *alpina*. Much of the material offered in commerce under this name may be A. *caucasica*, but the true type is superior in that the silvery-leaved clump does not spread excessively, and the short, compact racemes of white flowers bloom more consistently. 'Rosea' features a restrained 6-inch stature and soft pink flowers; it develops fairly true from seeds.

A. × *arendsii* (A. *albida* var. *rosea*). This German hybrid between A. *aubrietioides* and A. *caucasica* bears rose-pink flowers, and is probably a parent of modern garden cultivars such as 'Rosabella' and 'Pink Charm.' The latter two are choice garden forms that grow to 6 or 8 inches, with rose-pink blossoms, and crisp dark green leaves.

A. *blepharophylla*. Native to California. The tidy hummocks produce deep rose or nearly red flowers in florid tones. 'Spring Charm' is a fine carmine selection if propagated asexually, but it is not uniformly attractive when raised from seeds.

A. *caucasica* (A. *albida*). A rampant trailer, it may engulf nearby choice plants. Bloom is of short duration and is mediocre in wet years. In spite of the snowy mass of flowers under ideal conditions, it often offends by unkempt sprawling. The form known as 'Flore-Pleno'—the double arabis of the trade—has been a favorite since the turn of the century. It is more effective in the garden because of its double flowers; florists also prefer it for cutting. The pure white racemes reach 12 inches in height, and the woolly gray clumps may spread to 18 inches. 'Variegata' has leaves with conspicuous variegations of creamy white, although in time plants generally revert to the normal foliage of the species.

A. ferdinandi-coburgii. This rare gem is long-lived, and compactly mat-forming, with deep green leaves and 10-inch sprays of milky white blooms in June, perhaps recurring in autumn.

A. procurrens (*A. sturii*). More delicate in habit and flower than the common *A. caucasica,* this creeping species, 8 inches tall, has dark, shiny green foliage. Used in rock gardens, where it colonizes readily.

A. purpurascens. From the stony slopes of southwest Oregon, it is prolific of deep rose umbels, 6 inches above hairy, gray-green foliage.

A. × *sundermannii.* The parentage of this German hybrid is in doubt, but may be *A. ferdinandi-coburgii* and *A. procurrens.* At any rate, large pure white blossoms crown brilliant green leaves, making a fine plant for the rock garden.

Final Comment: The genus is to be praised for profusion of bloom, easy growth on poor soils, and restful summer foliage.

ARENARIA **Sandwort** **Caryophyllaceæ**

Arenaria, from the Latin for sand, is a genus of rock garden plants, of which *A. verna* var. *cæspitosa* is probably the best known. This is a valuable mat-forming type, almost mosslike in appearance, not over 2 inches tall, with tiny white flowers, about the size of a large pinhead, in June. It is sometimes grown as a ground cover in rock gardens, but is primarily used as a filler between flagstones or bricks on terraces, in paths, or around swimming pools because it will tolerate walking on without undue damage.

Best in shaded moist situations, it will not survive full sun unless watered almost daily during hot summers. A form with yellow-green foliage is called 'Aurea.' Propagated by division only; small sections or plugs root easily and spread quickly in flats of sand and peat if kept moist.

Most if not all of the material listed as *A. verna* var. *cæspitosa* in the trade north of the Mason-Dixon line is *Sagina subulata* or *S. procumbens.* Although this genus differs taxonomically from *Arenaria,* the horticultural effect of the species is identical.

ARMERIA **Sea-Pink, Thrift** **Plumbaginaceæ**

The armerias are neat, restricted plants with a place in any garden, large or small.

Armeria, from an old Latin name for one species, is a genus that has long floundered in a sea of botanical confusion; many catalogs still jumble *Armeria, Statice,* and *Limonium* in muddles of faulty nomenclature. Most of the accepted species are native to southern Europe, Eurasia, and North America.

Garden Value: Low evergreen tufts of narrow foliage and globular blooms on wiry stems in late spring and early summer stand out as characteristics. Practically all are splendid cut flowers. Smaller types serve well in rock gardens as restricted groups. However, the taller members of border stature are most effective in masses. For edgings, it is difficult to surpass thrifts with their symmetrical grassy mounds of foliage. As may be suspected from the sea-pink common name, plants also thrive in seacoast gardens.

Soil and Exposure: Full sun and dry, light soil are advisable; bloom becomes niggardly in rich ground, and stem rot often develops in continually moist areas.

Care: Plantings may be made in early spring or fall, with not over 12-inch spacings. Clumps require division at least every third year; otherwise vigor deteriorates.

Propagation: Fresh seeds are best soaked in water for several hours, sown thinly in August, and never allowed to dry out. Division in early spring or September is suggested for amateurs, as cuttings are not easily rooted.

Species

A. juniperifolia (*A. cæspitosa*). From warm Spanish mountains, this plant is dependent on sharp drainage for success. Tiny 4-inch tufts of grasslike foliage are dominated by small clear pink flowers.

A. maritima. The most frequently encountered species, it labors under numerous misnomers in trade circles. Typically, height is 12 inches or more; globular heads of flowers, 1 inch in diameter, vary from white to pink, red, and purple. Plants listed as the variety *laucheana* are distinguished by intensely rose-colored flowers. If prevented from seeding, plants may flower sporadically into September. The variety *alpina* has bright pink flowers on 8-inch stems. When obtainable, the rare white form is a rock garden treasure.

A. pseud-armeria (*A. formosa, A. cephalotes*). Most named selections grown by nurseries belong here. White, red, and pink variants, as well as intergradations are common. Floriferous, exceptionally sturdy plants with stems up to 2 feet in length typify the excellent cultivars available. 'Vindictive' is crimson, 'Glory of Holland,' a clear pink, and 'Bee's Ruby,' a sparkling cerise; all are fine cut flowers.

Final Comment: Sea-pinks must have a light, well-drained soil if good bloom is wanted.

ARTEMISIA Wormwood, Mugwort, Silverplume Compositæ

This genus, noted for its foliage rather than its flowers, was named for Artemisia, the wife of Mausolus in mythology. There are about 200 species native to the northern hemisphere, chiefly in arid regions. Only a few merit garden importance; many are weeds. *A. tridentata* is the sagebrush of western America, and *A. vulgaris* is the weedy mugwort, an escape in this country, with leaves resembling those of garden chrysanthemums.

Garden Value: By and large, the outstanding merit of several species is their attractive foliage, often finely divided and sometimes gray-white. Heights vary from a few inches to 5 feet or more, dictating use in rock gardens, borders, or semiwild landscapes. Several are cultivated in herb gardens.

Soil and Exposure: Light, well-drained locations in full sun are preferable, although the kinds grown only for foliage effects survive in partial shade.

Care: Spring-planting is recommended. Frequent division in spring is standard procedure. *A. albula,* in particular, may need winter protection in cold sections.

Propagation: Seeds are available for some species, and self-sowing often provides sufficient new plants, but cuttings, which are easily rooted in summer, or divisions in spring, are customary.

Species

A. *albula,* Silver King, Ghost Plant. Native from Colorado to Texas and Mexico, it is tremendously popular in spite of the fact that it does not tolerate wet winters. Normally 2 to 3 feet tall, it is a mass of silvery gray leaves all summer. Foliage may be cut for immediate arrangements, but is more often dried and used in winter. The insignificant white flowers are of negligible value; plants are grown only for their foliage. 'Silver Queen' is a garden selection, possibly a hybrid, with broader, more glistening foliage. Like the species, it may require annual spring division for survival.

A. *dracunculus,* Tarragon. Green-leaved plants 2 feet tall provide the foliage used for seasoning salads and meats. A subject for the herb garden.

A. *lactiflora,* White Mugwort. This 4-foot border perennial, with plumes of cream-white flowers in August and September, is valued for the texture of its inflorescences at a time when most garden subjects are somewhat coarser. The leaves are dark green and finely cut. In the rear of a border, it lightens the effect of heleniums, heliopsis, and chrysanthemums. Best in locations where summer moisture is available.

A. *pontica,* Roman Wormwood. Low-growing selections provide an adequate ground cover. The feathery, dissected gray-green leaves are quite effective, but the flowers are of no consequence.

A. *purshiana.* The decumbent stems, 1 to 2 feet long, are woolly white, as are the leaves. Planted only for foliage contrast.

A. *schmidtiana* var. *nana,* Angels-Hair. The gray hummock, only 2 inches high, of dissected, silken foliage is a novelty in rock gardens. 'Silver Mound' is supposed to be a selection, but the plants grow to 12 inches. Invaluable for foliage effect in dry rockeries, border foregrounds, or as an edging plant; the ineffective flowers are best removed.

A. stelleriana, Beach wormwood, Dunesilver, Old Woman. Native along the coast from Quebec to New Jersey, this species is quite hardy and may be used as a ground cover, as a subject for larger rock gardens, or at the seashore, where clumps growing to 2 feet, with silvery white leaves, create a handsome underplanting for pink *Tamarix.*

Final Comment: Of all members of this genus, the cultivar 'Silver Mound' seems most destined for a bright future.

ARUNCUS **Goatsbeard** **Rosaceæ**

The botanical name is from the Greek for goat's beard. *A. sylvester,* the only garden species, is a rather coarse perennial often sold under the name *Spiræa.* It is probably best suited to suburban or rural gardens as it forms a mass 4 feet or more in height. Resembling an overgrown astilbe, the compound foliage is surmounted by large, showy plumes of small white flowers in June. The sexes are separate; pistillate plants are somewhat more desirable, since they are more attractive than the staminate ones after the flowers have faded. Where space permits, aruncus may be used as a herbaceous substitute for a background of shrubbery. It can be grown in any location, but in dense shade plants do not grow so tall. Propagation is by division.

ASARUM **Wild Ginger** **Aristolochaceæ**

Wild ginger is one answer to the question, "What is good in the deep shade?" The various species, never over 1 foot in height and often less, are most successfully grown in rich, moist soils in half to deep shade. They may be used singly, in groups, as edging plants, or as ground covers.

While there is no certain derivation for the name *Asarum,* the common name refers to the pungent smell of cut roots.

A. canadense, native in northeastern America, spreads rapidly, and is of rather coarse texture. *A. caudatum,* from the West Coast, grows more slowly, and has evergreen leaves, flushed dark brown-

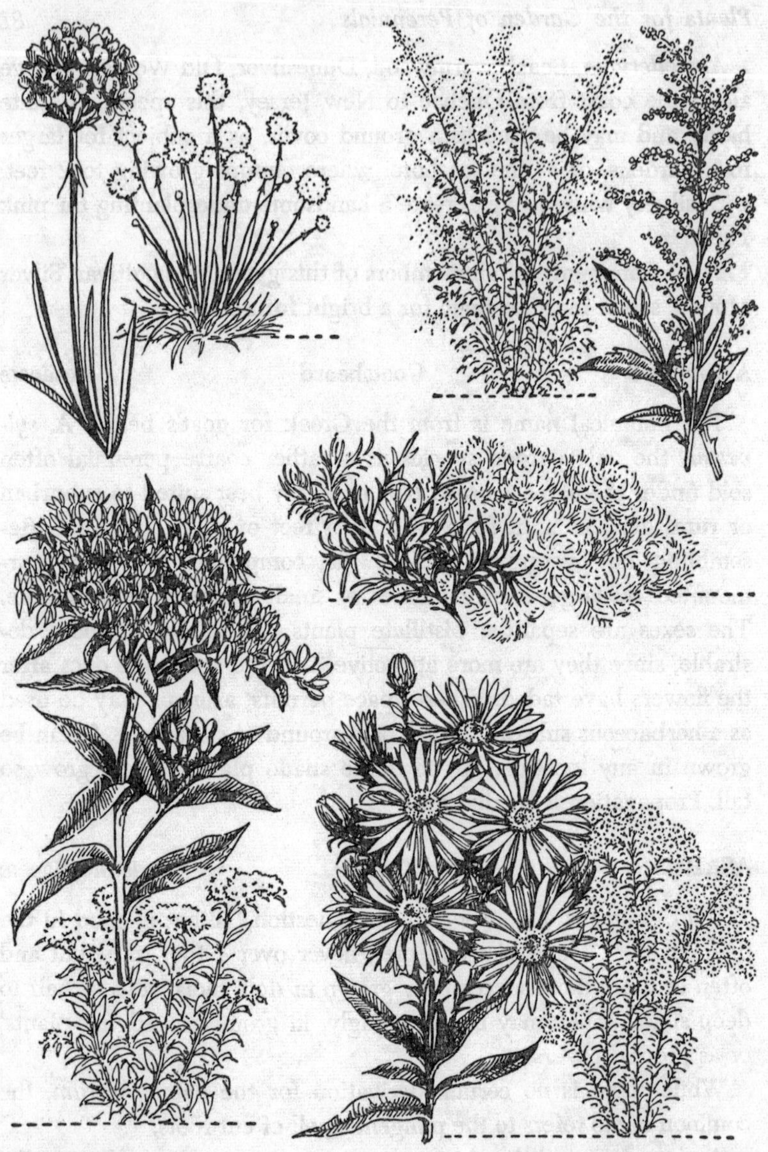

Armeria maritima
Asclepias tuberosa

Artemisia lactiflora
Artemisia schmidtiana 'Nana'
Aster novi-belgii

red all year. Another species from the Pacific Coast, *A. hartwegii*, is noted for the silver midribs of the leaves. *A. virginicum* differs in that the foliage, mottled with gray, tends to take on bronze tints in autumn.

The outstanding species, *A. europæum*, patrician of the genus, is not as well known as it should be. The leathery, kidney-shaped foliage, which persists over winter, is a glossy deep green. Plants spread slowly, and may take some time to become established, but the satisfaction gained is well worth any trouble or time. If in better supply, this superb plant would certainly be extensively utilized for ground cover purposes.

Division of large clumps is practical only in early spring before new growth develops. Seeds may be sown out of doors as soon as ripe, but germination will be delayed until the following year.

ASCLEPIAS Milkweed, Butterfly Weed Asclepiadaceæ

Many sun-baked American borders could be vastly enlivened by the butterfly weed, a certain antidote for monotony in the summer garden.

The scientific name refers to Asklepios, a legendary Greek physician. Although there are about 150 species native to Africa and both continents of the western hemisphere, only two are cultivated to any extent. Among the weeds of the genus, *A. syriaca*, the common milkweed, and *A. incarnata*, the swamp milkweed, are well known in this country.

Garden Value: Perhaps American gardeners take *A. tuberosa*, the native butterfly weed, for granted because they see it thriving in even the worst soils. However, it is indisputably a fine perennial for dry borders, and is without a serious fault. The bright display of orange flowers in midsummer makes it very effective, whether used singly or in groups of three. Hardy, showy, and never rampant, it can even be naturalized in sandy ground or along seacoasts. In addition, the unusual orange flowers last well when cut.

In southern gardens, *A. curassavica*, the vivid bloodflower, is a valued perennial, but in the North it is limited to growing under glass. Some species, such as *A. incarnata,* have limited use for naturalizing in moist gardens or swampy locations.

Soil and Exposure: *A. tuberosa* demands light, well-drained soil, and performance is best when it is planted in full sunlight.

Care: Planting may be done in spring or fall, but one should not be alarmed by the meager appearance of dormant roots. They are somewhat slow to sprout in spring, so cautious cultivation is necessary at that time. However, new eyes usually form in time, even if crowns are inadvertently cut off. Clumps increase slowly; hence, no attention is needed for a long time. The butterfly weed has a taproot, and once the plant is established, it is not readily transplanted.

Propagation: Seeds may be sown outdoors in spring or fall, but the young plants should remain undisturbed the first year. Root cuttings will increase any favored selection of *A. tuberosa,* if made in very early spring. A few may blossom sparingly the first summer, and all may be transplanted the following spring. Watering is advised only in very prolonged dry periods. Cuttings of *A. curassavica* root readily.

Species

A. tuberosa, Butterfly Weed. A score of blooming stalks may spring from a mature 2- or 3-foot plant, giving a broadly domed, symmetrical effect. While the orange display of July and August flowers is extremely showy, it seldom clashes with other garden flowers. Few summer flowers are more easily grown, prettier, or more enduring in light soils; soggy conditions usually lead to rotting. Scarlet and yellow variants are frequently reported, but to date named cultivars have not appeared in the trade. The seed pods, similar to those of the common milkweed, may be used for dried arrangements.

A. curassavica, Bloodflower. This 3-foot perennial, native in tropical America, has striking red and orange flowers, but it is satisfactory only in southern, frost-free gardens.

ASPERULA **Woodruff** **Rubiaceæ**

Asperula, from Latin, might translate to "roughish," in reference to the texture of the leaves. Of the 90 species that inhabit portions of Europe, Asia, and Africa, few are represented in American horticultural channels.

A. *odorata* is the only species widely grown at present. Plants 6 to 8 inches tall produce small white flowers in May and June, but the main attraction is the neat foliage which remains in excellent condition all season. An unmistakable odor of newly mown hay is intensified when stems are cut and dried; hence, the common name of *sweet* woodruff for this species. In Germany it was once utilized in a special May Day beverage, and is still cherished for flavoring wines and liqueurs.

Woodruff does well in any situation, although moist soil in partial shade is preferable. Well suited to rock gardens or naturalized areas, it is also useful as a ground cover or as an edging plant for the very front of the border. If kept clipped it creates a somewhat formal effect. Propagation by division is a simple matter in spring.

English growers are endeavoring to popularize several other species, especially the pink *A. lilaciflora* var. *cæspitosa.*

ASPHODELINE **Asphodel** **Liliaceæ**

Asphodeline lutea is an old-fashioned border plant, now grown mainly by those who "want something different." While sun and a light soil are preferable, it is easily grown in any border, and one plant is usually sufficient. From clumps of narrow, gray-green leaves, stiff upright stems grow to 3 feet, densely covered with 1-inch, fragrant, wide-spreading mustard-yellow flowers in June. Division in spring is the means of propagation, but a plant will increase so slowly that it can be left undisturbed for many years.

ASTER **Hardy Aster, Michaelmas Daisy** **Compositæ**

Hardly a garden can afford to be without some of the currently outstanding hardy asters. Some Americans are understandably irked by the realization that, while many species are weeds in our fields, practically all improvements have been made by Europeans, especially the English.

Aster, the Latin word for star, is the name given to this temperate zone genus of over 600 species. The majority are of North American origin, but the Orient and Europe have provided their share as well. The annual China aster is properly *Callistephus chinensis*.

Garden Value: Species vary from 6 inches to 6 feet, and blossom periodically, in all colors but yellow and orange, from May until killing frosts. Types are available for rock gardens, perennial borders, naturalized plantings, backgrounds, and even for screening purposes. However, only a few excel for cutting. The late-summer-flowering group makes an excellent transition in the border from summer to autumn, while still later ones vie with chrysanthemums for fall interest, and in many cases are longer-lived. Thus, it is regrettable that this genus is often neglected by American gardeners.

Soil and Exposure: Full sun and light soil are recommended for most species.

Care: Spring is the favored time for planting. For those which grow vigorously, frequent division is advisable. Some species, notably *A. novi-belgii*, are quite susceptible to rust and mildew, especially when overcrowded or neglected. Consequently, the use of a fungicide during the season results in better foliage at flowering time.

Propagation: Cuttings taken in summer are favored by the trade for all cultivars and selections. Plants of some species can be forced under glass for winter propagation. Division in spring is recommended for amateurs, since it fulfills most needs.

Species

This listing is not presumed to be all-inclusive, but covers those species which lead in appeal to the general public. Many others still not in great demand may please the serious gardener.

A. alpinus. From both the Rocky Mountains and European ranges, this species normally grows 6 to 12 inches tall, and is laden with purple daisy-like flowers in May and June. It does best in an alkaline soil in good sunlight, needs some moisture in summer, but will not tolerate wet soil in winter. Given ideal conditions, plants may require division each third year. Europe has a host of cultivars, but few are important elsewhere. All suit the rock garden, and are acceptable when cut. 'Roseus' is pink, 'Albus' is a cloudy white, and 'Dark Beauty' is a rich deep violet. 'Goliath' is noted for its lavender-blue flowers, 2½ inches in diameter.

A. *amellus,* Italian Aster. More appreciated in Europe than in America, it deserves attention in borders where small groups can be quite effective. The plant is typically about 18 inches tall, well-branched, with 2-inch flowers of purple rays and yellow disks. Neat gray foliage, a stalwart resistance to drought, and agreeable odor are traits to be admired, as is the late-July through September display. Sun, fairly good soil, and division each third year are advised.

Outstanding cultivars include: 'King George,' deep violet; 'Weinholzii,' rose softly flushed with purple; 'Perry's Variety,' almost red; 'Mauve Beauty,' with very large soft mauve blooms on 2½-foot plants; and 'Sonnenwende,' an early-flowering clear pink. 'Triumph,' a hybrid between A. *amellus* and A. *alpinus,* has striking blooms of violet-blue rays and bright yellow disks in June and July; height is 18 inches.

A. *cordifolius,* Blue Wood Aster. The tiny lavender-blue blossoms about a half inch in diameter will not please everyone, but this species can be a graceful 4-foot pyramid of arching sprays in the fall.

A. *ericoides,* Heath Aster. Comparatively slender, heathlike foliage gives rise to the common name; the dainty flowers, lavender or white, are also small. Numerous thin stems ranging from 2½ to 6 feet may be of value for naturalizing, or for dry patches at the rear of a border.

A. × *frikartii.* Carl Frikart, a nurseryman of Stäfa, Switzerland, named four seedlings derived from the cross of A. *thomsonii* and A. *amellus,* of which the finest is 'Wonder of Stäfa,' usually listed commercially as A. *frikartii.* It is extensively grown for the profusion of lavender-blue flowers that may extend from July to October. The loose, tumbling 2-foot growth complements bleeding heart, Oriental poppies, and Madonna lilies by hiding their lack of summer foliage. Superb cutting stems and clean gray foliage are likely, even in droughts. The plants require very porous soil and, in colder sections, winter protection. Staking is frequently required to curb ungainly sprawling in rich ground.

A. novæ-angliæ, New England Aster. Native from Quebec to South Carolina and westward to Colorado, it is frequently encountered along roadsides at 3- to 5-foot heights, bearing purple flowers. In the garden it becomes a pyramid of September bloom that requires 3 or 4 feet of ground space. Foliage is gray-green and pubescent. Division is needed every three or four years; pinching in early summer should forestall later demands for staking.

Since many variations occur in its widespread range, it is possible to locate forms of subtly improved coloring. For example, Millard Harrington, a farmer of Williamsburg, Iowa, repeatedly sowed seeds from the best pink individuals he could find, and in due time, selected an outstanding cultivar, now extensively grown as 'Harrington's Pink.' 'Survivor' is somewhat similar, but flowers a fortnight later. 'Mount Rainier' is white; 'Red Star,' dark carmine-rose; and 'Incomparabilis,' a fuchsia purple.

A. novi-belgii, New York Aster. Although found wild from Newfoundland to Georgia, it has received the most acclaim in England, where it arrived about 1700. Yet even there it evidently gained little attention until after 1900, for it scarcely appeared in catalogs of the intervening period.

In nature, it may vary from 1 to 3 feet in height, but usually has glossy leaves and flowers of blue-violet. However, English hybridizers—including Edwin Beckett (now American), W. Wood, and A. Harrison—gradually evolved finer, more diverse types, sometimes perhaps from breeding with *A. cordifolius.* Ernest Ballard, who was still actively hybridizing when he died in 1952 at the age of 81, became the leading popularizer of these plants with his unusually large-flowered cultivars, notably 'Eventide.' Formal records of his breeding projects seem to be non-existent.

These asters, extremely favored in England, and of increasing regard in America, are often called Michaelmas daisies, since they are showy around September 29, St. Michael's Day. Annual spring division produces neater habit, as does cutting back half way in midsummer, which also encourages greater flowering on the bushier specimens. Clumps are best situated at least 2 feet from neighboring plants, because crowding and poor air circulation encourage leaf diseases. In the border, hardy asters of this type complement chrysanthemums. As cut flowers they remain attractive only a short time.

Modern listings of cultivars, like Pliny's trees, "revel in rivalling each other," and only proven leaders are mentioned here to demonstrate the choices possible. 'Marie Ballard' is a large-flowered blue; 'Ernest Ballard,' a large mulberry-crimson; 'Clarity,' a spotless white; 'Winston Churchill,' a bushy, glowing beetroot-purple, almost red; 'Glorious,' a carmine-pink; and 'Eventide,' an imposing erect 3½-foot plant with dark violet-blue flowers.

There are several strains of dwarf hybrid plants with *A. novi-belgii* as one of the parents. The earliest to be developed is reported to be a cross with *A. dumosus*. H. V. Vokes of Southampton, England, specifically bred this strain for use in British military cemeteries of France and Belgium after World War I. The habit is rounded and compact, from 9 to 18 inches in height, but annual spring division is often essential to keep it so. Growers must be alert for foliage diseases, especially as late August bloom commences. The cushion-like masses of flowers are fine in rock garden or border. Of the numerous cultivars, 'Jean' is a clear lilac blue; 'Little Red Boy,' a rosy red; 'Peter Harrison,' a rosy pink; and 'Niobe,' a white.

Professor Leroy Breithaupt of Corvallis, Oregon, has produced a group of dwarfs by crossing *A. douglasii*, a native species there, with *A. novi-belgii*. Several cultivars appear promising and are under close scrutiny in many nurseries. All are more or less in the dwarf range. 'Pacific Amaranth' is of horizontal growth habit, with amaranth-colored flowers; 'Canterbury Carpet' is a gentian blue; 'Pink Bouquet,' an opalescent pink; and 'Persian Rose,' an excellent rose-pink cushion type. 'White Fairy' grows to 15 inches with snow-white flowers, and 'Romany' is very dwarf, having rich plum-purple coloring.

A. spectabilis, Showy Aster. This one is well known on sandy coast lines from Massachusetts to North Carolina. In the garden it becomes a 2-foot plant with blue-violet flowers from mid-August to the end of the season. Partial shade and somewhat heavier soil is acceptable, but unkempt habit results in rich soils. Relatively obscure in gardens, it is free of leaf diseases, and should be of interest to the breeder. Several selected forms are undergoing commercial tests at the present time.

A. yunnanensis 'Napsbury.' Here is an English improvement of a Chinese species. Coarse until leaves are fully formed, it is lavish with clear heliotrope-colored flowers borne singly on 18-inch stems, mostly in June and July. Requirements are the same as for *A. alpinus.*

Final Comment: Hardy asters are particularly recommended to those gardeners who find chrysanthemums distressingly short-lived. In time, asters other than those now available may assume even greater importance in the garden.

ASTILBE **False Spirea** **Saxifragaceæ**

All too frequently this herbaceous genus is still catalogued as *Spiræa,* which is actually a genus of deciduous shrubs in the Rosaceæ. Translated from the Greek, *Astilbe* means not shining, possibly a reference to the foliage. Two species inhabit eastern United States, and the others are found in Asia.

Garden Value: Minute flowers open in July and August, in dense narrow spikes or panicles which range in color from purple to red, pink, or white. Heights may vary from rock garden subjects of 6 inches to border plants 2 feet or more tall. Astilbes belong in every moist garden, where the spires combine well with Shasta daisies, hostas, and monardas. The neat compound foliage lightens any coarse plantings nearby. If first allowed to open to the tip, spikes may be cut and even dried. Florists frequently force plants under glass for holidays in late winter.

Soil and Exposure: A rich moist soil, well-drained in winter, yet with generous amounts of humus to retain moisture in summer is desirable. Since their roots are shallow, astilbes do not need deep fertility. Partial shade is recommended, although in moist situations full sun is not detrimental. Moist soil is more important than the exposure.

Care: Early spring or autumn planting is perfectly safe; specimens are easily transplanted, even when in flower. Protection in areas of unpredictable winters may be as important as either liberal watering during summer droughts or the use of summer mulches. Division of old, entangled plants quickly rejuvenates the stock.

Propagation: Seeds are very slow to germinate, and rarely come true to type. Division in early spring is customary; old clumps can be cut into sections of only one eye if desired. With *A.* × *arendsii,* the process is easiest when the new growth is about 1 inch high.

Species

A. × *arendsii.* George Arends, of Ronsdorf, Germany, intercrossed various species to produce most of the modern cultivars which are classed under this name. The majority grow about 2 feet tall, but may reach 3½ feet under ideal conditions. 'Fanal,' perhaps the best known, has narrowly erect, garnet-red spikes which glow above bronzed leaves. 'Red Sentinel,' a promising newcomer, produces loose, feathery carmine-to-Turkish-red panicles. 'Federsee,' a compact crimson-rose form, is somewhat more tolerant of drought than the others. 'Irrlicht' is a sturdy white, and 'Bonn' is a dainty pink. 'Peach Blossom' is noted for its elegant dense plumes of soft pink.

A. chinensis 'Pumila,' a dwarf, 8-inch form often seen in rock gardens, outranks the typical forms in worth. Rosy mauve flowers with a blue cast are produced in late summer.

A. × *crispa* (*A. simplicifolia* × *A.* × *arendsii*). This designation covers a dwarf group with deeply crinkled foliage of dark, almost bronzed tones. Cultivars grow to only 4 or 6 inches, and increase slowly. 'Perkeo' is a deep pink example.

A. *simplicifolia.* This small Japanese species was first erroneously included in a shipment of plants to England, but later proved desirable in itself. Glossy foliage and arching 6- to 12-inch spires of white to soft rose flowers are the main attributes. No doubt, hybrids such as *A.* × *crispa,* are even more promising.

Final Comment: If astilbes are neglected they become only haggard ghosts of their possible majesty.

AUBRIETA **False Rock-Cress** **Cruciferæ**

Aubrieta, named for Claude Aubriet, a French artist of the early eighteenth century, is somewhat comparable in form and purpose to arabis, to which it is closely related. Aubrietas are neater, more restrained, and somewhat more difficult to grow, but once established, they are indeed rewarding. The only significant garden species is *A. deltoidea,* a mat-forming native of Greece, not over 6 inches in height, flowering from April to June. Color variants range from red to purple.

Garden Value: Most appropriate for well-drained rock gardens or dry wall plantings, the false rock-cress can also be used at the front edge of a border, since the foliage is good throughout the growing season.

Soil and Exposure: Full sun and light porous soils are ideal, except on the West Coast, where partial shade is acceptable.

Care: After flowering, a gentle shearing promotes new growth, and often induces a fall display of flowers.

Propagation: Spring-sown seeds germinate easily, with plants flowering the following year. Cuttings can be made in midsummer, but division is best in spring.

Cultivars

The strain listed as Eyrei comprises forms with larger flowers and greater branching than other types. Many cultivars evolved from

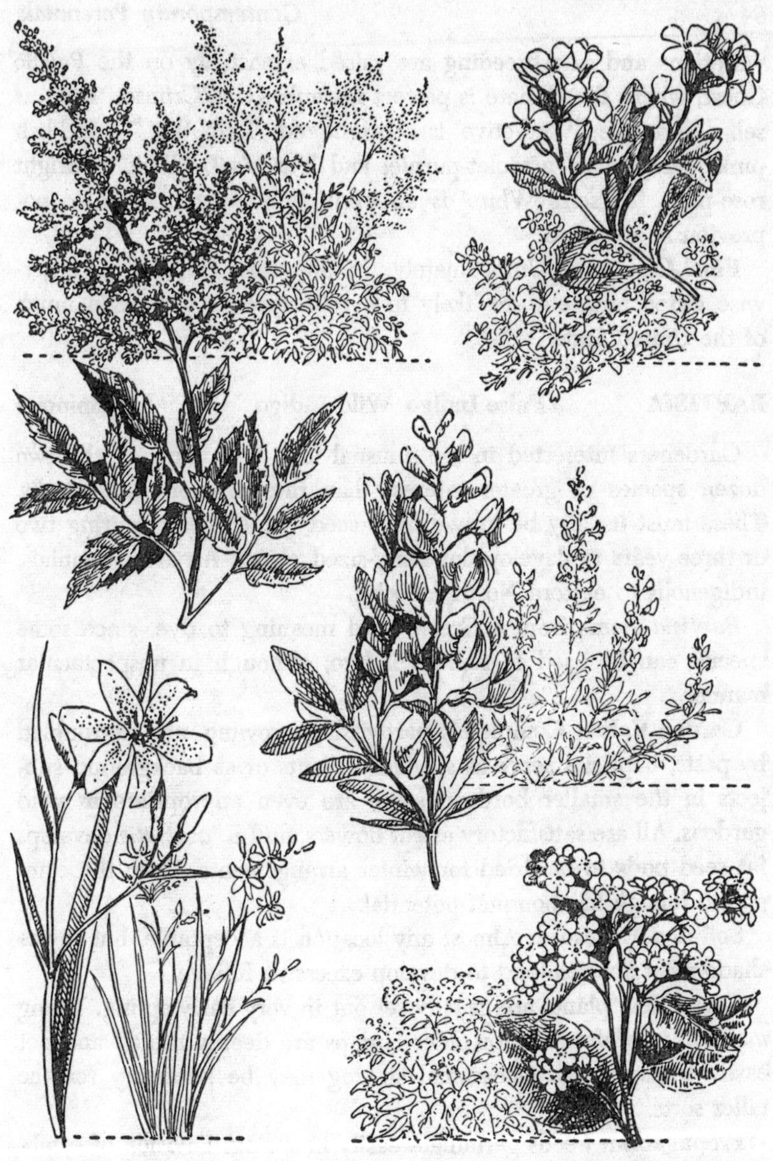

Astilbe arendsii
Belamcanda chinensis

Aubrieta deltoidea
Baptisia australis
Brunnera macrophylla

variations and interbreeding are raised extensively on the Pacific Coast, where the climate is perfect for aubrietas. 'Crimson King' is self-descriptive; 'Vindictive' is a bright red; 'Leichtlini," a reddish pink; 'Dr. Mules,' a violet-purple; and 'Purdy's Brilliant,' a bright rose-pink. 'Borsch's White' is an exciting novelty in a color not previously available.

Final Comment: Unfortunately, the querulous traits of the otherwise gifted aubrieta are likely to overbalance its virtues in much of the United States.

BAPTISIA False Indigo, Wild Indigo Leguminosæ

Gardeners interested in the unusual may find many of the two dozen species of greater interest than the common *B. australis.* These must usually be grown from seed, sometimes requiring two or three years to develop flowering-sized plants. All are perennials, indigenous to eastern North America.

Baptisia stems from a Greek word meaning to dye, since some species can be used to replace indigo, although in unspectacular manner.

Garden Value: Completely hardy, slow-growing, and untroubled by pests, baptisias serve as specimen plants or as background subjects in the smaller borders; some are even appropriate in wild gardens. All are satisfactory as cut flowers, and *B. australis* develops fat seed pods to be dried for winter arrangements. Even the compound foliage has bouquet potential.

Soil and Exposure: Almost any location is acceptable, but in the shade most species tend to develop excessive foliage.

Care: New plants are usually set out in very early spring. Young material is preferable, for older clumps are deeply rooted and not easily transplanted. Occasional staking may be necessary for the taller sorts.

Propagation: Seeds germinate easily in spring. Division of established plants is possible, but it is not an easy chore; however, unusual selections can be perpetuated only in this manner.

Species

B. australis. Colonies are found from Vermont to North Carolina. Although introduced into England in 1758, this species did not gain the coveted Award of Merit from the Royal Horticultural Society until 1948. Plants grow 3 to 4 feet in height, and in late May and June have arching terminal racemes of indigo-blue flowers. Foliage remains attractive until blackened by severe frosts. The strain, Old Orchard Hybrids, is believed to have originated in New Jersey from chance matings with an uncertain species growing nearby. The choice of colors includes tawny violet, buff, near yellow, and blue, as well as intermediate combinations. Seedlings of these hybrids vary widely, but normally do not exceed 3 feet in height.

B. bracteata. The comparatively restrained, 18-inch plants bear axillary racemes of soft yellow flowers. When more publicized, it may appear in many borders or even in larger rock gardens. The unique spread of foliage and subdued flower color combine to make this a valuable acquisition.

B. leucantha. The most demanding species of the genus, it prefers partial shade, and does not tolerate droughts. Still, the white racemes of flowers and the 4-foot habit are quite imposing.

B. tinctoria. Foliage on 4-foot plants is rather sparse, but the bright yellow racemes in June and July are redeeming features.

Final Comment: Baptisias may be one answer for those whose complaint is: "Nothing grows for me."

BELAMCANDA **Blackberry-Lily** **Iridaceæ**

Belamcanda is an east Asian name for a genus that is no doubt just as well known to gardeners by its common name, which refers to the shiny black seeds that remain in place when the pod splits open. Rhizomes and foliage resemble those of the German iris, but the flowering stems, often reaching 4 feet, carry numerous small, flat, star-shaped flowers.

Plants are most successful when grown in light, sandy soil in full sun. They may die out occasionally, and iris borer may be a problem, but plantings can be easily renewed by seeds sown in spring.

B. chinensis has exotic, 2-inch orange flowers spotted with red in July and August. Less common is the later-blooming, clear yellow-flowered species, *B. flabellata.* Both species fall into the category of uncommon material that adds midsummer interest to mundane gardens.

BELLIS **English Daisy** **Compositæ**

Bellis is from the Latin *bellus,* meaning pretty. The common naturalized form of *B. perennis* is considered a weed by turf specialists, but gardeners know it in its improved horticultural form, the completely double-flowered 'Monstrosa.' It is often planted in rock gardens or used in restricted foreground areas in a border; occasionally it is consciously naturalized in lawns.

Small plants, 6 inches high, with leaves in basal rosettes, produce white, pink, or red flowers from late April through July. Self-sowing occurs, and plantings have to be kept in check. Volunteer seedlings eventually revert to the common single form; they should be eliminated. After several years, new seeds should be purchased to renew plantings with the more desirable completely double form.

BERGENIA **Bergenia** **Saxifragaceæ**

Named for K. A. von Bergen, an eighteenth century German botanist, the genus is unfortunately still listed in many catalogs as *Saxifraga. B. cordifolia* is an extremely hardy perennial, interesting because of the large, loosely cabbage-like evergreen foliage which turns a purplish bronze in winter. In addition to the distinctive foliage, dense panicles 10 to 15 inches in height are covered with rose or purple flowers from late April through May, although in California they bloom during the winter months.

The plants grow in any situation. In moist, partially shaded areas colonies form quickly; in dry, sunny spots growth is retarded; and in dense shade it is very slow indeed. Bergenias are often planted in large rock gardens, along stream banks, around pools, and sometimes in borders. In colder sections, flowering may not be too dependable, but the foliage alone makes it worth having, especially if the gardener is interested in foliage effects for arrangements.

BOLTONIA **Boltonia** **Compositæ**

Boltonia honors James Bolton, an English botanist of the late eighteenth century.

Garden species are companion plants to the Michaelmas daisy, flowering about the same time and having similar flowers, but being taller, with a more restricted color range. Two species are easily grown in almost any situation: *B. asteroides* and *B. latisquama.* The latter is superior, with larger blue-violet flowers 1 inch or more in diameter, from mid-August through September. The 4- to 5-foot plants are acceptable in the background of larger gardens, but require staking.

Seeds sown in early spring produce flowering plants by autumn. Division every year or two, in spring, will result in neater clumps than the eyesores that may develop from neglected plantings.

B. asteroides 'Snowbank' is usually only 4 feet tall, with white flowers. *B. latisquama* 'Nana' grows to only 3 feet, with very pale pink blooms.

Boltonias are not indispensable, but have a purpose in large gardens where they relieve the possible monotony of late August and early September.

BRUNNERA **Siberian Bugloss** **Boraginaceæ**

In view of the undisputed excellence and solid popularity of *Brunnera macrophylla,* gardeners should be reminded that it is still widely distributed under the incorrect name of *Anchusa myosotidiflora.* The genus was named for S. Brunner, a Swiss botanist of the nineteenth century. There are three species native in Europe, but *B. macrophylla,* the only one of garden significance, is from Siberia and the Caucasus.

Garden Value: Hardiness and tolerance of neglect would be sufficient attributes, but the Siberian bugloss provides a spring display of blue rivaled only by myosotis. From April until early June, branched racemes of tiny blue, starlike flowers, darker than those of forget-me-nots, are strikingly colorful. Naturalized plantings in semishade often result from self-sowing. Effective combinations are possible when planted under forsythia or near doronicum, daffodils, and primroses. Plants usually attain a maximum height of 18 inches, with heart-shaped leaves which, when mature, may measure 8 inches across. The foliage may be somewhat coarse, but this is no drawback except in rock gardens, where it overwhelms more delicate plants.

Soil and Exposure: Plants survive in any location, but superior performance is obtained in partial shade and where there is adequate moisture.

Care: No special attention is needed except to note that when a clump deteriorates at the center, it should be divided early the next year. Seedlings may have to be weeded out occasionally.

Propagation: If additional plants are needed, root cuttings made of 1½-inch sections may be planted under glass in winter or outdoors in early spring. Seeds germinate best when sown in early fall; division is safest in spring.

Final Comment: Brunneras often find a place in a garden because they are one of the relatively few sources of true-blue flowers.

CALLIRHOË — Poppy Mallow — Malvaceæ

Callirhoë involucrata, native from Minnesota to Texas, is a sprawling, trailing plant with showy 2-inch saucer-shaped flowers that may vary from crimson-purple to cherry red. Prostrate stems may be 18 to 36 inches long at the end of the season, but they usually die back to the crown each winter.

Ideally adapted to hot, dry soil in full sun, this species is often planted in rock gardens with southern exposures to supply summer color from late June to early September. Plants are equally effective in dry-wall plantings or when naturalized on dry banks. As the roots are somewhat tuberous, heaving occurs during winter unless the soil is sandy and is provided with good drainage.

Renewal is by seeds or by cuttings taken in early summer.

CAMPANULA **Bellflower** **Campanulaceæ**

Campanula, meaning little bell in Latin, takes its name from the customary form of the flowers. There are about 250 species, mainly from European habitats. A few are annuals or biennials, some are common weeds, but many are garden favorites.

Garden Value: Briefly, the superior types of relatively tall growth are for the perennial border, spotted as individual heights dictate. Most lend themselves to naturalized areas where they are generally more impressive when groups replace lone specimens. A host of dwarf species and cultivars, many of which are tufted in habit, offer distinction for the better rock garden, where they supply the color needed in mid- and late summer. Several species are outstanding as cut flowers. Floriferous, colorful, and practically trouble-free, there is one or another bellflower for every garden.

Soil and Exposure: While specific quirks must be heeded, the general preference is for average fertility and well-drained soils. The belief that lime is essential is unsubstantiated if drainage is adequate. Most bellflowers thrive in full sun or light shade, but are surprisingly tolerant of additional shade.

Care: For the most part, spring-planting is desirable, although just about all may be transplanted carefully when in full bloom. Removal of seed pods decidedly prolongs flowering. At least every third year, renewal by division is a good practice. Winter protection may be needed for some in regions of severe climate.

Propagation: Seeds germinate readily from spring sowings, but the genus has many variants unlikely to reproduce true to type. Division in early spring or August is generally successful.

Species

C. carpatica, Carpathian Harebell. One of the leading rock garden members of the genus, it is treasured for the providential July and August flowers. The neat rotund tufts of foliage and blue, purple, or white cuplike blossoms, more or less erect on 6- to 12-inch stems, also promote its use for edging in perennial borders. Hardiness is unquestioned in well-drained sunny areas. Maurice Prichard of England has raised several of the finer cultivars. 'Wedgewood,' a blue-violet, and 'White Star,' a better white than the older 'Alba,' have flat flowers rather than cup- or bell-shaped ones. 'White Carpet' blooms in profusion, 'Blue Carpet' is a clear blue, and in 'Riverslea' the cups are purple.

The variety *turbinata,* from Transylvania, is essentially smaller than the species, about 4 inches tall, with deeper flowers resembling bells rather than cups. Unbranched stems carry solitary purple-blue flowers.

C. collina. This tufted 9-inch mound, rated by Farrer as "one of the most gorgeous campanulas we have," must be given two years of growth to merit the praise. Pendulous Tyrian-purple blooms occur in May and June.

C. elatines var. *garganica* (*C. garganica*). This sun-loving midget from Mt. Gargano, in Italy, far outweighs the species in value. Trailing stems press against rocks or walls, creep in rock gardens, and fan out like starfish in open ground. Starry, soft blue flowers on 6-inch stems open in June and July, but plants are points of interest all season because of the foliage.

C. glomerata, Clustered Bellflower. In some rural portions of England it is called "twelve apostles," because each floral head sometimes has a dozen flowers. After the terminal head blooms, axillary flowers continue to open. About 2 feet in height, it carries dense clusters of narrow bells in purple-blue shades, rarely white, primarily in June and July, although scattered blooms extend into August. In England, colonies are found on dry banks, but plants grow vigorously in shade, tending to spread quickly by runners. In poor soil, such activity is lessened.

The variety *dahurica*, called Danesblood in England, has larger clusters, 3 inches wide, of deep rich purple. For the rock garden, the variety *acaulis* is only 3 to 6 inches high, with sturdy little tufts of slender, pointed leaves. Small flower heads of blue-violet appear by July.

C. lactiflora. Easily grown and of robust 3-foot stature, this species may need staking in rich ground. Large panicles of milk white or pale blue, 1-inch flowers are in bloom from late June to August. They cut well if the stems are seared with a flame. Roots of this species were once beaten into pastes for cosmetics in England. 'Loddon Anna,' a variant from England in which the coloring is a pale mushroom pink, has not been adequately tested in America.

C. latifolia. Rather coarse, yet stately, it grows to 3 feet with stems bearing large bells of bishop's violet in terminal racemes in June and early July. The variety *macrantha* is usually taller, with flaring 2½-inch blooms of brilliant purple. 'Alba' is described as a white form, but the flowers are a disappointing off-white.

C. latiloba (*C. grandis*). The species is from Asia Minor and the Caucasus, but now has been largely superseded by a cultivar, 'Six Hills Giant,' which produces conical clusters of large starry saucers, light blue and prominent in midsummer. Tough, matted clumps commonly have 3-foot stems. Superficially, this species looks like a less spectacular *C. persicifolia.*

C. medium, Canterbury Bells. Although this species is definitely a biennial, it is included here because it is such a favorite that it becomes an integral part of many perennial gardens. Not over 2 feet tall, it forms heavy spikes of large, upfacing bells of white, pink, or blue-purple in June and July. Fine effects are achieved in front of delphiniums, hollyhocks, or similarly tall plants. Easily moved in full bloom, the white form is extremely useful for outdoor June weddings. Plants must be renewed by seeds sown in July or August, with care taken that the seedlings are not smothered by a mulch over winter. The variety *calycanthema* is best known for its cup-and-saucer race. Here a flattened petaloid calyx is transformed into an outer corolla-like structure, which acts as the saucer to an erect cup-shaped inner corolla. In another race, the petaloid calyx is also bell-shaped, creating the hose-in-hose or double type.

C. persicifolia. The specific epithet means peach-leaved, but in this instance the application seems rather fanciful. Slender, graceful plants are normally about 3 feet tall, with willowy stems neatly covered with broad bells, single or double, in shades of blue or white. Excellent for cutting, the stems may continue to flower well beyond July if kept free of seed pods.

This species is superb in a border of sun or partial shade, and is even a pleasant surprise in dry shady spots. If the basal tufts are divided each second August, bloom usually improves the following year. Seedlings vary, but horticultural selections, asexually propagated, are vastly better as a rule.

'Telham Beauty' is noted for its huge 3-inch single bells of a powdery porcelain blue which are typical from this English discovery of 1916. A doubled chromosome number accounts for the large flowers. The true form is scarce, as seeds do not reproduce it faithfully. Broader, heavier foliage than that of the type also marks this cultivar. In light shade it is unforgettable near iris, Oriental poppies, lupines, pyrethrum, or peonies. Rich soil and watering in dry periods will be rewarding. 'Wirral Belle,' a double of steely blue-violet, 'Blue Gardenia' a double deep blue, and 'Mt. Hood,' a double white that grows to but 30 inches, are other cultivars of importance.

Variety *moerheimei* is best represented by 'Summer Skies,' a double white flushed with azure.

C. portenschlagiana (*C. muralis*), Dalmatian Bellflower. Named for an Austrian botanist, it is closely akin to forms of *C. elatines.* Firm, compact 2-inch clumps of small foliage that is almost ivy-like are fine in rock gardens or dry walls. The tiny purple bells are in evidence from June to August.

C. poscharskyana. This Dalmatian species bears the unwieldy name of a Balkan botanist. It is extremely drought resistant, semi-prostrate, and is able to cling to dry walls. Larger rock gardens or sandy banks also permit the 2-foot stems to trail. In June and July, the open starry lavender-blue flowers are pleasingly colorful. Best in light shade.

C. rapunculoides, Rover Bellflower. This species is a rampant weed, and should not be grown in the border. If used at all, it should be restricted to wild plantings.

C. rotundifolia, Harebell, Bluebells of Scotland. Stems that may reach 15 inches carry many small nodding bells of blue, violet, or white in July and August. In tight crevices of the rock garden, growth may stop at 9 inches. Dotted among such mat-forming plants as thymes, they seem animated by each passing breeze. Medium soil in full sun is quite satisfactory. 'Purple Gem,' first raised in Vermont, is free-flowering with deep purple bells. 'Olympica,' a compact, profuse lavender variant, was discovered in the Olympic Mountains of Washington.

Final Comment: Only the readily available and proven species have been mentioned; many of these vary to the extent that deviations have been misnamed by some growers. Thus, a certain amount of confusion is inevitable. The connoisseur will profit from *The Garden of Bellflowers,* by L. H. Bailey. *Campanulas, Their Cultivation and Classification,* by H. Clifford Crook, while highly informative and readable, covers the more agreeable English gardening conditions.

CASSIA Wild Senna Leguminosæ

Adapted to sun or partial shade in well-drained areas, *Cassia marilandica* is an excellent 4-foot background perennial for the larger border or rural areas. Another species often distributed under this name, *C. hebecarpa,* is practically identical for garden purposes except that it grows to 6 feet or more. The fine-textured, compound foliage of both is most attractive throughout the season, and in August clusters of small bright yellow flowers appear in profusion. The textural contrast created by these species would make them worth while, even if they never flowered.

Of very easy culture, plants are free from pests or troubles, and can be left undisturbed for a long time. When necessary, clumps may be divided easily in early spring.

CATANANCHE **Cupid's Dart** **Compositæ**

The cupid's dart is an excellent cut flower, ideal for boutonnieres and excellent for drying; as an everlasting it is more graceful than the gaudier annual, *Helichrysum.*

Catananche is said to mean strong incentive in Greek, and as plants were used in love potions of early days, the common name of cupid's dart is easily explained. Native to Mediterranean sections, *C. cærulea,* which has been known in cultivation since 1596, is the only species of garden importance.

Garden Value: About 2 feet in height when in bloom, the plants bear masses of blue flowers in July and August and increase the interest in a border at that time. Groups of three to six are almost imperative to create the desired effect, because the plants are slim in outline. Gray foliage, wiry stems, and silvery buds, as well as the gray seed pods, all enhance garden interest. 'Alba' is the common white variant, now secondary to 'Perry's White.' 'Major,' also introduced by Amos Perry of England, is a sparkling violet-blue improvement.

Soil and Exposure: Full sunlight and a dry soil that need not be rich, but must be well drained are the only requirements. During severe winters plants may succumb, but they usually leave a legacy of volunteer seedlings to carry on. If the flower color of seedlings varies, the off-color types are often culled, as the deeper blues are usually more effective.

Propagation: Seeds sown in very early spring often produce flowering plants before the end of the season. Annual spring divisions of prized selections must be made to insure perpetuation of the stock.

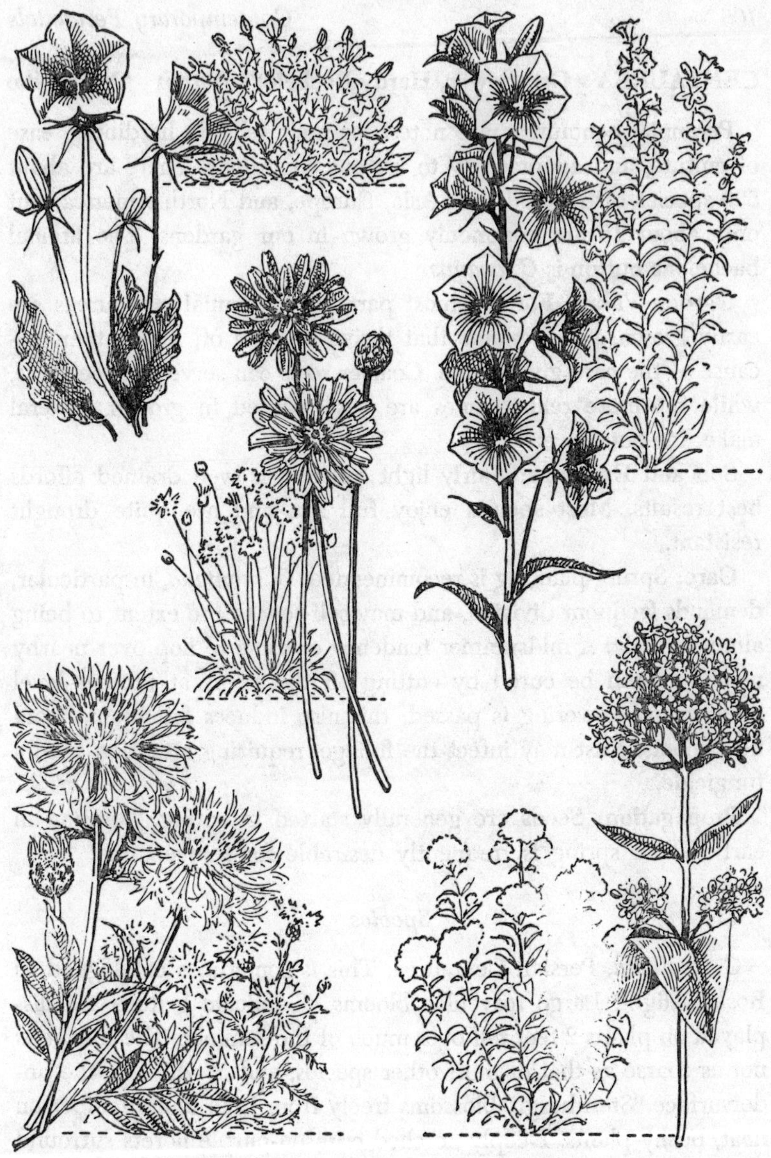

Campanula carpatica

Catananche cærulea

Campanula persicifolia

Centaurea dealbata

Centranthus ruber

CENTAUREA Cornflower, Hardy Bachelor's Button Compositæ

Perennial centaureas are noted for their reliable hardiness, ease of culture, and adaptability to various conditions. There are about 500 species distributed over Asia, Europe, and North America, but only about 15 are commonly grown in our gardens. The annual bachelor's button is *C. cyanus.*

Garden Value: For the most part, the perennial centaureas are easily grown, hardy plants that thrive in spite of, rather than because of the care given them. Coarser sorts can serve as specimens, while the more refined ones are best planted in groups. Several make fine cut flowers.

Soil and Exposure: Fairly light soil that is well drained affords best results. Most species enjoy full sun and are quite drought resistant.

Care: Spring-planting is recommended. *C. montana,* in particular, demands frequent division, and may self-sow to the extent to being almost weedy. A midsummer tendency of some to flop over nearby neighbors can be cured by cutting off the stems at ground level after spring flowering is passed; this also induces fall bloom from new shoots. Rust may infect the foliage, requiring attention with a fungicide.

Propagation: Seeds are generally started in spring. Division in early fall or spring is frequently desirable for rejuvenation.

Species

C. dealbata, Persian Centaurea. This is sometimes catalogued as Rose Delight. Large rosy lilac blooms of delicate texture are displayed on plants 2 feet tall over much of the summer. The foliage is not as coarse as that of most other species, and is white on the undersurface. 'Sternbergii' blossoms freely from June to September on neat, bushy plants. Deeply notched crimson-purple florets surround the gleaming white centers in attractive contrast.

C. macrocephala. This coarsely interesting Armenian species is almost too bizarre for formal plantings. Naturalized or highly individualistic settings can absorb the large ragged leaves and 3-inch, thistle-like blooms of golden yellow in June and July. Stiff, bulky 4-foot plants are the rule; usually used as specimens, not in groups.

C. montana, Mountain Bluet. Deep cornflower-blue flowers may reach 3-inch proportions on slender 2-foot stems, from May until midsummer. Secondary flowering occurs in September, especially if plants have been cut back earlier. 'Alba,' the white form, is less impressive, hence, seldom encountered. Care must be taken that this species does not encroach upon other areas of the border.

C. ruthenica. This yellow-flowered species, not as ungainly as *C. macrocephala,* grows to 3 feet in height. Foliage is deeply lobed. Suitable for large borders.

Final Comment: Most people will prefer the more delicate types to the coarse thistle-blossomed oddities.

CENTRANTHUS (*Kentranthus*) — **Red Valerian, Jupiter's Beard** — **Valerianaceæ**

Centranthus, Greek for spurred flower, is often confused in horticultural writings with *Valeriana,* a related genus, which differs by having deeply cut leaves and fragrant flowers without spurs. The genus *Centranthus* (sometimes spelled *Kentranthus*) is native to the Mediterranean region; only *C. ruber* is of commercial importance.

Garden Value: The gray-green foliage and red flowers provide interest in the border, and the plant belongs in every wild garden as well. Single clumps seem rather inconspicuous unless set off by green backgrounds.

Soil and Exposure: Poor soil or a dry location helps check the tendency to spread, but soggy winter conditions are detrimental, if not fatal. Full sun and partial shade are equally acceptable.

Care: Spring-planting is safest. Occasional division keeps the plants tidy over the years. In rich soil, staking is frequently essential. If old flowers are promptly removed, the blooming season is lengthened.

Propagation: Seeds must be sown in spring, although divisions will probably fulfill most needs.

Species

C. ruber. The first year or so plants will be only about a foot tall, but mature plantings may reach 3 feet. Dense terminal clusters of tiny trumpet-shaped flowers in showy reddish tones begin to open in early summer, becoming quite vivid later in the season. The form 'Albus' does not rate highly, as the white panicles are rather dingy.

C. angustifolius. Two feet tall, with clear rose flowers over a lengthy period, this species is usually very permanent and has some garden merit.

Final Comment: *C. ruber* is worth investigation for dry soils. Seldom will it fail to command attention in fall, even if largely ignored earlier.

CEPHALARIA Giant Scabiosa Dipsacaceæ

The reputation of this genus as a coarse weed is not fully justified. In fitting surroundings it becomes a tall, striking beauty. The midsummer primrose-yellow flowers resemble, in form but not in color, those of the scabiosas, which are in the same family. Individual florets are borne in heads; hence the significance of the scientific name, derived from the Greek *kephala,* meaning head.

C. tatarica, the only species of real importance, was first discovered in Siberia in 1759. Plants grow to a height of at least 6 feet, taking up 2 or 3 feet of ground space, so they might not be in scale for smaller gardens. Where space permits, they serve as background subjects and can be used in seminaturalized plantings. Wherever grown, they provide a profusion of cut flowers in July and early August. The blooming season will be lengthened if the faded flowers are removed.

Partial shade and moist soil, while not necessary, are desirable.

For propagation, divisions are customarily made in the spring, or fresh seeds are sown in early fall.

CERASTIUM **Mouse-Ear Chickweed, Snow-in-Summer** **Caryophyllaceæ**

The name of this genus of white-flowered rock garden standbys is derived from the Greek *keras,* or horn, a reference to the form of the seed pod. The species are very widely distributed in the temperate zone; many are common weeds.

Garden Value: Although valued for its mass of white flowers in June, *Cerastium's* desirable foliage should not be overlooked. However, a tendency to ramble in sprawling fashion calls for judicious selection of species. For edgings, walls, and ground covers, these little mat-forming plants excel.

Soil and Exposure: Dry soils are best, and the less fertile they are, the less spreading results. Maximum sunlight is advantageous.

Care: Field-grown material often rots badly in transit when shipped, but potted plants can normally be established in spring. Annual division may be needed to restrain aggressive specimens.

Propagation: Seeds germinate easily in spring or late summer. Division in spring or early fall requires some care, as roots are easily damaged.

Species

C. alpinum var. *lanatum.* A true alpine, it can be querulous if not in very well-drained, sunny situations. Comparatively large blooms on dense, woolly tufts compensate for the attention required.

C. arvense, Starry Grasswort. Green leaves form restrained tufts topped by 10-inch-high clusters of white flowers in April and May. The variety *compactum* is an extremely dense hummock of soft green, only 3 inches high, which may not flower until June.

C. biebersteinii. Asia Minor's mountains provide this fine species, named for a German-Russian botanist. In time it may prove preferable to *C. tomentosum,* as spreading is not objectionable. Moreover, the gray leaves and the slightly fragrant blossoms are larger than those of the common snow-in-summer.

C. grandiflorum (*C. argenteum*). White tomentose foliage and extra large blooms are the features of this lesser known species.

C. tomentosum, Snow-in-Summer. Probably seen to some excess, this is surely the public favorite of the genus. It should be used with caution and given plenty of room, since its 2-foot creeping stems may choke out weaker neighbors. The foliage is a sheet of silver all season long, but major interest is centered in June when a mass of white flowers opens about 6 inches above the leaves. It covers dry ground quickly, and drapes over walls attractively.

Final Comment: A breeding campaign in which the unbridled *C. tomentosum* might be crossed to less invasive types would make a laudable project for an experimental gardener.

CERATOSTIGMA Leadwort Plumbaginaceæ

Low habit and novelty appeal have gained some space for the blue leadwort, both in large rock gardens, where it is most useful for its late season bloom, and in the foreground of borders, where blue is welcome in late summer.

C. plumbaginoides, the only species extensively grown in American gardens, is often disseminated as *Plumbago larpentæ.* Plants were discovered growing in Shanghai's damaged ramparts by Robert Fortune, nineteenth century plant hunter. Seeds reached Sir George Larpent, who first exhibited blooming specimens in 1848 in London.

Garden Value: Broad 12- to 18-inch plants bear cobalt-blue clusters in late summer and early fall. Just below the flowers are leaves of a bronze-green, the color intensifying with the onset of cooler autumn weather. Interesting groupings can be made by planting the fall crocus, *Colchicum autumnale,* nearby.

Soil and Exposure: Rich soil provided with good drainage is necessary if the plants are to survive the winter. While they can be grown in part shade, full sun encourages better growth.

Care: Only spring-planting is recommended. Protection may be prudent in areas of severe winters. In the spring, new shoots are slow to appear; hence care in cultivation near the plants at that season is imperative.

Propagation: Propagation is by divisions made just as soon as the new shoots are in evidence, or by seeds sown in spring.

Final Comment: This is a worth-while garden subject, but it is essential to remember that wet conditions are fatal in cold climates.

CHRYSANTHEMUM Hardy Chrysanthemum, Mum Compositæ

Most gardeners are fully aware of the extensive choice in habit, flower size, form, and colors offered by chrysanthemums. Autumn would be sadly barren without the versatile mum. It is not idly called "the last smile of the departing year."

Chrysanthemum means golden flower in Greek, which leads some to believe that *C. indicum* was the original flower noted in the Orient. There are about 160 species, largely inhabitants of China, Japan, and portions of Europe, but only 25 or so are listed in catalogs; some of these are annuals.

While the history of the garden chrysanthemum dates back to at least 550 B.C. in China and later in Japan, popularity is presently at an all-time high. Moreover, a painstaking, thoughtful approach to breeding aims is increasingly apparent, thus holding incalculable future promise. So detailed a subject as that of chrysanthemum culture cannot be thoroughly discussed in a general work on perennials, but several excellent books have covered the matter in praiseworthy style.

Today's garden mums are generally classified under *C. morifolium*, which is perhaps a derivative of *C. indicum*. Several allied species, such as *C. arcticum*, *C. nipponicum*, *C. rubellum*, and *C. sibiricum*, have also entered into contemporary hybridizing patterns.

Garden Value: Careful choice and proper care allow a succession of bloom from early August to November. Areas free of hard frosts gain proportionately longer displays, for most cultivars continue to open buds at temperatures as low as 27°F. When frost reduces annuals, dahlias, and other flowers to oblivion, the mum comes into its own.

Wide variations in plant habit allow distribution over all parts of the border, but 4 feet is likely to be the tallest attractive height. Lower cushion types are being sought more and more for rock gardens, edgings, borders, and even for use in foundation plantings. Plants with a ball of soil may be freely moved in full bloom, to be reset in urns, tubs, pots, or other garden sites. Few cut flowers are lovelier or more lasting, and hundreds of cultivars are grown specifically for greenhouse culture and the cut flower market.

Soil and Exposure: A well-drained soil is essential for survival over winter. Organic matter in the form of manure, leaf mold, or compost is beneficial, as are such fertilizers as 5-10-10, to encourage deep root growth and added stolons. Once established, plants withstand droughts. Full sun is preferable although satisfactory performance can be expected if plants get direct sun for no less than six or seven hours a day.

Care: Newly acquired material is best planted in spring, after danger of frost is past, but early establishment leads to undesirably tall habit at times. June is ideal in New England. Small potted plants or rooted cuttings are suggested, spaced 18 to 24 inches apart. When growth has reached 6 or 8 inches, the tip of each shoot is pinched off to encourage bushy, floriferous clumps. Whenever new growth reaches 6 to 8 inches, this process should be repeated until July 15 or 30, after which flower buds are initiated. Deep weekly watering is helpful in dry spells. As flowering time approaches, tall, leggy plants may need staking.

Spraying or dusting with a complete pesticide formula every two weeks is desirable but not always necessary. On frosty autumn nights, structures of burlap, heavy cloth, or plastic can be erected several inches above and around the blooms to prevent injury.

Winter protection can be a sore point, in view of the shallow roots exposed to alternate freezing and thawing. About an inch of sand around each clump halts washing of soil, and 3 to 4 inches of hay or straw should be loosely blanketed over the plants after the ground is solidly frozen; it should be removed gradually in spring. Coldframes, if available, are superior for winter storage. Rot, heaving, and exposed roots cause more damage than sheer cold. The problem is most severe in areas with light snow cover during winter.

Cushion mums and a few selected cultivars famed for late summer bloom should be divided in alternate springs to preserve the early display. All others ought to be divided annually to insure compact growth.

The fancier seeking fewer blooms of large, well-shaped form resorts to disbudding. In this technique each plant is thinned to two to four stems, and all buds on the stem except one, the top or crown bud, are removed. Thus, the entire energy of the plant goes into only a few superior blossoms.

Shading with black cloth encourages earlier flowering. The method, in brief, is to completely cover the plant with the cloth, on supports, late each afternoon near the end of the summer, and remove it the next morning. The shortened period of daylight simulates conditions later in the season, and induces the plant to flower earlier than under normal conditions.

Insects that may have to be controlled include green, brown, or black aphids—at their worst in hot dry periods—and the tarnished plant bug, a small yellow and brown insect causing wilted, malformed shoot tips. Foliar nematodes—tiny microscopic insects that first cause browning of the leaf margins, and may eventually destroy all foliage—can be controlled by sprinkling the powdered form of sodium selenate about each plant in spring. The selenate is absorbed by the roots as a treatment of chemotherapy. Since it is very toxic to humans, it should not be used where vegetables are to be grown in the next several years. It is perhaps wisest to discard and burn affected plants, renewing a planting with clean stock set in a different location.

As for diseases, leaf spot—evidenced by brown or black blotches on the leaves—is apt to be a problem, especially on crowded plants in times of alternately hot and wet weather. Any good fungicide will check the spores quickly. Stunt is a virus disease which causes malformed, dwarfed plants with premature, off-color blooms. Affected plants should be carefully dug and burned. Clean cultivation, always wise in any case, may prove an important control of stunt by eliminating diseased weeds nearby.

Propagation: Seeds sown in early spring provide interesting variations. Cuttings made in spring readily multiply garden mums; commercial firms propagate by this method under glass all year. In the garden, division is always safest in spring.

Types and Cultivars

So widely grown a plant has naturally fostered flowers of many diverse sizes and forms over the years, with increasing doubleness apparent. As early as 1890, English commerce knew 3,250 cultivars of supposedly distinct identities. Increased breeding still produces a legion of newcomers annually, but more selectivity is in the offing. The one color conspicuously missing is blue, of which no form is yet available.

In 1932 Alex Cumming, of Bristol, Connecticut, introduced a new group called Korean Hybrids, from strains of *C. sibiricum.* Originally single-flowered, they brought increased vigor, novel shades, and greater hardiness, which vastly increased the mum's prestige. Doubled selections gradually evolved as well. Probably few recent cultivars are completely lacking of this heritage.

A few leading representatives of each class of chrysanthemums are mentioned here. Normal flowering dates are also given.

Decorative. Doubled flowers, over 2 inches across, with straplike rays, distinguish this outstanding border group. Customary height is 2 to 3 feet for well tended plants, most of which can be disbudded for larger blooms.

'Lee Powell'—3½-inch blossoms of China gold, Sept. 25
'Avalanche'—large, fluffy white, Sept. 20
'Huntsman'—a powerful-appearing plant, vivid scarlet, Oct. 5
'Fascination'—4-inch flowers of soft lavender-pink, Oct. 1
'Pheasant'—excellent bronze, Oct. 1

'King's Ransom'—extremely erect habit, 3-inch flowers of old gold, Oct. 1

Pompons. The globular, nearly rounded flowers, usually under 2 inches in size, make fine cutting sprays. The term "pompon," first applied to dahlias, was derived from small ornaments on French military headdress. Average heights are 2 to 2½ feet.

'Fred R. Rockwell'—vivid orange-scarlet-to-bronze, Oct. 1

'White Wonder'—immaculate white, late Sept.

'Masquerade'—mounds 18 to 24 inches in size, rosy lilac flowers with a red eye, Oct. 5

'Canary Wonder'—soft primrose-yellow, late Sept.

'Royalist'—velvety oxblood-scarlet, 18 to 20 inches tall, Oct. 1

'Blanche Litwiler'—vigorous, lavender-pink, Oct. 1

Singles. While these daisy-like flowers are exquisite to cut and bountiful in the garden, they are not as eagerly sought as are the doubles. Some of the original Korean Hybrids bloom rather late for northern regions.

'Summertime'—very hardy yellow, in bloom by July 25 when well established

'Daphne'—pastel old rose, Oct. 10

'Louise Schling'—red, Oct. 5

'Apollo'—orange-bronze, Oct. 10

'North Star'—white, Sept. 20

Further subdivisions of the single types include the Rubellum Hybrids, in which *C. rubellum* has been interbred with the Korean Hybrids, largely by the late Amos Perry of England. Very hardy, and often of fernlike leaf pattern, they are not outstanding for floral quality. 'Princess Margaret,' a salmon-shrimp, Sept. 20; 'Moira Goddard,' an old rose, Oct. 10; and 'Royal Command,' a wine-red, Oct. 1, are examples.

The Northland Daisies originated about 1903, at the Concordville, Pennsylvania, nursery of J. J. Styer, from a chance cross of *C. arcticum* and existing cultivars. In general, their display is too late for many northern areas, but they are tough, and boast handsome leathery foliage. Cultivars include: 'Astrid,' a salmon pink, Oct.

10; 'Kristina,' a rose, Oct. 10; 'Peer Gynt,' a coppery red, Oct. 15; and 'Igloo,' a white, Oct. 10.

Cushions. Low mounded clumps, seldom over 12 to 15 inches tall, form broad masses of flowers by September. Usually quite hardy, they become summer bloomers in their second year; hence their appeal is on a quantity basis, especially in northern states with early frosts. Their value for homes of small modern proportions is undenied, and breeders are improving the individual flower's quality each year.

It is said that the first cushion type ('Amelia') was observed at Mayhew's Nursery in Sherman, Texas, by Mrs. Sam Beatty, whose husband then operated R. M. Kellogg Co., of Three Rivers, Michigan. She compared the low growth to that of an azalea, and the astute Mr. Beatty swiftly trade-marked sole rights to the name "Azaleamum" for his firm. Thus, cushion and azaleamum are synonymous.

Among the many available are: 'Minnpink,' a superb pink; 'Lipstick,' strawberry-red; 'Twinkle,' fuchsia-purple; 'Bowl of Gold,' yellow; 'Powder Puff,' white; and 'Bronze Queen,' dark walnut-bronze, pompon-like.

Spoons. Delicately fashioned oddities have resulted from rays twisted into spoonlike forms resembling druggist's spatulas. Unique, well suited for cutting and lightening heavier flower or foliage masses, they are not always as robust as might be desired. However, they appeal strongly to women, especially flower arrangers. They bloom from October 1, and attain 2 feet in height. Some cultivars bloom very late for northern gardens. Many are self-descriptive, as 'Yellow Spoon.' 'Cardinal Spoon' is a flashing red and gold blend, while 'Garnet Spoon' is actually deep purple.

Commercials. These comprise the huge "football" mums, generally grown under glass, and disbudded for flowers often over 6 inches in size. Flowers of perfectly rounded form are possible outdoors —with considerable attention and protection from the elements. Cultivars that are attractive well into November are plentiful, but are not outstanding unless disbudded. For most practical purposes the so-called English Mums are simply earlier-flowering selections.

Popular cultivars include: 'Mrs. H. E. Kidder,' yellow; 'Major Edward Bowes,' deep orchid-pink; 'Superlative,' white; 'Regalia,' purple; 'Westfield Bronze,' orange-bronze; and 'Sultan,' red.

Anemones. Here, outer rays surround central cushion-like pads of modified disk flowers, often of gleaming yellow. Color contrasts are frequently breath-taking, but most cultivars are late-flowering. However, recent breeding efforts are beginning to produce blooms in September.

The following are among those available: 'Korean Princess,' a fine coral-bronze to strawberry-red, Oct. 15; 'Queen Victoria,' red, Sept. 20; 'Queen Elizabeth,' pink, Sept. 20; and 'Queen Anne,' white, Sept. 20.

Buttons. Tiny pompons, like ¾-inch buttons are usually seen on these plants very late in the season. They are so tolerant of frost that one is reminded of Coleridge's "living flowers that skirt the eternal frost," although the poet probably referred to alpine gentians. No longer in favor, this group is in need of hybridizing with earlier-blooming sorts to gain certain popularity.

Rayonnantes. These exotic creations have spidery, twisted rays, like colored shoestrings, but develop too late to bloom north of New York City. Moreover, only disbudding can produce those curious 6-inch flowers seen in flower shows.

Other Species

C. coccineum (pyrethrum), *C. maximum* (Shasta daisy), and *C. parthenium* (feverfew), are treated separately on subsequent pages.

C. arcticum. Very hardy, leathery-leaved plants from high northern and arctic regions grow to 15 inches in height. However, since the pink or white flowers of moderate beauty do not appear until late October, only the breeder and those in southern states are interested in them.

C. nipponicum, Nippon Daisy. This species is extensively grown on Long Island, for it enjoys seacoast conditions, and carries quantities of white 3-inch flowers on 2-foot plants in September and

Cerastium tomentosum *Ceratostigma plumbaginoides*

Chrysanthemum morifolium

Chrysanthemum maximum *Chrysanthemum coccineum*

Chrysanthemum parthenium

October. Thick spatulate leaves characterize this hardy subshrub which sprouts new growth from the lower stems each spring. It has frequently been utilized for breeding, with results still to be evaluated.

C. rubellum. Fairly pleasing pink-to-rose-red single flowers are borne on strong, hardy 2½-foot plants of pinnately divided foliage. 'Clara Curtis,' one of the best known cultivars, is undeniably hardy and long-lived.

C. sibiricum. While the breeding value of this species has been inestimable, the 2- to 3-foot individual is rather wild and unkempt. Coarse foliage and indefinite pink or white flowers after October 15 are not impressive either.

C. uliginosum. The specific epithet means moisture-loving, but this striking 6-foot plant is not insistent on wet conditions. Large white flowers, which can be cut, appear in early fall. Unless located in very rich soil, no staking is normally necessary. The tolerance toward wet winter conditions may offer a virtue to the hybridizer.

Final Comment: The All-America Chrysanthemum Selections promise increased attention to superior introductions of early bloom and bushy habit. With the chrysanthemum's inherent plasticity, future possibilities become endless. Even the lesser species offer great potentialities for new material in the border.

CHRYSANTHEMUM COCCINEUM — Pyrethrum, Painted Daisy — Compositæ

This species, native in Southwest Asia, is the season's first member of the genus to flower. It is a florist's favorite for cutting, as well as a gardener's choice border perennial.

Garden Value: The fine-textured foliage is as attractive as the colorful white, pink, or red flowers. June to early July is the primary blooming season, but scattered flowers may persist until frost. Flowers may be single, double, or of the anemone type, with tubular central disk flowers. In the doubles the central florets and horizontal rays frequently contrast in coloring, enhancing the effect. Cultivars range from 9 inches to almost 3 feet in height. Groups of three at 18-inch intervals can be richly rewarding, either by themselves or in combinations with practically all perennials.

Soil and Exposure: Considerable amounts of humus are an advantage, but the soil should not be continually wet in winter; some resistance to drought may be expected. The lustrous hues sparkle more luxuriantly in full sun, although light shade for part of the day is not harmful.

Care: Field-grown plants do not always withstand shipping, except in September; hence, potted plants are usually supplied in spring. Locally procured material, however, transplants readily almost all season long, even in full bloom, if a ball of soil is retained around the roots.

After the flowers fade, all stems should be cut to the ground to encourage new basal shoots and secondary flowering. Clumps should be divided every three or four years, preferably in late summer, with leaves trimmed by half to lessen wilting. Some protection may be desirable the first winter after division.

Propagation: Seeds, usually sown in spring, seldom produce flowering plants until the second year, and give a wide range of variability. It is unwise, however, to discard all plants with faulty blossoms until the following year, when improvement is often noted. Division, carried out in late summer, usually permits flowering the next year, and provides generous yields for amateurs, if not for nurserymen.

Leading Cultivars

England has a host of fine selections, but not all withstand American climatic extremes or the rigors of importation. Hence, only domestic cultivars are grown in great quantity.

Singles. The average flower is about 3 inches across, has a golden disk and is borne singly on each stem. Examples are: 'Crimson Giant,' with magnificent 4-inch blooms of velvety crimson on stalwart 3½-foot plants; 'Victoria,' a ruby red; 'Scarlet Glow,' a vivid scarlet-crimson; 'Mrs. D. C. Bliss,' an unusual coral-orange (but plants are not sturdy nor are the flowers large); and 'Eileen May Robinson,' an unsurpassed salmon pink from England.

Doubles. Popular cultivars include: 'Helen,' with full, 2½-inch, soft rose-pink flowers on 2½-foot plants; 'Rosary,' a rose-pink, with a silvery cushion in the center of each flower; 'Buckeye,' a deep rose-red, flecked white; 'Sensation,' with many small red blooms; 'Pink Bouquet' ('Miami Queen'), a rose-pink with silvery cushion; and 'Mrs. C. E. Beckwith,' a white with frail habit.

Final Comment: For ease of culture, beauty, and their hint of disciplined abandon, painted daisies warrant almost unlimited planting. Cultivars are far superior to most seedlings.

CHRYSANTHEMUM MAXIMUM Shasta Daisy Compositæ

While white flowers are notoriously low in sales appeal, the Shasta daisies remain extremely popular. Unfortunately, increased elegance and refinement at the hands of hybridizers have sometimes been accompanied by lessened vigor.

Luther Burbank, a much publicized plant breeder (1849–1926), is usually credited with evolving the type as we know it today. Since the Burbank experiments were conducted near Mt. Shasta's white peaks in California, the common name is understandable. It is reported that *C. maximum* from the Pyrenees, *C. lacustre* from Portugal, *C. leucanthemum*, America's ox-eye daisy, and *C. nipponicum* were intercrossed to give rise to the Shasta daisy we know. It is classified by botanists under the name *C. maximum.* Scores of later cultivars have been disseminated, and English hybridizers, in particular, are still diligent.

Garden Value: As a rule, plants attain 2 to 4 feet in height, and may flower from June until frost. Many flower types have been developed, with at least one selection carrying a hint of yellow shading. In general, recent cultivars do not fare well in the warmest inland states, but are splendid on the Pacific Coast and in much of the East.

As cut flowers, they are wonderfully productive and long-lasting; in the border, they are effective with practically all flowers. Astilbes, delphiniums, heliopsis, and echinops are typical good companions.

The foliage is always reasonably attractive, as well. Flower color is always white, but those raised commercially are sometimes dyed for florists' use.

Soil and Exposure: Rich, moist ground, neither unduly acid nor waterlogged, is necessary for optimum performance, but the nearly evergreen clumps seldom withstand poor drainage in winter. All Shasta daisies tolerate partial shade, and the doubles prefer it in sultry regions. Most singles do well in full sun.

Care: Small clumps or potted plants are desirable for planting in spring or early fall. Water should be supplied during droughts, for otherwise many wilt badly. Clumps are best divided after each second year's bloom, preferably in April.

Aphids may be a problem in warm, dry periods. Verticillium rot may develop in wet seasons; afflicted plants suddenly begin to rot during active growth. If quickly dug, trimmed of all diseased elements, soaked in fungicidal solutions, and reset in a new site, they may recover.

Propagation: Seeds, sown in spring, yield diverse yet often first-class plants. Division in spring is recommended for amateurs, both to increase and to revitalize cultivars of value.

Leading Cultivars

Singles. These daisies, which may have more than one row of white rays, range in diameter from 2 to 6 inches. Stiffly horizontal rays, overlapped to avoid gaping spaces, are desirable. With yellow disks, they bring to mind Francis Thompson's "drops of gold in whitened flames burning." Recent introductions have prolonged the blooming season notably, but they require regular division to persevere.

Among the most popular are: 'Majestic,' with perfect 4-inch blooms on plants 2½ feet tall; 'King Edward,' very hardy but flowering mainly in June and July; 'Mark Riegel,' with 4- to 5-inch flowers, which have two rows of rays; 'Edgebrook Giant,' which often bears 7-inch blooms; and 'Stone Mountain,' with fine 4-inch flowers on stocky 2½-foot plants.

Doubles. Here, central cushions of modified petaloids are surrounded by rays of normal character. The increased ornateness is frequently penalized by demands for light shade.

Double cultivars include: 'Esther Read,' popular since 1931, 2 feet high, and likely to bloom itself to death; 'Jennifer Read,' a sturdy 2-foot sport of 'Esther Read'; 'Wirral Supreme,' with blooms 4 inches across on strong 3-foot plants, at their best in June and July; 'Horace Read,' like a 4-inch snowball if in cool setting; and 'Cobham Gold,' a chance seedling from the gardens of the Earl of Darnley in England, actually a creamy white, but with a yellowish cushion effect caused by the anthers of the tubular disk flowers.

Frilled Selections. An informal flower with finely cut frilling gives interesting tousled effects.

Among them are: 'Marconi,' with fluffy 6-inch blooms of curly patterns; 'Chiffon,' a semidouble, crimped and flaring; 'Aglaya,' with long-blooming tasseled flowers; and 'Beauté Nivelloise'—like a 6-inch mop, fringed in white.

Final Comment: F. G. Read and George Murray, both Englishmen, are actively working for superior material. Breeding for sterner climates would also be advantageous.

CHRYSANTHEMUM PARTHENIUM	**Feverfew, Matricaria**	**Compositæ**

The specific epithet and the common name "feverfew" both have herbal significance, suggesting medicinal value. Indigenous from Europe to the Caucasus, the species has escaped into the wild in America.

Garden Value: Compact 12- to 15-inch high selections may be used in small groups with intervals of one foot between plants. The long flowering season may outweigh the short life span as a practical consideration; the plant is not reliably hardy in colder regions. Single-flowered forms may self-sow readily, becoming a nuisance. Florists prize it as an inexpensive cut flower. While some strains may reach 3 feet in height, the preferred forms are smaller, with ¾-inch, fully double flowers in July and August.

Soil and Exposure: Sandy, well-drained soil in full sun helps prolong life.

Care: Planting is feasible only in spring. Removal of faded flowers prevents spreading of volunteer seedlings. Winter protection is urged in northern areas.

Propagation: Spring sown seeds produce flowering material by midsummer. Cuttings root with ease in summer, but division is an operation for spring only.

Leading Cultivars

Among the best are: 'Aureum' ('Gold Feather'), so called because the foliage is a chartreuse or yellow-green color, single white flowers; 'Silver Ball,' gleaming white, fully double globular flowers; 'Golden Ball,' bright yellow disks, no ray flowers; and 'Lemon Ball,' elusive soft yellow disks, no rays.

Final Comment: The doubles have merit in borders, but the singles are largely to be scorned, except in naturalized areas.

CHRYSOGONUM Goldenstar Compositæ

Only one species, *C. virginianum,* found native from Pennsylvania to Florida, is worthy of garden space. It is noted for its prolonged summer production of 1-inch yellow, star-shaped flowers, from mid-June until September.

Chrysogonum, from the Greek, meaning golden knee, refers to the habit of bearing the yellow flowers at stem joints. The rounded light green leaves are both numerous and attractive. Average height is about 8 inches, in scale for rock garden nooks or edges of walks or borders.

Dry soil of medium fertility and full sunlight are preferred. Removal of seed pods and occasional watering during summer droughts help keep plants flowering. Propagation is by seeds or divisions.

With just a little care, this unsung little native becomes a rock garden delight, providing color at a time when there is likely to be a lull as far as flower interest goes.

CHRYSOPSIS **Golden Aster** **Compositæ**

Chrysopsis makes no pretense of splendor, yet it surely has its measure of garden worth. Compact habit, full hardiness, and pleasing yellow, daisy-like flowers in August and September are attributes not to be ignored. In rock gardens or in the border's front rank, perhaps in small groups, the late season color can be welcome.

Areas of light soil in sun or part shade are acceptable. Spring-planting is recommended; pinching shoots back 1 or 2 inches in June will increase branching, and the quantity of bloom.

In Greek, the generic name means resembling gold. Species range over North America, mainly in sandy ground, but few have been introduced into commerce.

C. falcata, from the seacoasts of Cape Cod down to New Jersey, grows 8 inches high. *C. mariana,* the showiest of the genus, at a height of 18 inches is suitable for most borders. *C. villosa,* to 2 feet tall, produces a mass of clear yellow flowers at summer's end.

Like several other unheralded wild flowers, chrysopsis will be a pleasant surprise to most gardeners.

CIMICIFUGA **Bugbane, Snakeroot** **Ranunculaceæ**

The rugged permanence of these statuesque plants, 5 or 6 feet tall, encourages their use as specimens in large borders.

Bugbane is a direct translation of the Latin name. Plants are found growing wild in Asia and in thin woodlands of North America.

Garden Value: The long racemes of small white flowers towering above glistening compound foliage are ornamental when the plants are properly situated. Waterside plantings or even spotting among green shrubbery is feasible. *C. simplex* excels as a cut flower.

Some gardeners complain of overly abundant foliage and unpleasant flower odor, but by and large, neither objection should deter the beginner from enjoying the months of elegance offered by bugbane.

Soil and Exposure: If plants are to persist, a rich, moist soil of high organic matter content is necessary. Partial shade is ideal, although sunlight is not detrimental under proper soil conditions. Survival in deep shade is customary, but the effect there is not so spectacular.

Care: Plantings must be made in very early spring, before new growth starts. Heavy watering in dry periods is beneficial, as are annual top-dressings of compost or old manure. Established clumps can be left undisturbed for many years.

Propagation: Division in early spring is recommended, since efforts with seeds are often fruitless.

Species

C. dahurica. This 5-foot Asian species, with relatively coarse foliage, is nicely fashioned with erect, finely drawn spikes of creamy white flowers from August into fall. The ebony stems present an admirable contrast to the flowers.

C. racemosa, Black Snakeroot, Cohosh Bugbane. Fairly common along some American roadsides near the forest's edge, it grows from 5 to 8 feet tall. In cool garden situations, a late-June to early-August showing is effectively prolonged by lateral branching of the bold stems.

C. simplex, Kamchatka Bugbane. Stately, yet delicate charm abounds in this excellent plant. Imposing spires, 3 feet tall, like white bottle brushes, appear in late September and October. 'Armleuchter' is a European introduction of even more substantial flower and robust habit.

CLEMATIS Clematis Ranunculaceæ

Most gardeners are familiar with the climbing woody forms of clematis, but it is a surprise to some that there are several erect herbaceous species suitable for the perennial border or rock garden.

Cimicifuga racemosa
Coreopsis lanceolata

Convallaria majalis
Corydalis lutea

Not overly showy specimens, they are likely to satisfy the gardener who enjoys the uncommon. Full sun or partial shade in rich, well-drained soil which is not very acid will provide the best location. Once established, they can be left undisturbed for a considerable time.

C. heracleifolia var. *davidiana,* from China, is superior to the species, and is suited to large borders. Stems to 3 feet or more bear terminal clusters of fragrant, blue tubular flowers in August and September. In addition, a few flowers are also prominent in the leaf axils. The ternately compound foliage is rather coarse but not distressingly so. A back corner of the garden is a good location, for plants are likely to take up considerable space.

C. integrifolia 'Cærulea' is likewise more desirable than the species, for the large bell-like flowers are a porcelain blue. These span the June-to-August weeks if watered during dry weather. Plants are usually 16 to 24 inches tall. In the perennial border, they may require staking; in the rock garden, the stems collapse, giving a prostrate effect; and in dry walls, stems trail in attractive manner.

C. recta var. *mandshurica* is a vigorous form with axillary, as well as terminal, clusters of white flowers in June and July. A doubled form is known in Europe. At a height of 3 or 4 feet, this plant is also at home in a large border. For the most part, single specimens are sufficient.

Propagation of all is by division in spring.

CONVALLARIA Lily-of-the-Valley Liliaceæ

As a fragrant cut flower or as a garden plant without a serious fault, the lily-of-the-valley is a prized harbinger of spring.

Convallaria is considered to be derived from the Latin, *Lilium convallium,* or lily-of-the-valley, although some persons believe *convallis* (valley) and *rica* (mantle) were combined to take into account the leaves as well as the flowers. Of the two species, only one, *C. majalis,* native to Europe and Asia, is planted. It has long been known in cultivation; in 1554 a woodcut of it appeared in

Dodoenaus' *Herbal.* Even by 1829, English florists were happily aware of its forcing possibilities, and the poets Thomson and Keats mentioned it.

Garden Value: Fragrance, freedom of bloom, ease of culture, success in shade, and colonizing tendencies combine to make this plant a universal favorite. As a ground cover, it is justly prized, even in such difficult spots as under trees, where little else will grow. The racemes of white bell-like flowers appear in May and early June, above or among the leaves, giving a height that rarely exceeds 1 foot. Occasionally, red berries develop in autumn. Special Dutch and German strains are extensively grown for commercial forcing in greenhouses.

Soil and Exposure: A fertile soil of leafy texture will retain the necessary summer moisture. Some shade is desirable, but exposure to the sun is not necessarily a drawback.

Care: Pips, or single eyes, with some roots attached, are planted in spring, at 9-inch intervals. In future years, applications of organic matter and fertilizer can be profitable. In certain situations where spreading is objectionable, a bit of trimming with a spade is a quick remedy.

Propagation: Division in early spring is common, but may be practiced at any time of the growing season, if care is used and the proper attention given until plants are established.

Species

C. majalis. While the species itself is far from wanting in beauty, several selections provide even more interest. 'Fortin's Giant' is larger than the type in every way. The double-flowered form is rather rare and expensive, but is easily grown when available. Occasional deviations toward pink in the flowers are offered for sale, the majority of them lacking in color purity; if grown in the full sun they fade considerably. There are also variegated types in which gold or silver margins frame the green leaves, but commercial sources are not easily located.

Final Comment: If some earnest collector would assemble and propagate all known variations, his service to horticulture would be valued. At least token efforts to this end are suggested in current English publications.

COREOPSIS **Coreopsis, Tickseed** **Compositæ**

Masses of simple yet effective yellow flowers during most of the summer contribute to the popularity of this genus.

Coreopsis, from the Greek, meaning buglike, was so named because the seeds resemble certain insects. About 100 species are native to America, tropical Africa, and the Hawaiian Islands. Several annuals still catalogued as *Calliopsis* and *Leptosyne* actually belong to *Coreopsis.*

Garden Value: The novice may grow certain coreopsis in unwarranted quantity, unaware of the habit of self-sowing and of the frequent lack of complete hardiness. Most of the perennial species are quite satisfactory for naturalizing or wild gardens, and a few have border merit. Showy yellow flowers on long, slender, wiry stems with reasonably attractive foliage are characteristic. The long blooming season and acceptability as a cut flower result in their being a common garden subject. The dwarf species are often used for summer color in rock gardens.

Soil and Exposure: In general, light sandy soil in full sun is ideal.

Care: Careful planting is successful in either spring or fall. Removal of faded flowers eliminates seeding and encourages longer flowering. Frequent separation of large clumps is advisable.

Propagation: Seeds sown in fall should provide flowers the next summer. Clones or cultivars should be divided in early spring.

Species

C. auriculata 'Nana.' This rock garden novelty has bright orange-yellow blossoms on 3-inch stems from June to August. Where summers are extremely hot, a trace of shade is advantageous.

C. grandiflora. Behavior is discouragingly biennial. The 2-foot plants may have flowers 3 inches in diameter, but the display lasts only from mid-June to late July, after which seedlings crop up all over, and the original clump begins to succumb.

C. lanceolata, Perennial Coreopsis. When true to type, this is a desirable perennial, thriving for years in a sunny spot. Seedsmen of the late nineteenth century were given to describing a wealth of 2-inch golden daisies on 2-foot plants, but unfortunately, named selections suffered from widespread crossing with the weaker *C. grandiflora.* Semidouble forms, such as 'Sunburst,' come fairly true from seed.

C. rosea 'Nana.' This comparatively fastidious dwarf form, 10 inches high, is the one generally observed in rock gardens. Pale rosy pink blossoms from July to September and creeping stems with aromatic foliage identify it. Flowering is negligible in the shade or in soil that is alkaline.

C. tripteris. Although likely to grow to 6 feet, this graceful species need not be staked. It is at its best in August, when the 1½-inch, slightly fragrant flowers are a soft lemon yellow with a disk that turns brown or purple. Mass plantings provide quick screening, and wild gardens are improved by it. However, it is not out of place in the rear of a border, where the compact clumps would not have to be disturbed for years.

C. verticillata, Thread-leaf Coreopsis. This is often sold as 'Golden Shower.' Dainty, fine-textured foliage of almost feathery quality is abundant on stocky 3-foot plants. In addition, flowers like clear yellow stars appear from June to September in clusters that are useful in short bouquets. While neither extremely weedy nor of dubious hardiness, it responds to annual division. Decided resistance to drought is an admirable feature.

Outstanding Cultivars

Although these may be garden hybrids, some will reproduce quite faithfully from seed.

'Sunburst' is a brilliant, semidouble yellow. 'Mayfield Giant,' an Australian introduction, grows to 3 feet with blossoms at least 3 inches across. 'Golden Wheel,' a German oddity with rays that are spaced like spokes of a wheel, proves very transient.

Final Comment: Too many coreopsis make the garden a refuge for mediocrity, but less formal areas benefit from liberal planting.

CORYDALIS **Corydalis** **Fumariaceæ**

Most species offer only early spring interest in small rock gardens, along walks, or in the very front of borders, but *C. lutea* excels until autumn. Many of the others die back to the ground by June. Shallow-rooted annuals then can fill the voids.

Corydalis comes from an old Greek name for the crested lark, which is suggested by the spurred flowers. Of the 100 species widely distributed in the temperate zone, very few are important in our gardens. The genus is closely related to *Dicentra;* resemblance is more than superficial.

Garden Value: The outstanding species, *C. lutea,* should be much more popular than it seems to be. It may take some searching to find commercial sources, but the result will be more than worth the trouble. Golden flowers on plants not over a foot in height are in bloom from late May through the month of August. They are effective in the garden, and are in scale for miniature arrangements. Lacy, almost fernlike foliage remains throughout the season, and would in itself be an attribute even if there were no flowers. Adaptable to heavy shade in rock gardens, dry walls, or borders, it is certain to please discriminating gardeners.

Other species for the specialist include *C. cava,* with purple flowers; *C. cashmireana,* blue; *C. angustifolia,* white; and *C. ophiocarpa,* yellow. However, with these and several others more often listed in foreign catalogs than in ours, foliage often dies back after flowering.

Soil and Exposure: All species are best in the shade and in well-drained soil that contains some organic matter.

Care: *C. lutea* should be moved in spring. For other species, early fall is an ideal time to plant the rhizomes, about 1 inch below the soil line, followed by protection the first winter. Those with foliage which disappears in summer should be marked to prevent injury when weeding.

Propagation: Seeds may be sown as soon as ripe in late summer, but divisions in early fall, or summer cuttings for those that retain their foliage all season, are sometimes more satisfactory.

CYCLAMEN **Cyclamen** **Primulaceæ**

Cyclamen, an ancient Greek name, was given by Linnæus to a genus of tuberous plants of the Mediterranean area and Central Europe. Best known is the common florists' pot plant, but there are two species that are hardy garden subjects. Although they are not particularly well known, they charm everyone who grows them.

Both species look like miniature versions of the florists' *C. persicum.* Perhaps the simplest to grow is *C. neopolitanum.* It has somewhat fragrant, rose or white flowers about ¾-inch long, from late August until October or even later, depending upon the weather. Scapes bearing the flowers are not over 6 inches high. The dark green, spotted leaves do not appear until late in autumn, and often persist over winter. Plants are dormant from the end of May to mid-August. *C. europæum* is similar except that the flowers are a bright red, and quite fragrant.

Tubers should be planted in groups of three, about 1½ inches below the soil surface, in rich, very well-drained soil to which liberal amounts of humus have been added. Light or partial shade will suffice. Because of the small stature and late flowering, plantings are often made close to paths, walks, or doorways, where the flowers can be noticed without having to tramp out to a muddy garden in which there is little else of interest late in the season.

The sophisticated gardener will find real pleasure in pointing out these delicate and unusual plants to his friends.

DELPHINIUM **Delphinium, Larkspur** **Ranunculaceæ**

In spite of their possibly transient nature in the garden, delphiniums are valued for their true-blue flowers, their stately form, and their excellence as cut flowers.

In this genus, the flower's resemblance to dolphins, or *delphin* in Greek, accounts for the name. Larkspur dates back to the seventeenth century and rural England, but presently is more likely to be applied only to the annual forms. There are at least 250 species indigenous, for the most part, to Asia, Europe, and North America. Only 15 or so are commonly grown in American gardens.

Garden Value: Few flowers evoke more lyrical outbursts than the statuesque delphiniums. In addition to true blues, there are also flawless whites, velvety purples, and novel raspberry shades. Perennial forms are an integral part of the border, especially the taller garden selections flowering in June and July. Proud and noble as accents, they blend admirably with many other subjects not of spike-like inflorescence. Madonna lilies, *Phlox* 'Miss Lingard,' Shasta daisies, coral bells, daylilies, and floribunda roses serve as examples. Secondary flowering in fall often occurs to complement such later-flowering plants as the early chrysanthemums. Many species are superb for cutting, and several are possibilities for spacious rock gardens.

Soil and Exposure: Rich, loose loam, very well drained and slightly alkaline, is needed. Humus, plus a light sprinkling of lime in acid soils, as well as some superphosphate, should be incorporated. Annual spring applications of a 5-10-10 fertilizer are desirable. While plants survive in partial shade, they may be more subject to mildew and other troubles in such a location, so full sun is usually recommended.

Care: Field-grown plants, one year old, may be set out in spring or early fall, or can be carefully moved when in full bloom. Spacing is usually at intervals of 2 feet. Deep planting sometimes causes rotting. Cultivation must be gentle, for the roots do not withstand rough treatment.

Staking is absolutely necessary for the taller, vertical sorts. Naturally, this must be done before winds or heavy rains topple the stalks.

As the blooms of the taller garden forms fade, the old spike is snipped off immediately below the bottom flower to forestall seed formation. Foliage is retained until new growths attain 6 or 8 inches, then the old stem is cut to the ground. Some growers apply a teaspoon of a nitrogen fertilizer at this time to produce better autumn flowers. If flowers are cut for purposes other than exhibition, three sets of leaves should be left on the plants for food production.

When winter approaches, an inch of sand or ashes placed around each crown wards off slugs, and prevents washing of soil. Later, when the ground is frozen hard, a 2- or 3-inch mulch of hay or straw forms good protection over winter. Clumps attaining considerable size after three or four years will be ready for spring division.

Garden delphiniums cannot be guaranteed long-lived plants; many are treated as biennials, and from Maryland south they are considered annuals for late season bloom. In order to have a good showing of delphiniums in the garden, it is often advisable to have a nursery area in which to grow plants for replacement.

Crown rot may be a problem in poorly drained areas. It is encouraged by overly deep planting, and by applications of green manures. The affected plants should be destroyed, and others placed elsewhere. A blight carried by tiny cyclamen mites may affect the entire plant, resulting in blackened, distorted leaves and buds. Mildew may be troublesome in areas of poor air circulation, especially when cool damp nights are followed by hot days. A complete spray program at ten-day intervals is advocated. Malathion plus a fungicide and a miticide make a versatile combination of materials.

Propagation: Seeds are the favored American method of propagation. Sowings should be made in a light soil in August or September when the seeds are fresh. However, seeds may be kept in airtight containers under refrigeration until spring, or even for several years. When outdoor sowings are made in the late summer, plants are moved to permanent locations in April. Springsown material is moved a year later.

If large clumps need division, it is best performed in spring when new growth has barely commenced. Sections of one or two sprouts are made, and the cut surfaces dusted with a fungicide.

Species

D. cheilanthum var. *formosum* (*D. belladonna, D. bellamosum*). The airy, openly branched stems of blue flowers differ greatly from the dense spikes of the *D. elatum* type. Lithe, 3- to 4-foot plants provide many short stems for cutting. Plants of this species must be given good air circulation, as they are susceptible to mildew. In the garden it provides particularly gratifying combinations with peonies.

Worthy cultivars include 'Cliveden Beauty,' a crisply deep turquoise blue; 'Lamartine,' which is a vivid gentian blue; and 'Sapphire,' a delicate pale blue.

'Pink Sensation' is a Dutch hybrid, one of the parents being the red-flowered *D. nudicaule*. It is not a clear pink; it increases slowly, is not altogether hardy, and is very subject to mildew.

D. elatum, Common Delphinium. Modern garden strains of aristocratic bearing have evolved from centuries of improvement of this species. Strong stems, 4 to 6 feet or more tall, abundantly covered with many individual flowers, 2 inches or more across, typify the selections. Flower types may be single or double, self-colored or bicolor, and may have a central "eye" or "bee" of contrasting shade. The bee is actually a formation of true petals; the showy parts surrounding the bee are sepals. Obviously, the original species from Siberia, with purple coloring, has been greatly modified over the years.

European breeders—Victor Lemoine, James Kelway, Watkins Samuel, the firm of Blackmore and Langdon, and the contemporary Frank Bishop—have worked wonders in delphinium development. In America, Luther Burbank, Major Newell Vanderbilt, Charles Barber, and Dr. Leon Leonian have made their contributions. At present, Frank Reinelt of Capitola, California, is renowned for his peerless Pacific Hybrids.

The Pacific Hybrids are sturdy plants 4 feet or more in height with dense spikes of large flowers having full, rounded bees. The original Round Table series was named for King Arthur's henchmen; since then other selections, which come virtually true from seed, have followed. A few examples are: 'Summer Skies,' a soft blue; 'Black Night,' a deep purple; and 'Galahad,' a white without the traditional black bee. Astolat and Elaine are strains resulting from fine efforts to obtain clearer pink forms. Mr. Reinelt's contributions to American gardens can hardly be praised too highly.

The Wrexham strains and those of Blackmore and Langdon are reputable English originations, the latter reported to be more perennial in habit than many others. In this country, the Jackson and Perkins Company has named cultivars resulting from a breeding program in northern New York, which was designed to create garden forms that are not so tall as some of the other types.

D. grandiflorum (*D. chinense*), Chinese Delphinium. Only 18 inches tall, this may bloom in late summer from spring-sown seeds. In the central Atlantic states the plants may be perennial, but in the North they are usually treated as biennials. 'Blue Butterfly' is a bright blue, 'Blue Mirror' a gentian blue; 'White Butterfly' is self-descriptive.

D. tatsienense. Here is another Oriential dwarf for sunny, porous sites, producing varying shades of blue or white flowers. Appealing white mottlings are often noticeable on the small, neat leaves.

Final Comment: Future garden strains promise more compact growth along with frilled flowers and added fragrance. In England, Frank Bishop is breeding *D. cheilanthum* var. *formosum* with brilliant American species to obtain types with petals and sepals that may contrast in harlequin style.

DIANTHUS **Pink, Carnation** **Caryophyllaceæ**

The garden boasts no more enchanting realm than that of the dianthus, with its beauty, clovelike fragrance, and striking foliage.

Linnæus took the name *Dianthus* from *dios anthos,* meaning flower of Zeus, or divine flower, a hint of the esteem in which it has always been held. Of the 300 species, which range in origin from Siberia and the Arctic through parts of Asia and much of Europe to the Cape of Good Hope, only about 30 are commonly grown in this country. American climatic extremes often prove too harsh for the

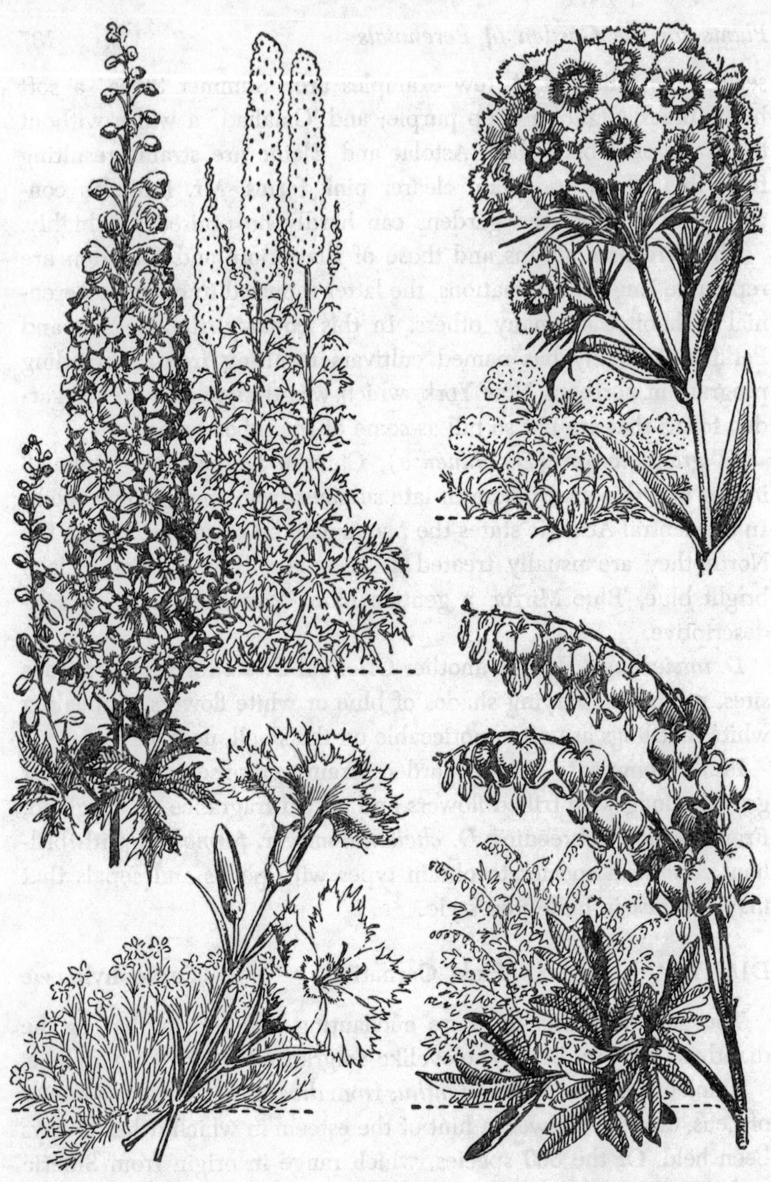

Delphinium elatum
Dianthus plumarius

Dianthus barbatus
Dicentra spectabilis

plants to make their finest performances. Here species range from the ragged annual *D. chinensis* to the wonderful greenhouse carnations developed from *D. caryophyllus.*

Garden Value: The leaves may be in close tufts, gray or bright green, usually spreading out in mat-forming clumps. Garden forms range in flower color from white to pink, red, and purple. Those of compact stature are best utilized in rock gardens or as edgings, while the ones with more upright habit look well in small groups at the front of the border. Charming cut material of varying size is available, primarily during the month of June, although some types produce scattered flowers until frost.

Soil and Exposure: Well-drained, sandy soil of alkaline tendency is basic. Working in small amounts of leafmold or rotted manure helps overcome dry American summers. Lime should be added to acid soil; superphosphate will encourage strong rooting. Full sun is often desirable. However, a large portion of the country is too hot in summer and too wet in winter for the enviable growth displayed in the British Isles. Along the coasts, as on Cape Cod, the Pacific Coast, and Maine ocean fronts, attempts to grow the various species are more liberally rewarded.

Care: Plants are best established in spring. Seeding is to be discouraged, except for propagation needs. Light shearing after the main blooming season encourages lively new growth. In areas of severe winters, a cover of evergreen boughs will protect the persistent foliage without causing rot. A few of the hardier species should be divided every third spring. Leaf spot in various forms may appear in muggy periods, especially on crowded shoots, and when noted, a fungicide should be quickly applied.

Propagation: Seeds sown in spring reproduce most species acceptably, and may provide interesting variants. Confusion in nomenclature is often due to carelessly collected seeds. In this connection, it should be noted that many times a packet of seeds will produce plants with other than the name indicated on the packet.

Cuttings taken in midsummer, from vegetative shoots only, provide the commercial means of propagation. Division in spring is common among amateurs, although layering works well on *D. plumarius.*

Species

Some nomenclatural changes have become necessary, and identities are often confused in commerce. Nearly any species will please the fancier.

D. alpinus, Alpine Pink. This perplexing 3-inch tuft seems to enjoy partial shade. When conditions duplicate those of its alpine habitat, rounded pink blossoms hide the leaves for a month in late spring. 'Little Joe' is a hybrid (*D. plumarius* × *D. alpinus*), created in Oregon, that produces stunning, single crimson flowers most of the summer. However, there is little foliage, and winter protection is vital.

D. arenarius, Sand Pink. Found in Finland, this is extremely hardy. Trim 4-inch tufts are characterized by blue-green foliage and fragrant pink or white flowers, which may reappear in autumn. To some it seems like a tiny *D. gratianopolitanus.*

D. barbatus, Sweet William. This popular plant is usually grown as a biennial, although there are strains that can be treated as annuals. It is of the clusterhead type, with many small odorless flowers in rounded clusters of several shades and colors. Fine for massed bedding, the 2-foot plants flower heavily in early summer, with riotous hues. Dwarf strains such as Indian Carpet, not over 6 inches high, are also available. Plants are apt to become straggly in habit after the second year and are usually renewed by seeds. Self-sowing is common, with seedlings reverting in time to uninteresting colors.

D. carthusianorum. This Hungarian species is exceptionally hardy, producing 2-foot stems with crimson clusters from June to early August. However, unless planted in the midst of other material, the leggy stems seem pitifully inadequate. The hardiness may inspire hybridizing efforts.

D. caryophyllus, Carnation, Clove Pink. Coming from southern Europe and Asia, it is not very hardy and is not recommended for northern gardens. This species has led to the majestic greenhouse carnations and the seed strains called hardy carnations. Such offerings as Chabaud's, Dwarf Vienna, and the Grenadins are typical. If grown in the garden at all, they should receive winter protection.

D. deltoides, Maiden Pink. Ancient England called this "sops-in-wine." From dense mounds of very narrow leaves, loose, wavy 10-inch stems carry many small blooms of reddish purple, rose, or white. A trailing habit favors its use in walls or rock gardens, where mild self-sowing may occur. It can also become a ground cover for a sunny spot. 'Brilliant' is a bright red selection.

D. gratianopolitanus (*D. cæsius*), Cheddar Pink (from stands in the Cheddar Gorge of western England). Good in walls or steps, it has small, usually fringed flowers in shades of pink, about 6 inches above thick mats of foliage. Occasional division is desirable. 'Rose Queen' is a pleasant double selection of bright rose coloring.

D. knappii. It may be that this is the only true yellow species, with lemon-yellow sprays on 10-inch stems. Foliage is scanty. Native to hot, dry hills of Hungary and Yugoslavia, it needs sandy soil. More of a novelty than a prize specimen.

D. × *latifolius.* Accepted as a hybrid, it is intermediate between *D. barbatus* and *D. chinensis* or *D. plumarius.* Plants grow to 10 inches high, with broad grassy leaves, and flowers normally 1 inch or less across in clusters. Splitting of the calyx is a common fault. While they bloom for several weeks, even the leading cultivars often flower themselves to death. 'Raven Rock Red' is a flashy crimson with spicy fragrance, 'Beatrix' is a salmon pink, and 'Silver Mine' is a white mutation of 'Beatrix.'

D. neglectus. Neat 2-inch cushions bear 6-inch stems laden with flowers of red, rose, cherry, or salmon. Petals overlap, and the reverse sides usually show buff tones. Soils need not be especially alkaline for this species. 'Henriette' is a choice deep salmon form.

D. plumarius, Cottage Pink, Grass Pink. This tenaciously hardy species, the backbone of most border carnations, was introduced from Europe in colonial days. Shades of red, pink, and white abound in May and June. Flowers are fringed, single to semidouble, 1½ inches in diameter, and very fragrant. Strong 12-inch clumps of polished gray foliage are fine for edging. There are countless cultivars of merit. A few outstanding ones include: 'Highland Queen,' a vivid scarlet, with a long blooming season; 'Cyclops,' with red flowers; 'Dinah,' a semidouble Persian rose with maroon center; and 'Evangeline,' which is softer toned than 'Dinah.' 'Pink Princess,' not to be confused with a garden carnation of similar name, is a superb addition from the U.S.D.A.'s extensive breeding campaign at Cheyenne, Wyoming. It produces fringed, fragrant 1½-inch blossoms of coral-rose for weeks beginning in May. Sturdy, hardy 15-inch plants are characteristic of this striking new perennial.

A hybrid between *D. plumarius* and *D. caryophyllus,* produced by Montague Allwood of England, is known in the trade as Allwoodii. Not hardy everywhere, this race produces flowers of good texture, color, and fragrance. Average height is 12 to 15 inches.

The so-called hardy or border carnations were bred largely from *D. plumarius, D. superbus, D. gratianopolitanus,* and *D. caryophyllus.* Around 1926, Alex Cumming hybridized *D. plumarius* and Allwoodii to achieve a group of border carnations free of calyx splitting. 'Bristol Jewel' and 'Bristol Purity' are examples, but as a rule, more recent introductions appear to be from haphazard seed collections.

For the most part, garden carnations have shapely, double flowers borne in successive crops during the summer. However, the desired blend of steady bloom and imperturbable hardiness has yet to be completely achieved. Of this group, 'Pink Princess' ('Old Spice') —not the U.S.D.A. introduction with the same name—is a brilliant salmon-orange; 'Spotlight,' a notably hardy crimson; 'Her Majesty,' a splendid white but seldom in flower after July; 'Dubonnet,' an exotic wine-purple; and 'Sweet Memory,' a red and white.

D. superbus. While the lacy, delicately fringed, pink or white flowers and brilliant leaves are most becoming, this plant should be treated as a biennial. The 18-inch stems offer so many frail clusters for summer bouquets that annual seed sowing is well repaid. 'White Loveliness' is especially good.

D. × *winteri.* This may not be a legitimate name, but the strain probably contains variants of *D. plumarius* from a particularly long-blooming, hardy race. Clumps 12 years of age have been known to thrive continuously. Selections from this strain should be worthy of asexual propagation.

Cultivars of Uncertain Parentage

'Rose Cushion,' a hedgehog-like 2-inch mound of blue-gray, produces tiny pink blooms in June. 'Tiny Rubies' bears small, bright red, fragrant flowers above dense gray cushions, while 'Sammy,' a hardy, spiny mound, produces dime-sized pink flowers on 5-inch stems in June and July. 'Rose Bowl,' with 4-inch clumps of brilliant green leaves, sports gay little purple-rose blooms from June until frost. 'Lacy Lass,' with semidouble white flowers quaintly marked with maroon, grows to 12 inches, and flowers in early summer.

'Napoleon III' is a sterile hybrid from the vicinity of Paris, where it was raised by M. Paré around 1858. It is believed to be the result of a natural cross between *D. chinensis* and the florists' carnation. Farrer berated it for "squawking carmine podginess." A short, hectic, but colorful life, and blooms with split calyces are characteristic. One-inch blossoms are startling red all summer.

Final Comment: Much could be accomplished by testing and interbreeding other species. It is unfortunate that all the latent beauty and hardiness of the genus are not combined to outwit the exacting American climate. In general, it should be remembered that the performance of this genus is superior where summers do not get too hot too quickly, if at all.

DICENTRA (*Dielytra*) **Bleeding Heart** **Fumariaceæ**

The attractive dissected foliage and the winsome delicate flowers of the dicentras often belie the staunchly permanent nature of most species. Plants are found native in Asia and North America, especially along the Pacific Coast. The name of the genus means two-spurred in Greek, referring to the form of the corolla.

Garden Value: Keeping in mind individual habit and culture, dicentras should be made integral parts of perennial borders or rock gardens. By proper selection of species, blooms are possible from May until frost. Attractive compound foliage, fine-textured in many species, is of merit even after the flowering season is over. Nearly everyone knows *D. spectabilis,* a patrician among plants, and the so-called "living valentine." *D. eximia* occasionally spreads to ground-cover proportions. All may be used as cut flowers.

Soil and Exposure: With few exceptions, the soil should be richly mellow, of considerable humus content, and neither dry in summer nor soggy in winter. Partial shade normally produces the best effects.

Care: Most species respond best to very early spring planting, before the young growth emerges. Division needs range widely: *D. formosa* needs almost annual separation, while *D. spectabilis* prefers to be undisturbed over a long period of time.

Propagation: Seeds should be sown in late summer. Division is safest in early spring, but is possible in fall with adequate winter protection. Root cuttings, made in early summer, and set 2 inches deep are sometimes the practice with *D. spectabilis*. Top cuttings or heel cuttings of vegetative shoots taken from this species also root well in midsummer.

Species

D. chrysantha, Golden Eardrops. This imposing 4-foot Californian produces arching showers of pure gold in full sunlight. As it is annoyingly difficult to transplant, seeds are best sown where plants are to stand.

D. cucullaria, Dutchman's Breeches. A midget often but 6 inches tall, it has white or pinkish heartlike flowers with yellow tips, normally from April until early June. The pale feathery leaves disappear in hot summers, but cool, moist areas may see a continuation of flowering. Shaded pockets of rich soil are favored for the species, native from Nova Scotia to Missouri and North Carolina.

D. eximia, Plume Bleeding Heart. From 12 to 18 inches tall, this East Coast native has excellent grayish blue, dissected leaves. Deep rose-pink flowers appear from May until August. Self-sowing may account for spreading tendencies in the shade, although it is quite tolerant of sunny areas. Preference is for a rather sandy loam. Best divided every three or four years.

The variety *alba* is a white form not yet in great demand, perhaps because of reports that it flowers sparingly. 'Clay's Variety' is a superb English selection that constantly bears vivid pink racemes all summer, and sets no seeds. The lacy foliage seems oblivious to heat. 'Bountiful,' obviously a hybrid with heavier, more bronzed leaves, seems most productive in full sun. However, the fuchsia-red flowers may fade in hot weather.

D. formosa, Western Bleeding Heart. While often confused with *D. eximia,* this species spreads by creeping underground rhizomes, and its bluish foliage is more substantial. Moreover, it usually insists on some shade, and demands frequent division. It generally has pale rose flowers tinted purple, on 12-inch stems. 'Sweetheart' is a pure white form that has been called "a fairy in the night garden," because the glistening blooms shine so brightly. Effective sea-green foliage and unceasing bloom from late May to September make it a choice selection for shaded rock gardens, especially when combined with primroses.

D. oregana (*D. glauca*). Never truly abundant in its West Coast haunts, this modern offering recalls a smaller *D. formosa.* Leaves are of a silver shade, and the flowers a pale cream or darker, with pink tips. In the wild, soils are gravelly; however, in the garden, flowering is increased if it is planted in partial shade and in soil to which peat has been added. It is most floriferous from May to July.

D. spectabilis, Bleeding Heart. This treasure was brought to England from Japan in 1847 by Robert Fortune, noted collector. It was also a favorite of Chinese mandarins, who called it Hong-pak-moutan-wha. Each blossom is doubly winged like a lyre; English gardeners may know it as lyre flower.

If well grown in partial shade, it should become a full-bodied 3-foot plant, glowing with arching sprays of pink hearts in May and June. In hot, sunny spots, the green leaves usually disappear in summer, but nearby plants like babys-breath can tactfully hide the gaps. It is effective with daffodils, primroses, lilies, and hostas. 'Alba' is a beautiful but fickle white variant, seldom grown in quantity.

Final Comment: *D. spectabilis* is a classical example of arching grace, although the whole genus exhibits refinement.

DICTAMNUS Gas Plant, Dittany, Fraxinella Rutaceæ

The popular name "gas plant" is derived from the fact that a volatile oil exuded from the plant, especially near the main stem just below the inflorescence, may be ignited on a calm, sultry night, producing a small burst of blue flame. While the name *Dictamnus* is of uncertain derivation, some botanists feel that Mt. Dikte, a Cretan habitat of the plant, is the logical source. John Keats mentions "the sacred Dittany," once believed able to frighten away serpents. There is only one species, prone to vary in some degree. The aromatic quality of foliage and seed pods is reminiscent of the citrus group, which are in the same family.

Garden Value: Incredible permanence and a solid, handsome frame of pinnate foliage make this plant a blue-chip investment for the border, where it is valued as a specimen plant. The 3-foot plants may serve as a herbaceous background for a small garden, since the glossy dark green foliage remains in good condition throughout the season. During the month of June, terminal racemes of flowers are at their best. In late summer, the seed pods are attractive; early settlers used them as holders for small candles.

Soil and Exposure: A rich soil in sun or partial shade is preferable. Plants withstand drought more surely than continued dampness.

Care: Almost 3 feet of ground space should be allotted each way. Small two-year-old plants, set out in spring, may not flower for another year or so. Young blooming plants can be moved with a ball of soil, but disturbing them thereafter is to be discouraged. An occasional spring top-dressing of a complete fertilizer is desirable, but beyond that plants are wisely left to their own devices.

Propagation: Seeds sown in fall germinate freely the next spring, but transplanting should be postponed for another year. Pods must be harvested as soon as they commence to turn brown, as the bursting pod expels seeds in all directions.

Species

D. albus (*D. fraxinella*). The white-flowered type is native from southern Europe to northern China. Individual flowers are grouped into sizable terminal racemes throughout June. The variety *ruber* has pink to purplish red colorings, making the flowers even more striking. A form with larger flowers is known as variety *caucasica*.

Final Comment: The gas plant is slow to become established, and is late in making an appearance in spring, but there is hardly another plant so satisfying to those who dodge maintenance chores.

DIGITALIS Foxglove Scrophulariaceæ

Foxgloves are old friends of the American gardener; he has long known the ornate, tapering racemes of large, almost tubular flowers as a conservative touch of early summer elegance.

There are many notions of origin for the common name, most of them connected with English superstitions of fairies. Most of the species come from Asia and Europe; horticulturally, those generally treated as biennials are the most valuable. The drug digitalis, so essential to victims of heart disease, is extracted from the leaves of certain species.

Garden Value: The vertical, spikelike effect of foxgloves is an attribute that relieves the horizontal forms of most garden plants. The common biennial, *D. purpurea,* is the one best fitted for the border, where 4- to 5-foot stems add dignity and color at the rear of a planting. The better strains form massive spikes that look well with sweet William or Canterbury bells. Darker shades give effective contrast with Madonna lilies, and all may be massed to perfection. Both biennial and perennial types may be naturalized in wild gardens. All are reasonably good for cutting.

Soil and Exposure: Gerard's *Herbal* (1597) states that "Foxgloves

Dictamnus albus
Dodecatheon meadia

Digitalis purpurea
Doronicum caucasicum

groweth in barren, sandie grounds, and under hedges, almost everywhere." This somewhat disdainful summary has now been modified to an extent. Mellow, well-nourished soil is preferred, but waterlogged conditions are fatal. Partial shade is ideal, although survival is frequent in full sun.

Care: The biennials must be renewed each August from seeds. Plants may be moved in fall or early spring. In areas where winter protection is necessary, care must be taken to prevent a wet soggy mulch from smothering the persistent basal foliage during the winter. Among the perennial species, seed setting is to be discouraged. An insecticide may be necessary in hot sunny areas to combat red spider.

Propagation: Seeds sown in late summer always produce blooming-sized plants the following year. Divisions of especially admired perennial sorts may be made in early spring.

Species

D. grandiflora (*D. ambigua*), Yellow Foxglove. This sound perennial, to 3 feet, suffers from lacklustre, pale yellow flowers. 'Canary Bird' is a more pleasing selection. If stems are cut down in late July, fall recurrence is possible.

D. minor. Only 20 inches tall, with deep purple flowers, this species fits into the foreground of a border—but without arousing undue enthusiasm. It must be grown in the shade.

D. purpurea, Common Foxglove. From a native English purple-pink form, the Rev. W. W. Wilkes, of Shirley, gradually evolved his Shirley Hybrids, long the accepted strain of foxgloves, with a full complement of shades, even apricot being available. Yet the blooms were massed in tiers on only one side of the stem, and hung downward in a depressed state.

Sutton's, a great English seed firm, secured an American variant in which the white flowers not only encircled the stem, but were even flaringly horizontal. This bit of fortune was assiduously bred to the Shirley Hybrids, finally resulting in the eminently superior strain known as Excelsior Hybrids. The latter could doom all other strains to eventual obscurity, now that segregation into separate colors is under way.

Although *D. purpurea* is a biennial, it self-sows and maintains itself in gardens much like hollyhocks.

D. thapsii. Unpretentious but engaging flowers of soft pink and cream cover the 2-foot stems of this agreeably hardy Spanish native.

Final Comment: By and large, the perennials are to the biennial Excelsior Hybrids as the inarticulate country cousin is to his assured, city-bred relative.

DODECATHEON   Shooting Star   Primulaceæ

There are probably 30 species of North American origin, yet they are more popular in England where they were first grown in 1774. There, only the primrose is considered superior for shade-tolerant brilliance in May. The scientific name comes from Pliny's writings, and means twelve gods in Greek.

Garden Value: As few specimens attain more than 1 or 2 feet in height, they are compatible with spring-flowering bulbs and primroses. Glabrous basal leaves and nodding flowers in umbels are characteristic. Acceptable for rock gardens, they can also be naturalized along shady brooks, or planted in tight groups in the front portion of a border. Since the foliage is prone to die down in July, after seeds have ripened, the resulting vacancy must not be overlooked, particularly in rock gardens.

Soil and Exposure: Soil enriched with leafmold is recommended, but it must be sufficiently well drained that water will not stand around the crowns in winter. Cool shade provides prosperous plants, although sunlight is not fatal.

Care: Plants are usually set out in August, while relatively dormant, as only potted plants transplant well in spring. Nine-inch spaces are needed between individuals. Foliage may be retained a bit longer if seed pods are removed early. The more hardy, vigorous specimens may need division after three or four years.

Propagation: Seeds are sown in late summer or early spring. Division of mature clumps is practicable.

Species

England cultivates and enjoys a dozen or more species, but few are handled in America by other than specialists.

D. meadia. This outstanding member, native from Pennsylvania to Georgia and Texas, was named for Dr. Richard Mead, a noted English physician of the eighteenth century. Flowers may show pinkish, white, or purple shadings, with beaklike anthers of reddish yellow. Plants are best situated where there is an effective background against which the delicate flowers can be viewed.

D. pulchellum (*D. pauciflorum, D. cusickii*). Here is a rather difficult shooting star, happiest along the Pacific Coast. On 10-inch stems there are deep rose and yellow flowers with dark purple tracing at the throat. Rosettes of fleshy, slightly toothed leaves are further assets. An acid, sandy leafmold yields the best results. If drainage is sharp and constant, success is assured.

Final Comment: This American genus could easily furnish limitless material for shaded naturalizing in its own country.

DORONICUM **Leopardsbane** **Compositæ**

Occasionally one is hard pressed to analyze the specific appeal of a flower. For example, doronicums offer merely simple, yellow, daisy-like flowers, and the month of May has almost a surfeit of that color. Nevertheless they always elicit favorable comments in the garden. Native to Europe and the less frigid portions of Asia, the species are reliably hardy.

Garden Value: All blend well with the spring-flowering bulbs, bleeding heart, primroses, spring phlox, and *Brunnera.* In general, most favored species grow about 2 feet in height, but *D. plantagineum* can stretch to 4 feet or more. In most cases, foliage all but disappears in summer, so conspicuous massing leads to later voids. No spring perennial offers finer cut flowers.

Soil and Exposure: Plants are shallow-rooted, but soil must be fairly rich at least a few inches deep. The presence of some humus aids in holding summer moisture. Open sunny spots, or those in partial shade, are generally prescribed.

Care: Planting time is either in earliest spring or late summer, with plant sections set at 12-inch intervals. Lacking long roots, the matted surface growths are divided each second August.

Propagation: Seeds germinate erratically regardless of the time of sowing, so division in late summer is the usual means of propagation.

Species

D. caucasicum. This native of the forest glens of southern Europe grows to 18 inches, with solitary flowers on each stem. A creeping, stoloniferous habit is very pronounced. 'Madam Mason' is a fine horticultural selection with flowers 2 inches in diameter, and foliage that tends to be more persistent during the summer than that of the species.

D. clusii. Named for Charles de l'Escluse, a Dutch professor of botany who died in 1609, it is indigenous to the Alps. Usually less than 2 feet high at the most, it is often offered for rock garden use.

D. cordatum. Known for over 100 years, this intriguing dwarf languished in obscurity until 1948 when it suddenly created a minor stir in England. Characteristically, striking 3-inch flowers are produced on stubby 9-inch stems for weeks in May and June. Rock garden trials promise future popularity here.

D. pardalianches. Here the name, from Greek words for panther and choke, stresses powers against animals. Instead of flowers borne singly, stems have clusters of canary-yellow flowers well into June. Height may vary from 2 to 3 feet.

D. plantagineum (*D. excelsum*). Coarser leaves and impressive 3-inch flower heads, on stems that may range from 3 to almost 5 feet in height, are typical. Acceptable in larger borders, its coarseness precludes extensive use in formal plantings. The English form called 'Harpur Crewe' is indistinguishable from the type for all practical purposes.

Final Comment: Any border could be improved by adding a doronicum if it does not already have one, *D. pardalianches* being a good one with which to start.

ECHINACEA **Purple Coneflower** **Compositæ**

In its native form this genus, indigenous to North America, can be dingy, coarse, and wholly out of place in self-respecting gardens, but the newer, more colorful products of the plant breeder will do justice to any sunny border.

The generic name comes from a Greek term for hedgehog, no doubt a reference to the central cone or disk, which is somewhat spiny.

Garden Value: Current forms of *E. purpurea* are useful for summer color, either as specimens or in spacious groups of three. Feathery blossoms of babys-breath or sea lavender aid immeasurably in toning down any suggestion of stiff rigidity. Open, semiwild plantings also benefit from its introduction. Colors vary from white to purple and crimson, in midsummer.

Soil and Exposure: Warm, light ground of sandy texture is called for; heavy soil poorly drained in winter is detrimental. While full sun is quite satisfactory, light shade enhances the richer colors in hot weather.

Care: Planting is done either in early fall or spring, at distances of 2 feet from neighboring subjects. Winter protection is prudent in extremely cold areas. Where growth is vigorous, clumps should be divided each third spring to forestall deterioration. In areas harassed by Japanese beetles, the flowers are sometimes badly riddled, and insecticides may be necessary.

Propagation: As seedlings do not come true to type, division in spring is recommended. Root cuttings give the speedy, liberal increase of commercial growers.

Species

E. angustifolia. Wild from Saskatchewan to Texas, it definitely offers possibilities for selective propagation. Growth usually approximates 18 inches, and rosy purple rays surround mahogany cones. Promising pink forms have often been reported, if not cultivated.

E. purpurea (*Rudbeckia purpurea*). Unsightly at its worst, this native of gravelly stretches from Pennsylvania to Georgia, grows from 2 to 5 feet tall. Foliage may be unkempt, and the nondescript flowers often fail to please; all too often the purplish rays droop listlessly. Tolerably good variants sometimes appear, but the named cultivars are generally superior. Most of these came into being after World War I, at the hands of English and German breeders. There is reason to believe that *E. dicksonii* and *E. heterophylla* from Mexico, *E. angustifolia,* and the old purple *E. intermedia* all played roles in this unsung breeding program.

Among the resulting cultivars is 'The King,' with splendid 3-inch flowers of coral-crimson that glow in arrangements under artificial light. The thick horizontal rays and brownish cones are of fine quality in August. Sturdy 3-foot plants are customary.

'Bright Star' ('Leuchstern') is more brightly colored than 'The King,' but it does not reproduce well from root cuttings, thus losing value in the eyes of the commercial grower. 'White King' ('White Lustre') has coarse leaves and dull white rays, which are prone to reflex and thus discourage wide acceptance. Floriferousness, even in drought areas, is the main virtue. White forms of *E. purpurea* are not unknown, but lighter foliage suggests the influence of other species.

Final Comment: Undoubtedly, added breeding and selection will one day provide doubled flowers as well as new pink tones. At present, named selections are a far better investment than indiscriminate seedlings.

ECHINOPS — Globe Thistle — Compositæ

Appropriately, the name *Echinops* is derived from two Greek words meaning like a hedgehog, for indeed the overall effect of the flower heads is prickly. While there are almost 100 species, native

Echinacea purpurea
Epimedium

Echinops
Eremurus

from the Iberian Peninsula to central Asia and Africa, only a limited few have garden significance.

Garden Value: The globe thistle represents a radical departure from the conventional perennial standbys. Globular heads of sharp, spiny bracts and flowers, predominantly blue, are borne on substantial stems during midsummer. The thistle-like leaves, white on the underside, could never be accused of lacking character. The very boldness of pattern usually eclipses any hasty condemnations of stiffness. The plants are recommended as accents for the middle or rear of a planting, where they are guaranteed to catch the eye. Foliage is robust enough at the base to choke out most adjacent weeds.

Globe thistles are favorite cut flowers for florists because of the contrast afforded by the spherical blooms. If cut just before the head begins to expand, flowers dry splendidly for winter arrangements.

Soil and Exposure: Soil should be fairly rich but on the light sandy side. Deep vigorous roots penetrate more than a foot in depth. Full sun is advantageous.

Care: Spring is the best time to plant the fleshy roots. At least 18 inches of open space should be reserved all around the plant. Division, while an arduous task, is wisely performed every three or four years.

Propagation: Cultivars should be divided in spring, with roots trimmed back to 6 or 8 inches. Root cuttings are used commercially. Inferior types often result from seeds, which may be sown in spring.

Species

E. exaltatus. Most catalogs continue to list *E. ritro* and *E. sphærocephalus,* but botanists have determined that the material so offered consists of selections of *E. exaltatus.* This species comes from Siberia. It is quite variable, ranging in height from 3 to 12 feet, with flowers of inconsistent blue colorings. Very fertile soils tend to encourage taller growth. Choice selections, if noted, should be propagated. The flowering season can extend from July to September.

'Taplow Blue' is far and away the best globe thistle available to date. It is an English selection, unsurpassed for arrangements or borders. Glistening steel-blue spheres with silvery overcasts are 3 inches in diameter. It makes a noble silhouette against an August sky at twilight.

E. humilis. Plants 3 to 4 feet tall have plump heads of blue flowers. The foliage is respectably ornamental, with a cobweb-like pubescence on the upperside; the undersides white-tomentose. Occasional white deviations in flower color seem lacking in durability.

Final Comment: Globe thistles will never command universal approval, but if used with discrimination they can make an unforgettable garden display.

EPIMEDIUM **Barrenwort** **Berberidaceæ**

Although the genus is not particularly well known, the delicate flowers and superb foliage it bears should delight all gardeners of refined taste. Most of the species are found native to the temperate regions of the northern hemisphere, but the majority of garden forms are of hybrid origin.

Garden Value: Perhaps the prime value is as a ground cover in shade, for the plants thrive even under trees if occasionally fertilized. In rock gardens or borders, combinations with primroses, phlox, and other dwarfs of spring prove engaging. Neat, compound, almost evergreen foliage forms trim plants about a foot high. In spring, leaves are usually a yellowish green tinted with a delicate rose, but they become grassy green, mottled purple during summer, and crimson or chestnut with the first frosts of autumn. Small flowers, in April and May, are red, yellow, or white. These, as well as the foliage, may be used for cutting.

Soil and Exposure: A sandy loam with added leafmold is recommended; very dry locations are to be avoided. Partial to deep shade is favored, but sun is no problem if the soil has sufficient organic matter to retain moisture.

Care: Potted plants are usually supplied in spring, even though clumps transplant readily in early fall. For massing, distances of 8 or 10 inches are good. Occasional division may be necessary, although plants can remain undisturbed for many years. If persistent foliage is cut back in late March, the growth of new leaves is hastened.

Propagation: Division is the usual method, in spring or fall.

Species

E. grandiflorum. An Asiatic jewel with 1- to 2-inch flowers, the largest in the genus. Outer sepals are red, inner sepals violet, and the spurred petals white. The variety *violaceum* grows to but 9 inches in height, with pure violet petals.

E. pinnatum. From the Caucasus and Persia. It has small vivid yellow flowers with reddened spurs. Plants in cultivation are usually those of the variety *colchicum*, which has fewer leaflets in the compound foliage than does the species.

E. × *rubrum* (*E. alpinum* × *E. grandiflorum*). This garden hybrid produces red juvenile foliage and large 1-inch blossoms of brilliant crimson, flushed yellow or white. It may well be the showiest of the genus, since stems carry more flowers in each cluster than do the others.

E. × *versicolor* (*E. grandiflorum* × *E. pinnatum* var. *colchicum*). A hybrid of garden origin, it has small flowers with rose-colored sepals and yellow petals with reddish spurs. Young foliage is mottled red, but in the variety *sulphureum* the foliage is not mottled, and the flowers are always yellow, vaguely reminiscent of a tiny columbine. In autumn, the leaves turn a pinkish red.

E. × *youngianum* var. *niveum.* Faultless 10-inch plants have white flowers and leathery foliage. The type is actually a garden hybrid between *E. diphyllum* and *E. grandiflorum*, which a man named Young brought to the Edinburgh Botanic Garden in 1838.

Final Comment: Just a bit of appreciative study will enslave many gardeners to this winsome group. It should be noted that, as with many other genera, catalogs do not always list plants under correct names.

ERANTHIS **Winter Aconite** **Ranunculaceæ**

Although often offered in catalogs as a bulb, *Eranthis hyemalis* is a perennial with a tuberous root. The great attraction of this plant, in either the border or the rock garden, is the fact that it flowers almost as soon as the snow disappears in March. In fact, the generic name is from the Greek, meaning an early flower.

Solitary flowers, always yellow, about 1½ inches across are borne on stems 3 or 4 inches high, subtended by a circular, dissected leaf. A sunny, well-drained spot is all that is necessary. Like its companions, the earliest crocuses and the snowdrops, it should be planted in close groups, as individual plants are so small that they appear lost if spaced singly. Dormant roots are planted in autumn. If seeds are sown out-of-doors as soon as ripe, colonizing is easily achieved. Foliage disappears by July.

Winter aconite intrigues those who anxiously await the first flower in the garden after a long winter.

EREMURUS **Foxtail-Lily** **Liliaceæ**

The foxtail-lilies are not overly popular in regions north of New York City, where winters are likely to be severe, but in sheltered locations, or where given winter protection, they can be striking subjects. Scapes of pink, yellow, or white flowers, varying from 3 to 6 feet tall, are most effective in large borders where they create vertical accents in June and July. The effect is even better if they are set off against a green background, such as a shrub border.

The name *Eremurus*, taken from the Greek, means solitary tail, and refers to the single flowering stem that develops from each plant. Twenty-five or so species come from Asia, but relatively few find their way into our gardens.

Cultural requirements include a light sandy soil, perfect drainage, especially in winter, and full sun. The best form of winter protection is coarse sand mounded over the crown; any mulch that retains moisture is detrimental. Without protection in the North, plants often produce leaves but no flowers. Buds that form very early are often killed by spring frosts. As soon as the roots are received from the nurseryman in the fall, they should be planted and protected. They are fleshy, brittle, and easily damaged, so should be handled with care. As field-grown plants are likely to be expensive, some gardeners prefer to raise their own from seeds.

E. robustus has pink flowers on a 3-foot stem, *E.* × *warei* grows to 6 feet with a very long inflorescence of salmon-pink flowers, and *E. himalaicus,* only 3 feet tall, has white flowers.

Eremurus are for painstaking gardeners who relish something unusual.

ERIGERON **Fleabane** **Compositæ**

Erigerons are much more favored in England than in this country, where they are often considered an uninspired lot. However, dwarf species can be useful in rock gardens, and the selected named cultivars of taller sorts make acceptable border plants if small groups are set at 12-inch intervals. Flowers are of the hardy aster or daisy type, but are abundant in early summer, combining well with single or Japanese peonies. They belong in full sun and light, sandy soils, low in organic matter. If old flowers are steadily picked off, the blooming season is prolonged.

The scientific name goes back to Theophrastus, and in Greek means old man in spring, an allusion to the downy young leaves of some species. Approximately 150 species are widely distributed in the temperate zone, often in mountains. Several are pesky weeds suspected of passing virus diseases on to cultivated plants.

E. aurantiacus, the double orange daisy, was mildly sensational about 1900 but is seldom grown today. About 9 inches high, it creates a generous display of semidouble flowers, 2 inches across, of dazzling orange-yellow.

E. compositus is a midget for rock gardens, with fine-textured, woolly foliage, and very small white or lavender flowers produced from May until late summer. Sharp drainage is imperative.

E. karvinskianus may be invasive in the open, but the trailing stems can be effective in dry walls. Semidouble white flowers, purplish on the reverse side, cover several weeks in late summer.

Selected cultivars of *E. speciosus* are far superior to chance seedlings or unnamed clones. Generally they are about 2 feet tall, with flowers 2 inches or more in size. 'Summertime' is a white; 'Wuppertal' a large amethyst-violet; and 'Azure Beauty' a nearly double lavender-blue.

Alan Bloom of England has introduced a set of 12 cultivars of long flowering season, strong habit, and large flowers, some of which are even pink. It is reported that initially his plan was merely to seek sturdier forms of *E. aurantiacus*, but his hybridizing efforts achieved even more than anticipated. 'Dimity,' 'Felicity,' and 'Sincerity' are typical names given these hybrids.

Perhaps the erigerons are not so popular in America because of the wealth of other material in flower at the time when they are at their best, but the gardener with a light sandy soil will find them rewarding.

ERYNGIUM Sea-Holly, Eryngo Umbelliferæ

Eryngiums are another answer to the problem of what to try in dry, sunny, rather poor sandy soils. In rich ground they tend to be oversized plants which lose the more restrained character that is desired. With a thistle-like appearance, they are not for massing, but serve best as small specimen plants.

There are over 200 species of this genus, found mainly in Mediterranean regions. Several are cultivated in Europe but only a very few are grown in American gardens. Plants in flower look something like a thistle, hence the name *Eryngium*, taken from the Greek name for one of the thistles.

E. amethystinum is one of the best, a low-branching type, not over 1½ feet in height. Flowers consist of small oval heads above narrow, almost spiny bracts. Flowers, bracts, and the upper stems are a steel gray shading to amethyst.

From July to September these exotic plants add a note of interest to larger rock gardens or sunny borders. Unfortunately, many plants offered under this name turn out to be *E. planum,* a taller species without interesting color, which belongs only in wild gardens. If possible, it is preferable to go to a nursery to select plants of the desired type, to be certain that *E. planum* is not being purchased.

Propagation is by root cuttings, or by division in early spring.

EUPATORIUM **Compositæ**

The perennials of this genus are, for the most part, adaptable to naturalizing in wild gardens or woodlands, although *E. cœlestinum* is an important border plant for fall color. The name *Eupatorium* is traced to Mithridates Eupator, a king of Pontus, who is said to have used one of this group as a medicinal plant. There are at least 600 species, largely from Mexico, the West Indies, and tropical South America; some are also native in eastern United States, and a few in Europe.

Garden Value: The greatest asset of the genus lies in the profusion of delicate flower clusters in late August and September. Unlike the majority of the members of the Compositæ, in this genus the heads are composed of fluffy, tubular flowers only; the rays are lacking. *E. cœlestinum* is one of autumn's outstanding blue cut flowers.

Soil and Exposure: Any good garden loam will do, provided it is well drained. Although some are tolerant of partial shade, full sun will increase flower production.

Care: Spring-planting is generally the rule, with about 2 feet allowed between adjacent specimens. Frequent division quells the rampant instincts in some, and rejuvenates failing clumps in others.

Propagation: Seeds germinate readily, but division in spring, the usual method, is very productive.

Species

E. cannabinum, Hemp Agrimony. Handsome downy foliage, intricately lobed, is a leading asset of this erect 5-foot species which inhabits damp English banks. Solid terminal corymbs of small reddish purple flowers can be quite striking in June and July. Only the form listed as 'Flore-pleno,' indicating double flowers, is cultivated.

E. cœlestinum, Mist-Flower, Hardy Ageratum. This valuable species is native from New Jersey south to Florida and Texas. Plants are 2 feet tall by late August, when flowers of blue or violet are formed in dense clusters. The unusual color for autumn makes an excellent combination with yellow or white chrysanthemums, either in gardens or arrangements. While it tends to spread rapidly, it never gets out of hand. Spring cultivation around the crown should be done with care so that the shallow roots near the surface are not damaged.

E. purpureum, Joe Pye-Weed. Joe Pye was an ingenious American Indian medicine man. The coarse plants that bear his name are very tall, up to 10 feet sometimes, with large, purple flower clusters in August and September. They are not garden subjects, but are useful for naturalizing.

E. rugosum, White Snakeroot. In autumn much of eastern America sees the wild forms of this species in bloom. Plants, to 4 feet in height, are covered with loose clusters of white flowers, even in the shade. It is too weedy for most cultivated gardens in the East.

Final Comment: If not asked to perform duties properly assigned to more gifted plants, eupatoriums volunteer a calm, softening presence in appropriate settings.

EUPHORBIA **Spurge** **Euphorbiaceæ**

Unquestioned hardiness and freedom from troubles are the principal attributes of garden forms of the spurges. The generic name comes from Pliny, and is said to honor Euphorbus, physician to a Mauritanian emperor. Under present classification, at least 1,000 species are recognized, comprising shrubs, greenhouse plants, and herbs. The weedy annual known as snow-on-the-mountain is *E. marginata;* the Christmas poinsettia is *E. pulcherrima.* Most species thrive in warmer parts of the temperate zone, but a few have garden significance in the North.

Eupatorium cœlestinum *Euphorbia epithymoides*

Filipendula rubra *Filipendula hexapetala* *Gaillardia × grandiflora*

Garden Value: Taller sorts may be used as border specimens, while the lower growing species are well suited for walls or rock gardens, and all remain ornamental over the entire season. If the cut end of the stem is charred with a match, then plunged in deep water, flowers can be used for cutting.

Soil and Exposure: Full sun and porous soil are ideal. In rich, moist loam, plants tend to spread badly.

Care: Unless plants are supplied in pots, very early spring is the time for planting. A long life and reluctance to be disturbed mean that no attention is needed, except for occasional division when spreading has become invasive.

Propagation: Seeds sown in fall or early spring are commonly recommended. Division is possible but must be done carefully, with minimum damage to the heavy roots.

Species

E. corollata, Flowering Spurge. This native from Ontario to Florida and Texas differs radically from the other species listed. Filmy clusters of white bloom, much like babys-breath, appear on slender 2-foot stems in July and August. Glossy, wine-red foliage in autumn, and a tough constitution further add to the garden importance. The value of the lacy relief is unquestioned for late summer.

E. cyparissias, Cypress Spurge. A rock garden subject, never over a foot in height, it is also sometimes used to hold the soil on dry banks. The narrow, linear leaves and the yellow-green bracts in May and June are not unattractive. As in the rest of the family, the actual flowers are inconspicuous, the effective color coming from enlarged bracts that surround the true flowers. This species will become rampant unless planted in dry soil.

E. epithymoides (*E. polychroma*). Here is a shapely 24-inch hemispherical mound with globular umbels of brilliant chartreuse-yellow bracts from late April until early June. The foliage, attractive all summer, turns a dark red in autumn. Neatly symmetrical, it enhances the front part of a border, generally as a specimen plant.

E. myrsinites. Strictly a weed in the Mediterranean area, this prostrate plant forms a large tumbled clump only a few inches high. Fleshy stems of gray-green foliage recline on the ground or trail from a dry wall. The early yellow bracts are far more decorative than the tiny flowers. Evergreen in all but the worst winters, it is unfailingly hardy in well-drained locations. Some believe the plants repel moles.

Final Comment: When used with discretion, spurges have much to offer, particularly in sandy gardens.

FILIPENDULA Meadowsweet Rosaceæ

Byron wrote, "The night shows stars and women in a better light." So, too, do nocturnal shadows enhance those filipendulas with white flowers, for they excel as garden accents at twilight.

The scientific name is from the Latin, meaning hanging thread, probably made logical by slender growths that join the root tubers of some species. All species are indigenous to the north temperate zone. In some horticultural literature several members of this group are incorrectly listed as *Spiræa,* a genus of woody shrubs.

Garden Value: In woodland plantings, along streams, or among partly shaded shrubbery, very effective pictures are created with filipendulas, especially the white-flowered species. Groups can be placed to advantage in the rear of a border, and *F. hexapetala* is small enough for widespread use in perennial combinations.

Soil and Exposure: In general, the genus is served best by moist soil well supplied with humus; but in contrast, *F. hexapetala* enjoys dry, sunny situations. All are tolerant of semishade.

Care: Watering in dry periods and infrequent division constitute all the care required, except that mildew may be a slight problem in wet weather. This can be readily controlled by an appropriate fungicide.

Propagation: Seeds sown out of doors in fall give better results than those stored until spring. Division of the tightly knit clumps is easily accomplished in spring, but a strong knife is needed.

Species

F. camtschatica, Kamchatka Meadowsweet. A picturesque giant from North Asia, it can tower to 10 feet yet remain airy and graceful. Huge white plumes throughout July fairly shimmer after dark. A rich, moist soil is necessary for top performance.

F. hexapetala, Dropwort. Barely 2 feet tall, it carries creamy white clusters of flowers, mainly in June. These, together with the fern-like foliage, blend favorably with poppies, baptisias, and iris. It is sometimes used for edging because of the excellent foliage even after flowering interest has passed. Barren, sandy ground is satisfactory if plants are fertilized occasionally. A dwarf, double-flowered form listed as 'Floropleno' (more correctly 'Flore-Plena') is a rare beauty that excels for edging, as it is not over 15 inches tall.

F. multijuga. Remarkably tiny, a mere 6 inches, it quickly ingratiates itself with little heads of soft pink flowers in late summer.

F. purpurea (*Spiræa palmata*). In early summer deep pink cymes appear on red stems 2 to 4 feet tall, depending upon soil conditions. In very cold areas, winter protection is needed for this Japanese native. The variety *elegans* has white flowers with brilliant red stamens.

F. rubra, Queen-of-the-Prairie. An outstanding plant for the rear of a border, it may grow to 4 or 6 feet in height, with large terminal clusters of very small pink flowers in late June and July. Flowering may be repeated later in the season. Variety *venusta* (*Spiræa venusta*), sometimes known as Martha Washington Plume, is a celebrated form that is superior to the species. Fragrant 12-inch clusters of bright carmine-pink are superb during July and early August if in fertile ground.

F. ulmaria, Queen-of-the-Meadow. From Europe and Asia, it has extensively naturalized itself in New England, but in a well-behaved way. Ancient druids cherished it as an herb, potent against stomach acidity. At heights averaging 4 feet, fragrant clouds of fragile white flowers are evident from June to mid-July. A double-flowered variant is rarely seen.

Final Comment: While many gardeners remain skeptical of the cut flower virtues claimed for this genus, the plants can be of infinite value in the right situation.

GAILLARDIA **Blanketflower** **Compositæ**

Spirited, all-summer displays characterize the gaillardias, which are scorned by some as being garish and barbaric. The botanical name honors M. Gaillard, a French patron of botany. Of the species, all native to America, there is only one perennial with garden merit. Although usually listed in catalogs as *G. aristata,* such plants are hybrids to which the name *G.* × *grandiflora* correctly applies.

Garden Value: Unfailing production of showy flowers over a long part of the growing season assures a place for gaillardias in many borders, either singly or in small groups. The red forms are particularly good near babys-breath, white phlox, Shasta daisies, deep blue veronicas, or delphiniums. The yellow types are notably pleasing near purple phlox. All are good cut flowers.

Soil and Exposure: Sandy, well-drained soil, with small amounts of organic matter, is desirable. Wet, rich loam leads to scanty bloom, excessive foliage, and a hasty death. Performance is best in full sun.

Care: Admittedly, permanence is not always strong, so a few precautions may help. Spring is the best planting time, with 15 inches of space allowed between individuals. Faded flowers should be cut off to eliminate seed formation. Winter protection may be needed, but the best precaution is to plant only in light soil with sharp drainage. If, during the summer, a spade is sunk in a circle 6 inches from the crown, the cut roots usually sprout into young material for spring transplanting.

Propagation: Seeds may be sown in fall or spring, usually yielding some creditable types. Division of large clumps is safest in spring. Root cuttings, the commercial means for propagating cultivars, are easiest for the amateur to make by the previously mentioned spade method.

Species

G. aristata. This native from Colorado to British Columbia and Oregon is the backbone of today's selections. In the wild, flowers are yellow, sometimes with purple at the base of the rays. Breeding has created many cultivars with at least token differences from each other. In England, Kelway's 1913 catalog listed 80 offerings of red and gold shades, all held to be distinct individuals. Unfortunately, some of the annual gaillardias have been hybridized with *G. aristata* to the extent that life expectancies have been lessened. Nonetheless, larger, neater blossoms have been achieved, and a seed packet often yields interesting forms with tubular or spatulate rays. Most if not all material in the trade is *G.* × *grandiflora.*

Cultivars and Seed Strains

'The Warrior' bears outstanding 3½-inch flowers of rich mahogany-ruby-red with delicate gold tips on stalwart 3-foot stems. It is majestic in gardens or when cut. 'Mr. Sherbrook' is the finest yellow and is relatively permanent; 'Sun God' is transient, but a good yellow.

Among the seed strains are: 'Portola,' a red and yellow blend; 'Tangerine,' terra-cotta to orange; 'The Sun,' with peach, butterscotch and yellow tones; and 'Golden Goblin,' a compact 12-inch mound for rock gardens or edgings, with pure yellow flowers all summer.

Final Comment: Stimulating colors, liberal output, and a blooming season that extends from June to September compensate for most flaws. Softer tints, perhaps gained from hybridizing with selections of 'The Sun,' would be welcome.

GALIUM — Bedstraw — Rubiaceæ

Bedstraws, while neither awe-inspiring nor fantastically beautiful, do add a pleasant lightness to borders or arrangements. Approximately 300 species abound over much of the world, but very few are important ornamentals. *Galium* is an old Greek name from Dioscorides, based on *gala* or milk, in reference to the fact that *Galium verum* was employed in Europe for the curdling of milk.

Garden Value: Drifts in borders or wild plantings present airy relief from the more domineering phlox, peonies, and heliopsis. Gently fragrant flowers prevail most of the summer, and like babys-breath, soften coarser material when used in the garden or as a cut flower. For best results, flowers are cut just prior to opening fully.

Soil and Exposure: While no definite demands need be heeded, fine colonies take shape in dry ground. Sun should predominate, though *G. boreale* does well in light shade.

Care: Planting, preferably in spring, should be at 9- to 12-inch intervals. A tendency to form spreading thickets often requires thinning or division when space becomes exhausted.

Propagation: Seeds or divisions in spring will more than supply any conceivable requirements.

Species

G. aristatum, False Babys-Breath. White flowers in panicles, on stems to 3 feet tall, are produced in July and August. Stems are often diffuse in growth habit and may need staking. A very easily grown plant that has an effect similar to gypsophila in the garden, this is usually erroneously offered as *G. mollugo,* a species far too weedy for the garden.

G. boreale, Northern Bedstraw. Not as vigorous as *G. verum,* it still forms sizable patches along rocky eastern slopes. The panicles of small white flowers are at their best in June and July. Fine-textured foliage adds to the fragility characteristic of the genus.

G. rubrum. Rare but useful, this quaint 6-inch wall or rockery plant produces a shower of reddish flowers.

G. verum, Yellow Bedstraw. This European immigrant has now made itself comfortably at home in many American fields, particularly along Lake Champlain. Tiny yellow blooms, on slender 2-foot, reedlike stems, have the fragrance of honey all summer. The foliage is somewhat reminiscent of asparagus.

Ancient legend has the yellow flowers portraying the golden star heralding Jesus' birth; moreover, Mary is believed to have rested on straw made from the dried stems. Hence, the species is still called Our Lady's bedstraw in portions of Europe. Another popular name, cheese rennet, harkens back to English farm use for curdling milk.

GAURA **Gaura** **Onagraceæ**

Gaura lindheimeri is a little known plant, native to Louisiana and Texas, that makes an excellent border subject as far north as New York State. In colder regions, it may winter-kill occasionally, but it grows so readily from seeds that it is quickly replaced. Full sun and average garden loam, adequately drained, provide optimum conditions. Established plants grow to 4 feet in height, the long slender stems producing pinkish white flowers from July until frost. The light, airy effect created by the delicate flowers contrasts favorably with coarser garden perennials. Incidentally, the generic name is from the Greek, meaning superb. Trouble-free, with no special cultural requirements, this is recommended to those interested in an unusual, yet desirable perennial with light texture.

GERANIUM **Cranesbill** **Geraniaceæ**

This inoffensive genus suffers from a multiplicity of species, and from coloring frequently too harsh for some or too insipid for others. Besides, some gardeners think it tender, since the popular bedding plant, in the genus *Pelargonium,* is commonly known as "geranium."

Derived from the Greek for crane, *Geranium* refers to the resemblance of the beaked fruit to the bill of a crane. About 260 species are found in temperate zones around the world. Some of the best are of difficult culture, others are annuals, and a number are quite weedy. For instance, *G. robertianum* is the herb Robert, a pesky, self-sowing annual or biennial weed.

Garden Value: There is considerable material of value, especially for summer color in the rock garden. A few species can be pleasing

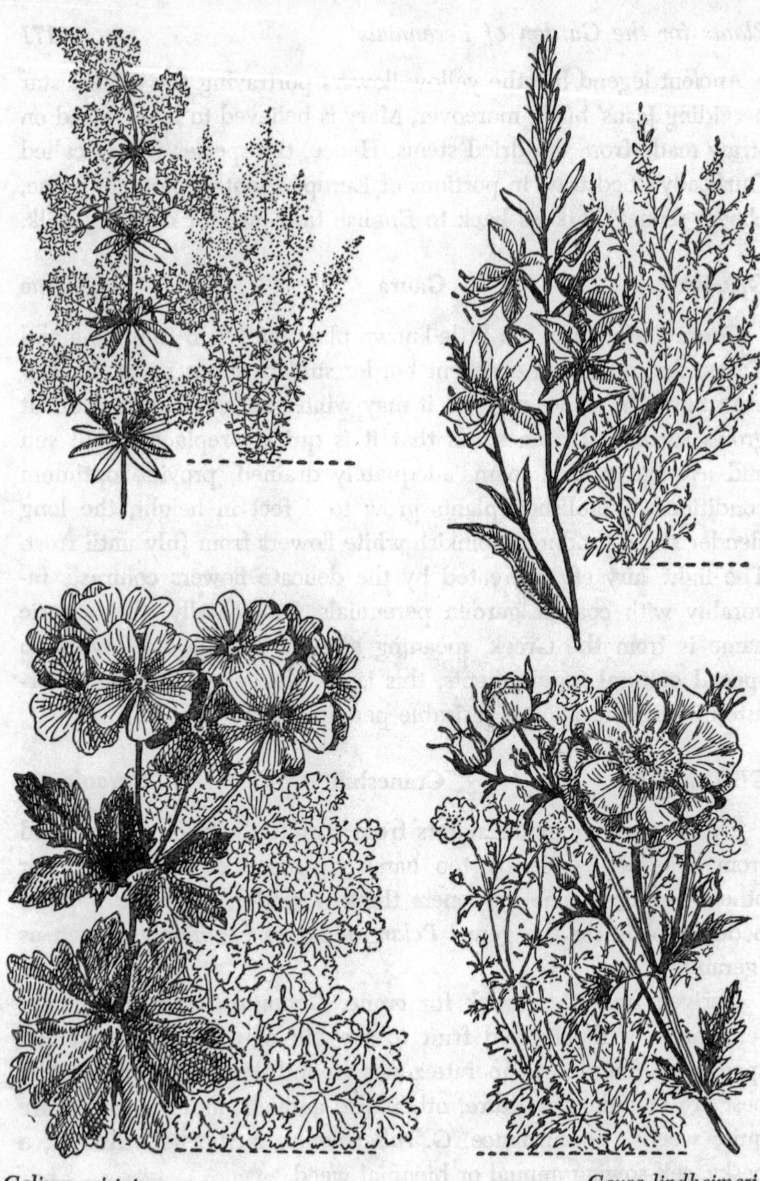

Galium aristatum
Geranium grandiflorum

Gaura lindheimeri
Geum coccineum

in small groups in the border. Many are attractive in foliage even when not in flower.

Soil and Exposure: An average garden loam is quite satisfactory. Flowering is more prolific in full sun, but partial shade is usually acceptable.

Care: Establishing the plants in spring, with a foot of ground space between them, is preferable. As a rule plants will need division every fourth year.

Propagation: Seeds sown in spring will provide an ample number of plants, but a tendency to hybridize with other species may result in surprising variation. Cuttings may be made in summer for several species, and root cuttings in spring will be satisfactory for *G. cinereum,* in particular. Division in spring is a simple method for all selections.

Species

G. argenteum. Silvery leaves on a neat plant, not over 5 inches high, are accented by large rosy pink blooms in June and July. Lime should be added to very acid soils.

G. cinereum var. *subcaulescens.* Unpredictable color sometimes condemns this 6-inch native of the Pyrenees. One indignant English writer proclaimed it "a screaming horror of wicked magenta," but the stray violet forms are not objectionable. Seeding freely, it is suspected of interbreeding with *G. sanguineum* when mongrel shades intrude. The selection 'Splendens' has attractive carmine flowers all summer, 1 inch across, with waxy dark blotches at the base of each petal to add a touch of glamour. This superb rock garden subject will not reproduce true to type from seed.

G. grandiflorum. Bold 15-inch clusters of large purple-blue flowers with reddish veins appear from May to July, and are eye-catching near anything yellow—early dwarf daylilies, for example. The plant is well-nigh indestructible. The variety *alpinum* has crinkly 1½-inch flowers, very nearly true blue, that cover a 12-inch framework of deeply lobed foliage. Rich soil encourages excessive spreading.

G. ibericum. Stems 2 feet tall, with strongly lobed leaves, support 2-inch flowers of purplish blue.

G. platypetalum (*G. ibericum* var. *platypetalum*). A much finer plant than the one above, it produces larger flowers of decisive purple-blue in profusion in midsummer. The handsome foliage becomes glowingly orange-crimson in autumn.

G. psilostemon (*G. armenum*). Since it may attain 2 feet in height, this easy Armenian species can go into the border. However, the red-violet flowers, mainly in July, are so nearly magenta that they will not please all; ebony blotches at the base of the petals add to the exotic effect.

G. sanguineum. Basically purple-red blossoms may vary to magenta, but are freely produced from May until early August. A gorgeous blood-red tint develops in the circular leaves after hard frosts. Although plants will not grow much over 12 inches in height, trailing stems may cover an area 2 feet in diameter. 'Album' is an acceptable counterpart with white flowers.

The popular variety *prostratum* (*G. lancastriense*) is native only to the Isle of Walney, off England's Lancashire coast. It is a compact dwarf plant that seldom exceeds 6 inches. Sunrise-pink blossoms, penciled with red veins, are freely borne all summer. The neat mat of foliage is likewise decorative throughout the season.

Final Comment: Seed lists, especially from England, offer the fancier many other species. Only a small fraction have been carefully tested in America, possibly to the detriment of serious gardeners.

GEUM — Geum — Rosaceæ

The modern roster of geums is a brilliantly arrayed one, including plants with almost ironclad hardiness. Most of the species are native to temperate and cold regions.

Garden Value: In general, the strongest displays cover the May to July period, with scattered flowers produced until frost, especially in cool summers. Flowers may be single or double, red, yellow, or orange, and heights may range from 4 inches to 3 feet. Dwarf forms are good either in rock gardens or in the front rank of borders. However, it is the taller forms that sparkle in the garden, especially in groups of three. Effective combinations may be created when planted near blue or purple salvias and veronicas. Crisp, dark foliage, almost evergreen, is an added attribute. As cut flowers, they are best picked when about half open.

Soil and Exposure: Well-drained soil, enriched with generous amounts of organic matter is necessary for outstanding performance. Sunlight is somewhat better than partial shade.

Care: Planting is possible in fall or spring, or even when in full bloom, at 18-inch distances for the larger types. Removal of seed pods, and watering during dry spells enhances the quantity and quality of flowering. Since recent introductions do not come into their own until the third season, they should neither be hastily judged nor repeatedly disturbed. Older selections need winter protection and biennial division.

Propagation: Cultivars are best increased by division, performed in late summer, after flowering. This will provide flowering-sized plants the following spring.

Species

The less common white and purple species are intentionally omitted as lacking in garden importance.

G. × *borisii* (*B. bulgaricum* × *G. reptans*). Named for King Boris of Bulgaria, this is ideal for rock gardens if not allowed to suffer during droughts. Typically, flowers are yellow. The erect, 10-inch plants with a profusion of orange-scarlet blossoms in May and June offered by the trade under this name are closer to *G. coccineum.*

G. chiloense. One parent of many of today's better cultivars, this Chilean species is only half hardy in rigorous climates. Variable single or double flowers, 1½ inches across, are borne on strong, 2-foot plants. In 1906 an English amateur, John Bradshaw, raised a dazzling scarlet, semidouble which he tactfully named 'Mrs. Bradshaw.' Soon a yellow mutation called 'Lady Stratheden,' sprang up. Until recently, these weaklings were the outstanding border geums.

Even today, seed-raised forms are still sold, but are neither consistently dependable nor necessary.

G. coccineum. Somewhat over 1 foot in height, this species from Asia Minor and southern Europe has intense orange-red flowers. European breeders selected hardier representatives and crossed them with *G. chiloense.* The resulting hybrids usually grow to 2½ feet, have a fresh, distinct appeal, and bloom at least from late May to July. They are fully hardy.

The form that is usually sold under the name *G. sibiricum* is quite possibly a variant of *G. coccineum;* it produces a sheet of scarlet flowers on 12-inch stems.

G. montanum. In the Alps, this species grows in alkaline soil alongside *Aster alpinus.* In a rock garden it needs part shade, or at least ample moisture. At heights of 6 inches, bright golden yellow flowers 1½ inches across appear in May and June, followed by interesting dainty seed pods.

Cultivars

Vegetatively propagated plants of the following cultivars are generally more satisfactory than seed strains offered under the same names. 'Dolly North' is a rich old gold, lightly veneered with orange; 'Princess Juliana' is a radiant, clear orange; 'Fire Opal,' a brilliant red with bronze overtones; 'Wilton Ruby,' a superb glowing ruby red; and 'Red Wings,' a scarlet. 'Golden West' ('Lady Stratheden' × *G.* × *borisii*) is two feet tall with yellow flowers from late April to August.

'Gladys Perry,' a precious 4-inch midget, of uncertain ancestry, cannot withstand neglect in prolonged droughts. A solid mass of semidouble, orange-yellow blossoms barely reach above the tufts of its foliage.

Final Comment: Here is a genus able to be completely showy without becoming blatant. Probably the better selections will never be in surplus, as the rate of increase is rather slow for modern nurserymen.

GYPSOPHILA Babys-Breath, Gypsophila Caryophyllaceæ

The generic name comes from the Greek for lime-loving, a clue to soil preference. About 140 species are indigenous to Europe, Asia, and North Africa.

Garden Value: While displaying strong individuality in stature and in the amount of care expected, the babys-breaths all share one trait in common: the misty grace of their filmy sprays. When cut, no flower is more cherished as a filler to lighten bulkier, dominant material. In varying degree, gypsophilas likewise serve in gardens to lessen the visual weight of bold masses and to harmonize harsh colors during the summer months. Smaller members provide cloudy pink or white subjects for rock gardens or, if they trail, for dry walls. However, the more robust types, especially those of *G. paniculata* parentage, are marvelous in the border, interspersed among contrasting perennials.

Soil and Exposure: None relish acid soils; lime should be added if tests indicate the need, but the thick roots should not come in actual contact with the lime. Well-drained porosity is imperative for winter survival. Predominant sunlight is preferable.

Care: With few exceptions, planting should be done in spring only. Once plants are established, they should not be disturbed. Winter protection is advised for all but the very hardiest, as those of *G. repens* ancestry.

Propagation: Spring-sown seeds effectively increase the species. Cuttings in midsummer root easily for selections of *G. repens.* The commercial practice for completely double-flowered types is to graft them onto the fleshy roots of *G. paniculata.* Experiments under way involve grafting onto *G. repens* for a more fibrous, compact root system.

Species

G. manginii. While not widely cultivated, this branching 3½-foot plant is desirable as a cut flower. A faint pink suffusion is cast over the basically white panicles.

G. oldhamiana. This Korean species, named for a collector of Oriental plants, grows to 3 feet, but not with complete grace. However, the large, dense clusters of pale pink flowers do not appear until August and September, when they work in well with asters and early mums. Comparatively hardy, it occasionally self-sows but not distressingly so. 'Flamingo' is a double-flowered Dutch origination which suffers from annoying mauve tints unless the late summer is unusually cool.

G. pacifica. This Siberian species is essentially similar to *G. oldhamiana* in garden effect. It lacks complete symmetry though. Rangy 4-foot plants are probable, and the numerous flowers occasionally verge on light purple shadings.

G. paniculata, Babys-Breath. Heavily branched stems, 3 feet or more tall, produce a tremendous number of small, single white flowers in huge hemispherical panicles. The major display occurs in July, but if kept cut to prevent seeding, blooms often repeat from August to October.

Double-flowered races are fairly common, and generally flower more freely than singles. 'Bristol Fairy,' perhaps the best known cultivar, was originated by Alex Cumming after repeated breeding and selecting. Still grown nearly all over the world, it has contributed millions of cut stems to arrangements, and has superseded the species in borders. The billowing panicles of snow-white double flowers tend to lighten the effect when combined with gaillardia, phlox, or coarse garden plants. They can also hide poor foliage of nearby neighbors. Since a plant can swell to an area of 4 feet, ample room is required. Invariably grafted onto the roots of *G. paniculata,* the graft union should be set 1 inch below the soil line, to encourage stem rooting. Plants take at least two years to become well established. They may have to be renewed occasionally after severe winters.

'Perfecta,' a recent Dutch novelty with larger flowers, is most promising in limited trials to date.

G. repens. Long, tough tap-roots and trailing, prostrate stems, often 18 inches in length, combine to make this alpine native supremely equipped for rock gardens or dry walls. Masses of white to pearl-pink flowers attract the eye in early summer. 'Rosea' is the form prevalent in the trade; it is seldom over 6 inches high, with rosy pink clusters of flowers. 'Fratensis' is practically indistinguishable from 'Rosea.' 'Sundermannii,' while rare, is very compact with white blooms larger than those of the species. Hybrid origin is suspected for 'Rosy Veil' ('Rosenchlier'), for it grows erectly to 18 inches, with smooth gray-blue foliage. From June to August, delicately soft pinkish to white clusters are borne on tangled, interwoven stems, making for difficult cutting. Exceptionally hardy, and quite double, it is an excellent border plant.

'Bodgeri' (*G. repens 'Rosea'* × *G. paniculata*) is a first-class California introduction that achieves 15 to 18 inches in height, and provides a profusion of bloom. The partially double flowers may be completely white, but will generally carry hints of pink. From late May through June, it is most showy, with spasmodic outbursts thereafter. Along with 'Rosy Veil,' it is splendid to cloak the absence of foliage of Oriental poppies during the summer.

Final Comment: The fact that the delicate rounded softness of this genus relieves vertical, horizontal, and coarse effects in the border makes it almost indispensable.

HELENIUM **Sneezeweed** **Compositæ**

The common name should deter no one from growing these plants, for they fit admirably into the late season picture, and no valid reason is apparent for the "sneezeweed" designation. The name of the genus is believed to honor either Helen of Troy or Helenus, the son of Priam.

Garden Value: Some gardeners are likely to ponder the status of the sneezeweeds, wondering if the good points outweigh faults. Unquestionably, the splurge of color takes place at a desirable period in late summer and early autumn. Yet, most of the older cultivars become tall, lanky, somewhat coarse, and if neglected, highly untidy. These are best consigned to wild gardens or spots among shrubbery. An occasional individual in the rear of a border may be satisfactory, but the medium-sized selections are far more suitable for well-kept plantings. Perhaps the more recent, dwarf cultivars are the best choice for smaller modern gardens.

Heights vary from 2 to 6 feet. Flowers with slightly drooping rays measure up to 2 inches in diameter; the colors are mainly tawny bronzes, reds, or yellows. If cut, they can be pleasantly bold in tall vases, and the cut-and-come-again quality is commendable.

Soil and Exposure: Average fertility suffices, but since most species dwell in moist, swampy areas in nature, the water-holding capacity of the soil is important. Full sunlight promotes bushier habit.

Care: Spring-planting, at 2-foot intervals, is recommended. Clumps should be divided every spring; otherwise unsightly bare centers develop. Pinching back all tips until mid-June creates a stockier habit and added flowers.

Propagation: Spring-sown seeds satisfy those not committed to exact reproduction. Cultivars are propagated by division in spring.

Species

H. autumnale. Most garden material stems from this species, native from Quebec to Florida and across to Arizona. In the wild it can vary from 2 to 6 feet, but the flowers are always yellow.

Among the popular cultivars are: 'Rubrum,' 4 feet, terra-cotta-red; 'Peregrinum,' 3 feet if divided annually, with rich coppery chestnut-red flowers; 'Pumilum,' 2 feet, a more recent introduction with yellow flowers; 'Riverton Beauty,' 4 feet, lemon-yellow heads with purplish central blotches; 'Crimson Beauty,' 2 to 3 feet, almost crimson; 'Moerheim Beauty,' a finer, more velvety 'Crimson Beauty' when true to name; and 'Golden Youth,' 3 feet, with large butter-yellow flowers.

H. hoopesii. Native from the Rocky Mountains westward to Oregon and California, this species bears the name of the collector, Thomas Hoopes. Rarely seen, it is really delightful in large urns or tubs on porches or terraces, and is pleasing in borders, as well.

Gypsophila paniculata

Heliopsis scabra

Helenium autumnale
Helleborus
Hemerocallis

About 2 feet tall, it flowers early, in May and June, with large, old gold to orange heads. Foliage is excellent. It will accept some shade.

HELIANTHUS **Sunflower** **Compositæ**

The Greek words *helios,* for sun, and *anthos,* meaning flower, are the roots for the botanical name. Although there are about 100 species, primarily natives of North America, relatively few are worthy of a place in the perennial garden. In light, well-drained soils and full sun, the less weedy types can be quite acceptable.

H. decapetalus var. *multiflorus* (*H. multiflorus* of the trade), the thinleaf sunflower, grows to 4 feet, with yellow flowers 3 to 4 inches across and somewhat like dahlias, in late summer. The double-flowered types are the most popular. European catalogs list several cultivars, among which 'Loddon Gold,' 'Meteor,' and 'Soleil d'Or' are the finest. Erect plants are well clothed with foliage all season, and the plants are bushy enough for one specimen to be usually sufficient. Mildew may require attention with an appropriate fungicide.

H. salicifolius (*H. orgyalis*), only for the large border, grows to 8 feet in height. It is an acceptable background specimen, with willowy stems and fine-textured, almost grasslike foliage. In fact, it is sometimes grown for its foliage effect alone, as the clusters of small yellow flowers in late August and September are in no way spectacular. Staking may be needed by midsummer to keep it erect. Both species, of easy culture, are propagated by division.

HELIOPSIS **Heliopsis** **Compositæ**

Weedy, chance seedlings of these plants seem both "rowdy and dowdy" alongside contemporary cultivars. As with hardy asters, just about all noteworthy improvements are credited to Europeans, in spite of the fact that the genus is native to North America. The botanical name means like the sun in Greek, in reference to the golden yellow flowers.

Garden Value: Experience and observation soon establish the fact that heliopsis is woefully mistreated in most gardens. Given ideal conditions, several recent introductions will produce sturdy plants, 3 feet in height, and a wealth of cutting material all summer long. Specimen plants or small commanding groups offer months of strong yellow accent that requires notice by itself or when combined with phlox, delphinium, or veronicas. Exceptional hardiness is an attribute not to be overlooked.

Soil and Exposure: The average gardener errs in believing the plant performs well on barren, parched soils, so becomes accustomed to miserly blossoms and somewhat ragged habit. Actually, only those with small single flowers are suited for such adverse conditions. A fairly rich soil, containing adequate organic matter, is to be preferred. Full sun is definitely recommended.

Care: Plants may be established in fall or spring, allowing 2-foot intervals. Liberal watering during dry periods is rewarding, especially for cultivars with large, fully double flowers. Division every three or four years has a revitalizing effect. Aphids, easily combatted, may appear in hot weather, particularly on under-fertilized material.

Propagation: Spring-sown seeds germinate quickly, but resulting plants may demonstrate considerable variation. Although division is the common method, cuttings of desirable types, taken in summer from vegetative shoots, root without difficulty.

Species

H. helianthoides. Native from Ontario south to Florida and west to Mississippi, it can be an inept weed of 5 feet, or a more presentable 3-foot plant. Flowers are only about 2 inches in size, frequently of a brassy yellow. 'Pitcheriana' is a selection with larger, deeper yellow blooms, frequently utilized for breeding.

H. scabra. In the wild, from Maine to New Jersey and Arkansas, it is a rather rank grower. Characteristic roughly hairy leaves and the habit of producing some solitary flowers on a stem have been handed down to some recent cultivars. Improved selections are usually desired for garden use.

'Excelsa' has nearly double flowers of chrome yellow; 'Vitellina' is similar. 'Eminens' is noted for the chrome-yellow flowers, 3 inches across, almost fully double, with some greenish central florets. The compact 3-foot plants are prolific bloomers from July to September. 'Gold Greenheart' may be even more completely double. 'Incomparabilis' is a superb semidouble, first offered in 1933, and sometimes listed as 'Summer Gold.' Brilliant, gold-yellow blossoms, 3 inches across, are well formed throughout the season. 'Patula,' often sold as 'Golden Rays,' is a semidouble that approaches cadmium-orange. Unfortunately, the 2½-foot habit is irregular, and sparsely flowered gaps are a possibility. 'Light of Loddon,' a newcomer from England, may be of hybrid origin. Medium-sized single flowers of a strong lemon-chrome, borne in large corymbs are most impressive in a mass. It is a good choice where drought and heat are problems.

Final Comment: Considering the gaunt parents, today's better forms of heliopsis are amazingly handsome.

HELLEBORUS **Hellebore** **Ranunculaceæ**

Perhaps no plant ever gripped gardener's imaginations more than the Christmas rose (*H. niger*) has in recent years. Unfortunately, certain advertising campaigns extolled and glamorized the plant so lavishly that many purchasers were confused and deluded. Some thought it a thorny shrub rose. Present promotions, with sound directions for proper culture, present the plant in its true value. Native to Europe and western Asia, the genus has only two species that are commonly cultivated in our gardens.

Garden Value: Certainly there is no more estimable subject for sheltered, yet conspicuous spots. Beaming owners proudly show off the plants and flowers, whenever snow melts during thaws, perhaps on any day from November through April. Because of this unusual period of bloom, plants are more effective if growing near a terrace, walk, driveway, or some other place near the house where they can be easily seen. Pride of possession, the off-season flowers, and the plant's distinguished evergreen foliage are sufficient cause for widespread planting. Flowers may be cut for indoor use.

Soil and Exposure: The soil must be well drained, and not too acid. Liberal amounts of compost or leafmold, as well as superphosphate, are advantageous. Summer shade is advisable, but at least partial sunlight is best during winter. Thus, a site under the seasonal protection of deciduous trees or shrubbery is ideal; areas where tree roots spread extensively should be avoided. Full exposure to summer sun and heat is usually detrimental.

Care: Spring-planting is safest. Clumps develop slowly and improve with age; any disturbance sets them back. Summer mulches of peat or leafmold will keep roots cool and moist, but watering is still required during protracted droughts. In regions of extreme winters, more certain bloom is assured if a small ventilated box with a glass top is set over the plant when buds begin to develop. Protection from snow or mud is thus provided, as is free circulation of air. A leaf spot sometimes develops, either from cold, wet autumn nights, or from soils that are extremely acid, but can easily be controlled by a fungicide. Lime will counteract the acid soil reaction.

Propagation: Seeds sown when fresh, in early autumn, may germinate by the following spring, but longer patience may be needed. Thousands are grown annually by this method in Holland alone.

Division is best attempted after flowering. Each carefully separated portion should have several roots and new leaf buds, or eyes, which are set about an inch below the soil level. No fresh manure should ever be in contact with the young roots.

Species

H. niger, Christmas Rose. Of fabled legend, this emblem of chaste perfection was first collected in Greece, arriving in England in 1596. *Niger* alludes to the black roots. Theophrastus' *History of Plants,* in the fourth century B.C., warned of the poisonous roots of allied species.

Plants are commonly 15 inches high, with dark evergreen foliage, and one to three white or faintly pink-flushed flowers that may be 2 to 4 inches in diameter. Environmental conditions govern time of bloom, but it usually starts in November and continues until April.

True material of variety *altifolius* is vastly preferable to the species. Slightly longer stems bear huge 4- to 5-inch flowers, and the foliage is more upright and impressive. Under ideal cultural conditions flowering should occur by Christmas. True material is scarce.

H. orientalis, Lenten Rose. As may be surmised, this species flowers later, from early March to mid-May. These colorful plants, indigenous to Asia Minor, are popular in Europe. Shadings vary from white to exotic purple hues, but have not excited many American gardeners as yet. Foliage is a lighter green, but the habit is similar to that of *H. niger*. Here, a worthy species may be unjustly suffering from indifference. The two species are easily differentiated by foliage alone, as *H. niger* has leaf margins with a few, very coarse teeth, while the margins of *H. orientalis* have many small teeth or serrations.

Final Comment: Because of the dignity and charm of these species, both can be strongly recommended to any discriminating gardener with a suitable location.

HEMEROCALLIS Daylily Liliaceæ

In comparatively few years daylilies have risen to exalted heights of popularity and excellence. Yesterday's orange and yellow mediocrities have given way to red, pink, and the whole range of tints and shades of orange and yellow. Some have deeply colored throats, others striped petals, and some are bicolors. One cultivar will usually remain in a flowering state for about one month, but by a selection of those with different blooming seasons, it is now possible to have one or another in flower at any time from May to October. Daylilies are sturdy plants with gracefully arching foliage of long, narrow, rushlike leaves. Dwarfs of but 20 inches contrast with stalwart members bearing scapes 4 or 5 feet high.

Hemerocallis is from the Greek, meaning beautiful for a day, a reference to the short duration of individual blooms. However, since there are so many flowers on each scape, and several scapes to each plant, this is no drawback. "Daylily" likewise refers to the fact that each flower usually remains open but one day. While there are about 15 species native to Europe, China, and Japan, most modern garden forms are cultivars of more or less hybrid origin, often not referable to any one species.

Garden Value: Daylilies are about the easiest perennial to grow, being almost indestructible and trouble-free. Plants are able to choke out weeds, and can remain undisturbed for several years. They are appropriate for foundation plantings, terraces, and brooksides; the dwarf types are suitable for rock gardens; some will naturalize in wild gardens, while choice cultivars are excellent border subjects. If picked just as the buds are about to open, cut stems will be fairly attractive in water for a few days. Aside from ornamental use, this genus was once used extensively for cattle fodder in England, and the Chinese find the petals useful in their culinary art.

Soil and Exposure: While daylilies may be shunted almost anywhere and still be effective, reasonably good soil, not soggy for long periods, is best. Very rich soil produces rank foliage and scanty bloom; an excess of lime causes the foliage to be pale green. Sunny areas or those in partial shade are suitable.

Care: Small divisions can be set out in fall or spring, allowing 2 feet between plants for eventual spreading. Occasional top-feeding or watering may be all the care needed for six or eight years, but after that time, division may be required. The average daylily is so hard to kill that it may one day become the symbol of abandoned or overgrown gardens. North of New York City, the evergreen types and some hybrids of *H. aurantiaca* may need winter protection.

Propagation: Seeds, sown in fall or early spring, seldom produce flowering plants before the second growing year, but this method is of interest mainly to the plant breeder. Division is slow commercially, necessitating high initial prices for introductions, but it is fine for amateurs. Clumps are dug, shaken free of soil, and the roots cut back halfway. Tops are cut to 2-inch stubs, and a sharp blade is used to divide the tough crowns into smaller segments. Early spring and August are equally satisfactory for the task.

Species

H. lilio-asphodelus (*H. flava*), Lemon Daylily. This species is still significant for the medium-sized, lemon-yellow blossoms of slight fragrance, in May. The slender 2-foot habit is not without merit.

H. fulva, Tawny Daylily. This species was introduced in England from Japan around 1600. It has now firmly escaped and settled along many American roadsides and by deserted homes. Stems of 4 feet bear reddish or orange flowers in July. A form known as 'Europa' is widely employed along Pennsylvania roadbanks to stem erosion and to run out weeds. The variety *kwanso* is a strange double-flowered variant known in Japan as early as 1912. Its sterility has continually thwarted breeders, perhaps thankfully so.

H. gracilis is a horticultural form similar to *H. minor.* It has narrow, reedy foliage, stems about 2 feet tall, and small lemon-yellow blossoms in May and June. It is prized for naturalistic plantings and for spacious rock gardens.

H. multiflora. This Chinese species, important to hybridizers because its blooming period extends from late August to October, has lengthened the flowering period of modern hybrids. Flowers, borne in clusters, are only 2 inches wide. The miniature appeal is noteworthy.

Outstanding Cultivars

George Yeld, an English schoolmaster, was far ahead of his time, producing 'Apricot' in 1891 by crossing *H. flava* and *H. middendorffii.* Previously only desultory Italian attempts at hybridizing had been recorded. Yeld introduced several hybrids, while Amos Perry also added to English listings.

However, the United States deserves top billing in the daylily's rise, chiefly from the accomplishments of the late Dr. A. B. Stout, of the New York Botanic Garden. About 1912, he systematically collected all the world's available species and hybrids, and began to hybridize on a monumental scale. Countless new shadings, petal formations, and blends soon resulted. For example, *H. fulva* var. *rosea* supplied decisive impetus toward pink tones. Beyond his fine breeding work, he wholeheartedly championed the daylily in writings and lectures, so that its popularity swelled with amazing celerity.

Other famed American breeders are Charles Betscher, Franklin Mead, H. M. Russell, Mr. and Mrs. Percy Merry, Mrs. Thomas Nesmith, Ralph W. Wheeler, Mrs. Bright Taylor, Stedman Buttrick, and many others, including gifted amateurs. The late Dr. E. J. Kraus, noted chrysanthemum hybridizer, raised up to 700,000 seedlings from hand pollinations in one year. Breeders are trying to eliminate the stubborn fulvous overcast, and to exploit newly twisted or crimped petals.

As to recommended cultivars, these lines from "The Walrus and the Carpenter" come to mind:

> "And thick and fast they came at last,
> And more, and more, and more."

Probably 4,000 named selections are in commerce, but only specialists can evaluate the annual torrent of new introductions. The following are tested and fully worthy of a place in the garden: 'Hyperion,' with superb 5- to 6-inch canary-yellow flowers, introduced in 1925; 'Painted Lady,' with large ruffled yellow petals flushed soft crimson; 'Potentate,' a dark, glistening, almost pansy-purple; 'Dauntless,' a soft yellow; 'Valiant,' with broad petals of clear orange; 'Caballero," a huge 6-inch red and gold bicolor; 'Georgia,' a buff, pink, and peach blend; 'Pink Charm,' a magnificent coral; 'Colonial Dame,' light apricot and tan; and 'Royal Ruby,' a glowing red.

Final Comment: For the specialist there is the thriving Hemerocallis Society of at least 1,500 avid members, and a fine book, *Daylilies* by Dr. Stout.

No one can adequately foresee the daylily's eventual zenith, with such newly introduced species as *H. exaltata* still being incorporated into present lines. Certainly more heed will be paid to the actual length of time a flower remains open, with day- and night-blooming types, as well as those with extended period of bloom, gaining in importance.

HESPERIS **Dames-Rocket** **Cruciferæ**

Hesperis indicates evening in Greek, and this flower is so named because it is more fragrant then than at any other time. *H. matronalis* is a common perennial that is better in naturalized areas than in borders. Lilac or white flowers are formed in clusters at the top of 3-foot stems in late May and June. Because of a slight resemblance to *Phlox paniculata,* it is sometimes called wild phlox, although there is no relationship. With no special cultural requirements, it self-sows rapidly, becoming practically a weed. Doubled forms are more desirable, though rare, and are not as rampant.

HEUCHERA **Coral Bells** **Saxifragaceæ**

Though not overpowering, heucheras are unquestionably endowed with that intangible something best called personality. From the first fiery red, pink, or white flowers in early summer to the bronzed foliage of autumn, coral bells are excellent subjects for gardens of any size. *Heuchera,* a genus of North American plants, honors a German botanist of the eighteenth century, J. H. von Heucher.

Garden Value: Beginning in late May and extending through most of the flowering season, wiry stems that may vary from 15 to 30 inches carry small but colorful bell-shaped flowers. The basal foliage alone is worth while; clumps of heart-shaped leaves, often at least 2 inches across, show veined, mottled, or crinkled patterns imposed on the rich green coloring. Restrained growth encourages massing or grouping in the border, where they are appropriate near any flower not of spikelike inflorescence. Those of more dwarf habit are fine as edging material or in rock gardens. Plants are easily forced in greenhouses, and the flowers last well when cut.

Soil and Exposure: While not demanding, coral bells behave best in well-drained soils of good humus content, for the roots are shallow. Full sunlight is usually suggested, but some shade is tolerated.

Care: Spring-planting is preferable, at 12-inch intervals. The crown should always be set about an inch below soil level, for heaving is a tendency in winter; each spring the crown may have to be pushed back into the soil. Watering in dry periods and prevention of seed formation prolong the June and July burst of flowers. Coral bells are not at their best until the second or third years, so plants will not require division for four years or so. If alternate freezing and thawing is to be expected, winter covering is prudent.

Propagation: The powdery seeds germinate freely in spring, usually providing blooming plants the following year. The tiny seedlings are best transplanted into flats or pots with tweezers. Cuttings in midsummer are favored by nurserymen. Any leaf with a portion of stem attached can form roots, as will top cuttings from each basal shoot. Division of the thick stock is practiced in spring. Each fat stem needs only a few roots to become a flourishing clump.

Species

Few species are of prime importance today, for hybrids and cultivars are far more floriferous. Several obscure species have decorative foliage but inferior blooms.

H. sanguinea. This blazing red native from Mexico and Arizona was once the outstanding garden type. However, the 20-inch stems are scantily branched and shy of bloom. Variety *alba* is an early white form, 'Rosea' a rosy pink, and 'Rosamundi' (*H. micrantha* var. *rosea* × *H. sanguinea*) a clear pink that may be in flower from June to August, but branching is still negligible.

'Brizoides' (probably *H. micrantha* × *H. sanguinea*) is a well-branched hybrid, often 2½ feet tall and exceedingly floriferous. However, the predominantly soft pink bells are rather small, even when gathered into generous clusters.

× *Heucherella tiarelloides* (*H.* 'Brizoides' × *Tiarella cordifolia*) is a curious bigeneric hybrid of which the best selections are European offerings; they may soon be available in this country.

Leading Cultivars

European breeders first crossed the branching *H.* 'Brizoides' and the vivid *H. sanguinea* to achieve larger, brighter blossoms on more productive stalks. However, Charles F. Barber of Hoodacres, Oregon, created the finest selection, named 'Queen of Hearts.' It was these vibrant, sizable red bells on long vigorous stems that really attracted gardeners to the genus. Barber also introduced others of undenied excellence.

At present, Alan Bloom of England is busily engaged in bringing out choices of lengthier display on sturdy 1½- to 3-foot plants. His Bressingham Hybrids constitute the finest seed strain available, with much diversity promised.

Available cultivars include: 'Pluie de Feu' ('Rain of Fire'), with scarlet flowers on dense 12-inch stems; 'Snowflakes,' 2½ feet tall, perhaps the best white; 'Garnet,' actually a deep rosy pink, with deeply marbled foliage on stocky 18-inch plants; 'Rakete' ('Rocket'), a new, scarlet-vermilion; 'Coral Mist,' tiny coral-pink bells of airy, corsage effect; 'Rhapsody,' possibly the finest clear rose-pink, to 20 inches, a persistent bloomer; and 'Scarlet Sentinel,' vigorous, upright, with scarlet flowers of great promise.

Final Comment: The potential riches of the genus have barely been scratched. Additional breeding is needed to gain freer, more striking bloom in association with the magnificent foliage possible.

HIBISCUS — Rose Mallow — Malvaceæ

Devotees of the gigantic exclaim over the hardy rose mallows because of their huge, platter-like flowers, lush foliage, and sturdy habit. Only a few native swamp-dwellers are suitably hardy for the bulk of American gardens. Of the 200 species native around the world, many are shrubs and trees from tropical regions. American veterans of World War II may recall the exotic double-flowered

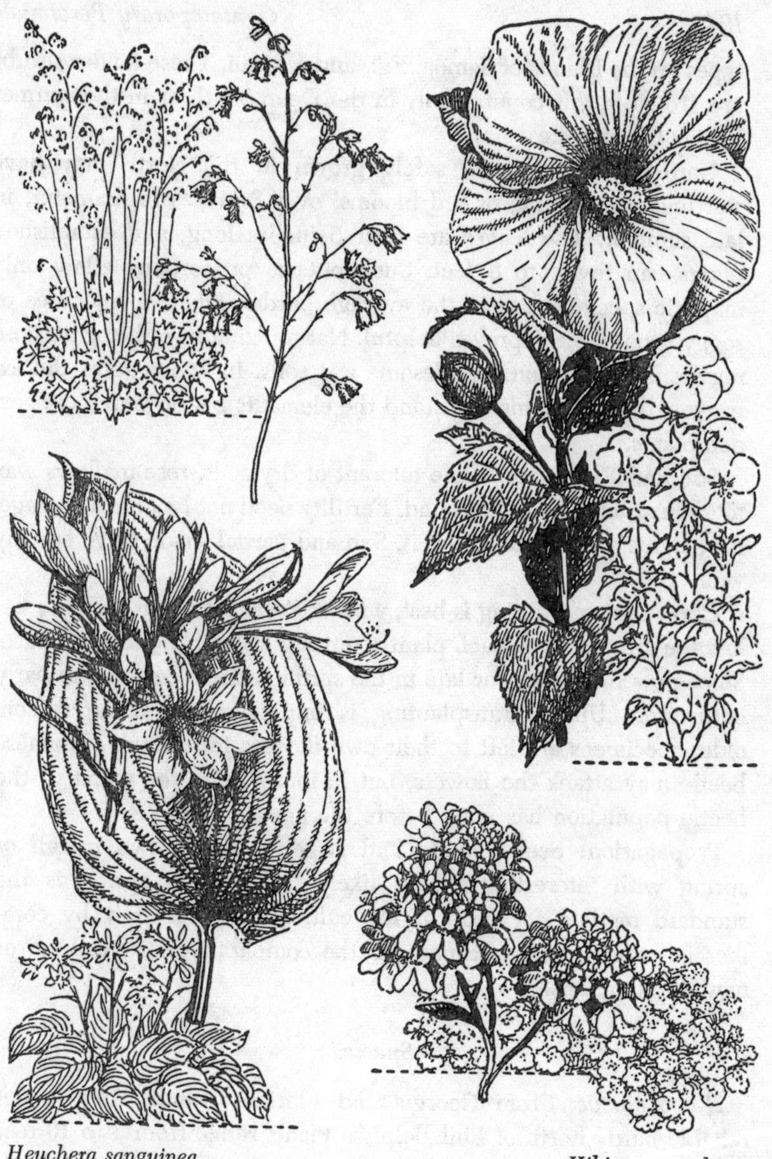

Heuchera sanguinea
Hosta plantaginea

Hibiscus moscheutos
Iberis sempervirens

types on the islands of Samoa, Fiji, and Hawaii. These tender shrubs are grown in this country only in the Deep South or in the warmer Pacific Coast States.

Garden Value: Plants safely grown in the North may have startling white, pink, or red blooms, over 8 inches in diameter, in late summer. The leaves are over 5 inches long, and established plants can tower to 8 feet. Such outsize proportions allow only majestic specimen use in the average border, where a tolerance of soggy ground often proves helpful. Naturalizing in rather grandiose masses is possible on troublesome wet soils. In windy spots the extremely durable stems withstand the elements better than most garden plants.

Soil and Exposure: While tolerant of dry soils, rose mallows wax more luxuriant in moist ground. Fertility need not be above average, for heights are sufficient as it is. Sun and partial shade serve equally well.

Care: Spring-planting is best, with the eyes set about 4 inches below the ground level, each plant requiring at least 2½ feet of space. Since new shoots appear late in the spring, care is essential in early cultivation. Unless transplanting is imperative for some reason, older specimens are left to their own devices indefinitely. Japanese beetle may attack the flowers, but in many areas the worst of the beetle population has gone before the flowers open.

Propagation: Seeds, round and large, may be sown in fall or spring with interesting results likely. Division in spring is the standard method for propagating cultivars. Rather slow by commercial standards, it accounts for the comparatively high price of new introductions.

Species

H. coccineus. From Georgia and Florida swamps, this is not reliably hardy north of Philadelphia. Plants range from 3 to 10 feet in height, and produce 5-inch blossoms of rose-red or crimson, with petals well spaced instead of overlapping, as in many of the other species.

H. militaris. Only 5 feet tall, it is native from Minnesota to Florida. The 4-inch flowers are either white or blush pink, and leaves are noticeably lobed. Seedlings vary in their resistance to severe winters.

H. moscheutos. By and large the hardiest species, which, with *H. palustris,* represents the base for today's better garden selections. White or cream flowers have distinct reddish purple centers.

Garden Cultivars

Interbreeding of the above species has given many desirable border types. J. Herbert Alexander of Middleboro, Massachusetts, and the late Ernest Hemming, of Easton, Maryland, did much of the initial spadework. At present, William Henderson, a Californian, is producing superb hardy material of gigantic blooms.

Cultivars include: 'Bessie Ross,' white with red eye; 'Mrs. William H. Allen,' bright pink; 'Annie Hemming,' flamboyant red, not fully hardy in the North; 'Radiation,' huge pink with maroon center, often 12 inches in size, 4 feet tall; 'Poinsettia,' giant red, 4 to 5 feet tall; 'Satan,' velvety maroon, in large clusters; and 'The Clown,' bizarre salmon-pink flushed white at the base, highlighted with deep crimson eye; 3 feet tall in poor soil.

HOSTA Plantain-Lily Liliaceæ

Hostas connote grandeur as well as excellent taste in the garden. Both flowers and foliage are extremely effective, and in appropriate situations the genus has an aristocratic, ageless stability. The various species, native to China and Japan, are unfortunately still often listed under *Funkia,* a name which is not valid. The common name loosely compares the foliar pattern to that of the noxious lawn weed.

Garden Value: The leaves are always ornamental in their broad, ribbed splendor; some are bright green, some gray, and quite a few are richly variegated. Mature foliage of some species often measures over 12 inches in each direction. The flowers, like small lilies of blue, purple, or white, are borne on scapes from July to October, according to the species chosen. The architectural mass can emphasize nearby structural features, such as driveways, entrances, and steps. Indeed, walks or driveways are sometimes completely edged with hostas, generally all of one kind. In mixed plantings, their solidity blends well with plants of delicate-textured foliage such as ferns, dicentras, astilbes, and thalictrums. Daffodils and their relatives add interest to a hosta border in spring. In midseason, the expanding foliage can cover voids left by these spring-flowering bulbs. Primroses, lungworts, daylilies, as well as such ground covers as ajuga, wild ginger, and myrtle are also appropriate companions.

As will be noted, the idea of a hosta border need be neither monotonous nor impossible. Varying habits of growth, the flowers, and the fascinating foliage, all become a joy to observe in succeeding years. Both flowers and foliage have cutting potential.

Soil and Exposure: Hostas survive in almost any soil, but for ideal performance it should be rich, with adequate humus for water retention, and should be well-drained in winter. Partial shade, such as that of tall deciduous trees, is far better than full sun. While deep shade produces lush growth, it also results in shy flowering. Full sun causes less luxuriant foliage which, except in cool moist areas, may turn pale green, or even burn to a degree.

Care: Spring-planting is recommended, but specimens set out in fall should survive if protected over the first winter. It is very important to realize the potential spread of the species purchased, as some can in time fan out to 3 or 4 feet in diameter. Thus, they need ample room to achieve symmetrical perfection. Light annual applications of rotted manure or compost, and slowly available fertilizers, especially superphosphate, are advised, as is heavy, infrequent watering during droughts.

Young plants, especially of *H. plantaginea,* often rot in open, wet winters, so are best mulched with hay or leaves after deep freezing has occurred. Except for propagation, clumps should be left undisturbed; life spans of 20 years are not uncommon.

Propagation: Seeds, sown in spring, will not produce flowering plants for two or three years. Variegated forms and the hybrid 'Honeybells' will not reproduce true to type.

Division, safe only in spring, is most rewarding with clumps not over three years old. Older, established specimens have very thick crowns which are not easily separated, and the new sections may be difficult to establish.

Species

Nomenclature in this genus has undergone several changes, is a source of confusion to many gardeners and nurserymen, and may not yet be stabilized.

H. decorata (often listed as *H.* 'Thomas Hogg'), Blunt-Leaved Plantain-Lily. The compact plant, never over 2 feet tall, has oval, blunt-tipped leaves about 6 inches long, with a prominent silvery white margin. The dark lilac blossoms are small and trim, appearing in August. Although other species radiate from an ever swelling crown, this one is unusual in that it spreads by stolons.

H. fortunei, Tall Cluster Plantain-Lily. Scapes 3 feet high with lavender to almost white flowers, 1½ inches long, appear in early July. Glaucous, pale green leaves, about 5 inches long and 3 inches wide, form an interesting contrast when planted among the other species. The variety *gigantea* is a massive form with tremendous 12-inch leaves almost like green elephants' ears. After a few years, when the leaves are fully expanded, a clump may measure 5 feet in diameter. This is a picturesque accent of real character. Variety *marginato-alba* has irregular shiny bands of white around the leaf edges. Another form, which may be listed as 'Marginata-aurea,' is a variant with yellow-bordered leaves.

H. glauca (*H. sieboldiana*), Blue-Leaved Plantain-Lily. Handsome 12-inch leaves are gray-green, slowly maturing to a powdery blue cast. The texture is somewhat like seersucker. The 3-foot clump that eventually develops would be valuable in any shaded border, on foliage merit alone. The nondescript lilac-white flowers in July are neither effective nor necessary, since they are often hidden by the foliage.

H. lancifolia, Narrow-Leaved Plantain-Lily. Comparatively slender lanceolate leaves, about 6 inches long, are dark green and rather striking in clumps with a 2-foot spread. Scapes 2 feet tall carry numerous pale lavender-lilac flowers in August. These are not too compelling, but the species is well worth growing.

Plants offered in the United States as *H. lancifolia* var. *minor* or *H. minor* var. *alba* may in part belong to *H. albomarginata* var. *alba.* White, funnel-shaped flowers are borne on slender 18-inch stems in September. Typically, the leaves are variegated, with a white margin, but there is a form with pure green foliage. The restrained habit and general daintiness can be utilized in shaded rock gardens, or as a contrast near the statuesque *H. plantaginea.* It has been described as "like a giant lily-of-the-valley, blooming in August and September."

H. albomarginata (*H. lancifolia* var. *albo-marginata*) is similar to *H. lancifolia,* except that the trim, narrow leaves are edged with white. It is one of the neatest variegated perennials to be found.

H. 'Honeybells' (*H. lancifolia* × *H. plantaginea*). This, the only known hybrid in the genus, was developed by Alex Cumming. In August, 3-foot stems carry medium-sized lilac-lavender flowers, striped by blue pencilings. A fragrance much like that of trailing arbutus enhances this outstanding novelty.

H. plantaginea (*H. subcordata, H. grandiflora*), Fragrant Plantain-Lily. This old favorite is still in great demand. Shiny rounded leaves, perhaps 6 inches broad and even longer, are pale green. They may be touched by early, unexpected frosts. From late August through September, lustrous, white trumpet-like flowers, 4 inches long, are borne on stems 2 feet high. Fragrance is a major asset of this species. Plants will spread to cover an area of 3 feet. Winter cover may be necessary in sections of very severe winters.

H. tardifolia (*H. lancifolia* var. *tardifolia*). The latest-blooming hosta, it flowers in October, with slender flowers of deep lavender-purple. The extremely late display and the 12-inch stature are the main virtues. Winter covering will be necessary in coldest sections.

H. undulata (*H. media picta, H. variegata*), Wavy-Leaved

Plantain-Lily. Medium-sized leaves with wavy margins are variegated, white on green. This is less pronounced in full sun. Pale lavender flowers in July, on stems that may reach 3 feet, are impressive. Plants rarely exceed 20 inches in width. The variety *univittata* (*H. univittata*) is quite rare, and is unique in that there is a white central stripe on each large waxy leaf. Clear lavender blooms in July add to the general effect.

H. ventricosa (*H. cærulea*). The nearest to true blue in the genus, this has large blossoms, lightly cast with purple in July and August. Sizable, shining, deep green leaves are twisted at the tips. One plant will spread to cover an area of 2 feet in diameter. Scapes may reach 3 feet in height.

Final Comment: Hostas—trouble-free, hardy, dignified, and worthy—are plants for every garden with suitable conditions.

IBERIS **Candytuft** **Cruciferæ**

A restrained habit, evergreen foliage, and flowers the whitest white of any perennial justify the popularity of the common candytuft.

Iberis refers to Iberia, once a name for Spain. Some of the species are native there, the rest in other parts of the Mediterranean region. "Candytuft" is derived from "Candie," the old English designation for Crete, where early forms were noted, and "tuft," from the moundlike habit of most species. Gerard received the first seeds in England in the sixteenth century, and called his plants Candie-mustard.

Garden Value: For the most part these are small perennials, often evergreen, somewhat woody at the base, that rarely attain more than 9 inches in height, but can spread to 2 feet. Superior hardy types are mainly a sparkling white, the small flowers in corymbs making a spectacular display from late April to early June. A second fall bloom frequently occurs in the South.

For rock garden nooks, individual plants will suffice. In large borders, small masses are probably more attractive, particularly when combined with spring-flowering bulbs. The neat evergreen hummocks make splendid edging material, as well. The use as a ground cover in the sun may prove disappointing, especially after really severe winters.

Soil and Exposure: As may be expected from the native habitat, a light, well-drained soil is necessary. Full sunlight is customary, but slight shade is not detrimental.

Care: Plants are set out in early spring, fall, or even when in full bloom if they have been either potted or dug with a ball of soil. Severe trimming of the tops after flowering and light fertilizer applications encourage new bushy growth. Without pruning, noticeable gaps or voids at the center may develop. In cold, snowless regions, most candytufts should be protected against winter burning. The less hardy species, such as *I. gibraltarica* and *I. tenoreana,* require a winter cover of evergreen branches in most northern states.

Propagation: Seeds germinate well in fall or spring, with variation in seedlings to be expected. Cuttings made in midsummer root easily. While division is safest in spring, it is not always possible to retain sturdy roots during the process.

Species

I. gibraltarica. Rather lax 12-inch plants flower well into summer in handsome lilac to light purple shades. While not notably hardy, this species sometimes self-sows, thereby perpetuating itself. Valuable for its color and the extended period of bloom, it is worthy of winter protection.

I. saxatilis. Minute, 2-inch clumps that spread very slowly are best established in gravelly soil in which some lime has been incorporated. White, flat-topped clusters are produced throughout the month of May. 'Little Cushion' is a scarce, tiny, 3-inch powderpuff of a plant that is a prize in the rock garden.

I. sempervirens. Without a doubt the most common species, it varies from seeds, but normally forms an irregular circle, 2 feet in diameter, with pure chalk-white flowers on 8-inch stems.

'Snowflake,' when true to name (from asexual propagation), is a desirable form with large clusters of flowers and deep green leaves. 'Purity'—far and away the finest selection—is much whiter, more floriferous, and persistently long flowering. Also, the luxuriant, dark green foliage is always ornamental. Plants are quite hardy. 'Christmas Snow' is of interest mainly because of a tendency to rebloom in autumn. 'Little Gem,' a compact, densely-flowered plant, makes a clump not over 8 inches in diameter.

I. tenoreana. The name honors an Italian botanist of the last century. The sizable umbel-like inflorescence opens as a cloudy white, but gradually assumes purplish pink tints. Growth is inconsistent, governed mainly by climatic factors; hence, protection is required in the North.

Final Comment: Practically every rock garden and many a border contain the common candytuft, but more attention to superior cultivars, such as 'Purity,' and to the other species, would improve most plantings.

IRIS **Iris** **Iridaceæ**

Although the average gardener's first thoughts of iris undoubtedly swing to the tall bearded types, the genus has a wealth of other material, and only cursory discussions are possible in a general work of this kind. Probably everyone is familiar with the showy flowers and the swordlike leaves typically encountered, but there are also excellent midgets for rock gardens, tender bulbous sorts for warm climates (not treated here), and moisture-loving types for naturalizing in damp areas. In view of the wide diversity of character and cultural needs, garden groups will be discussed separately.

The name *Iris* is generally considered to signify the rainbow in Greek, a tribute to the brilliant colors found in the genus. Legend has it that Iris, a messenger to Juno, used the rainbow as a travel route between heaven and earth, and eventually Juno transformed her into a rainbow. There are at least 150 species, but many are only for the fancier or for those who garden in warm climates. As a testimony to their antiquity, Pliny spoke of them as a source of perfume.

Tall Bearded Iris

Quite possibly no perennial is more enthusiastically grown in American gardens. The large flowers are composed of three erect inner segments, called *standards,* and three reflexed outer segments known as *falls,* on the upper surface of which is the *beard.* Blooming is largely confined to May and June, stems may reach 3 feet or more, and the foliage is of strong, gray, sword-shaped character.

With the advent of the promising flamingo pinks, colors available today duplicate the rainbow. All manner of blends and pastels are to be had, as well as types with ruffled or laciniated falls. "Amœna" is a term covering types with white standards and colored falls. "Selfs" are of solid, uniform color, and the "plicatas" are basically yellow or white, with contrasting dots or stippling. "Variegata" is used to designate yellow standards and dark colored falls.

The tall bearded iris were formerly referred to as *I. germanica,* or the German iris. However, hybridizing with other species, such as *I. pallida, I. variegata, I. cypriara,* and *I. trojana,* plus the development of tetraploids, with four sets of chromosomes rather than two, have resulted in the adoption of the term "pogoniris" to signify the bearded types, since they are no longer typical of *Iris germanica.*

Garden Value: Plantings near other perennials that bloom at the same time are always effective, but because their days of glory are comparatively brief, only the specialist will devote a great amount of prime display space to them. Nonetheless, for early color in the border, after the spring-flowering bulbs have finished, these iris are peerless.

Soil and Exposure: Average, well-drained soil, not pronouncedly acid is required. Strong fertilizers or lime should not actually touch the roots. Overly acid soils may be corrected by the use of limestone chips. Full sun produces sturdy, erect stalks and maximum flowering.

Care: Planting is best undertaken after flowering but no later than August. However, early spring is also a safe time, although flowers may be sacrificed the first summer. If a group of three of one cultivar is planted, the usual procedure is to set the rhizomes so that the new leaves, and hence the main direction of growth, face outward away from the center of the group. Rhizomes are set 1 inch deep, and foliage cut back to 6 inches. Clumps should be divided at least every fourth summer to prevent deterioration. One set of leaves in a fan, plus several feeding roots below the rhizome, constitute a suitable division.

Iris borer may be a source of trouble. The worm leaves a trail of slime along the leaf edge before it tunnels down the central portion into the rhizome. It may be squeezed or pinched out where leaf swellings are noted, but affected rhizomes must be dug, cut clear of borers, and reset. DDT as a dust or spray will help to prevent reinfestation. Destruction of old foliage each fall helps, too, as it eliminates the borer eggs.

Bacterial soft rot begins on the rhizome, and can soon destroy the entire plant. Poor drainage or harsh chemical fertilizers promote the trouble. If diseased areas are cut from the rhizome, and fungicidal powders applied to the cut surfaces, recovery usually ensues.

Recommended Cultivars

With hundreds of new cultivars registered every year, it is all but impossible for any one except a specialist to keep up with all the new introductions. Prices ranging from the customary "nominal" to those which may seem exorbitant to many are quite naturally governed by supply and demand.

The highest recognition an iris can receive is the Dykes Medal (DM) which is awarded one outstanding selection each year. The American Iris Society also makes several Awards of Merit (AM) to other outstanding cultivars. Both of these awards are noted in specialists' catalogs. Here it must suffice to list but a few of the excellent introductions, which far surpass the garden types of a generation ago.

'Violet Harmony'—DM, large flower, ruffled, light violet

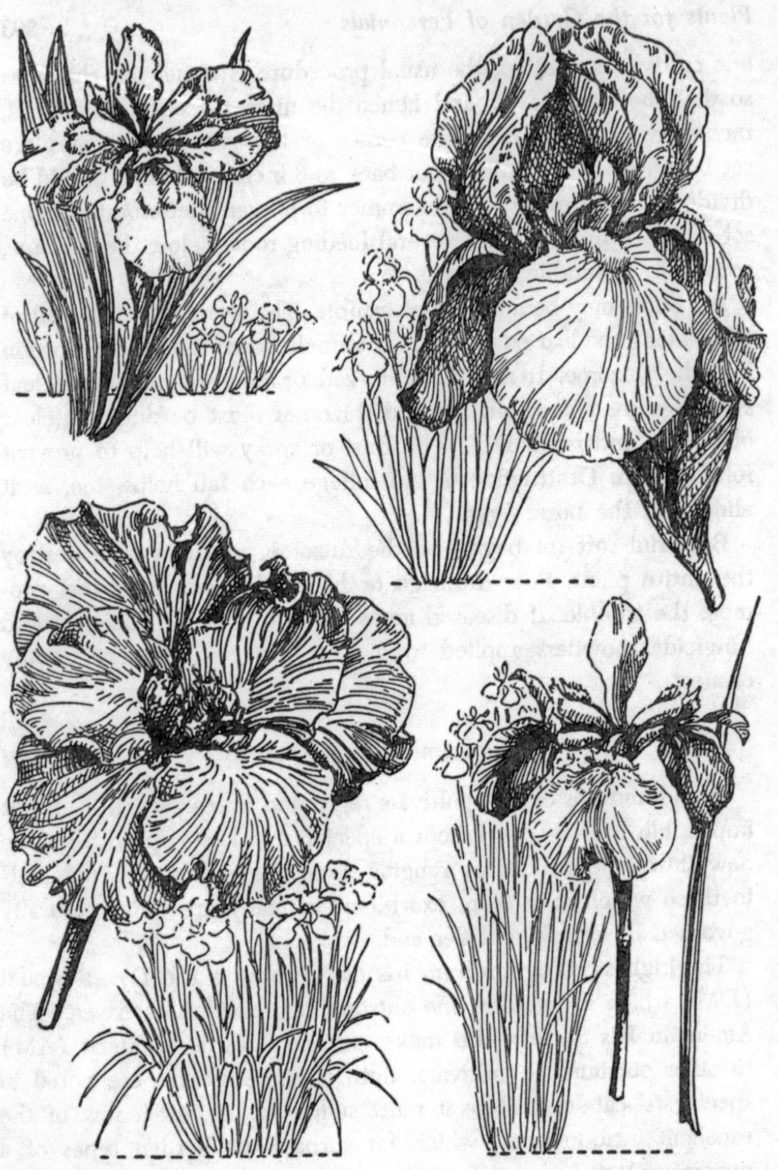

Iris cristata
Iris kaempferi

Tall Bearded Iris
Iris siberica

'Truly Yours'—DM, large, yellow shading to white, late-flowering
'Sable Night'—DM, velvety purple-black falls, reddish purple standards and bronze beard
'Mary Randall'—DM, rose-pink with tangerine beard
'First Violet'—DM, uniform light violet self
'Helen McGregor'—DM, ruffled light blue, lemon-yellow beard
'Ola Kala'—DM, deep rich yellow
'Blue Rhythm'—DM, elegant cornflower blue
'Ranger'—AM, dark crimson, bronze-orange beard
'Black Forest'—AM, velvety blue-black
'New Snow'—AM, white with light yellow beard
'Bryce Canyon'—AM, strong coppery bronze

A very significant development of recent years is the crossing of tall bearded iris with the oncocyclus tribe. The latter consists of species from around Palestine which feature very large, rounded flowers of striking form and coloring. William Mohr of Capitola, California, succeeded in making the initial crosses between 'Purissima,' a fine old white bearded cultivar, and *I. gatesii*. Later, Mohr also used 'Capitola,' a seedling of *I. iberica*, as a parent. Several desirable selections of mammoth blossoms, exotic blendings, and odd venation are now extensively grown. These are usually listed under the tall bearded group in catalogs. 'Elmohr' (DM) has 7-inch blooms of bishop's purple, 'Lady Mohr' (AM) combines lavender-white standards and chartreuse falls, while 'Bluemohr' (AM) is a large, rounded plumbago-blue.

Dwarf Bearded Iris

There are several species and an ever increasing number of hybrids which are 6 to 12 inches tall, flower very early—often by late April—and continue for about five weeks. Ideal for rock gardens or the foreground of a border, they have a charm quite apart from that of the tall ones. Their culture is the same as for the other bearded types.

Species

I. chamæiris. Native to southern France and northern Italy, this species is of interest now primarily as one of the prominent parents of garden cultivars. While flowers vary in color, there nearly always is a contrasting beard. Much of the material listed in catalogs as *I. pumila* belongs here.

I. arenaria. One of the tiniest bearded iris in commerce, it usually bears bright canary-yellow flowers with an orange beard, on stems less than 4 inches high. It is to be seen in flower only by early risers.

I. mellita. This produces relatively large, white-bearded flowers of crimson-purple on 2-inch stems. Recurrence of bloom in fall is not unknown. The sickle-shaped leaves of dull green are edged with crimson.

I. pumila. Colors range from primrose yellow to blue, purple, and deep reddish purple. This is a densely spreading type that will not tolerate lime near the roots.

The above species have all contributed to today's dwarf selections. Paul Cook and Walter Welch of Indiana are largely credited with increasing the possibilities of this type, especially of the blue tones. Today the dwarf bearded iris are available in all colors and patterns found in the tall group, except tangerine and plicatas.

A few representative garden cultivars include: 'Atroviolacea,' a very early reddish purple; 'Primus,' with yellow standards and yellow-rimmed falls of red; 'Little Jewel,' a red; 'Cream Delight,' a large ivory; and 'Winsome,' a blue and violet. The smallest is 'Little Bit,' only 2 inches tall.

Intermediate Iris

Not appreciated to the extent deserved, these are hybrids between the tall and dwarf types, chiefly *I. chamæiris*. They bridge the gap in flowering period of the parents, and are intermediate in size and height. In addition, several will also repeat flowering in September; they are known as Fall Bloomers, and were originated by Charles André of France and the Sasses of this country. They require adequate moisture in dry summers if they are to be noteworthy in autumn.

In America, Paul Cook and Geddes Douglas have collaborated on a very new group which they call the Lilliputs, bred from tall bearded iris and *I. pumila.* These forerunners of even more promising types are considered highly decorative, but are still scarce. Several good intermediate cultivars are: 'Lieut. de Chavagnac,' reddish purple and velvety black, repeating blooms in fall; 'Ruby Glow,' a fine red; 'Cosette,' a gleaming white; 'Black Magic,' which is dark, almost ebony, and repeats, and 'Dorcas Hutchinson,' a violet and purple repeater.

Japanese Iris

The Japanese iris, native to Japan, Korea, and Manchuria, are classed under *I. kaempferi,* so named for a Swedish consul who studied Japanese flora in the late seventeenth century. It is possible that *I. lævigata* and others have entered into the cultivars of the present day.

This group is sometimes called the "flat-top iris" because the standards are either short or else resemble the falls, which may be almost horizontal. In late June and July, 3- to 4-foot stalks carry large beardless flowers, often over 6 inches across, in colors ranging from white to blue, lavender-pink, reddish purple, and purple. Willowy, slender leaves form graceful clumps.

Garden Value: Moist soil is preferable; hence, this type is beautiful around pools, fountains, and streams, especially when reflected in the water. They add an aristocratic note in borders when well grown. As cut flowers they are only fair, usually of short duration.

Soil and Exposure: Plantings should be in rich, mellow soil that retains abundant moisture throughout the growing season. Lime is fatal; peatmoss or other acidifying agents should be used in neutral or alkaline soils. Yellowing of the foliage may be caused by soils that are not sufficiently acid, or by overly deep planting. Full sun or partial shade will be equally acceptable.

Care: Young plants, established in spring or late summer, should be set 1 inch or so deep, and about 2 feet apart. At least two growing seasons are needed before the plants will be at their best. They can be left undisturbed for a long time.

Cultivars

Most early selections were of Japanese origin, and their names did not always translate into workable English, so slight differences in nomenclature are often encountered in catalogs.

A recent step forward has been the Higo strain, a vastly improved galaxy from an isolated portion of Japan. The flowers may exceed 12 inches in size, and are magnificently colored, with a velvety texture. Still in short supply, they may supersede all current favorites in time. Typical selections include: 'Norma,' a double orchid-pink; 'La Favorite,' a large white flushed with lilac; 'Mahogany,' a deep red double; 'Margaret S. Hendricksen,' medium blue double; and 'Rose Anna,' a unique mauve veined with rich purple. The Marhigo strain, originated by the Walter Marx Gardens of Oregon, is a more recent development with large flowers, both single and double, in a wide range of colors and patterns.

Siberian Iris

Botanically the group is referable to *I. sibirica,* a beardless blue- or white-flowered species of Europe. However, Japanese hybridizers evidently did all their work on *I. sanguinea* (*I. orientalis*). Their better types were dispatched to England about 1900, and Messrs. Barr and Wallace added *I. sibirica,* thus introducing new luster. Since 1920, Americans and Canadians, including F. Cleveland Morgan, Isabella Preston, and Frances Cleveland, have produced better cultivars, some of which approach red coloring.

Garden Value: These iris bridge the gap in sequence of bloom between the bearded and the Japanese types. Tall, slender foliage, topped by medium-sized, delicate flowers makes splendid groupings in borders or in naturalized colonies.

Soil and Exposure: While able to survive in poor soil, they perform better in rich, moist, slightly acid soils. Sun or light shade will suffice.

Care: When clumps begin to die out in the center, division is in order. Very early spring is preferable, since plants divided after flowering are sometimes difficult to get established again before winter.

Cultivars

'Snow Crest' is a ruffled white. Like Miss Preston's other introductions, 'Gatineau,' a medium blue, is named for a Canadian river. 'Tycoon' is largest of all and a deep violet-blue. 'Eric the Red' is the best red to date; 'Caesar's Brother' is a deep pansy-purple.

Bulbous Iris

Another group, outside the scope of this work, is the bulbous iris. For the most part the Dutch iris (*I. xiphium*), English or Spanish iris (*I. xiphioides*) and the Wedgewood iris (*I. xiphium* × *I. tingitana*) are satisfactory garden subjects only in warmer sections of the country where the winters are mild, as in the South and on the West Coast. The hardy bulbous iris such as *I. histrioides* (blue), *I. reticulata* (purple) and *I. danfordiæ* (yellow) are dwarf types that flower early in the spring, and are appropriate in rock gardens or in colonies in the front of a border.

Miscellaneous Species

I. cristata, Crested Iris. The crested iris have a crest of petaloid tissue on the falls, in place of a beard. Small pale lilac flowers open in late May on diminutive plants about 6 inches high. A white form is less common. They are ideal for rock gardens.

I. dichotoma, Vesper Iris. One of the latest to flower, it is more or less a novelty. In August small purple, white, or coppery lavender flowers, on branched 3-foot stems, open about four o'clock in the afternoon, and last but the one day.

I. graminea. This seems to grow anywhere, even in the shade. In its European habitat it is described as yellowish white, but commercial forms show reddish purple to violet shadings. Fragrant flowers on 10-inch stems are partially hidden by the foliage. Mat-forming, it demands occasional division.

I. minuta. Here is a Japanese midget for the really appreciative gardener. Tiny yellow blossoms appear in late April, hardly above ground level. After flowering, the narrow grassy leaves elongate to 15 inches when grown in shade and rich soils.

I. orientalis (*I. ochroleuca*). This species is suitable for colder areas only if given winter protection. Stems approach 3½ feet in height, and generally produce white flowers with yellow throats, although other selections are also available. Rich, moist soils are a necessity. 'Mrs. A. W. Tait' is a blue, 'Lord Wolsely' a purple, 'Mt. Whitney' a white, and 'Shelford Giant' a creamy yellow.

I. pseudacorus, Water Flag Iris. From Europe and North Africa, this iris is occasionally found naturalized in North America. Excellent in boggy poolsides or waterways, it likewise flourishes in garden soils if adequate humus has been incorporated. The 3-foot stems are normally topped by vivid yellow flowers. A good companion plant is the native blue-flowered *I. versicolor.*

I. tectorum. The roof iris of Japan is frequently raised on thatched roofs there, where space for garden flowers is at a premium. It is about the largest crested iris, growing to 15 inches. The wavy, flattened, lavender-purple flowers in May and June develop best in good loam and full sun. Variety *alba* is a seldom distributed, pure white variant that has possible rock garden value, but needs winter protection in colder areas.

Final Comment: The discussion has merely skimmed the surface of this outstanding genus. While the great progress in improvement and variety of the past is to be stressed, the avid gardener will be on the alert for new developments. Those particularly interested should consult the literature of either the American Iris Society or the Dwarf Iris Society.

KNIPHOFIA (*Tritoma*) Torch-Lily, Red-Hot Poker Liliaceæ

With the recent improvements in color, season of bloom, and hardiness, there is no reason to avoid this genus because of the weaknesses and limitations of earlier garden types. All of the species, native to Africa, present an exotic, tropical effect. The name of the genus pays tribute to J. J. Kniphof, an eighteenth century professor in Germany.

Garden Value: Stout plants of long, grassy leaves and terminal, poker-shaped racemes, about 3 feet tall, in vivid hues are typical. The individual floret is drooping, slender, and tubular. Florets are massed along the top 12 inches of the scape, opening mainly in midsummer. Formerly, only red and yellow were common, but today's developments have increased the range and softened the colors. Groupings are adaptable to small borders, red forms are conspicuous near shrubbery, while the newer dwarfs are suitable in rock gardens. When in bloom, they are striking near white lilies, and the stately growth can be effective for landscape accents. All have cut flower possibilities.

Soil and Exposure: Sandy, well-drained spots are needed, soggy areas being fatal. Full sunlight is recommended, and windy areas are to be avoided.

Care: Only spring-planting is advised, at about 18-inch spacing. Most recent introductions are quite reliably hardy, yet mulching until spring may be wise in cold regions. Large clumps should be divided about every third or fourth spring.

Propagation: Seeds may be sown in spring, but the resulting plants will probably take two or three years to reach flowering size. Division in early spring is the preferred method.

Species

Most true species are important in America only as they have contributed to hybridizing.

K. caulescens. Often 4 to 5 feet tall, as are few modern selections, it has glaucous gray leaves, and flowers that range from reddish salmon to yellow-white. Most significant is the habit of blooming both in June and in autumn.

K. foliosa. This species is evidently one source of the increased hardiness in hybrids. It grows to 2 or 3 feet, with racemes of reddish yellow flowers.

K. galpinii. Winter protection is imperative for this plant, but it remains popular with many American gardeners. Only 2 feet tall, it carries tiny pokers of saffron-buff tinted salmon-orange, and supplies excellent cut flowers from July to frost.

K. tubergenii. Creamy yellow shadings have led to current white flowers and others of subdued tones.

K. uvaria (K. pfitzeri). This species, once the only garden form in commerce, is the prime source of today's cultivars. Usually it grows to 3 feet, with gaudy spikelike racemes of scarlet upper flowers and yellow lower ones. Blooming in late autumn, it has been disapprovingly castigated as a "glare of the garden." Although it is seldom completely hardy, some nurseries still offer seedlings of this type only. The variety *erecta* is notable for erect spikes that remain attractive until all flowers are open.

Dwarf species of 1- or 2-foot stature, such as *K. rufa* and *K. tuckii*, red and yellow bicolors, *K. nelsonii*, an orange-scarlet, and *K. macowanii*, an orange-red, have contributed their low habit and, in some cases, a tendency to bloom as early as May, to modern hybrids.

Leading Cultivars

'White Fairy' bears slender 2-foot spikes of cream color in June and July. The artistically blended coral-red and deep rose flowers of 2½ feet tall 'Coral Seas' are best in June and July. On 'Springtime,' a hardy, vigorous 3-foot plant, the inflorescence is divided into solid coral-red and ivory-white halves. 'Primrose Beauty,' 2½ feet, bears primrose-yellow flowers in early summer. 'Summer Sunshine' produces bold, clean flame-red blossoms on 3-foot stems in midsummer; it is hardy.

Final Comment: It behooves the gardener to swallow old prejudices and try the newly glamorized selections. Those who seek the flamboyant can still find bold colors to satisfy their needs.

LAMIUM — Dead Nettle — Labiatæ

Dead nettles are filler plants, in that they spread adequately, but are not weedy, are sufficiently ornamental but not indispensable, and will grow almost anywhere. The genus comprises annuals and perennials native to Europe, with very few grown as ornamentals.

Garden Value: In habit, the lamiums are low and informal, sometimes to the point of straggling, but the foliage is interesting, and the blooming season extends from late April to the end of August. Usually less than a foot in height, they can be used in rock gardens or in the foreground of a border.

Soil and Exposure: An average garden loam is adequate. Partial shade will produce a better effect than full sun, although in the latter situation a soil with moisture-holding capacity is to be preferred.

Care: Spring-planting is generally suggested. Midsummer shearing encourages a dwarf, compact mass.

Propagation: Spring-sown seeds are productive, but division in early spring is the only practical method for desirable forms or variants.

Species

L. maculatum, Spotted Dead Nettle. Half trailing, unless sheared annually, this 12-inch hummock is engaging in foliage and flower. Leaves are basically green, but in the form usually found in cultivation, there is a white blotch along the midrib. Other forms may be marbled with red and silver. Flowers in whorls are purple, deep rose, or rarely pure white. The latter form is particularly useful in shaded areas.

L. veronicæfolium. While relatively unknown, this hardy, showy Spanish native is seemingly easy to raise. Large, bright, rose-pink flowers bloom on 6-inch stems almost until fall. The foliage is coarser than that of *L. maculatum* and a rusty green. Best in the sun.

Final Comment: With judicious use in controlled quantities, the less common forms of *L. maculatum* afford a touch of welcome novelty in the shade.

LAVANDULA **Lavender** **Labiatæ**

Flowers and foliage are pungently aromatic, the fragrance lingering for years after stems are cut and dried. Lavender sachet is well known, and a precious oil was formerly distilled from the bloom in England. There, wines, confectionery, and medicine were thus flavored. Hence, the plant belongs in every herb garden; it has justly been called the "queen of all herbs."

Lavandula is derived from the Latin *lavo*, to wash, since the ancient Romans used the perfume in baths. The correct name of the commonly grown species is *L. officinalis*, although often still listed in catalogs as *L. vera* or *L. spica*. Actually, it is a subshrub with woody stems, native to the Mediterranean region.

Garden Value: Because of the low stature, ornamental foliage, and flowers, it is not out of place in rock gardens or in the front rank of a border. Untrimmed, dwarf hedges along walks or borders are pleasing, but one must remember that plants in full bloom will spill outward, so space must be allowed accordingly. The persistent gray or gray-green foliage forms a pleasing contrast with the green of nearby subjects, the lavender to purple flowers adding interest from late June to August.

Soil and Exposure: A light, sandy soil and full sun are desirable. In heavier, fertile soils, growth becomes lax and soft, creating a hardiness problem.

Care: Plantings at 12-inch intervals are best made in early spring before new, active growth commences. Trimming after flowering induces a desirable compact habit.

Propagation: Clones are propagated by cuttings taken in summer.

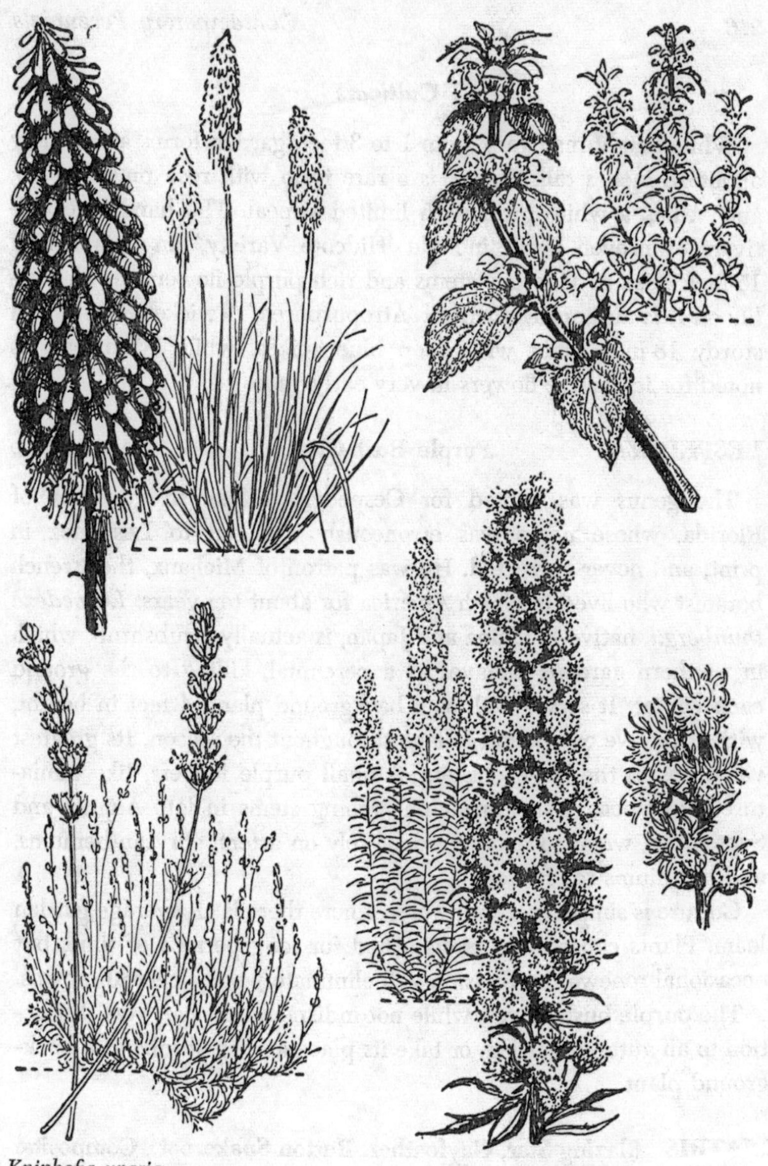

Kniphofia uvaria
Lavandula officinalis

Lamium maculatum
Liatris 'September Glory'

Cultivars

While height may vary from 1 to 3 feet, garden forms are usually about 18 inches tall. 'Rosea' is a rare form with rosy pink flowers, and 'Alba,' a white form with limited appeal. The handsome cultivars of proven merit include 'Hidcote Variety,' an outstanding 15-inch bush of vigorous stems and rich purple flowers. In all likelihood it is an improvement of 'Atropurpurea.' 'Twickel Purple' is a sturdy 18-inch plant with deep blue spikes, while 'Munstead' is noted for its mauve flowers in very early June.

LESPEDEZA Purple Bush-Clover Leguminosæ

The genus was named for Cespedez, a Spanish governor of Florida, whose name was erroneously changed to Lespedez in print, and never corrected. He was patron of Michaux, the French botanist who lived in North America for about ten years. *Lespedeza thunbergii,* native to China and Japan, is actually a subshrub, which in northern gardens behaves as a perennial, killing to the ground each winter. It serves well as a background plant, 4 feet in height, with attractive compound foliage throughout the season. Its greatest value lies in the large clusters of small purple flowers, like miniature sweet peas, that appear on arching stems in late August and September, when so many gardens rely on asters, chrysanthemums, and heleniums for flowers.

Culture is simple in a sunny area where there is an average garden loam. Plants can remain undisturbed for long periods of time, but occasional renewal by division will eliminate woody central crowns.

The purple bush-clover, while not indispensable, can give distinction to an autumn garden, or take its place among shrubs as a background plant.

LIATRIS Blazing Star, Gayfeather, Button Snakeroot Compositæ

In the main, liatris are a starkly upright, elongated group, definitely of stiff, vertical effect. Spikes in flower usually evoke comment because the uppermost flowerheads open first, and flowering progresses down the stem. No valid derivation is evident for the botanical name, but the common names are in keeping with the appearance of the plants.

Garden Value: Heights range from 1½ to 5 feet, according to the species or cultivar. The heads of rosy purple or white florets, massed into terminal racemes or spikes 18 inches long for the taller types, are striking in August and September. Foliage is narrow and grass-like.

For narrow niches in the rear of the border, the sentinel-like growth is perfect, but excessive massing gives an austere, regimented feeling. Gypsophilas near the colored forms and sea-lavenders close to white ones relieve the stiff effect. When cut, the long stems last well in water. Secondary racemes usually develop after cutting the main stem.

Soil and Exposure: Ordinarily, a sandy soil of above average fertility is best, although *L. spicata* will survive in quite moist ground. Soil must be well drained in winter, as soggy conditions limit hardiness. Full sun is to be preferred.

Care: One may plant liatris in early spring, at 12-inch intervals. If flowering is to begin in really dry periods, occasional deep watering is necessary. At least one-third of each stem used for cutting should remain on the plant for continued manufacture of food; otherwise clumps die. When a planting becomes overgrown, about every fourth spring, the tuberous root mass should be divided.

Propagation: Seeds sown in spring give more than adequate increase. Even white forms reproduce reasonably true to type. Division in early spring is common practice for named selections.

Species

L. graminifolia, Grassleaf Gayfeather. This is not widely distributed in commerce, although the modest purple spikes on wiry 2-foot stems find some favor. The foliage is extremely narrow. It is native from New Jersey south to Florida.

L. punctata, Dwarf Gayfeather. Native over broad expanses from

Manitoba to New Mexico, it varies from 1 to 2½ feet, flowering mainly in August.

L. pycnostachya, Cattail Gayfeather. Native from Wisconsin to Louisiana, this is perhaps the tallest species in general cultivation, where 5 feet is not uncommon. Stems well clothed with foliage produce dense spikes of purple or pinkish lavender flowers in August and September. The form 'Alba' is a white, infrequently seen counterpart. This species is particularly subject to deterioration in wet winters.

L. scariosa. Most of the plants or seeds listed in catalogs under this name do not belong to this species, but to *L. aspera*. In the wild, from North Dakota and Ohio to Texas and Florida, variations in height of 1 to 3 feet are found, although in garden forms 3 or 4 feet is the rule. The liberally spaced flowers are perhaps more interesting and graceful upon closer inspection than are those with tightly massed spikes. Flowering usually begins in late August. 'September Glory' is notable for the simultaneous opening of all flowers on each spike for a total display of purple. 'White Spire,' said to be a sport of the former, is self-descriptive. 'Nana' is a form found by Dr. Edgar T. Wherry of the University of Pennsylvania. It remains preciously rare. Tiny 8-inch racemes of reddish purple persist from September to late October, but only in poor soils are such miniature proportions likely.

L. spicata. Even though heights range from 1 to 6 feet in its eastern habitat, a fairly well-knit 3-foot plant is customary in gardens. Again, coloring is purple, except in the rare white forms. 'Kobold' is a compact, dark purple hybrid.

Final Comment: As with all plants leaning slightly to the bizarre, gayfeathers are for strategic placement, not for lavish colonization.

LILIUM Lily Liliaceæ

Lilies, having a bulbous rootstock, are technically outside the scope of this work, but are included because of their popularity and because they are, or should be, an integral part of any perennial planting. So much could be written on this superb genus that the fancier will do well to secure an expertly prepared book on the subject alone, such as *Lilies for American Gardens* by George L. Slate or *The New Book of Lilies* by Jan de Graaff.

Lilium is the ancient Latin name passed on over the years. There are about 100 species, indigenous to the north temperate zone in general. Today, interspecific hybrids are assuming as much, or more importance for the gardener than the straight species.

There are various classifications of the species, but a good working one based on the form of the flowers follows:

1. Upright or cup-shaped flowers, as in *L. hollandicum*
2. Trumpet types, with funnel-shaped flowers like those of the regal lily
3. Turk's-cap or martagons, in which the flower segments are recurved, as in the tiger lily
4. Wide open, outward facing types, typified by *L. auratum*

Garden Value: Maeterlinck spoke of "the great white lily, the lord of the gardens, the only authentic prince among all commonalty issuing from the kitchen garden." While most lilies are superb as lone specimens or as solid masses, they are always stately garden subjects. Heights range from 1 to 6 feet or more, colors extend from white through yellow and orange to red and even purple. The blooming season encompasses a lengthy May to October period. Most lilies excel for cutting, especially when picked just as buds swell noticeably. At least one-third, and better two-thirds, of the stem should be left to supply nourishment for the bulb.

Soil and Exposure: Drainage is unquestionably the paramount consideration. Average soils, slightly acid in reaction, are appropriate. Leafmold, compost, or peatmoss (the last not for *L. candidum*) supply essential humus. Deep green foliage denotes proper nutrition; yellowed leaves indicate a lack of essential elements or perhaps excessive lime.

Sunlight is normally recommended, but when it is filtered by high-branching trees such as elms, the resulting shade will not be harmful. In fact, such relief enhances the recent pink hybrids and such delicately tinted species as *L. henryi*.

Care: Fall-planting is most desirable, for bulbs are freshly dug and relatively dormant at that time. Carefully stored bulbs, which are not shriveled by exposure, can also be set out in early spring. An exception is *L. candidum,* which has evergreen leaves over winter, and is dormant only in August and early September. Only potted specimens of this species are safely moved in spring. This practice, becoming more prevalent, allows purchase of all lilies, even when in full bloom.

Most growers believe that the depth of planting is not as important as was once supposed, since the contractile roots pull the bulb to desired levels. Roughly, a depth of 4 inches is suitable for the smaller-growing types, and 6 inches for taller sorts. Again *L. candidum* is the exception; it is never set over 2 inches below the soil line. Spacings usually average 18 to 24 inches.

A tablespoon of a complete fertilizer may be worked into the soil around each bulb every spring. An inch of peatmoss makes a fine summer mulch to keep roots cool and moist and to control weeds. Seed pods should not be allowed to develop unless needed for propagation.

In areas of late spring frosts, tender new shoots may be damaged unless covered by baskets at night. Some growers mulch the planting with hay after the ground freezes hard in fall, to prevent damage to tender precocious growth in warm periods during March.

After six or eight years, a large clump of lilies is best dug and separated to prevent crowding and to allow better aeration.

Diseases and Insects: Mosaic—Caused by a virus and spread by aphids, this is the worst disease of lilies. Symptoms vary from light green, mottled, or malformed foliage to drooping leaves and split or distorted buds and flowers. Infected bulbs must be destroyed. The disease is not soil borne, so replanting in the same area is safe. Dusting or spraying with insecticides to control the aphids is a wise preventive measure, but there is no cure. Resistant strains are more common today, and bulbs produced from seedlings are less prone to pass on the disease than are asexually propagated forms.

Botrytis—This blight appears most often on *L. candidum* but not exclusively so. It flourishes in cold wet springs, forming swelling brown spots on leaves, stems, and buds. As the affected leaves fall, the source of nourishment for the bulb disappears, leaving weakened specimens. Overcrowding, with resultant poor circulation of air, is a prime cause; damp cool periods intensify the problem. Hence, bulbs should not be planted in crowded surroundings. Diseased leaves should be removed at first signs of the trouble, and a fungicide used at weekly intervals.

Basal Rot—A slimy fungus may be noted on newly purchased bulbs or on old colonies dug for separation. Excessively deep planting or poor drainage is often at fault. All infected portions should be cut off, and the clean tissue dusted with a germicide, or dipped in a comparable solution.

Propagation: Seeds—sown in early spring in shallow outdoor rows, some seeds will germinate in a short time, others not for several months. In the succeeding spring the little bulblets that develop may be set at proper depths and distances for the species in question, but flowering may not occur for two or three years. Some species take a considerable time for seedlings to appear above ground, more than a year in some cases.

Division—Matted clumps are lifted either in very early spring, before active growth starts, or in autumn, and are shaken free of soil and split into individual bulbs, preferably with roots attached. These should be reset in newly prepared sites. Bulbs of dubious condition should be discarded.

Bulbils—*L. tigrinum* and some others produce ebony bulbils in the leaf axils. In August these may be picked from the plants and sown an inch deep. The following spring, or when leaves appear, they can be reset, and will be of blooming size in a few years.

Scales—These are loose, fleshy growths, peculiar to lily bulbs. They may be removed from the mother bulb after bloom has ceased, and each protectively dusted with a fungicide. Bulbs may be lifted and completely stripped, or merely uncovered and a few scales removed, depending upon the number of additional plants desired. Each scale is set 2 inches deep in sand, sphagnum moss, or vermiculite in greenhouse pots or flats, or directly outdoors in partially shaded spots. Winter protection is required outside. During the following spring, each is moved to more spacious quarters, planted 1 or 2 inches deep, then reset in fall where deeper, permanent plantings are made.

While any vegetative means of propagation will provide rapid increase of outstanding selections, the possibility of passing on the virus disease cannot be overemphasized. Seed-grown material is much more likely to be disease-free than that propagated by any other method.

Species

In spite of the countless advances of spectacular hybrids, strains, and selections, many true species still compare favorably with the modern derivations. They are reliable, popular, and decorative, with amazing diversity.

L. auratum, Gold-Banded Lily. Ever since 1862, when first exhibited in London, the huge, extremely fragrant, 10-inch bowl-shaped flowers have awed onlookers. Carried on 5- or 6-foot stems, the basically white flowers are flecked with crimson-bronze, with a central gold band on each perianth segment.

Today, stock raised from seeds in America is less difficult and more rewarding to grow than was once the case when bulbs were subjected to long sea voyages from Japan. The Esperanza strain, raised by Alwyne Buckley of British Columbia, from seeds collected in the wild in Japan, is a notable advance. Clean, floriferous stock, able to sustain 20 or more fine blooms on each stem, complements the August scene immeasurably. The variety *platyphyllum* is a magnificent giant, now grown from seeds on the Pacific Coast.

It should be noted that *L. auratum* is susceptible to the mosaic disease, so it is imperative that it never be grown near infected lilies.

L. canadense, Meadow Lily. Native in eastern America, it grows to 4 feet in height, with stems of bell-shaped flowers, normally

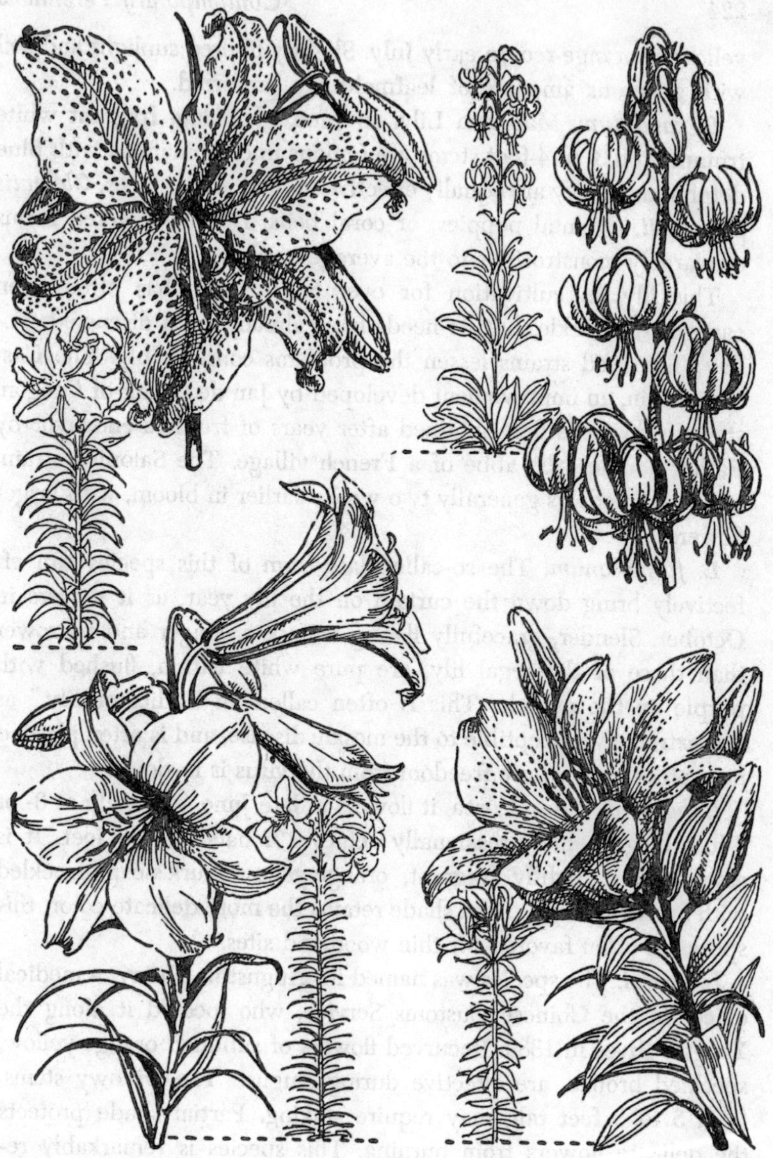

Lilium auratum
Lilium regale

Lilium martagon
Lilium hollandicum

yellow or orange-red, in early July. Slightly filtered sunlight and soil with generous amounts of leafmold are preferred.

L. candidum, Madonna Lily. In June, gleaming, fragrant white trumpets on 3- or 4-foot stems are famous in combinations with blue delphinium. They are equally effective with climbing roses, *Clematis jackmanii,* Oriental poppies, or coral bells. Double-flowered forms are largely monstrosities to the average gardener.

This lily, in cultivation for over 6,000 years, has often been castigated as fickle, but its needs have already been discussed. Today's fine seed strains lessen the problems considerably. The Cascade strain, an improvement developed by Jan de Graaff of Oregon, stems from seeds first obtained after years of fruitless endeavor by Father Souillet, the abbé of a French village. The Salonika strain, also from seeds, is generally two weeks earlier in bloom, with larger flowers.

L. formosanum. The so-called late form of this species can effectively bring down the curtain on the lily year, as it flowers in October. Slender, gracefully flaring trumpets, longer and narrower than those of the regal lily, are pure white within, flushed with purple on the outside. This is often called an "indicator lily," as it is extremely susceptible to the mosaic disease, and is often planted near other lilies whose freedom from the virus is in doubt.

L. hansonii. From Korea, it flowers in late June, generally at 3- or 4-foot heights, but occasionally achieves a handsome 5 feet. It is essentially a slightly fragrant, orange-yellow Turk's-cap, freckled with brown spots. As light shade retains the more delicate color, this species is often favored for thin woodland sites.

L. henryi. The species was named for Augustine Henry, a medical officer in the Chinese Customs Service, who located it along the Yangtse River in 1889. Recurved flowers of subdued orange-yellow, speckled bronze, are effective during August. The willowy stems, from 5 to 8 feet tall, may require staking. Partial shade protects the delicate flowers from burning. This species is remarkably resistant to mosaic. Besides its own inherent value, it has frequently entered into far-reaching breeding efforts.

L. hollandicum (*L. umbellatum*), Candlestick Lily. Today this is noted as one parent of the more sophisticated Mid-Century Hybrids. In June and July, stiffly erect cup-shaped blossoms appear on rigid stems 2 feet or so in height. Bright scarlet, vermilion, and orange flowers make vivid effects when massed.

L. leucanthum var. *centifolium* (*L. centifolium*). Because of the stalwart 5-foot stems and the numerous large white trumpets of good substance, many prefer it to the regal lily.

L. longiflorum var. *eximium*. The hallowed Easter lily, formerly Bermuda-grown, is famed for its large, fragrant, pure white trumpets. Horticultural selections such as the 'Croft Lily' and 'Estate Lily' are better both for forcing in the greenhouse and for outdoor plantings, although even these are not always reliably hardy in northern gardens. When they do survive, flowering is in late July and August.

L. martagon 'Album.' Martagon denotes a style of turban, and typifies these waxy white blossoms of mid-June. They really need a green background to be effective. Vigilant selection has greatly improved the white parental stock, though *L. martagon* itself is no longer very important, except to breeders and to those who find the purple flowers interesting.

L. pumilum (*L. tenuifolium*), Coral Lily. A miniature among lilies, the 18-inch wiry stems, with grasslike leaves, produce small, scarlet Turk's-caps in early June. Groups of four or five at 8-inch spacing make an effective display. Soil must be well drained. Plants may not be long-lived, but this is balanced by the ease of quickly raising more from seed. 'Golden Gleam' is an orange-yellow selection, and 'Red Star' a mid-June type with a broad, deep red corolla.

L. regale, Regal Lily. Dr. E. H. ("Chinese") Wilson, the great plant explorer, first located this widely grown species in 1903, far up the Yangtse River near the China-Tibet border. Speedy production from seeds, aggressive sales promotion, and ease of culture soon led it to general popularity. Graceful 4- to 5-foot stems bear quantities of lightly fragrant white trumpets. Various pink to purple colorings are usually seen on the outside of the flower. While still extensively cultivated, the regal lily may be about to give way to more ornate hybrids to which it has contributed.

L. × *imperiale* (*L. princeps*) is a hybrid between *L. regale* and *L. sargentiæ*. The cross was made in 1919 at the Ontario Agricultural College. Finer white trumpets, larger, and more leathery in texture, bloom about ten days after *L. regale*. 'George C. Creelman,' honoring the Canadian college's president, is an even more choice cultivar of this outstanding hybrid. Six-foot stems and golden yellow throats are characteristic.

L. rubellum. This dainty 2-foot specimen from Japan needs partial shade and fairly heavy soil. Flowering in May, the small, pink funnel-shaped flowers are about the earliest of the genus.

L. speciosum 'Rubrum.' Spectacular and glamorous, this is one of the outstanding lilies. Pink suffusions and crimson spottings on an undercast of white are typical. The recurved flowers open from late August through September, with 4 feet the customary height. Protection from the midday sun by light shade is advantageous. 'Red Champion,' from escaped stock on Oregon's Mt. Hood, is even more striking and vigorous. 'Album' is a pure white. Both forms are quite susceptible to the mosaic disease so it would not be prudent to plant them near tiger lilies or any other bulb that might possibly carry the virus.

L. superbum, American Turk's-Cap Lily. This needs cool, peaty soil and full sun. From 4 to 8 feet in height, it usually bears large, pendant, orange-crimson flowers, beginning in mid-July. Mrs. J. Norman Henry of Gladwynne, Pennsylvania, has segregated several colorful orange and yellow forms.

L. tigrinum, Tiger Lily. Its August blaze of orange-red flowers, spotted black or brown, is most familiar in the United States, where it often escapes. However, it originally came from the Orient. No cultural problems are posed, plants growing to 5 feet even in medium soils. This lily is a Typhoid Mary of the garden, as it is tolerant of mosaic, and survives in spite of it, acting as a possible source of infection for other lilies in the vicinity.

Recent Hybrids

There is a growing tendency to offer strains of hybrids (in which there may be some variation) rather than selected clones. These strains often exhibit hybrid vigor, unusual flower forms, and pleasing colors, as well as an extended season of bloom.

Sulphureum Hybrids. These are mainly the result of crossing *L. myriophyllum* and *L. regale* in attempts to obtain yellow trumpet lilies. In time, desirable sulphur- to canary-yellow selections seem assured. Light shade in warm sections retains the delicate coloring.

Shelburne Pink Hybrids. Fred Abbey of Shelburne, Vermont, has carefully intensified the pink flushes seen in many of the regals. His race, notable for pink trumpets of pleasing, varied tints, is easily grown.

Mid-Century Hybrids. This is Jan de Graaff's much publicized group, raised mainly from *L. tigrinum* and *L. hollandicum* crosses. Remarkably simple to grow, seldom over 3½ feet tall, they bloom in late June and July. Erect, up-facing flowers blend with out-facing types, often in orange, red, or tawny yellow. Softer yellows also occur in this bold race, with pastel shades to be expected one day.

Aurelian Hybrids. In these, *L. henryi* has been crossed to some of the species with trumpet-like flowers. The habit and height, as well as the manner in which the flowers are borne on the stem, resemble *L. henryi,* with larger blooms of varying shape common. Colors ranging from yellow to orange or apricot, in August, are best in light shade.

Havemeyer Hybrids. Pale cream-ivory, lemon and burnt-orange-yellow colorings predominate in the crosses between *L. henryi* and *L. myriophyllum.* Plants 5 to 6 feet tall are to be expected. Again, light shade from the noon sun is helpful.

Olympic Hybrids. Here several trumpet-flowered types have been interbred, chiefly to *L. leucanthum* var. *centifolium,* resulting in crisp flowers that are quite large, with intriguing ruffling prominent.

Gradually yellow and pink shadings are being introduced. Segregated pink selections need a little shade to hold their color in warm inland areas.

Sunburst Lilies. This promising strain, developed by crossing the Olympic hybrids with *L. henryi,* comprises tall plants with large recurving flowers of orange and yellow.

Pfeiffer Hybrids. Dr. Norma Pfeiffer of Yonkers, New York, is responsible for these crosses between *L. auratum,* the pink *L. rubellum,* and *L. japonicum.* All manner of intermediate forms, covering a wide range of flower type, size, coloring, and habit have cropped up, but these are still in the trial stage. Further refinements and selections promise to be of considerable interest.

'Jillian Wallace' (*L. auratum* × *L. speciosum* 'Rubrum'). At present, this Australian import is the loveliest red lily, a brilliant 10-inch crimson jewel, somewhat reflexed.

Final Comment: No hardy plant has advanced so far as has the lily in recent years, with the end far from evident. Those particularly interested in the genus should make it a point to visit the annual flower show of the North American Lily Society whenever possible, to see prize specimens, as well as new hybrids.

LIMONIUM Sea-Lavender, Hardy Statice Plumbaginaceæ

No better subject exists for relieving the monotony of late summer gardens, and only gypsophilas equal its airy effect in the garden. *Statice* is a botanical name often erroneously applied to this genus. The 180 species are widely distributed around the world, and include the annuals grown in gardens and by florists under the common name statice.

Garden Value: Dwarf species enliven rock gardens; the taller ones are appropriate in borders. A profusion of tiny blossoms are carried on tremendous panicles that vary from 2½ to 4 feet in height. Foliage, in basal rosettes, is leathery and partially evergreen. These patricians, like babys-breath, are airy masses that lighten effects made by coarser material, and tone down stiff forms or gaudy colors. The sprays may be cut and effectively used either fresh or dried for winter arrangements.

Soil and Exposure: Plants thrive indefinitely in light sandy loam in full sun. Heavy soils may lead to weak stems that require staking.

Care: Planting is possible in early spring or fall, in holes large enough to accommodate the surprisingly long roots. At least 18-inch distances from other plants are required for the large panicles of flowers to be effective. Plants do not assume their true majestic beauty until well established, so it is not a good idea to move them often. Side-dressings of compost and light commercial fertilizer annually are the only attention needed.

Propagation: Seeds sown when soils are cool in early spring or late fall are the accepted method, with three or four years needed to obtain a flowering-sized plant. Division is possible in very early spring. Root cuttings, sown erectly, are possible, but not too successful.

Species

L. bellidifolium. Stems 8 to 12 inches high form trusses of lilac flowers in late July and August.

L. gmelinii. Named for an eighteenth century German botanist, but native around the Caspian Sea, it is essentially a shorter *L. latifolium* as far as garden effect goes. The smaller clusters, under 2 feet in height, are lavender-blue.

L. latifolium. From July through August, this outstanding perennial bears great misty panicles of bright mauve-lavender flowers on stems to 2½ feet high. In time, each clump may have a dozen sprays making a spectacular yard-wide canopy. This species overshadows the rest of the genus, for it is one of the finest and hardiest of all perennials.

L. minimum. A rock garden gem from which stems 3 or 4 inches high produce clusters of flowers with white calyces and reddish lilac corollas. Glistening gray-green foliage is also decorative.

L. tataricum var. *angustifolium* (*L. dumosum*). At a height of

20 inches, this is a billowy mass of silvery gray-lavender in August and September. *L. tataricum* 'Nanum' is a diminutive 9-inch form, with fluffy pinkish flowers in late summer, that is preferable to the species.

Final Comment: Most borders would benefit from the lasting, stabilizing sea-lavenders if sufficient time were allowed for the plants to prove themselves.

LINUM Flax Linaceæ

Though of no use as cut flowers, the linums serve well in the garden because of the abundance of delicate blue or yellow they provide during much of the summer. Many species abound on warm Mediterranean hillsides, a point to remember in their culture. *Linum* is derived from *linon,* the classical term for flax and the root of linen, for flax was a recognized clothing fiber from ancient times. *L. usitatissimum* is the common flax, noted both for its fiber and for the seeds which are the source of linseed oil.

Garden Value: Primarily for rock gardens or foregrounds of borders, the linums are noted for a long season of bloom. Although individual flowers may last but one day, they are produced in such profusion that the plants are unfailingly colorful. Their delicate texture is another attribute not to be overlooked.

Soil and Exposure: A light, well-drained soil and full sun are ideal.

Care: Spring-planting is advisable. In areas where plants tend to die out over winter, a light winter mulch may prove helpful. However, self-sown seeds usually insure perpetuation of garden forms.

Propagation: Seeds germinate readily; when sown in spring, the resulting plants will not flower until the following year.

Species

L. alpinum. For rock gardens, it looks like a miniature edition of *L. perenne,* the common blue flax.

Limonium latifolium
Linum flavum

Linum perenne
Lobelia cardinalis

L. capitatum. When fully established, this glistening 18-inch mass of golden flowers is striking in early summer. Reliably hardy.

L. flavum, Yellow Flax. Compact plants, about 18 inches in height, are covered with golden yellow flowers from late June to mid-August. Foliage is greener than that of the blue flax. 'Cloth of Gold,' a 9-inch dwarf, makes a bright summer spot in the rock garden.

L. narbonense. In effect a more robust plant with larger flowers than *L. perenne.* Plants reach a maximum of 2 feet in height, and the azure flowers with a white eye measure 1 inch across.

L. perenne, Common Blue Flax. This is probably the species most often encountered. Graceful, arching 2-foot stems bear many sky-blue flowers from June through August. 'Album' is a white-flowered counterpart.

L. salsoloides and the form 'Nanum' are trailing plants from the Alps that may not persist too long. White flowers with blue veins occasionally vary to light pink.

Two European favorites, *L. iberidifolium* and 'Gremmel's Hybrid' (*L. iberidifolium* × *L. flavum*), both of which have very large yellow flowers, are still unknown in America.

LOBELIA — Lobelia — Lobeliaceæ

Several of the 250 widely distributed species are found in eastern United States, where they are well known to collectors of wild flowers. The name *Lobelia* was given to this genus by Linnæus in honor of Matthias de Lobel, a noted Belgian botanist of the sixteenth century.

Garden Value: When well established, lobelias provide colorful spots in August gardens. Perhaps their greatest attributes are the colors—scarlet-red and blue—and the fact that they do well in shade. Many favor them because they attract hummingbirds. As cut flowers they are satisfactory if the stems are seared.

Soil and Exposure: Moist but well-drained sandy loam is best. Shade is preferable but not absolutely necessary. In the wild they are often found in large colonies along streams or in damp meadows.

Care: Young divisions may be purchased in early spring and set at 12-inch spacings. After the flowering stalk dies out in early fall, the cluster of new basal growth should be divided and reset. A light covering over winter may be wise. If self-sowing does not occur naturally, garden colonies do not persist in the average border.

Propagation: Seeds germinate easily when sown in midspring. As mentioned above, basal shoots may be reset in fall to increase the number of plants, as well as to insure survival of some for the next year.

Species

L. cardinalis, Cardinal Flower. Found in damp terrain all along eastern America, it attains a height of 3 to 4 feet, and blossoms with a dramatic flare from late July until early September. The scarlet-red flowers create a vivid splash of color in the shade, where the erect spikes may be vertical accent points.

L. siphilitica, Great Blue Lobelia. Somewhat more weedy than the one above, the leaves are rather coarse, the height 2 or 3 feet, and the flowers a deep blue. The same conditions, treatment, and drawbacks noted for the cardinal flower are largely duplicated here.

Final Comment: Because the lobelias self-sow, they may move around in the garden. Hence, it is wise to be familiar with the young foliage so that plants are not weeded out in the spring.

LUPINUS Lupine Leguminosæ

Where lupines thrive, the columnar racemes of dazzling colors are unequaled during June, but they can cause untold chagrin to hopeful gardeners in areas where the plants sulk and finally succumb to hot summers. To have a stately profusion of flowers highlighting a perennial border is a real challenge.

The scientific name comes from *lupo,* Latin for wolf, an allusion to ancient legend that claimed the plants despoiled soil fertility. However, today some of the species are actually used for building up exhausted ground, and for fodder. Moreover, as a member of the legume family, the lupine utilizes nitrogen from the air, storing it in root nodules. This fact enters into the culture, especially in regard to fertilization.

There are 300 species, largely confined to North America, but also found in Europe and Africa. As for garden forms, England's modern Russell Hybrids have largely superseded all other types.

Garden Value: Small groups of three or four are most effective; overplanting will leave great gaps in the border after the relatively short flowering season. Nevertheless, the digitately compound foliage creates a pleasant contrast with other material in the garden. The racemes of pealike flowers, magnificent for cutting, cover an extremely wide range of colors, bicolored flowers predominating.

Soil and Exposure: Lupines thrive in cool areas with high humidity, as in the Pacific Northwest, parts of northern New England, and in Great Britain, where most of the recent advances have been made. However, hot days inland can exact a toll that results in poor plants and sad flower stems with many skips in a raceme where flowers failed to develop. A light, well-drained soil near the neutral point, low in nitrogen but high in phosphorus, and containing small amounts of leafmold or compost is desirable. Either sun or light shade will suffice.

Care: Planting may be carried out in early spring or fall, at 18-inch intervals. Seed pods should be removed, and when stems are cut, all possible foliage should be left on the plant. During dry periods, occasional watering is helpful. Light winter protection is good insurance where winters are severe. If the large California aphid is troublesome, rotenone or malathion will be effective.

Propagation: Seeds, which if hand pollinated may be expensive, are best sown after ripening in late summer, with transplanting left until early spring. Division of large clumps is possible in early spring. Stem cuttings of hardened side growths in late spring are sometimes made commercially, but special attention is required.

Species

L. cytisoides, Canyon Lupine. This California native, which has naturalized itself in parts of New York, should interest the patient breeder. Admittedly the 4-foot plants with pink-lavender flowers are not to be compared with the Russell lupines, but the general ease of culture and hardiness might well be bred into the Russell strain.

L. polyphyllus. Unquestionably this 3- to 5-foot West Coast native is the basis of all superior garden offerings. Originally purple and blue, horticultural variants have now greatly increased the color range. Yellow evidently entered by way of the Kelway Hybrids of *L. arboreus,* the tree lupine. At the present time such earlier strains as Downers and Moerheim have yielded to the more exciting Russell Hybrids. *L.* × *regalis* is the name given to these hybrid strains.

George Russell of York, England, was a humble working gardener, who, in 1911, at the age of 60 was stirred by the common blue and white lupine, and decided to try to improve it. Collecting all known forms in England, and procuring seeds of diverse species from elsewhere, he began to build his master race.

By 1925 his seedlings were renowned; he refused as much as $250 for a thimbleful of seed. All offers were turned down until the firm of Baker persuaded him to grant them dissemination rights. Immediately his fame spread over the gardening world, and all existing strains became less important.

Since Russell kept no records, the exact parentage of his group is not certain. Experts believe such annuals as *L. lepidus, L. laxiflorus, L. nootkatensis, L. mutabilis,* and *L. leucophyllus* all added distinctive traits. Large flowers with full keels and broad standards completely encircle the stem. Just about every color, shading, and combination thereof is to be found. In cool, moist areas their popularity is tremendous, and in the British Isles scores of named cultivars are raised by means of vegetative propagation. Even in Vermont, they have been known to stray into nearby fields by self-sowing. Unfortunately, in the Russell strain, no added sturdiness or heat resistance is discernible.

Final Comment: Where the climate is ideal for lupines, they will be a most decided asset to any plantings; elsewhere, they may be a disappointing shadow of their possible perfection.

LYCHNIS **Campion, Maltese Cross, German Catchfly** **Caryophyllaceæ**

The name of the genus is from the Greek, meaning lamp, in recognition of the fiery red of the flowers of some species. Today, occasional catalogs list campions erroneously as *Agrostemma;* certain species are even distributed as *Silene.* The various species are indigenous to north temperate and arctic zones.

Garden Value: Gardeners satisfied with merely a bright display of color, plus comparatively restrained stature, may be smitten with the lychnis. However, shortcomings include a brief span of life and rather harsh coloring. Small groups add brilliance to the border, primarily in July.

Soil and Exposure: Very light and very well-drained soil is imperative; wet winters can be fatal. Full exposure to the sun is recommended.

Care: Several transplant well only if potted, or as young field-grown plants moved in early spring. Self-sowing of some species must be kept under control by elimination of seedlings that are crowded or that extend beyond their range. Some gardeners prefer to sow a few seeds in the fall as insurance against possible winter casualties.

Propagation: Seeds are relied upon for all except the double-flowered types. Division should be made every third year of those that may develop large crowns, such as *L. alpina* and *L. viscaria.*

Species

L. alpina. From arctic and alpine regions, it has the low habit to be expected. Its 10-inch growth and persistent tenacity redeem it for rock gardens. From dense rosettes of foliage, stems with pink or white flowers appear in June and until late July.

L. chalcedonica, Maltese Cross. Brought to England from Russia in 1593, it was later established by homesick American pioneer women in plantings along the westward trail; hence, it prevails over much of this country. Vermilion-scarlet flowers are aggregated into dense heads on stems about 3 feet tall, mainly in June and July. Removal of faded flower heads induces continued flowering. The form known as 'Salmonea' is an unusual pastel salmon. The white variants are not particularly interesting.

L. coronaria (*Agrostemma coronaria*). The ancient rose campion, dusty miller, or mullein-pink of England often behaves as a biennial, but perpetuates itself by volunteer seedlings. Gerard's *Herbal* found it "growing plentifully in most gardens" even in 1597. Deep crimson flowers on 2-foot stems contrast with the silvery gray foliage; white and bicolor forms are also available. Flowering is spasmodic from June to the end of August.

L. flos-jovis, Flower of Jove. From southern European mountains, this is a fully presentable, well behaved 18-inch plant with gray foliage and attractive pink to carmine clusters of flowers.

L. × *haageana* (*L. fulgens* × *L. coronata* var. *sieboldii*). In spite of its hybrid origin, seeds reproduce the plant quite true to form. Less than a foot in height, it becomes a mass of orange-scarlet in early summer. With winter protection survival is possible in northern gardens. A hybrid of this with *L. chalcedonica*, known as 'Arkwrightii,' frequently listed as a *Silene*, was raised in 1912 by J. S. Arkwright of Prestleigh, England. It often behaves as a biennial, but to its credit must be mentioned the large scarlet flowers of midsummer, developing from compact 12-inch plants.

L. viscaria, German Catchfly. Hardy tufts of grasslike foliage give rise to 18-inch stems with red-purple clusters, mostly in late May and June. Better known is the form 'Splendens,' a rose-pink variant found in alpine meadows of Europe. 'Zulu' is not as deep a red as the name might indicate. 'Splendens Flore-Pleno' is a double form that has become popular; clusters of magenta flowers either appall or enthrall—no indecision is possible.

Final Comment: While glaring colors and transient behavior typify the bulk of the genus, *L. viscaria* might furnish the hybridizer with a source of hardiness to be combined with the flamboyance of other species in the production of worthy strains.

LYSIMACHIA Loosestrife Primulaceæ

Ease of culture and general adaptability to almost any situation are the probable reasons for the popularity of these undemanding loosestrifes. About 100 species inhabit diverse sections of the temperate and subtropical regions, frequently in bogs and damp terrain. The genus may have been named for King Lysimachus of old, or the name may be directly translated from the Greek as loosestrife, with the implication of peacemaking. Pliny stated that branches laid on the shoulders of quarreling, yoked oxen caused "instantaneous and perfect reconciliation." He further considered the genus able to dye hair yellow, while Gerard averred that smoke created by its burning drove away serpents. Culpeper praised the ability to stem the flow from bleeding wounds. Whatever their early use, today the lysimachias make good hardy garden perennials.

Garden Value: Small groups established at 15-inch intervals add summer interest to borders that are not too rigidly formal. Several lend themselves to naturalizing in sparse, moist woodlands or in partial shade. Some have cutting value, and one, *L. nummularia*, is a possible ground cover. The commonly grown species may be somewhat invasive unless controlled.

Soil and Exposure: In general, soils of moist, fairly rich make-up are preferable, but not always required if in partial shade. None will thrive in parched, baked soil.

Care: Spring-planting is favored. Occasional division or reduction in size of clump is the only attention needed.

Propagation: Divisions are usually adequate, but seeds sown in spring are also quite productive.

Species

L. clethroides, Gooseneck Loosestrife. Interesting indeed, in gardens or when cut, are the July and August spikes of white flowers, curiously bent into gooseneck form. Originally from China and Japan, the plant is largely confined to old-fashioned American gardens or to rural areas where space is not a problem. Height when in

Lupinus polyphyllus

Lysimachia clethroides

Lychnis coronaria

Lychnis chalcedonica

Lysimachia punctata

full flower is about 3 feet. Plants are of some value in the fall, when foliage oftens turns a bronzy yellow. Ornamental in the average semishaded border, it may spread rapidly.

L. nummularia, Moneywort, Creeping Jenny. With vinca and pachysandra, this could be one of the best ground covers for the shade, if it were not for its weedy tendency. It will even tolerate considerable sunlight in heavy soil. On a wall, where naturally restrained, it can be most effective, with many small flowers of bright yellow from June to August. It has been used to advantage under apple trees to cushion fallen fruit, and will bring a bright spot to darkened corners anywhere that its invasive habit is not objectionable. Caution: creeping stems can be a nuisance in lawns.

L. punctata, Yellow Loosestrife. This import from Europe has naturalized itself to a certain extent in some of the eastern states. Rather rigid, sturdy 3-foot plants have axillary whorls of yellow flowers for most of their length in June and early July. In heavily composted soils, full sun is tolerated, but some shade is customary.

L. vulgaris. Somewhat imaginatively dubbed golden phlox on occasion, it has terminal panicles of butter-yellow flowers. It does not do as well in sunny locations as *L. punctata.*

Final Comment: Breeders might evolve worth-while new material from other species in the genus. Some rare sorts, as the crimson-spiked *L. leschenaultii* and the yellow pigmy, *L. pseudo-henryi,* might be potential sources of added interest or variety.

LYTHRUM — Purple Loosestrife — Lythraceæ

Recent cultivars are annually increasing the prestige of the lythrums; finer selections are infinitely better than the wild, swamp natives that are primarily rosy magenta weeds. *Lythrum,* from blood or gore in Greek, refers to the underlying flower color. Most of the species inhabit the northern hemisphere; several are heavily naturalized in the eastern states.

Garden Value: Today's improvements are excellent border plants averaging 3 feet in height, with individual flowers about ¾ inch across, forming dense terminal spikes throughout July and August.

Perhaps to be ruled out for strictly formal plantings, the superior forms are welcome in most gardens for their long season of bloom and possible cutting virtues. Single specimens are attractive, but groups of three at 2-foot intervals provide colorful masses. All are excellent for naturalizing along streams or in difficult, soggy terrain.

Soil and Exposure: Even the better selections are equally content in poor, sunny ground or in rich, shaded locations, a fact not wholly appreciated by amateurs. These plants answer the puzzling problem presented by wet, shaded situations.

Care: Save for the possible removal of faded blooms or seed pods, little attention is needed. Few plants are as self-sufficient or as hardy over a period of years.

Propagation: Since seedlings exhibit some variation, division in spring of named cultivars is customary, although softwood cuttings root easily in summer.

Species

L. salicaria, Purple Loosestrife. Shakespeare knew this plant as "long purples," and Hamlet's mother wove it into garlands. Naturalized in Australia as well as in American swamps, it can grow to 6 feet in cultivated gardens with good soil. Predominantly rosy purple, and spreading rapidly, it is best in naturalized plantings.

The variety *roseum superbum* has larger, brighter carmine-rose flowers, a somewhat tidier habit, and more persistent bloom; several named cultivars apparently stem from this form.

L. virgatum, Wand Loosestrife. From Europe and Asia, this is now occasionally naturalized in Massachusetts. The 3-foot plant is quite attractive, if seldom cultivated, with purple flowers on branched, twiggy racemes.

Cultivars

'Morden Pink' is a reputed bud sport of *L. virgatum* that originated at the Dominion Experiment Station in Morden, Manitoba. A truly first-class plant, it produces trim spikes of rose-pink flowers almost all summer. Although sterile, so producing no seeds, clumps increase rapidly. Tolerant of wetness and drought alike, the comparatively restrained 3-foot plants are good subjects for the average border.

'Morden Gleam' gives much promise, even as a cut flower, as a leading, so-called red. Deep carmine flowers and ruddy rhubarb-colored juvenile foliage always attract attention.

Other cultivars include: 'Morden Rose,' a very recent deep rose-pink of sparkling effect; 'Dropmore Purple,' whose popularity is hindered by varying color, purple in cool areas to muddy dark pink in hot situations; 'Robert,' an outstanding rose-red dwarf, only 2 feet high, but not too floriferous; 'Brightness,' brilliant rose-pink, with dark foliage, 3 feet; and 'The Beacon,' weedy, fading red, now secondary to 'Morden Gleam.'

Final Comment: Occasionally, white and true red variants have been reported, but evidently not exploited. Several species unavailable commercially may have breeding potential, particularly for dwarfness.

MACLEAYA (*Bocconia*) Plume-Poppy Papaveraceæ

Catalogs still list this plant under the invalid name *Bocconia.* There are only two species, native to Japan and China, with but one, *M. cordata,* of garden importance. The scientific name honors Alexander Macleay, a British colonial secretary in the early nineteenth century.

The elegantly shaped leaves of the plume-poppy are most impressive, and are vaguely reminiscent of fig leaves. Light green on the upper surface and gray-white on the underside, they exhibit this interesting contrast in a light breeze. Erect, elongated panicles of small buff to cream-pink flowers appear in July and August. While the foliage may be a bit on the bold side, the plumelike effect of the flowers is quite delicate. Even without flowers, the foliage alone would be sufficient reason to use this species in proper settings.

Because of the 6 to 8 feet heights expected, and the fact that plants can spread to a sizable mass, the rear of a border is the appropriate site. As a tall, robust specimen, it warrants consideration for the larger garden, although among shrubbery or spotted in semiwild landscapes, it seems more conspicuous.

Only full sun and soil of average fertility can be recommended, for the definite tendency is to spread at redoubled rates in rich soil or in shade. In open exposures, some protection from the wind is an advantage. Spring planting is favored. No further attention is needed, other than to reduce the size of large clumps every three or four years. Division in spring gives adequate increase, as do seeds sown in spring.

MERTENSIA Bluebells Boraginaceæ

This genus, named for Franz Mertens, a German botantist, is one of the relatively few in which the flowers are a true blue. In general, the species favor cooler portions of the northern hemisphere, particularly in North America. No man-made hybrids, and only a few natural variants, are on record.

Garden Value: Unassuming, yet often inimitably engaging, the bluebells tend to be of semidwarf proportions. Thus, various nooks and crannies in the rock garden, border, or along foundation plantings are possible settings. A few will readily colonize.

Soil and Exposure: Cool, moist, shaded areas where the soil has adequate leafmold are best for most species.

Care: Many break dormancy so early in the year that spring planting is reliable only if potted plants are used. Dormant roots, set in the garden from August to October, are not at all reassuring in appearance, but seldom fail to survive. Plants are set 1 inch deep for permanence. The foliage of some species, particularly *M. virginica,* dies down in midsummer, necessitating care in cultivation. This tendency must also be considered in gardens where sizable plantings would leave obvious voids in midseason.

Propagation: Seeds may be sown in spring or fall. Division is restricted to early autumn. Root cuttings from 2-inch sections are often set shallowly in early fall and protected over winter. In very early spring they may be planted in permanent locations.

Species

M. ciliata. The mountain bluebell is native from Montana and Oregon to New Mexico. The 2-foot stems carry shining blue flowers well into the summer. Glaucous leaves of considerable size are not shed after blossoming if the soil is adequately moist.

M. lanceolata, Prairie Bluebell. This species, about 10 inches high, withstands drought and neglect. Sky-blue flowers open in April and May.

M. longiflora. Found in the wild from Montana and British Columbia to Northern California, plants vary from 4 to 12 inches in height. They are classed as exquisite dwarfs with bell-shaped blossoms that form blue clusters during April and May. The pale green leaves sometimes disappear in summer, especially in dry, sunny locations.

M. oblongifolia. A Rocky Mountain dwarf about 8 inches tall, this needs shade and fertile, rather acid soil. Narrow pale green foliage and nodding blue flowers are prominent in early spring.

M. paniculata. This species, native from Quebec to Alaska and south to Washington, is also very much at home around Lake Superior. Coral red buds develop into blue flowers on sturdy stems that are 3 feet tall in dry areas, but may reach 5 feet in wet seasons. The rugged, dark green leaves linger all season. In the Chicago parks it is used as a ground cover in the shade of large trees; it deserves added distribution for such problem spots where rainfall is not excessive.

M. virginica, Virginia Bluebells. These dwell along rivers and in bogs from New York to Alabama, often covering large areas. Arching clusters of funnel-shaped, clear blue bells harmonize with bright pink buds on stems not over 2 feet tall. Bloom is very early, a cheery note of a new spring. By June, all foliage may die back until the next year; hence, it is best planted among primroses, hostas, vinca, and others with spreading summer foliage, so that voids will not be obvious later in the season. Partial shade in rich mellow soil is preferable, but sun is not detrimental if plants have adequate moisture during the summer.

'Alba,' a rare white treasure which is very slow to increase, is of fragile pure beauty. In all probability, it will remain a connoisseur's pet. Random pink forms have not propagated true to type; the coloring may be caused by soil conditions.

Final Comment: If for no other reason than as a symbol of spring, the bluebells should be popular. It should be noted that they can rarely, if ever, be successfully transplanted from the wild when in flower.

MONARDA Beebalm, Bergamot Labiatæ

The common wild beebalm makes an acceptable garden plant but, as with so many other genera, the modern, improved cultivars are far superior. The genus was named for Nicolás Monardes, a Spanish physician and botanist of the sixteenth century. All of the species are indigenous to North America, but only two are of garden merit. As usual, practically all improvements have originated in Europe.

Garden Value: For bold groups or for naturalizing, especially along streams, *M. didyma* is a wise choice. The vivid red flower heads may also be striking accents among evergreens or against a shrub border. The better selections and hybrids with *M. fistulosa* are well advised in borders at 2-foot intervals. Combinations can be effected with anthemis, heliopsis, phlox, and delphinium. The 3-foot stems produce terminal flowers, and later, secondary side shoots which extend the blooming season from June to August. A pungent, aromatic quality pervades both leaf and flower. In spite of the hollow stems, they are splendid cut flowers.

Soil and Exposure: The species naturally inhabit areas of shaded, moist, fairly rich ground, but modern cultivars prosper in full sun if given adequate moisture.

Care: Beebalms form mats of shallow roots, and may spread rapidly. Thus, division every three or four years, and resetting in newly prepared soil becomes imperative. Moving is perfectly safe at almost any time during the growing season if proper care is used. Neglected plants in gardens take revenge by degenerating into irregular thickets of gaunt, bean-pole effect.

Propagation: Division in spring or late summer is recommended for cultivars. Seeds of unselected types germinate well in spring.

Species

M. didyma. This is sometimes known as Oswego tea because John Bartram found early settlers near Oswego, New York, steeping the leaves to make a tea. Bees are attracted by the fragrance, hence the common name, beebalm. From Quebec and Michigan south to Georgia, it inhabits moist woodlands and river banks. In 1752 John Collinson introduced it to England, where it held strong favor until the late nineteenth century. Then William Robinson, a noted writer of the day, praised it so highly for naturalizing that gardeners began to fear it as merely a gaily colored weed.

Shades of red predominate in the wild; the old Indian name of O-gee-chee meant fiery flower. Variants in pink, violet, purple, salmon, and white are common.

M. fistulosa. No beauty itself but an important parent of recent cultivars, the 3- to 4-foot bergamot has a natural range that extends farther south and west than that of *M. didyma.* Smaller, less decorative flowers are usually purple but may vary from crimson to lilac. Significant is the ability to settle in bleak sandy banks or on sawdust piles, for it implies tolerance toward privation. It has contributed its adaptability and tolerance of the full sun to many of today's offerings.

Leading Cultivars

Among them are: 'Cambridge Scarlet,' with very effective heads of blazing scarlet; 'Croftway Pink,' a clear rose-pink, of sturdy habit; 'Granite Pink,' a very recent introduction from the University

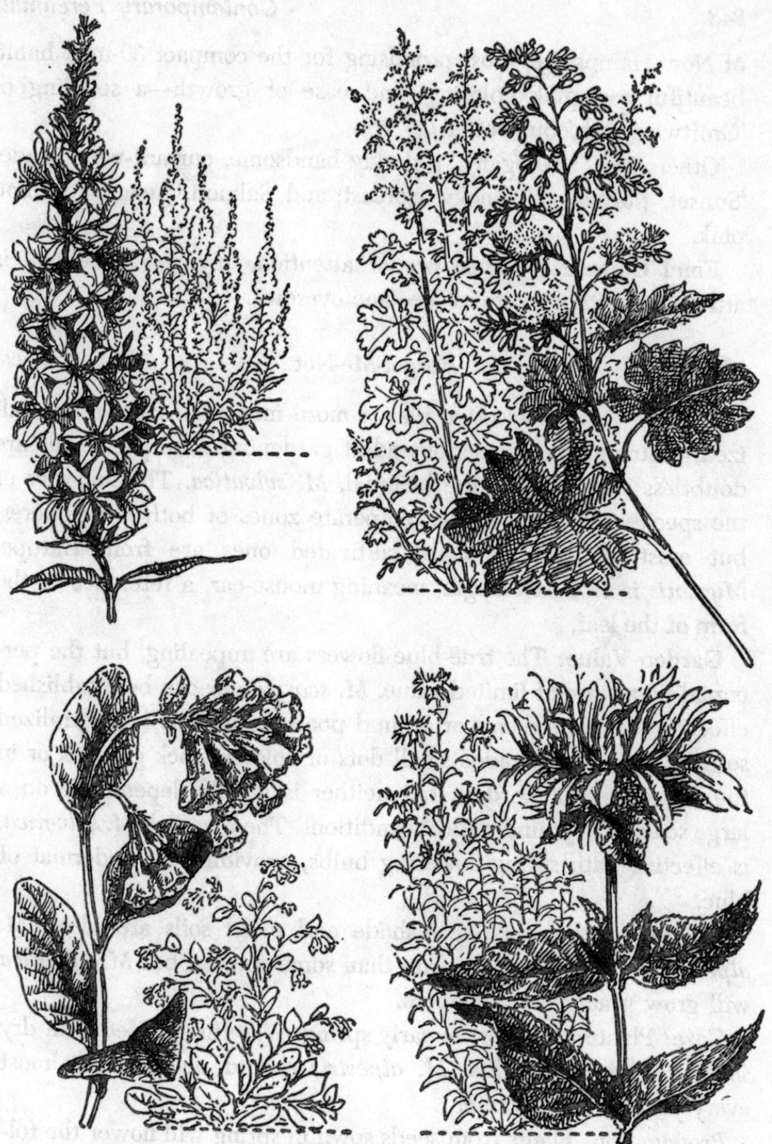

Lythrum salicaria
Mertensia virginica

Macleaya cordata
Monarda didyma

of New Hampshire, most promising for the compact 30-inch habit, beautiful rose-pink coloring, and ease of growth—a seedling of 'Croftway Pink,' but better.

Others are: 'Mahogany,' a darkly handsome, currant-wine shade; 'Sunset,' purple with smoky overcast; and 'Salmon Queen,' a salmon pink.

Final Comment: Given proper attention, any good beebalm is attractive; without care all become eyesores.

MYOSOTIS — Forget-Me-Not — Boraginaceæ

The forget-me-nots often play a more important role in naturalized treatment than in serious adult gardening. The perennials are doubtless secondary to the biennial, *M. sylvatica*. The majority of the species are found in the temperate zones of both hemispheres, but most of the commonly cultivated ones are from Europe. *Myosotis* is of Greek origin, meaning mouse-ear, a reference to the form of the leaf.

Garden Value: The true-blue flowers are appealing, but the perennial plants are of limited value. *M. scorpioides* can be established effectively along streams or around pools, as well as in naturalized settings. *M. alpestris* adds small dots of color to rock gardens or in the foreground of borders, but neither is wholly dependable on a large scale, except under ideal conditions. The biennial, *M. sylvatica*, is effective with spring-flowering bulbs, providing an undermat of blue.

Soil and Exposure: Some shade and moist soils are ideal. *M. alpestris* is more tolerant of sun than some species, but *M. sylvatica* will grow practically anywhere.

Care: Planting is safest in early spring. Watering is needed in dry soils or during droughts. *M. alpestris* should be divided almost every year, in late summer.

Propagation: Plants from seeds sown in spring will flower the following year. Division in late summer is by far the best method, although cuttings root easily in summer.

Species

M. alpestris. The true species comes from the arctic regions of Europe and North America. It grows in dense tufts not over 8 inches tall, and is in full bloom from May until September. It will fail in prolonged drought, in spite of the fact that it is accustomed to drier soils. Usually a light blue, there are several variants in the trade. 'Ruth Fisher' has dark foliage and azure flowers, while 'Pink Beauty' is a shell pink. Regular division is required. Gardeners are cautioned that much of the material in the trade listed as *M. alpestris* is actually *M. sylvatica,* a biennial that self-sows so readily that once it is planted, it spreads and comes up every year, flowering in May. This is the common spring forget-me-not, mainly blue, but pink and white forms always appear from any packet of seeds.

M. scorpioides (*M. palustris*). The true forget-me-not of Europe and Asia, it is also known as scorpion-grass in England, as the twisted stems recall a scorpion's tail. Many escaped colonies are found in matted disarray along shaded American streams. In spring, sprawling stems 6 to 18 inches long bear loose racemes of little, bright blue flowers with yellow eyes. These blossoms have often been modeled by jewelers for turquoise work. Narrow oblong foliage is notably clean. The variety *semperflorens* is noted for its prolonged season of bloom, from May until frost. Stems are usually but 8 inches or so long.

Final Comment: Myosotis will perhaps impress those appreciative of a precious type of beauty, more than those who are discriminating gardeners.

NEPETA — Catmint — Labiatæ

Primarily cultivated for one outstanding species, *N.* × *faassenii,* this genus is noted for its pungent gray foliage. Of the 150 species, the majority come from the northern hemisphere. The name *Nepeta* is credited to Pliny, perhaps from Nepete, an Etrurian city. Catnip, of interest to herb gardeners or to those owning cats, is *N. cataria.*

Garden Value: Low-growing forms with gray foliage are striking in walls, edgings, rock gardens, or borders, mainly because of the foliage color. Other species often serve as ground covers. Small flowers, mainly blue or white, are effective in early summer.

Soil and Exposure: Well-drained, rather light soil is recommended. Sun or partial shade is suitable.

Care: Most may be planted in spring or fall, at distances dictated by individual growth characteristics. *N.* × *faassenii* should be pruned of at least one-third its foliage in summer. This encourages new basal shoots and a bushier habit. All species need division about each third year.

Propagation: Spring-sown seeds will be satisfactory for the species, but cuttings of selections and sterile hybrids should be made in midsummer. A poorly drained rooting medium quickly causes damping off. Divisions can be made in early spring or fall.

Species

N. × *faassenii* (*N. mussinii*). This hybrid is the result of a cross between *N. nepetella* and *N. mussinii* which is reported to have occurred spontaneously at the Copenhagen Botanic Gardens. It is sterile, hence plants do not ordinarily set seeds. Even though this hybrid was correctly named in 1939, scarcely a grower or amateur has dropped the outdated name of *N. mussinii.*

Twelve-inch stems carry attractive blue-violet flowers from late May until the end of July, but spikes often continue to bloom more or less until September. Small, toothed gray leaves are most pleasing, even if the aromatic qualities may leave something to be desired. The silvery foliage effect and blue flowers are suitable near anthemis, phlox, lilies, and delphiniums. Often used as an edging, this plant is far superior to the true *N. mussinii,* which is an inoffensive sprawling clump of gray-green foliage and blue flowers, having a much shorter blooming season than that of *N.* × *faassenii.*

N. nuda. Some promise is seen in this rarity from southern Europe, an erect type that may attain 3 feet. Leaves are larger than those of the other species mentioned, and are green. Floriferous panicles are either violet or white with purple spots.

Cultivars

'Blue Beauty' ('Souvenir d'André Chaudron' in Europe) is probably a hybrid referable to *N. grandiflora*. Stems 2 feet high produce rich blue flowers, airy in effect, that are fair for cutting in early summer.

'Six Hills Giant' is an English hybrid about 2 feet tall, with gray leaves, short branches, and fringed blossoms of light blue from June to August. Rampant habit outlaws it for purposes beyond a ground cover in the sun.

Final Comment: *N.* × *faassenii* is commendable, *N. nuda* has possibilities, but little solid value can be claimed for the rest of the genus.

ŒNOTHERA Evening-Primrose, Sundrop Onagraceæ

When buds on plants of this genus open at night, they are called evening-primroses; sundrop is applied to those species in which the flowers open during the day. *Œnothera* is reported to mean wine-scenting in Greek, although the plants to which reference is made are no longer known. Legend tells of the roots of certain species which were used as relishes with after-dinner wines. As presently constituted, the genus comprises at least 200 species. Most are from the north temperate zone, rarely from the tropics; some are native or have escaped in America. Annuals, biennials, perennials, and pestiferous weeds are all to be encountered.

Garden Value: A formidable array, a botanical welter, and a genus of much unspoiled charm—all describe this group in varying degrees. Some garden forms are trailing, others are 2 feet tall; the common flower color is yellow, although a few are white, and pink is rare. With the few exceptions noted, the perennials are best suited for naturalizing; the smaller types add summer color to spacious rock gardens. Moths, incidentally, are often attracted to the night-blooming species.

Soil and Exposure: Well-drained, light soil is essential, but some humus is helpful in areas where prolonged dry periods are common. Full sun is preferable.

Care: Planting is possible in fall or spring. Removal of seed pods extends the blooming period. Frequent division is a necessity.

Propagation: Seeds are plentiful on most species, and can be sown in fall or spring. Cuttings taken in late summer are customary for named cultivars. Division in early fall or spring prevents deterioration of perennial types.

Species

Œ. missouriensis, Ozark Sundrop. Native from Missouri and Kansas to Texas, it is reliable in the northeastern states. Astounding flowers of tissue-paper texture can swell to 5-inch cups of golden yellow over many weeks from June through August. Stems tend to trail, with ascending tips. Perhaps an occasional plant is permissible in the border or in the larger rock garden, for the sake of its light fragrance and very showy blossoms.

Œ. pilosella. Native in some of the North Central States, it is satisfactory in borders, where it grows about 2 feet in height with a mass of yellow blooms in June. It will spread rapidly but is easily controlled.

Œ. speciosa, Wind-Primrose. Found from Missouri south and west, it is usually 18 inches tall, with long narrow leaves. Fair-sized white flowers are the rule, but rose suffusions are also possible. The variety *childsii* (*Œ. rosea* var. *mexicana*) is not reliably hardy very far north; it comes from warmer Texas and Mexico. The 1½-inch flowers are a lovely shade of pink for many weeks. Rather prostrate branches measure only 6 to 12 inches in length. Often grown as a conservatory plant. In the border it repays winter attention.

Œ. tetragona (*Œ. fruticosa* var. *youngii*). Native from Nova Scotia to Georgia and Tennessee, local variants could conceivably differ in hardiness. Stems about 2 feet tall bear quantities of 1½-inch, lemon-yellow, cup-shaped flowers from June to August. Shiny foliage can be 4 inches long and fairly decorative. Usually plants are reliably perennial. 'Yellow River' is a garden selection of larger blooms and well-spaced stems.

Variety *fraseri,* from the southern Appalachians, is satisfactorily hardy. Slender red stems and buds blend well with butter-yellow flowers and rich leathery leaves. 'Illumination' ('Fyrverkeri' in Europe) is a horticultural selection that is an excellent choice for rockery or border. Fine yellow flowers abound on tough 12-inch plants.

Final Comment: The œnotheras, rarely specimen plants, might be called fillers, unassuming but always colorful when in flower.

PACHYSANDRA **Pachysandra, Japanese Spurge** **Buxaceæ**

Pachysandra, from the Greek for thick stamens, provides a valuable 8-inch-high ground cover that will grow in deep shade where few other plants thrive. Very short terminal spikes of insignificant white flowers appear in spring. Fruits like small white beads may follow in midsummer, but the primary value of the plant lies in the handsome foliage.

P. terminalis, from Japan, is the species commonly grown. Glossy, deep evergreen foliage and absolute hardiness account for its popularity. Nurserymen propagate it by the thousands, landscape architects use it on massive scales, and homeowners plant it where even grass is unsuccessful, as under trees. Average soil containing some humus is adequate. While shade is not absolutely necessary, full sun in hot summers may scald the foliage. A form known as variety *variegata* has white variegations on the leaves. This grows more slowly than the type, but is good in small patches or even in dish gardens.

P. procumbens, native from West Virginia to Florida and Louisiana, has gray-green leaves that are not completely evergreen. A slower spreading plant, it can be used in rock gardens, mainly for foliage effect.

Propagation is by cuttings or division. Small rooted cuttings may be set in spring at 6-inch intervals. Spreading by underground runners, plants will fill in an area nicely in time. Small rooted stems brought indoors late in the season and set in a bowl of water provide a refreshing novelty all winter.

Although usually trouble-free, plants may be attacked by euonymus scale, evidenced by small whitish encrustations on stems. Spraying with miscible oils in late winter and early spring, or later treatment with malathion are suggested.

With *Vinca minor*, pachysandra can be safely regarded as almost indispensable for covering shaded areas.

PÆONIA Peony Pæoniaceæ

Peonies were cultivated in China over 2,000 years ago; Marco Polo is said to have mentioned the size of peony flowers observed there to the skeptical Venetians of the thirteenth century. Most of the species are natives of Asia.

In the publication *The American Garden* of February, 1891, the following statement appeared: "The peony is no longer anything but a beautiful and splendid flower, despised by amateurs and seldom seen but in poor gardens." This quotation should discourage similar dogmatic statements on the part of gardeners, for today the hardiness, the comparative ease of culture, and the permanent nature of a peony planting combine to make this flower one of the most prized of perennials. Nearly all the species have decorative value.

The name honors Pæon, who is said to have been an ancient Greek physician. One old legend has it that Pluto gratefully changed Pæon into a flower to repay his successful treatments after Pluto's losing battle with Hercules.

The genus was included in the Ranunculaceæ, or buttercup family, until recently. Detailed studies on the anatomy, morphology, and cytology of the species have shown that it belongs in a family of its own.

Since both herbaceous and tree peonies enjoy widespread garden prominence, they will be discussed separately.

Herbaceous Peonies

Today's favorite cultivars stem largely from *P. lactiflora*, formerly known as *P. albiflora*. The original colors were pink and white, but red is now common, and yellow is being introduced by hybridizers. The American Peony Society recognizes five basic types: the single or Chinese, Japanese, anemone, semidouble, and double.

Garden Value: If not treated as a dominating specimen and allowed 2 or 3 feet of space between plants, a peony's true accent value is diminished. However, planted fairly near iris, poppies, coral bells, or in front of climbing roses, they afford elegant contrast. Some people are pleased by hedges exclusively of one cultivar, but others would decry such military precision.

Complete peony borders of the confirmed fancier need not be as rigid or confining as might be imagined. Spring-flowering bulbs can precede the main display, with interspersed annuals to supply summer bloom. Medium height dahlias interplanted would not be out of place. Finally, chrysanthemums in full bloom could be transplanted to available spots for a glorious autumn finale. For so ambitious a scheme, peonies would require 3- to 4-foot spacing.

Plants that may range from 2 to 4 feet in height will flower from May through June, depending upon the cultivar. In addition, the foliage is always a great asset, from the reddish young shoots of April through summer's lustrous green, to the crimson tints often seen in autumn.

As cut flowers, peonies are renowned, with vast acreage of the doubles commercially cultivated for this purpose. Flowers should be cut as the buds swell halfway open, and the stems quickly plunged into deep water. At least three full sets of leaves should be left on the plant to manufacture food for storage in the roots. When the buds just start to show color, the stems may be cut and

Myosotis scorpioides

Pæonia lactiflora
Japanese type

Œnothera tetragona

Nepeta faassenii

Pæonia tenuifolia

stored in containers without water in a cold refrigerator room, for use later in the summer.

Soil and Exposure: Plants so enduring should have a deep, rich soil that is well-drained. Manure should never actually touch the roots, but some form of humus is required in most soils. Success with peonies will be meager in poorly drained areas, as it would be for any fleshy rooted plant.

Sunny exposures are advisable although light shade prevents fading of delicately tinted individuals. If planted too near light-colored buildings, the radiating heat may result in precocious spring foliage that might occasionally be injured by late frosts.

Care: Planting of divisions with three to five eyes is best done during August or in early September. The eye is the reddish bud at the top of the tuberous roots; this should be set about 1 inch below the soil line. Peonies may take a while to become established in a new planting, so judgment should be reserved for three years. Annual side-dressings of fertilizers and some form of humus are beneficial in view of the fact that these plants do not have to be disturbed until deterioration is obvious. Twenty years of productive beauty is not an uncommon life span.

Botrytis and phytophthora blight may affect peonies. Shriveled buds that turn brown and never mature are the major symptoms. Regular treatment with a good fungicide or with Bordeaux spray will help in the control, but clean culture is essential. All wilting or rotting stems should be cut off at the soil line and burned to prevent overwintering of the disease. If affected plants are in the shade, they should be moved to an area that receives more sunlight, especially in the morning, so that the dew will evaporate quickly.

Common Peony Problems

1. Failure to bloom: Caused by too much shade, divisions that were too small, starvation or competition, excessively deep planting, blight, or a late spring freeze.

2. Weak stems: Some cultivars have inherently weak stems, espe-

cially in poor soils. Too much shade or a deficiency of phosphorus also might be the cause.

3. Collapsing stems: Spring droughts can be responsible, particularly in light soils. Because of the large flowers to be supported, watering may become a requirement. Extremely heavy, double-flowered types may require staking by means of a hoop supported on three stakes.

Propagation: Seeds take five to seven years to produce a flowering plant; hence, division is the usual method. In August or early September, a sharp knife is used to cut the heavy root mass into sections with three to five eyes. If the foliage is damaged or wilts, it is usually cut off at the ground level. Old, disintegrating roots may be cut back so that 6 inches or so remain on the section.

Breeders will find that the technique of culturing excised embryos on nutrient agar under aseptic conditions may shorten the time required to develop flowering plants from seed.

Hybridizers of Note

Many breeders, often purely amateur and too numerous to mention, are still very active. However, early pioneers like the Lemoines of France should not be slighted, for countless older cultivars are still highly satisfactory. In this country, Van Wert, Ohio has been dubbed the Peony City from the activities of Charles Wassenburg, a onetime haberdasher.

A. M. Brand, of Faribault, Minnesota, did no actual breeding, but annually raised several acres of seedlings from leading garden forms. He was responsible for several outstanding cultivars. Myrtle Gentry, his partner since 1918, has been honored by a gracious pink peony named for her.

The late Professor A. P. Saunders of Clinton, New York, a former member of the Hamilton College faculty, had neither space nor time for such grandiose procedures, but did hybridize with scientific thoroughness. He intercrossed hitherto neglected species, and is credited with introducing some excellent tree peonies.

Recommended Cultivars

Doubles: The stamens and sometimes the carpels are petaloid so that a fully double flower results.

White

'Festiva Maxima,' one of the oldest, is still wonderful for landscape effects, but crimson flecks modify its whiteness. 'Couronne d'Or' is a midseason white with yellow stamens evident. 'Le Cygne' has huge, milky, bomb-shaped flowers, prone to droop in poor soil. 'Baroness Schroeder' shows some flesh tints in its midseason bloom. 'Flower Girl' is a fine 2-foot dwarf with blush to white flowers, and 'Victory' is an outstanding new introduction.

Pink

'Milton Hill' is a shell pink; 'Raoul Dessert,' an erratic but beautiful shell pink; 'La France' is fantastically enormous; 'Albert Crousse,' a light rose. Other pinks include: 'Mons. Jules Elie,' a handsome silvery pink; 'Sarah Bernhardt,' an apple blossom pink; 'Mattie Lafuze,' very new, with blush tones; and 'Doris Cooper,' a light pink.

Red

Among the best are: 'Karl Rosenfeld,' the leading crimson cut flower; 'Richard Carvel,' intensely fragrant; 'Cherry Hill,' early, deep maroon, slow to develop its true majesty; 'Mons. Martin Cahuzac,' darkest garnet; 'Lowell Thomas,' a new, dramatically deep color, a fine grower; and 'King Midas,' novel, with yellow flashes at the petal tips.

Yellow

Two previously unavailable introductions were initially exhibited in 1954: 'Oriental Gold' and 'Clair de Lune.' Louis Smirnow of Sands Point, New York, had long tried to track down Japanese rumors of yellow forms, but with only vexation and expense for his pains. Finally, after repeated failures, he secured 'Oriental Gold' in 1951. Slightly fragrant, clear yellow 4- to 5-inch flowers, fully double, appear on 3-foot stems. The foliage is dark green without the customary red venation. The roots are yellow, not black or sooty as is common. Smirnow also has 'Knisui,' a yellow-rooted import still unflowered here. Widespread breeding is anticipated that will develop other new tints.

'Clair de Lune' is a hybrid created by Dr. Earle B. White, now of Daytona Beach, Florida. He made over 4,000 attempts to obtain a yellow peony, but not until 1939 did he get even a seed. 'Mons. Jules Elie' crossed with *P. mlokosewitschii,* a yellow-flowered species, contributed this one seedling able to reach maturity. It has pale creamy yellow flowers of 10 to 12 rounded, cup-shaped petals, highlighted by orange-yellow anthers. Under test, it reaches medium height.

Singles: The single or Chinese type, is characterized by one or more rows of petals surrounding a center of many yellow stamens that contain pollen. If one considers the doubles too gross, he may enjoy the daintier simplicity of the singles. They withstand drenching rains better than the heavy doubles, and are more adaptable in arrangements. Flowering is usually earlier than that of the doubles.

Relatively few cultivars are commonly listed today as compared to those once available. While the Japanese spoke of these as "Imperial peonies" they are now likely to be considered by some as only season-extending curiosities, in spite of their unquestioned beauty.

Leading white selections include: 'Pico,' 'Snowsprite,' 'Puritan Maid,' 'Cygnet,' and 'Opha.' Fine pinks are 'Champlain' and 'Dawn Pink.'

Japanese and anemones: The Japanese type is characterized by five or more large petals surrounding a center of stamens bearing abortive anthers, devoid of pollen. Filaments are thick and enlarged. The anemone peonies are similar, and are often included in catalogs with the Japanese group. The filaments of the stamens in the anemones have been transformed into narrow, incurved petal-like parts.

Many of these types are of matchless ornate symmetry, and deserve far greater popularity. Their behavior in the garden and their appearance in arrangements is beyond reproach.

Leading cultivars include 'Nippon Brilliant,' a magnificent red, and 'Mikado,' also red. 'Ama-no-sode' and 'Alstead' are stately pinks, while a more sedate white form of value is 'Fuji-no-mine.' 'Bowl of Beauty,' from Europe, is a Japanese type that may be a star of the future.

Species

P. anomala. This species will startle no one, but its May-flowering habit affords some interest. Single, bright crimson flowers, 3½ inches across, are borne on 2½-foot stems. The foliage is deeply divided. As a cut flower it combines nicely and lasts well.

P. mlokosewitschii. It is a pity that this yellow species of keen interest to hybridizers is burdened with such a name. From the Caucasus, it bears 4-inch, eight-petaled flowers of citron-yellow, followed by open seed pods with double rows of shiny black seeds interspersed with unfertilized ovules of scarlet. The foliage, blue-green above and paler on the underside, turns brown by September, restricting its effectiveness. Light shade seems best for this 2-foot oddity.

P. officinalis. This species is perhaps the one described by Pliny. It is of amazing longevity; in Oberlin, Ohio, a clump over 80 years of age still thrives and blooms each Memorial Day. The type grows to 2 or 3 feet, with single red flowers. Gradual variations have been noted, and at present, quite acceptable forms in white, pink, and red are cultivated as 'Alba,' 'Rosea,' and 'Rubra' respectively. The latter sometimes passes as the Memorial Day peony because of the fragrant early display of double flowers about the end of May.

P. tenuifolia, Fernleaf Peony. So-called because of the fine-textured, lacy foliage of fernlike delicacy, it seldom grows over

20 inches in height, swelling into rounded clumps over the years. Single and double forms, shaded dark crimson, flower in May. The double form, known as 'Flore-pleno' is far more showy than the type. It is an outstanding garden ornamental all season, for its flowers in May, and for its foliage later in the season.

P. wittmanniana. Actually cream-colored, this so-called yellow species could captivate the fancier. Essentially single blooms of medium size are formed on 2-foot stems. Glaucous leaves are handsome, but tend to deteriorate too early in autumn.

Tree Peonies

These noble aristocrats are actually deciduous shrubs that will grow to 6 feet in time, mature plants having from 25 to 100 flowers each May. Woody stems survive all but the harshest winters; success has been reported as far north as Keene, New Hampshire. For the most part, they are derived from *P. suffruticosa* (*P. moutan*), the ancient tree peony of China.

Almost worshipped in the China of 500 A.D., and jealously guarded against export, they nonetheless reached Japan by the eighth century, and England by 1787. An initial price of $400 for a single root was often levied even in those pre-inflation days. Thomas Oberlin and B. H. Farr pioneered in their introduction to America, where they remain comparatively expensive but increasingly appreciated.

Garden Value: Such regal plants are entitled to focal points in large perennial borders or among evergreen plantings. Furthermore, they become stately accents near steps or entrances, and often become intermediate specimens between herbaceous gardens and shrubbery.

Soil and Exposure: Requirements are similar to those of the herbaceous types. A windbreak may help prevent injury to larger specimens.

Care: Young plants are set 6 to 8 inches deep, in early fall. They are always grafted onto roots of the herbaceous type, and deep planting encourages the grafted portion to send out its own roots in time. During the first winter a protective cover of hay or leaves is advised. As with the herbaceous peonies, botrytis may develop. The San Jose scale is another possible pest, evidenced by starchy deposits along the stems. Winter sprays of miscible oils or lime sulfur, as well as malathion applied during the growing season, promise control.

Propagation: Seeds demand great patience. Grafting, the usual method, is a difficult procedure which is scarcely for amateurs. This accounts for the seemingly high prices of the plants. With the best of luck, there may be a high percentage of failures. Old established specimens can be lifted and divided in August; winter protection must follow.

Cultivars

European type: Very double, thickly petaled flowers and broad, leathery leaves. Some of the more popular cultivars are: white—'Lactea,' 'Bijou de Chusan'; pink—'Athlete,' 'Banksi'; salmon—'Reine Elizabeth,' 'Madame Stuart Low'; red—'Robert Fortune,' 'Osiris.'

Japanese type: Single to semidouble, often with crinkled petals and mounded cushion-like centers. Cultivars include: white—'Gesaekai,' 'Renkaku'; pink—'Beikoku,' 'Nira'; salmon—'Panama,' 'Miyo-no-Hikari'; red—'Nishiki-jishi,' 'Koukkoshi.' 'Kamada-Fuji' is wisteria-colored.

Lutea hybrids: *P. lutea,* from China, has some yellow strains which have been utilized by breeders. Lemoine crossed it to existing cultivars to widen the color range, but the gigantic flowers of many of his hybrids droop to some extent. Professor Saunders created a group of less pendulous habit with smaller, less doubled flowers. 'Argosy' is a clear yellow, 'Souvenir de Maxime Cornu' a yellow-streaked orange, and 'La Lorraine' a sulfur yellow.

Final Comment: Detailed studies could go to much greater lengths. Those particularly interested should join the American Peony Society. This organization maintained a rating of cultivars on the basis of 1 to 10, with 10 being a perfect specimen. Unfortunately, no recent evaluations have been issued for the newer cultivars.

PAPAVER **Poppy** **Papaveraceæ**

There is no reason for tolerating the common, second-rate, orange-scarlet Oriental poppies in contemporary gardens when so many modern improvements are available. *P. orientale* is the only perennial of true garden merit, although the genus contains several annuals that are commonly grown; all have a milky sap.

Papaver is the old Latin name for poppy. The common name is thought to be derived from *popig*, an Anglo-Saxon term for sleep. A drink made from the seeds of certain species was once prescribed to induce slumber. Early poets, including Robert Burns, always associated poppies with sleep. This may have been through association with the annual *P. somniferum*, the opium poppy of Greece and the Middle East.

Oriental Poppies

In the early eighteenth century, the raging red *P. orientale* reached England from Armenia, to be followed by *P. bracteatum* from Turkey a hundred years later. These interbred naturally to afford some variety, but seedlings stubbornly remained barbaric red. A writer of the early part of this century bemoaned the "burning cressets like signals of alarm" as spoiling all nearby refinement. Gradually sports began to appear; a salmon form sprang up in a Virginia yard, and a deep crimson enlivened the Boston garden of Francis Parkman, the famed historian.

Amos Perry, the late English plantsman, found 'Blush Queen,' the first light pink, around 1880 in a bed of seedlings. Not until 1906 was a really fine pink offered, under the name 'Mrs. Perry.' In 1912 a hitherto undreamed of white appeared as an unwanted volunteer in the London border of a Perry customer. The angry gardener, desirous of only scarlet poppies, was neither appeased by Perry's delight nor impressed by the pale color. Finally, however, a trade was effected for some montbretias.

'Perry's White' is thought to be a spontaneous hybrid with an annual species, for its life span, as with many whites to follow, is frequently short.

Ruys of Holland, Pfitzer in Germany, and Cayeux of France produced 'Mahony,' 'Wurtembergia,' and 'Watteau' respectively, all noteworthy cultivars still widely circulated. In America, Dr. John Neeley of Paulding, Ohio, was a zealous hybridizer until his death in 1934. 'Beauty of Livermore,' 'Lulu A. Neeley,' 'Echo,' 'Cavalier,' and 'Mary Jane Miller' are all Neeley prize-winners. John Siebenthaler, Karl Lorenz, the Sasses, Mrs. Thomas Nesmith, and A. E. Curtis, who produced the giant-flowered types, are recent or still active breeders.

Garden Value: The better cultivars of today offer taut 2- to 4-foot stems with 6- to 12-inch blossoms in shades of white, pink, and red, with hints of lavender and near yellow. Plump, hairy buds gradually swell into flowers with elegant petals of tissue-paper texture. Waxy black blotches usually, but not always, mark the bases of the petals. A few double forms also exist.

The coarse, hairy, lobed leaves are ruggedly handsome while they last, but they disappear from July to September, leaving open border spaces that cause the inexperienced gardener to think the plants are dead. New foliage usually starts growth in the autumn, persisting over winter.

Oriental poppies are spectacular plants that do not need to be combined with others that flower at the same time in June. Better neighbors would be those that spread and fill in the voids left when the poppy foliage dies. Gypsophila, *Artemisia lactiflora,* hybrid anemones, phlox, dwarf asters, and most daylilies, as well as sundry annuals are suggestions. When used as cut flowers, the stems must be thoroughly charred by flame to last effectively in water.

Soil and Exposure: Well-drained soils, with small amounts of humus are suitable, but soggy winter conditions will cause the fleshy roots to rot. Full sun and partial shade are equally rewarding.

Care: Field-grown roots are best, and August to September is the only desirable season for planting or moving. If transplanted in spring, foliage wilts badly when the long taproot is severed, and survival is doubtful. Potted material, if available, may be established at this time of year, however.

The root crown is set 3 inches deep and lightly mulched during the first winter. The mulch should not be packed over the foliage so as to cause decay or suffocation. After five years or so, division in late summer may be necessary for rejuvenation.

Because of the lack of foliage in summer, careless cultivation may injure unseen clumps. Even so, new shoots slowly form. Hence, it is unwise to set poppies near recent casualties, for fear of later conflict. A summer mulch will be doubly useful to mark their sites and to keep the soil cool and moist.

Propagation: Seeds are of interest only to the breeder, for open-pollinated seeds of valuable cultivars do not breed true, and often revert to undesirable types.

Root cuttings are made in late summer. The brittle roots are cut into 4-inch lengths, dipped in sand to halt bleeding, and planted in pots or set 3 inches deep, right end up, at 15-inch intervals in the open. If protected the first winter, they will bloom the second spring. Division is also practical, in late summer.

Leading Cultivars

Red: 'G. I. Joe' is cerise overlaid with watermelon-red; 'Cavalier' is a deep red; 'Lulu A. Neeley,' a radiant dark red; 'Mahony,' a mahogany, but not the easiest one to grow well; and 'Henry Cayeux,' a unique mulberry-wine color with ashy cast; while 'Curtis Giant Flame' is self-descriptive.

Pink: 'Cheerio' is a shell-coral with red at base of petals, 'Helen Elizabeth' is geranium-pink, 'Spotless' has pastel tones with no central blotch, 'Watteau' is a dwarf coral, and 'John III' sports crinkled coral petals.

White: Most whites are generally not as long-lived as the others

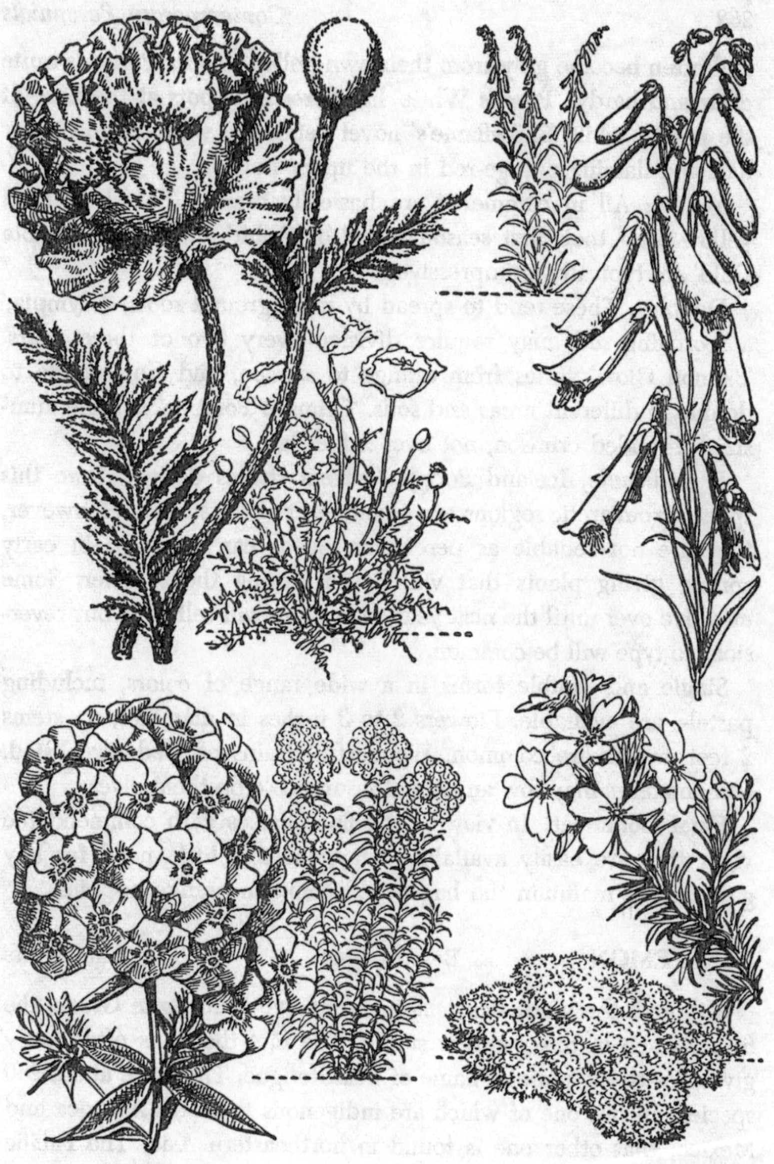

Papaver orientale
Phlox paniculata

Penstemon torreyi
Phlox subulata

and often become gray from their own pollen. 'Thora Perry' is quite clear and hardy; 'Perry's White' has fierce red spots at the base of the petals; while 'Snowflame's' novel petals are white in the lower half and flaming orange-red in the upper portion.

Yellow: All in commerce are basically orange, but show faint yellow after their first season. 'Gold of Ophir' and 'North Dakota Gold' are typically unimpressive.

Doubles: These tend to spread by underground roots. 'Olympia,' a scorching red, may require division every two or three years. 'Salmon Glow' varies from orange to salmon, and from single to double in different areas and soils. 'Crimson Pompon' is a medium-sized, rounded crimson, not over 2 feet tall.

P. nudicaule, Iceland Poppy. Current strains derived from this species from arctic regions can bloom most of the summer. However, they are not reliable as perennials. Seeds can be sown in early spring, giving plants that will flower during the summer. Some may live over until the next year, and many will self-sow, but reversions to type will be common.

Single and double forms in a wide range of colors, including pastels, are available. Flowers 2 to 3 inches in diameter, on stems 2 feet or less are common. Wonderful strains of seeds are listed, and amateurs may sow an annual insurance crop themselves.

Final Comment: In view of the fine choices with commendable vigor that are easily available today, there is little need for any gardener to maintain the hackneyed common orange poppies.

PENSTEMON **Beardtongue** Scrophulariaceæ

Although the word *Penstemon* means five stamens in Greek, the fifth stamen in this genus is sterile. The fact that it is often hairy gives rise to the popular name of beardtongue. There are about 250 species, all but one of which are indigenous to North America and Mexico; that other one is found in northeastern Asia. The Pacific Coast and the Rocky Mountains are virtual storehouses of penstemons but many are not successfully grown elsewhere. Vast confusion is evident in identification, nomenclature, and evaluation of true worth across the country. The American Penstemon Society hopes to create order from this chaos.

Garden Value: Flowers in various colors appear generally as small, trumpet-like bells clinging to slender stems. Some penstemons flower in May, others progress with the season until late summer. Heights range from a few inches to over 5 feet.

Areas of moist air and not too severe winters, such as on the western, northeastern, and southern coasts, are more suitable for penstemons than the inland states, where only a few really thrive unless conditions are ideal. Groups of three display to advantage their free flowering, slim grace, good foliage, and harmonious effect with other plants. The majority naturalize readily where conditions suit them; several dwarf species have rock garden merit. Fine cutting stems are frequently possible, although some require charring of the cut stems.

Soil and Exposure: In the wild, they normally favor light, gritty soil that is well drained and not too fertile. In the border, sharp drainage is essential if winterkilling is to be avoided. Full sun is ordinarily desirable, but light shade is not detrimental.

Care: In most cases spring-planting, with 12 or 18 inches between specimens, is best. Specialists often grow penstemons in raised portions of the garden which have better drainage. Adequate watering during droughts improves performance. After flowering, stems should be cut to prevent seed formation. Division every second year may help the touchier sorts, as will winter protection.

Propagation: Seeds sown in late summer are the common means of propagation. Cuttings made in midsummer are feasible for nearly all choice forms, but these must be wintered carefully in harsh climates. When necessary, division is safest in early spring.

Species

P. barbatus. A sound constitution and colorful spikes distinguish this native of the western mountains. Height averages 3 feet or so, foliage is slender and linear, flowers in thin spires are red or deep rose in color and narrowly tubular in form. They are superb for early summer cutting. Horticultural selections in salmon or pink have been noted, along with occasional dwarf types. These mix nicely with short delphiniums. 'Rose Elf' is a grand 2½-foot cultivar with radiant deep rose flowers from June to August. It rates as a trouble-free, hardy, well-groomed perennial worthy of space in any sunny border.

P. cobæa. Native from Missouri to Texas, it varies in hardiness depending on the area of seed harvest. In any case, it offers about the largest flowers of any species, perhaps 2 inches across. The finest purple selections are quite showy. Lavender and white variants also occur, in foxglove-like racemes on stout 2-foot stems, mainly in July. Regular division may perpetuate a fair border addition. 'Ozark' is a splendid deep purple form that must be propagated asexually to remain constant.

P. crandallii. Only 12 inches high, forming a mat of narrow evergreen leaves, it is in favor with some rock gardeners. Upturned little bells of sky blue or lilac are at their peak in June. This Colorado mountain dwarf must have perfect drainage, but it is nearly immune to drought injury.

P. digitalis. Despite uncommon volunteers of white or silvery lavender, this 4-foot stalwart often suffers from muddy purple-pink flowers. Colonies on banks or in semishaded naturalistic areas are best. The range extends from Maine to Texas.

P. × gloxinoides. This stunning race of hybrids between *P. hartwegii* and *P. cobæa* produces magnificent 2-inch flowers, rich in red and pink tones, all summer long. However, plants seldom survive hard winters, even if protected, unless in coldframes. Large vivid blooms on trim 2-foot stems will induce the fancier to coddle the plants. Florists on the West Coast and in the British Isles raise large quantities of them. 'Garnet,' 'Ruby King,' and 'Firebird' are excellent red selections, propagated annually by cuttings.

P. grandiflorus. From Illinois to Wyoming, it effects a towering grandeur by dint of 3-foot spikes of large flowers, usually lavender-blue but with infrequent white variants. Thick blue-green leaves, oddly spoon-shaped, add to the early summer effect.

Two recent strains of hybrid seeds resulted from crosses of *P. grandiflorus* and *P. murrayanus.* The Fate Hybrids were originated by Mr. F. Fate of Columbia, Missouri, and the Seeba strain by Mrs. Henry Seeba of Cook, Nebraska. In addition, Mr. Glenn Viehmeyer of the University of Nebraska is trying to build seed lines that will reproduce true to color type.

Although not at their best in wet summers, these hybrids can be quite spectacular, with 4-foot heights and large early summer flowers in colors ranging from white to pink, red, and purple. The glossy leaves are tilted vertically like those of some eucalyptus. Midwestern gardeners may find these well worth a trial.

P. heterophyllus. This 4-foot native of California is wanting in hardiness in the East, but the splashes of color from the narrow blue flowers repay frequent replacement.

P. murrayanus. Often spectacular, this shoulder-high native of the Southwest has fiery red flowers and bluish foliage. Careful protection is worth while in cold regions.

P. ovatus. The tendency of this West Coast species toward biennial habit perhaps restricts its use to massing in seminaturalized areas where it can self-sow. Small lavender flowers, often tinted blue or pink, are effective only in masses. Attractive broad leaves are flushed crimson at winter's approach. Height ranges from 2½ to 4 feet.

P. palmeri. Also from the Far West, it behaves as a sturdy perennial. In June and July large pink and white flowers bloom in profusion on 4-foot stems. Flowering may be repeated later in the season.

P. torreyi **(*P. barbatus*** **var.** ***torreyi*).** Almost identical to *P. barbatus* in garden effect, except that the larger flowers are scarlet. As sold by the trade, *P. torreyi* is more colorful and handsome. Considerable deviation is evident from seed-grown material.

P. unilateralis. Bright blue flowers on wiry 2- or 3-foot stems in May and June make a sparkling display in garden or arrangement. Native from Wyoming to New Mexico.

Final Comment: Many other species have pleased collectors, but are generally erratic in behavior. An extensive breeding program might well attempt to combine the hardiness of some species with large colorful flowers of others.

PHLOX Phlox Polemoniaceæ

Almost exclusively American in habitat, the phloxes are, horticulturally, one of our most important native flowers. The generic name means fire in Greek, but in ancient days this name was applied to the plants we now know as *Lychnis,* in a different family. Of the approximately 50 species of phlox, all but one from Siberia are native to North America.

Bright flowers, self-colored or enhanced by a contrasting eye, are borne in cymes or panicles of varying size; some are fragrant. All colors but orange are represented in the genus, though the annual *P. drummondii* contains pale yellow forms. Leggy 4-foot subjects, dwarf spiny evergreen mats, and intermediate types are to be found, with bloom spanning the season from May to October, according to the species.

In view of the wide diversity to be found among the various species, and the relatively greater importance of the tall summer-blooming ones, they will be discussed separately.

Tall Summer-Blooming Phlox

P. paniculata (*P. decussata*). The immensely popular summer phlox, native from New York to Georgia and Arkansas, is likely to have pinched, mediocre panicles of dubious pink-purple or magenta flowers in the wild. However, transferred to a decent border, many take a new lease on life, and are scarcely distinguishable from some garden cultivars. In native habitats, as in the garden, heights may range from 2 to 4 feet.

As is true for so many others, this plant gained most of its current character in Europe, where it was introduced in the nineteenth century. Crosses between isolated selections soon produced superior types. Until 1959, the late Captain B. Symons-Jeune, of England, was the man most engrossed with still greater advances.

Garden Value: In comparison with earlier forms, modern cultivars have larger flowers, more shapely panicles, more attractive colors, and a blooming period that has been considerably lengthened. With care, well-branched specimens remain attractive from late June to September, whereas once only August benefited from their display. With proper culture, just one stalk is a virtual bouquet. A plant of several stems can enhance any planting, but groups of three are almost indispensable for summer color in large perennial gardens. Taller forms are best in the background, lower ones are suited to the midportion, and the shorter types belong nearer the foreground.

Phloxes are compatible with most garden flowers, tiger lilies excepted. Also, the bright salmon-orange group needs careful placement to prevent clashing with some of the dark-colored flowers, such as aconitums. Coral bells, gypsophila, and sea lavender are attractive softening influences. White cultivars are ideal for picking up highlights at twilight or early evening.

As cut flowers they are imposing but transient; after a few days, the flowers shrivel and drop.

Soil and Exposure: In the average garden, phlox becomes "A wretched soul, bruised with adversity," as a result of neglect and barren ground. Deep, fertile soil with ample organic matter is needed, with applications of superphosphate a possible help toward deeper rooting. Full sun produces optimum effect, but light shade is not detrimental. In fact, the so-called blue forms deteriorate into a slate lilac under hot sun.

Care: Phlox can be planted from spring to fall, if seasonal precautions are heeded. Two-foot intervals are adequate. Watering is required during droughts, and regular spraying with an all-purpose compound is helpful. Faded flower clusters should be snapped off just below the lowest flowers to encourage side branching and the formation of additional buds. This also prevents seeding, the cause for reversion to the common magenta.

Clumps should be divided every three or four years without fail, and reset in newly enriched ground; otherwise flower size diminishes and generally shabby disarray results.

Red spiders, signified by brown spottings on the undersides of gradually yellowing leaves, may be a problem in hot weather if the soil is poor and watering is neglected. Mildew, evidenced by a white powdery covering on leaves or stems, as well as rust, which is indicated by brown-black spots on the foliage, are the worst diseases. Using an all-purpose spray every two weeks is a wise preventive measure.

Propagation: Seeds, of interest only to the breeder, must be stratified if sown in the spring; otherwise they can be sown outdoors in the fall. Division, the common method, can be practiced in spring or fall, but only thrifty outer shoots should be retained.

Root cuttings provide speedy increase commercially. Two-inch sections of the fleshier roots are sown upright or horizontally, under ¾ inch of sandy loam—in outside frames in fall, or in cool greenhouses during winter. Ready for planting in late spring, most will bloom by August.

Leading Cultivars

Red: 'Fanal' is a new, clear flame red; 'Red Glory' is a deep ruddy shade; 'Brigadier' has brick red tones; 'Leo Schlageter' vacillates from scarlet to crimson; and 'Spitfire' is a flamboyant orange-scarlet. 'Charles Curtis' may vary, depending upon the source. From some nurseries it will be identical with 'Red Glory' but from others it may be the same as 'Spitfire.'

Pink: 'Sir John Falstaff' bears huge salmon 1¾-inch florets; 'Elizabeth Arden' is an elegant pastel; 'Dresden China,' with soft shades, is seldom over 2 feet tall; 'Windsor' is a salmon-tinted carmine-rose; while 'B. Symons-Jeune' is a rigidly erect rose-pink, with red eye.

White: 'Mia Ruys' is dwarf, not over 2 feet; 'Mary Louise' is snow white; 'White Admiral' is very fragrant; and 'Rembrandt' has a compact habit.

Wine and purple: 'Aida' is crimson-purple; 'San Antonio' an unfading plum shade; and 'Progress,' almost blue if in partial shade. 'Lilac Time' has an excellent constitution, with sizable clear lilac flowers. 'Blue Moon' is a promising Symons-Jeune selection. (The Symons-Jeune group appears to be gaining a solid foothold, but requires more testing under American conditions.)

P. carolina (*P. suffruticosa*). While found native in the warmer states from Ohio south, this species is hardy almost anywhere. The narrowly ovate leaves are rather glossy and quite disease-free; stems have reddish purple mottlings. The slender panicles are more conical than those of *P. paniculata* but bloom earlier, possibly by late May.

Unfortunately, even today, shades are largely restricted to white and rose-purple, with all sorts of uninspiring intermediates. Wild forms often attain 4 feet in height, but cultivars are generally of a more shapely 3-foot habit. Spreading is not overly aggressive.

Superior types are fairly useful for cutting and are fine for border groups. Flowering is of six weeks duration, perhaps recurring in autumn. Culture is identical to that for *P. paniculata*.

Collected plants from the wild, sent to Europe in the nineteenth century, were intercrossed and the resulting improvements became known as *P. suffruticosa*. While a score or more bear cultivar names, most, like 'Burns' and 'Miss Verboom,' are perilously close to magenta. Only 'Miss Lingard,' the superb white, deserves solid praise as one of the finest border subjects extant. However, it sets no seeds, so is valueless to the breeder.

P. carolina types are propagated by top cuttings in summer or by divisions in spring or early fall.

Other Species

P. adsurgens, Periwinkle Phlox. If the conditions of its western mountain habitat are reproduced, acid soil and partial shade in particular, it becomes quite ornamental. Shining leaves, often bronze in winter, form neat mats topped with domelike clusters of pale pink to salmon flowers on 6-inch stems for several weeks in spring.

White central eyes are an interesting departure from the prevalent red.

P. amœna. A doughty Spartan from dry southern wastelands, it soon degenerates in fertile loams. About 12 inches or less in height, the wiry stems produce vivid rose-pink flowers in the better selections. These remain colorful well into summer. Plants with bright purple flowers, often sold under this name, are probably hybrids of *P. subulata* and *P. stolonifera,* which should be correctly called *P. procumbens.*

P. divaricata, Spring Phlox, Wild Sweet William, Blue Phlox. This species imparts blue vivacity to the spring pageant when featured with daffodils, primroses, pink tulips, and lungworts. In moist woods, from Canada south to Florida, as in cultivation, semishade is the preference. Stems 12 to 15 inches high usually carry somewhat fragrant pale blue clusters in early spring. Plants may creep and self-sow into almost ground cover proportions. Shearing after bloom causes thrifty branching. Frequent division in late summer prevents deterioration.

The variety *canadensis,* an easterner, is dwarf, with notched corolla lobes ("petals"); variety *laphamii,* from the West, is a distinctive periwinkle blue with rounded corolla lobes.

The strain known as *P. arendsii* is a group of hybrids between *P. divaricata* and *P. paniculata* that is primarily of botanical interest, as the several weeks of informally clustered bloom do not wholly compensate for the insipid colorings. Susceptibility to mildew is a prominent weakness.

P. glaberrima. Most of the material offered under this name is *P. carolina.* 'Buckeye' is an interesting selection, growing to 18 inches, with rosy purple flowers.

P. maculata, Meadow Phlox. It is encountered in moist, sunny fields from Connecticut south to North Carolina and west to Missouri, usually varying from 3 to 5 feet in height. Cylindrical panicles of normally mediocre purple or white flowers sometimes sport to fair carmine shades, but the cultivars of former days seem nonexistent today. While naturalizing is possible, drought produces thin flower clusters and dull, stringy foliage.

P. nivalis, Trailing Phlox. Some confuse this southern native with *P. subulata* but its habit is looser, its hardiness less reliable, and flowering is later, not until June. A second blooming period may occur in the fall. In cold areas of harsh winter winds, sandy soil is needed to condition flowering shoots, and protection with evergreen boughs is prudent. Relatively large clusters of white, pink, purplish, or almost red are common.

A selection named 'Dixie Brilliant' has watermelon-red flowers, 1½ inches across, but unless protected it is useless in the North. 'Camla' is an excellent salmon pink of iron constitution that produces fine, airy 9-inch clusters, likely to repeat in September. It is assumed to be of mixed parentage. 'Camla Alba' is really pale lilac. 'Gladwynne,' with large creamy cymes, is an outstanding white.

A strain known as *P.* × *henryæ* represents variants from a spontaneous cross between *P. nivalis* and *P. bifida.* It develops into a pink cushion that seems content in hot arid ground. Further blue and lavender forms have been reported. Breeding attempts with other species might bring startling advances.

P. ovata, Mountain Phlox. From high terrain in Pennsylvania and southward, this species produces dense cymes, ranging from rosy pink to reddish purple, in June and July, and sometimes again in fall. Height averages about 15 inches. Attractive variants are easily perpetuated by division. 'Pulchra,' a pale pink noted in 1929 in Alabama, may eventually be given species rank as *P. pulchra.* It does not easily adjust to garden conditions, but some shade, well-drained peaty soils, and biennial division may help. An excellent cut flower.

P. pilosa. Dry sandy stretches from Connecticut to Texas often sustain this erect 15-inch species. The corymbs are rather small but showy in spring, especially in the royal purple shades. White, pink, and rose forms also occur. Natural crosses with *P. divaricata* are reported, but evidently have not been propagated for sale.

P. stolonifera, Creeping Phlox. In the woods of Pennsylvania to Georgia it forms a solid mat. Such aggressive behavior declares it suitable only for ground cover purposes in the shade. Nevertheless, the small cymes of purple or violet flowers are engaging during

April and May. 'Blue Ridge' and 'Lavender Lady' are self-descriptive commercial selections.

P. subulata, Moss Pink, Ground Pink. Native from New York and Michigan south to North Carolina, it has yielded scores of named selections. Prickly narrow leaves clothe the dense evergreen hummocks, often 2 feet across, from which a mass of early spring bloom creates a carpet-like effect. Pink, white, and lavender-purple forms are in the majority.

For walls, edging, and rock gardens, a few plants are pleasing if they are not over-exploited. Their ground cover value is undeniable. Sunny, porous soil is best; summer shearing, top-dressing with compost, and occasional division all prove worth while.

Cultivars in gardens are often outdated mediocrities. Today's superior offerings frequently have flowers 1 inch across, with clean colors, that may recur in fall. Hybridizing with *P. nivalis,* chiefly by J. Herbert Alexander of Middleboro, Massachusetts, is tending to increase the autumn display.

Good pink selections include 'Emerald Cushion,' 'Alexander's Beauty,' 'Chuckles,' and 'Alexander's Surprise.' 'Alexander's White' and 'Schneewitchen' are typical of the palest sorts, while 'Intensity,' a cerise, and 'Brilliant,' a magenta, are approaches to red. Violet shades creep into 'Blue Hills' and 'Sky Blue.' Local favorites are legion and often choice. 'Scarlet Flame' is a brilliant, scarlet-ruby of excellent behavior, the first true red.

Final Comment: This genus is easily a complete subject in itself. *Phlox* by Captain B. Symons-Jeune is a diverting book, while Dr. Edgar Wherry's *The Genus Phlox* is a scientifically prepared work for the botanist.

Considerably more testing and breeding of America's great store of phlox would be a worthy project.

PHYSOSTEGIA False Dragonhead Labitæ

Each gardener must carefully weigh the assets and drawbacks of the physostegias to determine his own attitude toward the genus. In its favor are invaluable late summer bloom, ample long-stemmed

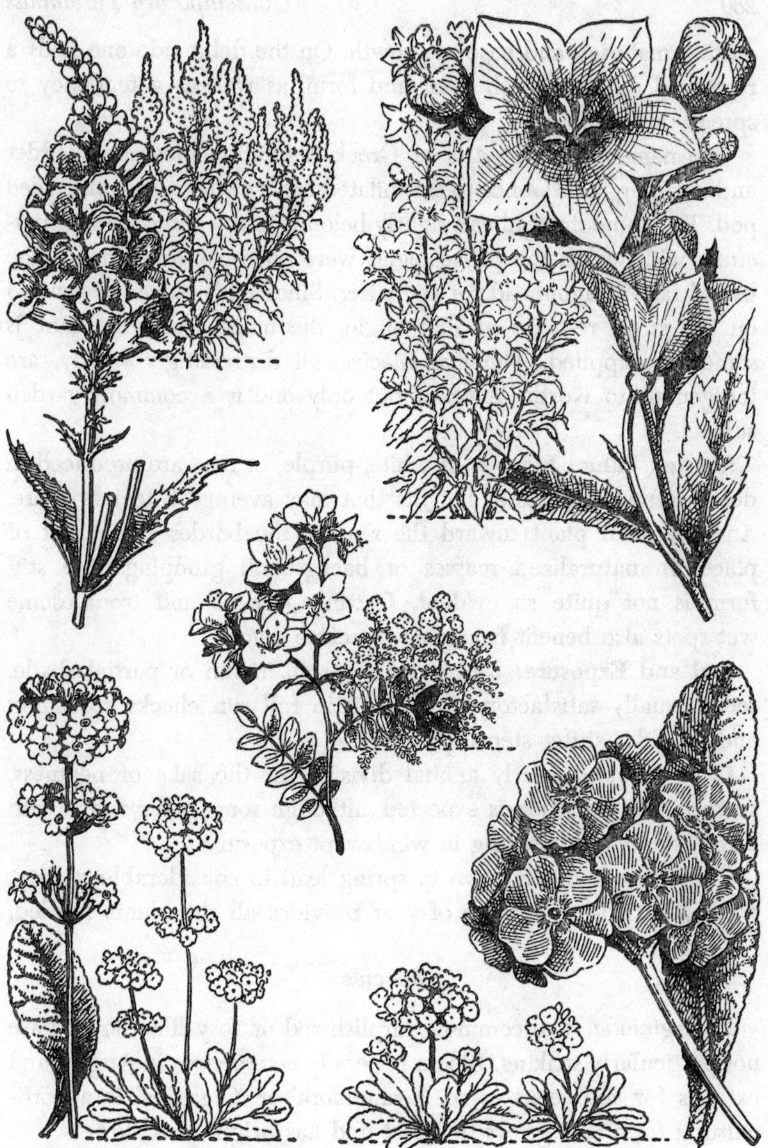

Physostegia virginiana
Primula japonica

Polemonium cæruleum

Platycodon grandiflorum
Primula polyantha

cutting material, and ease of growth. On the debit side one finds a restricted range of both color and form, as well as a tendency to spread rampantly.

The name *Physostegia* is of Greek derivation meaning bladder and covering, a reference to the inflated calyx of the developing seed pod. The name dragonhead rightly belongs to the genus *Dracocephalum,* with which the physostegias were once confused; hence the use of false dragonhead for the latter. Since each flower, if twisted on the stem, remains at that angle, the name obedient plant is sometimes applied. The five species, all distressingly weedy, are indigenous to North America, but only one is a common garden subject.

Garden Value: Flowers of white, purple, or rose are produced in dense terminal spikes at heights that may average 3 feet or more. An occasional plant toward the rear of the border is not out of place. In naturalized masses or background groupings the stiff form is not quite so evident. Cutting gardens and troublesome wet spots also benefit from their carefree vigor.

Soil and Exposure: Moist and dry soil, in sun or partial shade, seem equally satisfactory. Light soil in full sun checks spreading and provides stiffer stems.

Care: Beyond nearly annual division for the sake of neatness, scarcely any attention is expected, although some taller forms with brittle stems need staking in windswept exposures.

Propagation: Seeds sown in spring lead to considerable variety. Division at the same time of year provides all the plants needed.

Species

P. virginiana. The common purplish red or rosy lilac flowers are not particularly striking. Bloom generally commences in August and extends for six weeks or so. 'Grandiflora' or 'Gigantea' is a horticultural form that grows to 5 feet and has bright pink flowers.

'Vivid,' a cultivar found in a St. Louis nursery by the waterlily expert, August Koch, became very popular around 1935, but soon proved typically invasive. Only about 24 inches high, it has deep rosy pink flowers, usually in September. Crossed to 'Grandiflora' by Alex Cumming, it produced the forms know as 'Rosy Spire,' to 3½ feet with rose-pink spikes in early September, and 'Summer Glow,' a taller, earlier-flowering cultivar with rosy crimson flowers.

'Summer Snow,' a white of medium height, is less objectionable in roaming, but it still needs frequent division. The clean ivory-white flowers, at their best in August, combine happily with *Lilium speciosum* 'Rubrum.'

Final Comment: If just one species of tidy habit could be found and hybridized, very desirable border plants might result.

PLATYCODON **Balloon Flower** **Campanulaceæ**

The genus takes its name from words meaning broad bell in Greek, an allusion to the shape of the flower. The inflated ballon-like buds, which can be resoundingly popped when squeezed, give the plant its popular name. There is but one species, *P. grandiflorum*, from eastern Asia. All modern cultivars stem from variations found within this species.

Garden Value: Few plants boast more satisfying traits than the relatively unsung balloon flowers. They are perfectly hardy, long-lived, and have been known to blossom in one spot for 20 years. They stay in place with no vagabond instinct for spreading, and perhaps as important an attribute as any, they bloom in habitually dry, hot sections.

In most cases, mature plants averaging 3 feet in height begin to flower in late June, continuing until early September. There is a dwarf form for larger rock gardens and both single- and double-flowered types for borders. Single clumps, about 2 feet in breadth, or small groups make good companions for phlox, yellow daylilies, and anthemis. They also extend the season of their relatives, the campanulas, into the later part of the summer. For cutting, the stems are useful only if well charred, or if allowed to wilt freely before being placed in deep water.

Soil and Exposure: Light, well-drained soils are ideal. Just about the only cause of sudden death is stagnant, damp ground, which is likely to encourage winter rotting. Full sun is satisfactory, as is partial shade, especially for some of those with pink tones.

Care: Spring-planting should be such that the crown is barely covered with soil. Seed pod removal adds to the length of the flowering season. Since new shoots emerge slowly, early cultivation must be done with care. New plantings are rather slow to exhibit the expected performance, but after two or three years results will be justly rewarding.

Propagation: Seeds give liberal increase, but plants develop slowly. Division is a touchy process, for spring only. If outer sections of the thick crown are cut off with buds and roots present, some will survive resetting. Cut surfaces should be dusted with a fungicide to forestall disease problems.

Species

P. grandiflorum. Originally, flowers were merely open bells of blue or white, 2 to 3 inches across. Now a soft pink named 'Shell Pink' has been added. Double selections with petaloids in the throat, which are also comparatively new, are increasing in public favor.

The variety *japonicum* is a double-flowered form usually listed in catalogs under cultivar names. A Japanese dwarf, variety *mariesii,* is not over 18 inches tall, with large blossoms of bright blue or white. 'New Alpine' is apparently a constant blue variant, breeding true from seeds and remaining effective all summer.

Named double forms were created by Alex Cumming from crosses of a chance double blue with singles in all colors. Cataloged as 'Bristol Bell,' a lavender; 'Bristol Bride,' a white; 'Bristol Blush,' flesh pink; and 'Bristol Bluebird,' a deep blue, they bring added attraction to the genus. More polished and urbane, they remain both productive and drought tolerant to become a real treat for gardeners.

Final Comment: Odd variations which still appear from Asiatic seeds are being tested. In the meantime, the border material now available should not be disregarded.

POLEMONIUM Jacob's Ladder, Greek Valerian Polemoniaceæ

Polemoniums play their role in the garden by helping to overcome the dearth of blue flowers, and by offering compound foliage that in itself lends interest. Most of the species are from western North America, with others scattered in Europe, Asia, and South America.

Garden Value: These relatively small subjects will hardly set pulses racing, but a few of the low-growing species are significant when situated in rock gardens or in the front of borders. The pinnate foliage provides leathery, tufted hummocks all season. Predominantly blue flowers are small, cup-shaped, and clustered into loose corymbs, mainly in spring or early summer.

Soil and Exposure: Unless otherwise noted, soils of medium fertility and reliable drainage suffice. Sun and partial shade are generally of equal advantage, although several do not thrive in abnormal heat.

Care: Planting is safest in spring, with about 18 inches of space allowed for vigorous spreaders. Watering in dry periods keeps the foliage neat and trim during the summer.

Propagation: Seeds are usually sown in spring. Cuttings in midsummer are customary with 'Blue Pearl' and other cultivars. Large clumps can be divided in late summer.

Species

P. cæruleum, Jacob's Ladder. The pinnate leaves, with up to 20 leaflets, are supposed to resemble the ladder of Jacob's dream. The species is native to Europe. Plants average 15 inches in height, and have erect stems with many nodding blue panicles from May to July.

'Blue Pearl,' a fine selection highly effective with doronicums, is notably floriferous. Each little flower is a shiny cobalt blue with a yellow eye. Variety *lacteum,* sometimes listed as 'Album' in catalogs, is a white-flowered form.

P. carneum. Here is a rather fussy treasure from cool Oregon and

California mountain ranges. Blends of flesh, cream, apricot, and pink, effective in late spring, are loosely carried on rather weak, slender 15-inch stems. It cannot withstand long periods of drought, it fades in hot sun, and can seed itself to death if so allowed.

P. pauciflorum. This oddity from Chile is accustomed to moist conditions and some shade; hence ample watering is required in gardens. Strict 2-foot stems produce narrow amber-apricot flowers in July and August. Prevention of seed formation is again advised.

P. pulcherrimum. From western mountains, this is a beauty with light blue flowers of bright golden throats, on frail 6-inch stems in May and June. Considering the added charm of the fine-textured fernlike leaves, the effect is delicate, yet bloom is appreciable. In slightly acid, porous soil, it may attain 10 inches.

P. reptans. In spite of its name, it does not creep; but the weak stems sprawl so that the garden effect is almost that of a creeping type. Plants form dark green mounds 2 feet in breadth, from which soft blue flowers with white eyes appear from May to July. It is found native from New York south to Alabama.

P. richardsonii. Belated flowering in June serves well for a rock garden when the spring burst of color begins to wane. Plants creep slightly with many very small leaflets on 9-inch stems, and blue or purple flowers in medium-sized clusters. As befits an arctic native, it is reliably hardy.

POLYGONATUM — Solomon's Seal — Liliaceæ

This genus provides one of the answers to the problem presented by gardening in the shade. Cool moist soil is the only other requirement. Naturalized areas, wild gardens, and the shadiest part of a border all benefit from the 3-foot, gracefully arching stems. Small white tubular flowers hang below the leaves along the stems. The flowers, in late May and June, are not conspicuous, but the foliage is effective throughout the season.

Two species commonly encountered in gardens are *P. commutatum* and *P. multiflorum.* The former is taller, to 4 feet, and has slightly larger flowers. Both tend to spread by underground rootstocks but are never nuisances. Forms with variegated leaves are occasionally available. Propagation is by division in early spring.

The botanical name is taken from the Greek for many kneed, because of the nature of the jointed rootstock. Native in the temperate zone, many species are well known to collectors of local flora in this country.

PRIMULA **Primrose** **Primulaceæ**

Scarcely a flower better expresses the exuberance of spring than primroses; significant are the extensive references to them by earlier poets. Just about every color, shade, and tint can be found in the genus.

The botanical name is derived from *primus,* or first in Latin, presumably so named because of the early flowering. Well over 400 species are known, with newly discovered ones from Asia still being disseminated. Loosely speaking, temperate regions of the northern hemisphere supply the bulk, including some of widespread greenhouse culture. A few comparatively easily grown species are found in Europe, but those from the rain-drenched Himalayas often prove recalcitrant in much of this country. Areas similar in climate to the British Isles and the Pacific Northwest sustain many more species than the inland regions. In this genus there is no lack of exotic aristocrats for the fancier to pamper.

Flowers may be in heads, umbels, or solitary on individual stems. Earliest forms bloom in April, May has the greatest profusion, and lesser known species continue until late summer.

Garden Value: Shaded spots in rock gardens or in the forepart of a border are suitable, but some enthusiasts give over a whole edging to the polyanthus type. Single plants are seldom arresting. Under flowering dogwoods, crabapples, or apple trees, they complement the canopy above. Naturalizing along shaded brooks is possible, as is carpeting a shrubbery planting if the soil is sufficiently moist and well fertilized.

Soil and Exposure: Unless otherwise noted, a rich soil of liberal organic content, able to retain moisture during the summer, is desirable. Partial shade is imperative, but if dense, it leads to excessive foliage at the expense of bloom. Species at home in Himalayan bogs may not adapt to attempts at duplicating the situation. Nature provides aeration and drainage in her works, but man's efforts usually produce disastrous stagnation.

Care: Plants may be set out in spring, early fall, or, with care, when in full bloom. Individual spacing of 6 inches is the minimum for massed groupings. Deep watering is prescribed during droughts. Division is suggested about every fourth year, immediately after flowering.

Red spider may attack plantings in the sun, especially during hot, dry summers. Underfertilized plants are also susceptible. The underside of the leaf becomes rusty brown, the top portions turning a sickly yellow. One or two sprays with a good miticide and attention to watering should clear up the trouble. Growing conditions should also be checked, and modified if necessary.

Propagation: Seeds usually germinate best if sown as soon as ripe. Spring-sown seeds should be pretreated by several periods of alternate freezing and thawing in an ice-cube tray of a refrigerator; the treatment should be spread over three or four days. January sowings in cool greenhouses are common. Division of choice forms is quick by amateur standards but slow and costly to the trade. After flowering, the clumps can be separated into individual sections and reset. Root cuttings in early spring can be made of *P. denticulata.*

Species

P. auricula. Growers seeking an exquisite, refined novelty, and willing to supply extra attention should be tempted by this species. In the Alps, it flourishes with *P. hirsuta,* and natural crosses are probable. Many mutations have appeared in cultivation so that there is now a far wider selection of colors than was found in the original yellows. Their highest popularity came in Victorian England, where British hybridizers played important roles. A revival of interest is under way on the Pacific Coast.

Rosettes of thick, smooth evergreen leaves and slightly fragrant flowers with contrasting eye colors predominate. Winter protection is advised; plants have swollen roots that tend to heave out of the soil.

P. denticulata. Rounded flower heads in lilac, violet, or white appear so early that they often precede the foliage. Scapes may be 10 inches high by the time the last floret opens. Precocious bloom is not uncommon in warm autumns or winters. The white-flowered form is a choice acquisition, easily raised from seeds, that would improve any planting when combined with the more common type.

Variety *cachemiriana* (*P. cashmeriana*) is a form with showy purple to lilac-rose flowers with yellow throats. It blooms somewhat later than the species, and so has more leaves expanded at that time.

P. elatior. The oxlip of England is native as far east as Iran. It is not unlike the cowslip, *P. veris,* except that the flowers are larger and the corolla lobes open out flat. It is important as one parent of the polyanthus group.

P. florindæ. F. Kingdon-Ward, the plant explorer, called this "the giant cowslip of Sikkimensis," and named it for his wife. Fantastic 3-foot scapes wait until July or August to produce flowers of cream, apricot, or yellow in great umbels. Fragrance reminiscent of vanilla is noticeable. In the Himalayas of Tibet growth is rampant enough to choke ditches; but it is deserving of bog or waterside conditions elsewhere.

P. japonica. This species is probably the most popular of the candelabra section of the genus, wherein many umbels are superimposed in tiers. Stems often reach 2 feet in height, blooming from late May to early July. Colors include intense crimson, pink, magenta, and white. Continued shade and moisture are needed.

P. juliæ. This primrose was named for Julia L. Mlokossjewicz, who collected it in the Caucasus in 1900. Dwarf plants are a mass of solitary rose, red, or stunning crimson-purple flowers, practically making a carpet effect in April and May. Small, glossy, wrinkled leaves form more or less rounded tufts. Plants with slightly creeping rootstocks offer some value for shaded ground covering, as they are tolerant of dry periods.

The Juliana Hybrids are often the result of crossings with *P. polyantha*. The globular, moundlike types are perhaps most popularly acclaimed, but taller clustered types also have garden charm. A splendid range of colors is available. 'Wanda' and 'Gloria' are crimson-purple, 'Snow White' and 'Mrs. McGillivray,' rose-pink; all four are favorites.

P. × polyantha. This embraces all the polyanthus types that amateurs overwhelmingly connect with the genus, for they are widely cultivated. *P. elatior, P. veris,* and *P. vulgaris* have been interbred for many years, originally in England by Sutton's, also by Gertrude Jekyll and others, to produce this elegant race. Clumps average 6 to 12 inches in height when in flower. There is a fantastic range of colors in the finer strains. Pastel forms are increasingly offered, and dwarfs, mainly of *P. vulgaris* parentage, add still more variety. Fragrance, flowers larger than a silver half-dollar, and healthy vigor characterize any carefully selected group.

Fine strains such as Clarke's and the Barnhaven's originate in the ideal climate of the Pacific Coast. Ellen Carder Hybrids from Mrs. Frederick C. H. Carder of Cheshire, Connecticut, are accustomed to surly New England weather. England, Australia, and New Zealand all have splendid offerings, for their climates, at least.

Double forms, such as the rich burgundy 'Marie Crousse,' sometimes appear but they do not reproduce faithfully from seeds. Asexual propagation restricts their distribution mainly to the West Coast.

P. pulverulenta. From clumps of striking leaves, often a foot or more in length, strong, silver-coated 2½-foot scapes grow with tiered whorls of usually purple flowers in early summer. English strains have added more attractive coloring; the Bartley strain is strongly pink, while 'Mrs. R. V. Berkeley' is a pretty white with orange eyes. The Lissadell Hybrids (*P. pulverulenta × P. cockburiana*) feature sharp purple and scarlet flowers.

P. sieboldii. This Japanese species, 9 inches tall when in flower, is more tolerant of sun, heat, and drought than are most of the others. Nevertheless, the ornately scalloped leaves often disappear during summer. Large 1½-inch flowers of white, rose, or purple do not open until late spring. The white forms are spectacular in their stark purity, rare for the genus.

P. veris. The cowslip of England has scapes 8 inches tall that carry loose nodding umbels of bell-shaped flowers, usually bright yellow but sometimes purple. A curious variant known as "hose-in-hose" is made up of two corollas, one inside the other. This species has been somewhat superseded by the polyanthus type.

P. vulgaris (*P. acaulis*). From small tufts of foliage, solitary peduncles bear single flowers in pale yellow, blue, or purple. Probably best known are the cherished blue forms, frequently sold as *P. acaulis.*

Final Comment: Only the most common and most widely grown species have been discussed. Fanciers who join the American Primrose Society will find that it distributes interesting rare species. At present, the polyanthus primrose is very well known, but time may see many more species becoming popular, and additional ones introduced in commerce.

PULMONARIA Lungwort Boraginaceæ

Lungworts bloom so early in spring that even primroses seem laggards by comparison. While largely taken for granted, they have much to offer for shaded areas. Flowers are attractive during April and May, and the foliage is uniquely becoming all season.

The Latin word for lung gives the scientific name, no doubt because one species was once believed to cure lung disorders. The common name follows the same pattern. Culpeper, the famed herbalist, pronounced it able "to help the diseases of the lungs, and for coughs, wheezings, and shortness of breath, which it cureth both in man and beast." Leaves were even boiled in beer to treat afflicted horses. Various species are indigenous to Europe and Asia.

Garden Value: The small flowers, roughly trumpet-shaped, frequently contrast in color with the buds. In fact, pink buds and blue flowers are common in this family. Height seldom exceeds 12 inches. The indifferent gardener enjoys this genus because it thrives on neglect.

Compact structure and preference for shade permit lungworts to be used in rock gardens, borders, edgings, or as an undercarpet for shrubs. Such a treatment with forsythia makes a happy combination. Small border groupings can be made with daffodils or primroses.

Soil and Exposure: Cool, peaty ground is best, but it need not be high in fertilizer content. At least partial shade is ideal, although a struggling existence may be eked out in full sun, with a listless appearance probable by late summer.

Care: Planting is satisfactory in early fall, very early spring, or—with careful handling—when plants are in full bloom. Watering is helpful in prolonged dry periods. Division every fourth year will prevent overcrowding.

Propagation: Seeds sown in late summer may give widespread variation. Division is recommended for late summer, so that the spring display will not be impeded. Heavy watering must follow.

Species

P. angustifolia (*P. azurea*). It is sometimes known as soldiers-and-sailors or Mary-and-Joseph in England. The leaves are plain green but decorative. Stems not over 12 inches high carry blue flowers or, rarely, white ones. The occasional designation of *P. azurea* was applied to certain intensely blue forms. These are sometimes cataloged as 'April Opals.' 'Johnston's Blue' is a first-class gentian-blue offering. 'Rubra' is a name that covers horticultural deviations to nearly reddish shades. 'Salmon Glory' is notably choice, for its clean-cut coral to salmon blossoms are never dingy.

P. saccharata, Bethlehem Sage. Striking foliage is the feature of this European native. The rather oval leaf is basically dark green, but is spotted with white, making it more conspicuous in the shade.

Pulmonaria saccharata
Salvia hæmatodes

Rudbeckia sullivantii
Saponaria ocymoides

Flowers vary from white to blue or reddish violet. 'Mrs. Moon' is a fine selection with large pink buds and showy gentian-blue flowers. A spurious 'Mrs. Moon' with startling dark crimson blossoms has also been reported.

Final Comment: Another solution for the would-be gardener who feels he is doomed to failure is found in this genus.

RUDBECKIA Coneflower Compositæ

American prejudice against this genus can probably be traced to the fact that one member, the black-eyed Susan, is a common field weed. Similarly, *Solidago,* which has won abiding respect in English gardens, in this country is merely scorned as goldenrod, supposedly (but unjustifiably) the arch foe of hayfever victims. In truth, the coneflowers are a rather coarse lot, with liberal splashes of yellow from July to September that can be an unqualified asset.

Rudbeckia honors Olof Rudbeck, a Swedish botanist of the late seventeenth century and a counselor to Linnæus. The species are all native to North America, some of them well known as common weeds. Nomenclature has been unbelievably confused among growers, who usually include the more colorful echinaceas in this group. Even the true coneflowers may not always be listed by correct name.

Garden Value: Occasional spottings of plants in borders yield an attractive summer display, but excessive use may lead to coarseness. With certain asters in the blue range, such as *A.* × *frikartii* and *A. amellus* as well as with some of the dwarf asters, pleasing effects are possible. For spacious, open naturalizing, their effect is less likely to offend. Most are acceptable for cutting.

Soil and Exposure: Soils of only average fertility but with adequate summer moisture are necessary, as is full sunlight.

Care: Spring-planting is safest for the better sorts. Division is suggested for every third spring. Aphids may appear in quantity, but an insecticide should quickly dispose of them.

Propagation: Seeds should be sown in spring; division is also recommended at this season.

Species

R. laciniata var. *hortensis.* This rampant hoodlum is known far and wide as goldenglow, a spreading, weedy 7-foot menace to all nearby plants of refinement in the border. While the brilliant yellow flowers, 2 or 3 inches in diameter, are appealing, and good as cut material, they hardly justify the need for almost annual division in gardens. As color interest near rural buildings or for naturalizing, plants can be useful if not allowed to develop into a weedy thicket.

'Golden Globe' grows to only 4 or 5 feet but its invasive spirit is pronounced. 'Goldquelle,' a contemporary European selection now available in this country, is said to attain but 2½ feet and to make only restrained clumps, as it increases slowly. In early tests it seems worth while.

R. purpurea. Correctly *Echinacea purpurea,* under which it was discussed.

R. speciosa (*R. newmanii*). Superior forms are prevalent in Europe, but seem to excite little attention here. Ordinarily, compact 2-foot clumps yield generous quantities of 3-inch, bright yellow flowers with jet black cones, in late summer. The plants known in the trade as *R. sullivantii* may be a form of *R. fulgida* or may belong here as a form of *R. speciosa.* At any rate, they are fine border plants, especially the cultivar 'Goldsturm.' Large flowers, 3 or 4 inches across, are deep rich yellow, with rays that are faintly twisted. Well-branched 2½-foot plants are very floriferous, and the foliage is not overly domineering.

In passing, *R. serotina, R. hirta,* and *R. triloba* might be mentioned as the biennial (or annual) plants commonly known as the black-eyed Susans that sometimes pop up in neglected borders and are allowed to remain until the display of flowers is finished. They should not be left until they self-sow, or a weeding problem is promised for the future.

Final Comment: New and improved cultivars far outshine the common garden subjects of this genus, some of which might be more properly classed as weeds.

RUELLIA **Ruellia** **Acanthaceæ**

Ruellia, named for Jean de la Ruelle, who first described it in 1530, is a genus better known in the South, since many of the 200 species are native to tropical and subtropical zones; many excellent greenhouse subjects come from Brazil, in particular.

The hardy section of the genus is best suited for rock gardens, small border groups, or limited naturalized colonies. Funnel-shaped flowers, up to 2 inches across, are vaguely like petunias in form. The foliage is not particularly exciting; large masses would be somewhat dull. Full sun and porous soil that is not too fertile are desirable.

R. ciliosa, native from South Carolina to Florida, is hardy as far north as New England, especially in barren soils. From late June to mid-August, stocky plants 1 foot in height produce flowers of lavender-blue. Although each blossom may last but a day, a plant is seldom devoid of color. The species has ground cover potential on sunny well-drained banks.

R. strepens is lankier, to 2 feet, much-branched, with deep blue-purple flowers from June to late July. A third species, *R. græcizans* (*R. amœna*), somewhat over a foot in height, provides brilliant red clusters in early summer.

Progagation of all three is by seeds, cuttings taken in late summer, or by division in spring.

Those species mentioned are useful, but new glamour might be attained by a breeding project using *R. ciliosa* as one of the parents to be combined with more exotic but less hardy subjects.

SALVIA **Sage, Salvia** **Labiatæ**

Little ornamental value can be claimed for the majority of the 700 species in this genus, but when they are good, they are outstanding. Salvias are found native in both temperate and warm regions in many parts of the world. There are annuals, biennials, perennials and subshrubs; some are grown for culinary or medicinal uses and a few are used as ornamentals in the garden. S. *officinalis* is the common sage, a subshrub whose culinary virtue makes it a household word. *Salvia* is probably from the Latin "salvare" meaning to heal. Medicinal uses have been attributed to some species.

Garden Value: Most salvias do exceptionally well in the South, but only a few are reliable farther north. By and large, occasional specimens in borders or rock gardens, as individual stature dictates, are preferable, although some can be naturalized, and a few are good cut flowers.

Soil and Exposure: Drainage is the important feature needed in the soil, for most salvias are found in light, sandy, well-drained places in the wild. Wet footing in winter is dangerous, but drought seldom harms them. Full sun is recommended.

Care: In general, spring-planting is desirable. While those of short life spans may require regular renewal from seeds, division of vigorous types may be required each second spring. Light winter covering is advised for the less hardy sorts.

Propagation: Seeds must be sown annually in the fall to maintain the biennials and tender species. Cuttings are often difficult to root except with a mist system because pronounced wilting is otherwise encountered. Division is practical only in spring, as the long stringy roots are slow to take hold.

Species

Since the more vivid, red-flowered perennials are notably transient in colder areas, they are merely mentioned in passing. These include S. *coccinea*, S. *greggii*, and S. *microphylla* (S. *grahamii*). They are primarily for southern gardens where they can be quite colorful. Several biennials are included, in view of their popularity in gardens.

S. *azurea*. From sandy areas of the Southeast, it attains heights of 3 or 4 feet in gardens, but is far more variable in the wild. In August and September, the slim stems are well covered by whorls of icy blue flowers and slender leaves that are faintly blue on the underside. While proven satisfactorily hardy in Vermont, it cannot be considered a reliable perennial in many northern areas, especially where open winters are the rule. The white-flowered forms are of but moderate appeal.

The variety *grandiflora*, often listed as S. *pitcheri*, native as far north as Missouri and Nebraska, is the form most often grown. Brilliant gentian-blue flowers are doubly welcome amid the tawnier shades of early autumn. It arches gently, combining well with late lilies, roses, or early chrysanthemums. Pruning back to 6 or 8 inches in early June may forestall a need for staking later in the season. This variety also is not reliably hardy.

S. *farinacea*, Mealy-Cup Sage. Perennial in southern gardens, it is usually treated as an annual north of Maryland. Mostly lavender-blue flowers on gray-blue stems 2½ feet tall open in late summer. 'Blue Bedder' and 'Royal Blue' are superior selections for cutting.

S. *glutinosa*. This species is unusual in that the large blossoms, as well as the leaf tips, are pale yellow. Flowering in July on rough 3-foot stems, it is perhaps best mixed in with equally coarse shrubbery.

S. *hæmatodes*. Some botanists consider this closely allied to S. *tenorii*. It was brought to England from the Mediterranean in 1699 but practically disappeared until 1940, when E. K. Balls reintroduced it from Grecian hills. The nearly horizontal leaves, forming coarsely attractive rosettes, may be 6 inches long with prominent red veins. Spectacularly large panicles of handsome lavender-blue flowers appear in whorls on 3-foot stems, primarily during the month of June. In some areas, the plant may have a tendency to behave as a biennial, but sowing a few seeds when ripe will easily perpetuate this fine specimen.

S. *jurisicii*. This curious little 12-inch oddity is a particularly appropriate choice for rock gardens, where the matlike clumps of feathery leaves are a foil for clusters of violet flowers. If seeding is discouraged and water supplied in dry weather, blossoming flows steadily from June to August, and wintering is no problem.

S. *pratensis*. Native to Europe, it is hardy in most American gardens. It may spread and self-sow, an attribute when naturalized, but the invasive tendencies can be easily controlled in gardens. Well-spaced whorls of flowers range from blue to purple, rose-pink, and white. The mottled leaves are also distinctive. Purple forms are often combined with geums, which flower about the same time, from late May to early July.

S. *sclarea,* Clary, Vatican Sage. The large silvery leaves of this often grown biennial are quite coarse, but are effective for color contrast. However, the aroma of the foliage could hardly be described as a pleasing fragrance. An herb wine is still made from the leaves in rural England. Flowers are white or rosy purple in late summer. Height will vary from 2 to 3 feet. The variety *turkestanica,* often listed as S. *turkestanica,* is possibly more common, or at least more showy because of the enlarged pinkish purple bracts immediately beneath the flowers.

S. × *superba* (S. *nemerosa*). This hybrid between two obscure species blends favorably with white or soft pink phlox, and will bloom from mid-June until late August if not allowed to go to seed. Two-and-a-half-foot stems carry violet or purple flowers with reddish purple calyces. 'Purple Glory' is a very recent introduction of outstanding qualities that should soon gain wide popularity.

Final Comment: Those unfamiliar with the perennials in this genus should try 'Purple Glory' and S. *hæmatodes* to acquaint themselves with the admirable qualities of the salvias.

SANGUINARIA Bloodroot Papaveraceæ

Both scientific and common names refer to the orange-red juice exuded from cut roots. Bloodroot is a well-known wild flower from Nova Scotia in the North to Nebraska in the Midwest and Florida in the South. It is often transferred to cultivated gardens because of the attractive white flowers in early spring. The stray pink or pale purple variants reported at times have not been commercially exploited.

S. *canadensis,* the only species in the genus, is often grown in naturalized areas or in larger rock gardens, in spite of the rather coarse leaves. Height is never over 1 foot. Fairly rich, well-drained soil with adequate organic matter is desirable, as is summer shade. The petals shatter readily in heavy rains, so sheltered locations are preferable.

S. *canadensis* var. *multiplex* is an exceptionally beautiful double form. A Professor Dillenius of Oxford University, who studied the genus in 1732, reported doubles with 14 petals, but today forms with 30 or more are available. Scarce and rather expensive, it will repay a prolonged search with its sheer refinement.

Seeds should be sown in fall. Divisions are best made in August when the plant is dormant, particularly for prized double forms. While the doubles have an exceptional but transient beauty, the singles should not be scorned for naturalized areas.

SAPONARIA **Soapwort** **Caryophyllaceæ**

The cultivated saponarias are of prime interest in rock gardens where their June flowers provide color needed during that month. Plants are native to Europe, Asia, and North Africa. The botanical name is of Latin extraction, from a word meaning soap. Several species have root juices that create lather with water, and in earlier days in England they were supposed to be effective against grease spots.

Garden Value: Soapworts, with bright, usually pink flowers, clean foliage, and low habit, fit into rock gardens, dry walls, or sandy borders. While individual flowers are small, the June clusters are large enough to be quite effective.

Soil and Exposure: Full sun and sandy soil with perfect drainage are best. Overwintering will be difficult in wet areas.

Care: In general, potted material, especially if it is to be received through the mail, is best for spring planting. Winter protection is advisable in regions of variable winters.

Propagation: Seeds of most may be sown in early fall or spring. Cuttings root with ease in midsummer, but division is safest in very early spring.

Species

S. × *boissieri* (S. *cæspitosa* × S. *ocymoides*). Developed by F. Sundermann, noted Bavarian plantsman, and named for a Swiss botanist, it is roughly intermediate between the two parents. Clear pink flowers are sizable and freely produced. Neat mat-forming plants make for over-all tidiness.

S. *cæspitosa.* One of the nicest soapworts is this dwarf, only 5 inches high, even when in bloom. The large, brilliant rose-pink flowers are colorful in May and June. During the rest of the season, glossy bright green foliage is decorative in the rock garden.

S. *lutea.* Reginald Farrer called this "a rarity that suffers from the anticipations aroused by its name." Indeed, the yellow tints prove to be of creamy-straw quality, although lilac stamens afford some contrast. Perhaps this unobtrusive 3-inch midget will most satisfy the connoisseur of novelties for rockeries.

S. *ocymoides.* This, the most widely cultivated soapwort, forms a trailing branched plant with small oval to lanceolate leaves and reddened stems. In June, the mass of pink flowers add interest to a dry wall or rock garden; flowering may continue spasmodically until September. 'Splendens' has larger deeper rose flowers, and 'Alba' is a less interesting white form.

S. *officinalis,* Bouncing Bet. Native to Europe and Western Asia, it has become widely naturalized in North America where it is all too common along roadsides in rural areas. Occasionally planted in naturalized areas, the 2½-foot plants have terminal clusters of pink or white flowers. The double form is sometimes used in borders with very sandy soil, where other plants might present serious problems.

S. *pumilio.* The fancier may enjoy the challenge presented by this alpine subject, with emerald-green mat-forming foliage and relatively large, deep pink flowers on 1-inch stems. It needs the sharpest drainage and neutral soils to persist.

Final Comment: Because of the drainage requirement for most of this genus, hillside gardeners may find them more acceptable than will others.

SAXIFRAGA **Saxifrage** **Saxifragaceæ**

Of the 300 species found in the subarctic and temperate zones, the majority are true rock garden plants for the collector or specialist, but a few are of sufficiently easy culture to be rather commonly grown. *Saxifraga* means rock-breaking in Latin.

In the wild the plants are usually found in mountains, or at least on rocky soils of the moraine type. Consequently they can be used in wall gardens, rock crevices, or rock outcrops.

Plants are mostly dwarf, the leaves commonly basal and clustered, often forming evergreen rosettes, although some are mat-forming. Flowers are predominantly white, pink, or purple; a few are yellow.

Saxifrages grow best in light shade, where drainage is perfect and the moisture adequate. They are definitely not for hot, dry locations. The encrusted type, which has encrustations of lime along the leaf margins, needs an alkaline soil, or one to which limestone chips have been added. It tolerates more sun than the other types.

The mossy type will thrive in heavier shade and richer soil, but the need for moisture is just as great as for the others. Beyond those species native in the eastern states, all need attention, and no doubt, occasional replacements.

S. *aizoon* is one of the easiest to grow, and is thus the commonest. Plants 3 to 8 inches high form a clump of many rosettes somewhat like sempervivums. Leaves are a bluish gray-green with white encrustations of lime along the margins. The flowers, in June, vary from white or pink to red or rose-purple. Other satisfactory encrusted types include S. *hostii* var. *altissima* (S. *altissima*), which has larger rosettes and large white flowers, S. *lingulata,* which is similar but smaller, and S. *macnabiana,* with long leaves in large rosettes and white flowers flushed with pink.

As for the mossy type, a good one to try as an introduction to the group is S. *rosacea* (S. *decipiens*), 2 to 8 inches high, spreading, with fresh green leaves in rosettes, and white, pink, or red flowers in May and June. It can serve as a ground cover where soil, drainage, moisture, and shade create ideal conditions.

In the eastern states it is relatively simple to grow the native S. *virginiensis*. Flat rosettes of slender dark green leaves turn bronzy red in late summer or early autumn. White flowers on 10-inch stems light up shaded, moist rock crevices in May.

If the rock gardener begins with the saxifrages of easy culture, he may soon find himself with a new hobby.

SCABIOSA **Pincushion Flower** **Dipsacaceæ**

The sophisticated-looking flowers of S. *caucasica* easily overshadow those of the other perennials in the genus; in fact they represent the entire genus to some gardeners. The globular shape of the blossoms has given the name pincushion flower, the protruding stamens representing the pins. Native habitats range from Europe and Asia southward to Africa.

Garden Value: Scabiosas can be used both in borders and rock gardens, providing a source of fine cut flowers. Where it can become well established, S. *caucasica* is worthy of generous massing in the summer border, if for no other reason than the attractive flowers from June to September.

Soil and Exposure: Sandy loam, with added humus and perfect drainage, should be the basic medium, for summer moisture and winter dryness are equally imperative. Lime should be added to acid ground.

Care: Planting is advised in spring, usually at 15-inch intervals. In addition to a summer mulch, watering is necessary during dry periods for superior performance. Faded flowers should be removed before seeds form. Where open winters are common, winter cover may be helpful.

Propagation: Seeds should be sown as soon as ripe in the early fall. Division in spring is standard, but slow, for cultivars. Cuttings rot badly for many growers.

Species

S. *caucasica*. Native in the Caucasus, it flourishes in areas of cool, humid climate, such as in the British Isles and Pacific North-

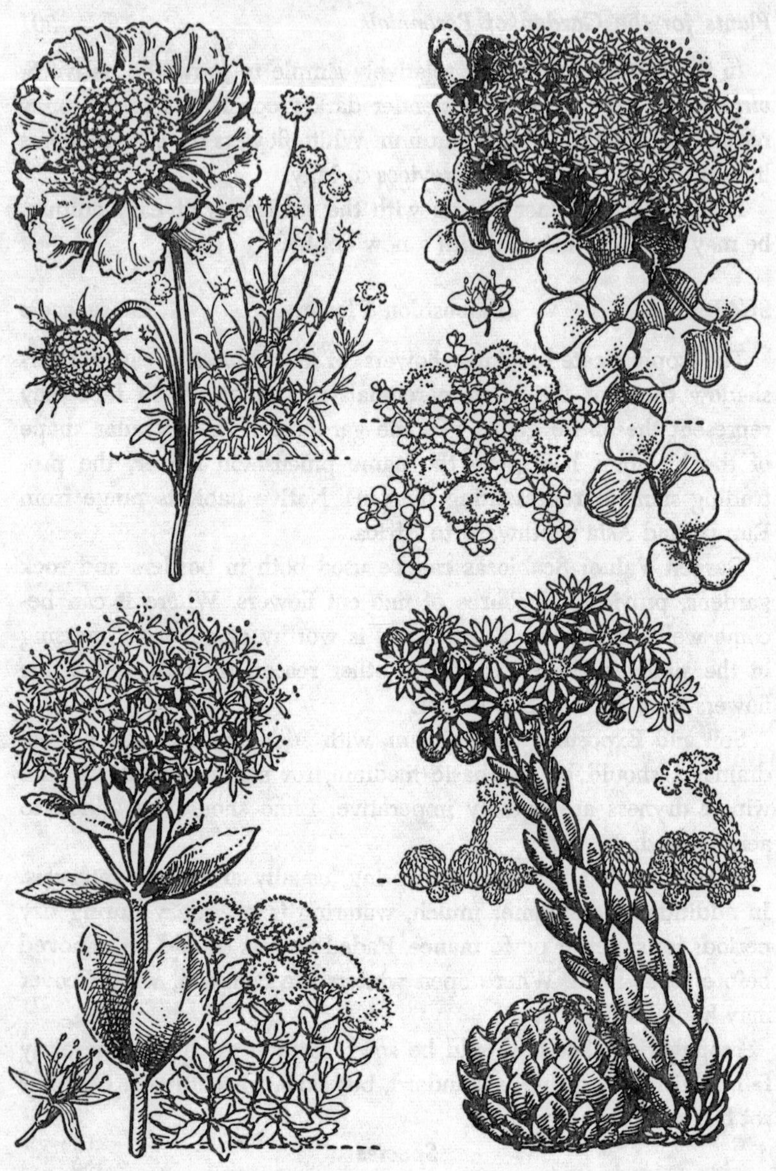

Scabiosa caucasica
Sedum spectabile

Sedum sieboldii
Sempervivum

west. In sultry regions, special attentions are necessary for its survival.

Flowers are mostly blue, flat, 3 inches across, with tufted central cushions from which gray stamens protrude, frequently adding a neat contrast. Plants are normally 2 feet or slightly more in height.

Fine English strains, especially from Isaac House of Bristol, are superior to those available in America. Unfortunately the British cultivars withstand neither trans-oceanic travel nor importation ordeals. Furthermore, named selections increase slowly by American standards. Good seed strains, however, promise an excellent range. 'Miss Willmott' is a snow white, 'Blue Lady' a gentian blue, and 'Constancy' an amethyst.

S. *columbaria.* Flowers are about 1½ inches in diameter, a soft clear pink or lilac, and globular rather than flattened. They are in bloom in July and August on 20-inch stems. Plants may not survive rough winters, but annual replacement is worth while in view of the shapely, distinctive flowers.

S. *fischeri.* This fairly tough Manchurian plant, with its 2½-inch blue-lavender flowers, is less handsome than S. *caucasica,* and with the foliage which is only passable, indiscriminate exploitation is hardly advisable.

S. *graminifolia,* Grassleaf Scabiosa. The grassy foliage is silvery gray and somewhat pubescent. Soft violet-pink flowers on 12-inch stems are appropriate in rock gardens.

S. *lucida.* Not over a foot high, it too can serve in rock gardens. The small, attractive lilac-blue pincushions are formed all summer long, with occasional rose tones noted. Long life can be anticipated if the drainage is perfect.

S. *ochroleuca.* Sometimes this one is stubbornly hardy but at other times it behaves as a biennial. Tiny, 1-inch globes of creamy yellow are produced on wiry 2-foot stems from June to September.

S. *rummelica.* Too recent an introduction for positive appraisal, it appears to be a bushy 2½-foot plant producing unusual crimson globular flowers all summer. The unusual coloring encourages further testing.

Final Comment: Since vegetative propagation of these plants is a slow process, it has perhaps discouraged hybridization and selection on the part of nurserymen; therefore it may be up to amateurs to make improvements.

SEDUM **Stonecrop** **Crassulaceæ**

Sedums join the saxifrages and sempervivums in providing fascinating and diverse material for the specialist, collector, or enthusiast with sufficient space in ideal locations. The majority of the 350 species of *Sedum* inhabit the north temperate zone, although several are found in tropical mountains. The ornamental features of many are strictly limited. The common name of stonecrop refers to the ability of some species to flourish on or around stony ledges.

Garden Value: Not all sedums are a plebian lot, if assigned duties for which they are fitted. Weedy, carpet-forming plants, menaces in the formalized garden, could be ideal for sunny ground covers or wall gardens. Fleshy, succulent foliage is attractive for months, flower colors range from white to pink, red, and purple, and the blooming season, with an appropriate choice of species, can extend from May to October. While most are for rock garden treatment, preferably in masses, a scant few have sufficient merit and stature for perennial gardens.

Soil and Exposure: In general, a gritty, sandy loam of good drainage is preferable, but some of the very succulent types do better when humus is added to the soil. For the most part, full sun is desirable.

Care: It is well to learn the character of any stonecrop to avoid using it unwisely. Spring is the usual time to plant, but some move easily at almost any time of the growing season. Those grown in borders may need division about each third year.

Propagation: Nearly all except named cultivars may be reproduced by spring-sown seeds. However, the tiny seeds wash easily if not protected from rains. Summer cuttings and spring divisions are rewarding.

Species

S. *acre*. This is the common stonecrop, crawling over rocks, walls, and yards. Although of European origin, it has strayed widely in America, where creeping mats of glabrous light green leaves, fully evergreen, are quite invasive except when used as ground cover in the open sun. Multitudes of bright yellow blossoms span the late May to July period. 'Minus' is a restrained, cushion-like miniature, refined enough for rock gardens.

S. *cauticolum*. Being a confirmed cliff dweller in Japan, this little trailer has merit in walls or on banks. Similar to S. *sieboldii* but only 3 inches high, it blooms a fortnight earlier, with rosy red cymes, and has a greater tolerance toward soil moisture.

S. *ewersii*. Somewhat like a dwarf edition of S. *spectabile*, the purplish pink flower clusters develop equally late in the season, and the 6-inch plants have blue-green foliage on twiggy red stems.

S. *kamtschaticum*. A shrubby tendency is noted, for the 9-inch stems remain alive over winter. Neat clumps of scalloped leaves are the rule, and intensely orange-yellow flowers appear from July to September. Forms with pure yellow flowers, and with variegated leaves are listed in rare-plant catalogs.

S. *maximum*. The form listed as 'Atropurpureum,' grown in Europe for years, is now available in America. Large leaves tinted a rich deep purple with an overcast of mahogany, and rather informal flower clusters of soft creamy rose tones all summer are supported on 24-inch stems. For borders and arrangements the foliage interest is unquestioned.

S. *sieboldii*. Interest starts in early spring, when young red leaf buds pierce the soil, later forming glaucous blue-green foliage, except in those forms in which leaves are edged with pink. Nine-inch stems arch gently as the flowers open in August. The pink flowers add much to rock gardens or walls until October. Lean, well-drained soil is essential. Variegated forms with yellow blotches on the leaves interest some fanciers.

S. *spathulifolium* 'Capa Blanca' is superior to the species, for the fleshy leaves are thickly coated with white farina, while 3-inch stems bear yellow flowers in May and June. Creeping is not a problem, and the foliage makes interesting contrast with any green plants. Some humus can be added to the soil where this is grown.

S. *spectabile.* Originally from Japan, this is perhaps the showiest and most extensively cultivated sedum. Ordinarily it grows in compact form, 18 inches high, and does not spread to any extent. Bold, fleshy 3-inch leaves, obovate in form and gray in coloring, are normal. Thick stems produce flat cymes, 3 or 4 inches across, of rosy pink flowers, although variations are possible. Flowering from August until frost, it is very useful in borders. Fairly good soil adds to the lustre, and slight shade does no harm; few plants are easier to raise.

Cultivars of value include the following: 'Brilliant,' the favored raspberry-carmine form, which often attracts butterflies; 'Carmen,' carmine-rose to red; 'Meteor,' almost wine red, with very large flower clusters. 'Alba' is a creamy white that would be more attractive if the color were pure. 'Variegatum,' or ice-plant, has white and yellow markings on the foliage. In time, reversion to the normal may occur. In addition, the muddy white flowers are of sorry character.

S. *spurium.* All forms creep diligently, with reddish 9-inch stems that bear rounded 1-inch leaves. Late summer sees a prolific production of pink or white flowers. Ground cover value for arid banks or sunny open spots is suggested. 'Album' is an innocuous white, 'Coccineum' a name that covers a number of deep pink or red variations. 'Bronze Carpet' has reddish bronze foliage all season, and 'Schorbusser Blut' ('Dragon's Blood') has ruby-red blossoms and scarlet leaves after midsummer. If less invasive, the latter selection would be a real acquisition.

SEMPERVIVUM **Hen-and-Chickens** **Crassulaceæ**

The Latin origin of the botanical name, which means live forever, well characterizes many of the species. Most of them are native to Eurasia. The many interspecific hybrids all offer interesting variations in color of foliage and flowers.

Primarily rock garden subjects with leaves in dense basal rosettes, they are also sometimes seen in front of borders, as edgings, or even planted to cover old, low stumps. They are companion plants for sedums, as their requirements are similar.

Sempervivums are ideal for poor soils, thin rock outcroppings, or dry walls. A few offsets wedged between thin layers of rock will take hold and spread surprisingly well in what appears to be an almost total lack of soil. Good drainage and full sun are their only requirements. Propagation is by separation of the small outer rosettes, or offsets, from the mother cluster.

The midsummer flowers, on stout stems 3 to 10 inches high, may be white, pink, red, purple, or yellow. Even if these plants never flowered, the foliage forms and colors alone would make the genus intriguing. Many are varying shades of green, some are tipped with red or purple, others may be bronzy red or a glaucous blue.

One of the more vigorous species is the common hen-and-chickens, S. *tectorum,* with large green rosettes and pink or red flowers. The variety *calcareum* differs in having glaucous leaves tipped with brown-purple. S. *arenarium* is fast-growing, with green leaves and yellow flowers sometimes flushed with red. S. *arachnoideum,* not over 4 inches high, has red flowers, and leaves covered with cobwebby gray hairs.

Those interested will find long lists of variations handled by specialists, and once a small collection is started, there will always be room for one more that is different.

SIDALCEA — Prairie Mallow — Malvaceæ

The sidalceas, native to the western states, are largely neglected as border plants, but can be very useful. Most of the garden forms commonly cultivated are hybrids, so no attempt will be made to discuss the various species.

Strict, narrowly upright plants about 3 feet tall look somewhat like miniature hollyhocks, but without the hollyhock rust. They have similar flowers and the same vertical effect in the garden, although they are far more delicate. Never weedy, they are ideal for contemporary gardens where space may be at a premium.

Our pink, rose, and purple flowers, which open along branching stems in July and August, are not quite up to some named cultivars available in England, but they make good garden subjects in groups of three, with 12-inch spacing. 'Rosy Gem' and 'Pink Beauty' are old favorites. More recent offerings include 'Rose Queen,' 'Scarlet Beauty' and 'Pompadour.'

Plants thrive in any good loam having adequate moisture-holding capacity during hot summers. Flowering stems should be cut back when the flowers have faded, to induce later bloom. Seeds do not breed true, good selections being propagated by division in early spring.

STACHYS **Betony** **Labiatæ**

Flowers of this genus are arranged in whorls on spikes, hence the scientific name, which was probably derived from an old Greek word for spike. There are over 200 species, rather widely distributed. Herbal use once caused esteem for a fair number, but very few are seen in modern gardens. Several species are sometimes listed under *Betonica*, now an invalid name.

Garden Value: The common desire for borders that never become stereotyped is favorable to these plants. While no startling display is claimed, the contrasting foliage color of some and the quaint flowers of Old World flavor should not be disregarded. An occasional group adds interest to borders or even to large rock gardens. *S. officinalis* is above average for cutting.

Soil and Exposure: Light loamy soils and predominant sunlight are preferable for most species.

Care: Beyond occasional division, little maintenance is required.

Propagation: Spring-sown seeds give adequate increase, but division in spring usually covers all normal requirements.

Species

S. *grandiflora* (*Betonica grandiflora*), Betony. Rich purple-violet flowers appear in whorls in early summer on plants 18 inches high. Plants tolerate partial shade; in fact, flowering may be prolonged in such a situation. There is a tendency toward spreading, but it never gets out of hand.

S. *officinalis* (*Betonica officinalis, S. betonica*). The rather hairy leaves are grouped into closely packed tufts. In July and August, rosy purple flowers appear in whorls on 2½-foot stems. Hot, dry soils are best.

S. *olympica* (S. *lanata*), Lambs-Ear. The name comes from the silky, woolly leaf, shaped somewhat like a lamb's ear. The tight pink or purplish red flowers are not outstanding, but they continue to open from July until frost on stout woolly stems a foot or more in height. As an unusual accent, the gray foliage has much to commend it. Plants are usually set in the foreground, and flowering stems are often cut back, leaving the low foliage for color contrast and texture.

STOKESIA Stokes Aster Compositæ

In dry ground, a thrifty habit, glossy foliage, and welcome late season displays of unique flowers are offered by this genus. There is but one species, S. *lævis,* native from South Carolina to Florida and Louisiana. There, in sandy soils the flowers may be only a paltry inch in diameter. Some have strayed to moist pine barrens, but survive in the absence of severe winter temperatures. The genus was named for Dr. Jonathan Stokes, an English botanist of the early nineteenth century.

Back in the thirties, stokesias were in the public eye, and were much sought after and heartily enjoyed. Nurserymen almost feverishly built up stocks and bickered over the respective merits of their pet cultivars. At present, however, the genus is indifferently regarded by many, and demand has dwindled to a trickle. Apparently, widespread climatic shifts to open, wet winters are the cause, for sogginess spells doom for the plants.

Spring-planting at 15-inch intervals is recommended. Where freezing and thawing alternate in winter, protection is advisable. Propagation is by spring-sown seeds, divisions, or root cuttings. Commercially, 2-inch root sections are started under glass. Amateurs could sow the seeds outdoors in April.

Small groups of three plants, set in the full sun, lend decided late appeal in the garden. This is especially true of those with flowers of bright metallic blue. Seldom over 18 inches tall, they blend well with annuals and cushion chrysanthemums, since they begin to flower in mid-July and continue through August. In Florida gardens, plants bloom practically all winter. Flowers are usually 3 inches in diameter when well grown.

'Præcox' is the trade classification given to early-flowering forms, often in bloom by late July. 'Alba' is a white variant not consistent in purity; 'Silver Moon' is much more reliable. 'Lilacina' tends to lilac shading. 'Blue Moon,' a very large-flowered selection, blends silvery blue casts into its lilac background. 'Blue Danube' is a leading example of the decisive blue forms, 'Lutea' is a very rare sulfur yellow, and 'Rosea' a soft pink.

Stokesias can be heartily recommended to gardeners who have soil conditions that meet the requirements.

SYMPHYTUM **Comfrey** **Boraginaceæ**

Symphytum asperum, the prickly comfrey, from western Asia, is an acceptable plant for large borders where it can fill in a rear corner, or for rural gardens where space is not limiting. Most often planted in full sun, it is sometimes set at the base of fence posts to which the taller stems can be secured. It is practically indestructible. Staking may be necessary, especially in rich, moist soils, where it grows rapidly.

Plants are rather coarse, to 5 feet, with many clusters of pink buds and light blue tubular flowers. The main value is the long blooming

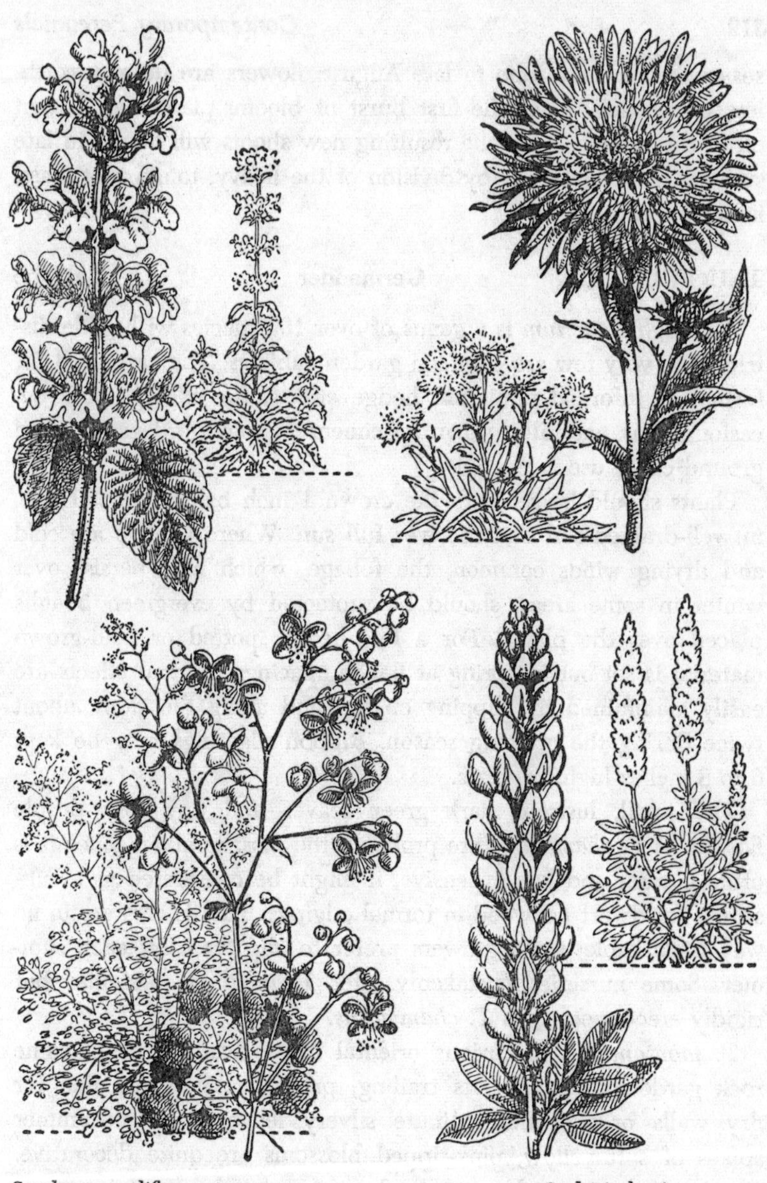

Stachys grandiflora
Thalictrum rochebrunianum

Stokesia lævis
Thermopsis caroliniana

season, from early June to late August; flowers are utterly worthless for cutting. After the first burst of bloom, plants can be cut off at the ground level; the resulting new shoots will flower in late summer. Propagation is by division of the heavy, tough root mass, in early spring.

TEUCRIUM **Germander** **Labiatæ**

Although *Teucrium* is a genus of over 100 species with wide distribution, very few are common garden subjects. They are used for formal or informal miniature hedge effects, for edgings, and occasionally as naturally grown specimens in rock gardens. Limited ground cover use is possible.

Plants should be set with the crown 1 inch below the soil line, in well-drained soil that receives full sun. Where winters are cold and drying winds common, the foliage, which may persist over winter in some areas, should be protected by evergreen boughs placed over the plants. For a low hedge, potted or field-grown material is set out in spring at 6-inch spacings. Formal effects are easily maintained by clipping on top and along the sides, about twice during the growing season. Ribbon plantings may be kept 6 to 8 inches high for years.

The small, lustrous dark green leaves and tiny rosy purple flowers of *T. chamædrys* are probably the most familiar. Since it is often hardier and less expensive, it might be considered as a substitute for dwarf boxwood in formal edgings. The flowers are in no way remarkable; some growers prefer to clip them off each summer. Some nurseries mistakenly offer *T. lucidum,* a similar but rigidly erect species, as *T. chamædrys.*

T. montanum is a curious oriental rarity available from some rock garden specialists. Its trailing, prostrate stems are fine for dry walls or rockeries. Minute silvery leaves and midsummer spikes of soft yellow, pink-tipped blossoms are quite decorative. The hardiness factor has not yet been adequately ascertained.

Seeds germinate well but slowly. Cuttings are easily rooted in summer, and division of deeply planted, old established clumps is possible in spring.

THALICTRUM **Meadow-Rue** **Ranunculaceæ**

The meadow-rues are esteemed for their delicately compound foliage and their light airy flowers. There are no petals; the color is provided by petaloid sepals, which often fall quickly, and by numerous colored stamens. Not many species are presently cultivated, but European nurserymen are still investigating new Asiatic introductions.

Garden Value: Being of predominantly tall habit, the average plant belongs near the rear of the border. There, the delicate tracery of foliage and feathery bloom adds refined grace. Behind heliopsis, phlox, echinacea, or iris, they tone down obvious dominance; near Oriental poppies, they disguise the withering summer foliage. Most are well suited to wild gardens or even to lighten heavy shrubbery effects. As cut flowers, the same airy effect is worthy.

Soil and Exposure: Since most species are found in thin woodlands, they are accustomed to light shade. In borders, full sun is no handicap provided soils are fairly moist, with rich peaty content. In no instance will meager, rocky ground sustain them.

Care: Planting may be done in fall or spring, with spacing at least 2 feet from nearby subjects, to allow for natural spreading. Every fourth or fifth spring, the congested root mass should be divided. Unless planted deeply, winter protection may be needed, especially for *T. dipterocarpum.*

Propagation: Seeds should be sown in fall, when fresh. Division is best in spring, but can be done in early fall if winter protection is given.

Species

T. aquilegifolium. Three-foot plants flower from late May through June. Many small lilac-purple blossoms are gathered in a loose inflorescence of countless small umbels. There are white and rose forms as well, the colored stamens furnishing most of the color. Foliage is similar to that of the columbines, but is slightly gray-green. Effective combinations are made with tulips, columbines, and painted daisies; the white variant is often seen complementing bearded iris.

T. delavayi. This species resembles *T. dipterocarpum,* but is smaller, never over 3 feet. The willowy, purple-tinged stems carry nodding pale lilac flowers. It was named for a French missionary in China.

T. diffusiflorum. A recent addition from Tibet, this one is noted for very large overlapping, cup-shaped blossoms, an inch long, of clear, delicate mauve-blue. Plants grow 3 to 4 feet in height, and tolerate considerable sunlight. They are still in limited cultivation.

T. dipterocarpum. Dr. Ernest Wilson found this beauty in Yunnan Province, China, where it towered to 10 feet in height. In American gardens, 3 to 5 feet is the range observed, depending upon soil conditions. Floriferous sprays of lavender to bishop's-violet flowers with yellow stamens appear in August as the last of the meadow-rues. The showy sepals do not fall as quickly from this species as from some of the others. 'Album' is a less commonly grown white form.

T. kiusianum. An uncommon Japanese midget, it is not over 5 inches high, with purplish leaves, pink-lilac sepals, and striking blue stamens. Part shade and leafy soil encourage sporadic bloom until fall. In an ideal situation, it may act as a limited ground cover.

T. minus (*T. adiantifolium, T. majus*). The exquisite ferny leaves of this species are as attractive when cut as they are in the garden. In comparison, the insignificant greenish yellow flowers in June and early July are secondary. A variable species, it may range in height from 1 to 3 feet. Massing among shrubbery or on moist banks is possible.

T. rochebrunianum, Lavender Mist. In every way, this plant is superior to *T. dipterocarpum.* A soybean trader in North Japan first brought it to garden attention. The lusty 4- to 6-foot clumps bear huge masses of lavender-violet blossoms with primrose-yellow stamens from mid-July to early September. It may become one of the finest of all perennials, hardier than *T. dipterocarpum*, and overshadowing all other thalictrums.

T. rugosum (*T. glaucum*), Dusty Meadow-Rue. Native to southern Europe, this species features blue-gray leaves that are superb for cut-flower work. The plumy panicles consist of slightly fragrant, soft yellow flowers. At heights of 4 to 6 feet, clumps are splendid with delphiniums or *Campanula persicifolia* in early summer.

Final Comment: The captivating and tasteful meadow-rues fit well into almost any border. Special attention is directed to the relatively new *T. rochebrunianum*.

THERMOPSIS False Lupine Leguminosæ

The name *Thermopsis* signifies lupine-like in Greek, the plant being so named because the pealike flowers are formed in dense tapering spikes that resemble a yellow lupine.

Garden Value: Exceptionally hardy, little troubled by insect or disease, never invasive, thermopsis can be useful in the border for both its yellow flowers and its good foliage. All species supply useful racemes for cutting, and in general, can replace yellow lupines.

Soil and Exposure: A sandy loam and full sun are ideal, but partial shade will allow adequate performance.

Care: Fall-planting is often preferable, since spring growth is both early and rapid. Division more often than every eight years is hardly necessary.

Propagation: Seeds germinate readily if sown in late summer. When necessary, divisions can be made in very early spring or autumn, but old clumps are hard to dig and split.

Species

T. caroliniana. Although native from North Carolina to Georgia, it is enduringly hardy almost anywhere. Strong 4-foot clumps are topped by 12-inch racemes of sparkling yellow flowers in June and early July, allowing effective combination with blue or purple delphiniums.

T. montana. Where room is at a premium, this more restrained 2½-foot species is suggested. Racemes are less solid, seldom over 8 inches long. Native to the western Rocky Mountains, it is suitably hardy in the rest of the country.

T. rhombifolia. Here is an uncommon little 8-inch possibility for rock gardens. It colonizes agreeably if allowed to self-sow. Color and season of bloom are the same as for the other species.

Final Comment: Attention is called to the fact that this genus is in the pea family, which means that nitrogenous fertilizers should be used very sparingly around the plants; otherwise yellow foliage results.

THYMUS Thyme Labiatæ

The thymes are tiny subshrubs, but because they are grown in rock gardens, treated as perennials, and often so listed in catalogs, they are included here. Many are planted in herb gardens, particularly *T. vulgaris,* a favored herb for seasoning pork and poultry. *Thymus* is an old Greek name of uncertain derivation. The species, spread widely over the temperate zone, are most prevalent in the warm Mediterranean region.

Garden Value: Nearly all have rock garden value, many are used for planting among paving stones, while others become shrubby little specimens to be spotted in crevices or included in herb gardens. Inasmuch as the majority are only inches high, no problems of height plague the gardener. Aromatic foliage is attractive throughout the season. Small clusters of flowers, which may be pink, rose-purple, or white, are most effective in June and July.

Soil and Exposure: In general, a gritty, loose sandy loam with some organic matter is suitable. Performance is best in fairly sunny areas.

Care: Spring or early fall is ideal for planting, yet many thymes can be transplanted in full bloom. Where winters are extremely severe, light winter protection may be necessary.

Propagation: Seeds germinate well but cannot always be expected to produce seedlings true to type. Cuttings root easily in early summer, and division is possible in spring.

Species

More than normal confusion in identification and nomenclature is noted in many trade listings. A degree of the uncertainty is no doubt due to natural variations encountered, especially in *T. serpyllum.*

T. lanuginosus, Woolly Mountain Thyme. This sturdy native of northern Europe was once included under *T. serpyllum.* Minute, woolly, gray leaves make attractive but sprawling plants on which the scanty pinkish flower heads do not have much appeal. It resents being trodden on even though it is often used among paving stones or along walks or steps. 'Hall's Variety' is liberal with red flowers, but it lacks the type's full beauty.

T. nitidus. From Sicily, it becomes an aromatic little shrub in our gardens, 9 inches high, with silvery gray leaves and tight rose-lilac flowers in June. Older clumps do not transplant well; thus young material from cuttings is preferable. Self-sowing to some extent is likely.

T. serpyllum, Mother-of-Thyme, Creeping Thyme. This species seems to have been a general dumping ground for any thyme able to creep. Basically it is a creeping subshrub, invaluable for ground covering, planting in terraces, or displaying in wall chinks. It may be walked on, even mowed. Tiny rose-lilac flowers are customary, but deviation is common.

Variety *vulgaris* (*T. citridorus*) is the famed lemon-scented form, a fine creeping ground cover for full sun. Propagation of good clones by division assures more uniformly aromatic stock than does seed-grown material. This variety of *T. serpyllum* should not be confused with the species *T. vulgaris,* which spreads rampantly, becoming practically a weed.

'Argenteus' has silver markings on the leaves, is relatively erect and quite fragrant. 'Albus' has white flowers, 'Coccineus,' bright crimson flowers over deep green foliage, and 'Splendens' may be a thick, fluffy carpet, almost a foot high and a yard wide when the brilliant rosy red clusters are in bloom in July and August. 'Annie Hall' is a very freely flowering pink form.

TRADESCANTIA Spiderwort Commelinaceæ

Ease of culture, longevity, and length of flowering season are virtues no one can deny the spiderworts. John Tradescant, a plant collector for whom the genus was named, sent material of *T. virginiana* back to England in the seventeenth century, when Virginia extended to the Mississippi. There is only the one species of real garden importance.

Garden Value: Undeniably hardy and well suited to survival in gardens that may be neglected, the spiderwort likewise has a long blooming season to commend it. While slightly weedy, it can be easily controlled.

Near foundations of buildings or in poor soil, these plants have their uses. Groups of three are the minimum that will create any sort of an impression. Not exactly the neat plant for a formal garden, one or two of the better cultivars would not be out of place in the average garden.

Soil and Exposure: Spiderworts grow wherever planted, in spite of, rather than because of what is done for them.

Care: Fairly regular division is necessary to restrain excessive spreading. If the stems flop in midsummer, they can be cut off at ground level; the new shoots that come up will flower during autumn.

Propagation: Division in spring is recommended for cultivars.

Species

T. virginiana. The species is found throughout the central states, and has escaped even farther south. Erect habit, to 3 feet, is expected from native plants. Grassy spears of linear 15-inch leaves, and terminal umbels of violet-purple flowers are the rule. While

Thymus serpyllum
Trollius europæus

Tradescantia virginiana
Tunica saxifraga

each flower lasts but a day, there are always more to come. For the most part, garden cultivars are a vast improvement over plants found in the wild. Both European breeders and those at the United States Department of Agriculture have named a fair quantity. Heights of 18 inches are average for the following: 'Pauline,' a large rosy mauve type; 'James C. Weguelin,' a large porcelain blue; 'Blue Stone,' a strong, deep blue; 'Purple Dome,' a spectacular rosy purple; 'James Stratton,' which is more subdued than 'Purple Dome'; 'Iris Prichard,' a white with blue flush; and 'Osprey,' a huge feathery white, shaded blue in the center.

TROLLIUS **Globeflower** **Ranunculaceæ**

The undemanding, trouble-free globeflowers should find a place in any garden with moist, heavy soil. In this genus, the showy part of the flower is composed of sepals; the petals are narrow, erect structures somewhat resembling the stamens. Although all the species are commendable, a number of cultivars, mostly of European origin, are especially admirable.

Garden Value: Where soil is suitably rich and heavy, globeflowers can be spectacularly successful. Small groups dress up the border. The earlier-flowering types combine well with myosotis and tulips. Practically all are good when cut. Since they flourish along streams and around pools, their garden effectiveness can be greatly expanded if the owner is willing to supply water when needed.

Soil and Exposure: Rich, peaty soil with high moisture content is imperative, although stagnant, boglike conditions are hardly to be recommended. Liberal additions of organic matter are necessary in sandy soils. While partial shade is quite satisfactory, trollius, like astilbes, thrive in full sun if soil conditions are ideal.

Care: Clumps may be planted in spring or fall and should be well watered in dry periods. Removal of seed pods prolongs flowering. When plants get oversized, perhaps in five years, division can be safely accomplished in late summer.

Propagation: If seeds are used, they should be sown as soon as collected. Late summer sowings of seeds frozen in a refrigerator for two days usually germinate before winter arrives. Divisions made in August produce enough growth to permit flowering the next year, but careful retention of roots on the sections is imperative.

Species

T. asiaticus. Not fully globular, the flowers are bright orange-yellow with colorful orange-red anthers; foliage is a bronzy green. This species grows to 3 feet where native in Siberia, but it is usually 18 inches or so in most gardens. 'Byrne's Giant' is a favored European selection that gives a fine performance in this country.

T. chinensis. Cup-shaped flowers of golden yellow open on 2-foot stems in May. The lower leaves are often extremely large, sometimes 7 inches long and 5 inches wide.

T. europæus. This familiar globeflower is native to northern Europe, being especially prominent in English hills and Welsh river valleys. The Scottish know them as butterballs. Unfortunately, indiscriminate collecting, as with many wild flowers, has impoverished many British stands.

Normally, plants grow to 1 or 2 feet, with globular 1½-inch yellow blooms during May and June. Fascinating variants of orange and intermediate tones are also probable on plants of this species. Neatly divided foliage remains attractive all season. The form 'Superbus' is a horticultural selection with bright lemon blossoms 2 inches across.

T. laxus (*T. albiflorus*). This species is distinguished by the novelty of its creamy white sepals surrounding small, narrow yellowish petals in 1½-inch flowers. Height is 15 to 20 inches.

T. ledebouri. This native of Siberia has orange-gold sepals that fan wide open to 2 inches or more, with very thin, narrow petals around brilliant, erect stamens. Flowering is in June, extending the season of the common earlier species. Flowers may appear periodically until the end of August if summers are not too hot. Two-foot stems and neatly lobed foliage are the rule. 'Golden

Queen' is an outstanding cultivar, taller, to almost 4 feet, with larger flowers, sometimes 4 inches across, that are butter yellow in color. It reproduces quite reliably from seeds.

T. pumilus. Not over 8 inches tall, this tiny Himalayan is ideal for moist rock gardens, since the glossy lobed foliage has a delicate pattern. One-inch blooms are clear yellow, rounded, and a trifle flattened on top.

T. yunnanensis. From West China, this species produces 3-inch blooms of bright yellow that open flat on 20-inch stems in early summer. Large mottled leaves add interest to a species likely to self-sow where it is contented.

Cultivars of Hybrid Parentage

Those available include: 'Prichard's Giant,' an excellent English hybrid, a fine 3-foot plant of vivid orange-yellow; 'Earliest of All,' early, naturally, with spherical yellow flowers; 'Lemon Queen,' darker than the name suggests; 'Orange Princess,' with bright old-gold coloring; and 'Fire Globe,' a tawny burnt orange.

Final Comment: Always reliable but never objectionable in any way, the slow-growing trollius deserves a place in modern gardens, where space is not boundless and where maintenance may be neglected.

TUNICA Tunic-Flower Caryophyllaceæ

Tunica saxifraga, a small tufted perennial native to the Mediterranean region of Europe, is of value for summer color in rock gardens, where one all too often sees a burst of color in spring, then only green foliage the rest of the season. While in no way conspicuous, this species invites closer inspection from those who favor plants in miniature. Superior selections are excellent for walls or any stony, sunny nook. In summer, the profusion of tiny flowers of modest charm justifies its use in appropriate settings.

Threadlike, wiry stems, seemingly almost leafless, are about 10 inches in length when the lilac blooms appear. The double-flowered forms are somewhat more effective. 'Rosette' is a robust form with doubled rose-pink flowers. 'Alba' is a white variant that may have doubled as well as single flowers, some of which may show a faint pink edging to the petals.

Full sun and a light porous soil yield the best performance. No attention need be given, other than to remove old flowers to prevent seed formation. Outstanding forms are propagated by division in spring, although cuttings may be taken from non-flowering shoots all season.

VALERIANA Valerian, Garden-Heliotrope Valerianaceæ

This is an old-fashioned border plant that persists by repeated self-sowings, even after the garden itself may have disappeared. While 175 species are found in the northern hemisphere, only one, *V. officinalis*, is of garden importance. Derived from the Latin, *Valeriana*, meaning to be strong, was applied to this genus because certain species had medicinal uses.

When planted in moist soils, in either sun or semishade, it grows to 4 feet and produces small fragrant flowers in large panicles that may vary from white to lavender, sometimes with pink tints; fragrance in July and early August is commendable. The deeply lobed foliage is not unattractive during most of the season.

It is satisfactory for wild gardens, and its tolerance toward shade suggests its use in moist shaded borders. The flowers are creditable when cut, but excessive use in more formal designs is to be discouraged. In other than naturalized areas, volunteer seedlings must be eliminated; otherwise the plants' weediness will become objectionable.

VERBASCUM Mullein Scrophulariaceæ

Most of the 250 species are native to the Mediterranean regions; many are biennials. The common garden forms are hybrids, offered mainly as cultivars.

Full sun and sharp drainage, especially in winter, are necessary for survival. Saucer-shaped flowers 1 inch in diameter are borne on terminal racemes about 3 feet tall, from mid-June through July. Propagation of hybrids is primarily by root cuttings, in early spring.

The most common cultivars are 'Pink Domino,' with rose-colored flowers, and 'Cotswold Gem,' which has terra-cotta shadings.

While not spectacular, and often outclassed by other plants in bloom at the same time, the verbascums in groups of three relieve more stereotyped materials.

VERONICA Speedwell Scrophulariaceæ

With a judicious selection of species and hybrids, gardens can now have a display of veronicas almost throughout the season. Since there is a scarcity of blue-flowered perennials, the speedwells may well be prized for this reason alone. The genus was named for St. Veronica. There are about 150 species, mainly from temperate and colder regions.

Garden Value: The taller, spike-flowered veronicas of summer are unquestionably the elite for borders, particularly when well established. They blend well with other materials and usually furnish agreeable cut flowers. The dwarf or trailing members have value for walls or rock gardens. Those species and cultivars with gray stems and leaves provide additional interest throughout the season by creating foliage color contrast.

Soil and Exposure: Soils of average fertility and texture suffice, but winter sogginess must be avoided. Predominant sunlight is best, although plants tolerate partial shade.

Care: Most species can be planted in spring or early fall; the trailing group is easier to establish if the plants were grown in pots. Removal of seed pods adds to the flowering season. Occasional division preserves the good appearance of most types.

Propagation: Seeds are best sown in late spring, but will no doubt produce some variation. Cuttings are usually easily rooted in summer; however, divisions, possible in fall or spring, will supply all normal garden needs.

Valeriana officinalis

Veronica latifolia

Veronica pectinata

Verbascum

Veronica spicata

Species

V. filiformis. This pernicious, invasive weed should never be purposely planted. It invades lawns and gardens, choking out everything in its path. Invulnerable to applications of 2,4-D, it persists in spite of attempts to eradicate it, although some promising new chemicals being tested show hopeful signs of control.

V. holophylla. This rotund Japanese newcomer promises well for the polished leathery foliage and the 12-inch spires of velvety deep blue in late summer. Hardiness appears unquestioned.

V. incana, Woolly Speedwell. The white woolly foliage and 6-inch stems of porcelain-blue flowers in June and July make an attractive contrast in rock gardens or in the front rank of a border. Plants vary from 12 to 18 inches in height when in flower. Perfect drainage is necessary. 'Rosea' is a form considered by many to be more desirable because of the rose-pink flowers; seedlings are not reliable. 'Wendy' is a pleasing hybrid between *V. incana* and *V. spicata,* growing to 18 inches, with striking violet-blue flowers and gray foliage.

V. latifolia (*V. teucrium*), Hungarian Speedwell. Some forms are reasonably erect 2-foot plants while others may tumble informally. Slender, tangled stems usually have lengthy axillary racemes of blue, but white and pink variants are on record. If plants are trimmed after flowering, bloom will often repeat in fall. 'Crater Lake Blue' is a cultivar first sent to Amos Perry by an Oregon resident. It boasts vivid gentian-blue spires in early summer.

V. longifolia (*V. maritima*). While this species is the foundation for the better garden forms, it is now secondary to hybrid cultivars. The variety *subsessilis* (*V. subsessilis*), said to have been found in Japan around 1878, is extremely popular. In late July, dense terminal racemes of royal-blue flowers are striking, particularly near red phlox or yellow anthemis. Poor drainage and severe cold may be fatal. A white form, which is actually ivory-colored, was first noted in a Montreal garden about 1945; it seems less hardy than the others.

The majority of garden cultivars appear to be hybrids of *V. longifolia* and *V. spicata.* They may begin to flower in June, continuing most of the summer.

'Blue Champion,' a 2½-foot-tall plant with medium-blue flowers, blooms about July 1 and continues until almost Labor Day, making a good combination with *Coreopsis verticillata.* It must have good drainage.

'Icicle' produces 2-foot clumps of neat gray-green leaves and white flowers from June to September; a very hardy, productive, and wholly desirable plant.

'Sunny Border Blue' is a stocky 18- to 24-inch plant with navy-blue spikes from July to September. 'Blue Spires' is a deep blue of medium height, flowering over the same period.

V. pectinata. A prostrate mat from Asia Minor, with small woolly leaves, it can appropriately fit into restricted wall crevices. Racemes of blue flowers with white eyes are produced in early summer. 'Rosea' is a showier pink form.

V. prostrata (*V. rupestris*). Tufted plants produce many creeping, prostrate shoots, as well as some erect ones to 8 inches high. Frail racemes of pale blue begin to open in June. 'Shirley Blue' has dense, brilliant blue flowers; 'Hav-a-Look' may have blue and white blossoms on the same plant. None trail to excess.

V. repens. Coming from Corsica and Spain, this dainty, mossy creeper needs sandy soil and water during droughts. Slender stems of pale blue, milky white, or soft rose flowers are produced for a month in late spring. Because the roots are shallow and the leaves small, it can be planted with spring-flowering bulbs.

V. spicata. Well-branched plants are more restrained and with shorter racemes than *V. longifolia.* The maximum height is 18 inches. From late June to early August, the blue flowers are quite showy. 'Nana' is a midget form. There is also a white-flowered variant; its dwarf form is only 6 inches high. Pink-flowered types are also available. 'Blue Peter,' named for the flags displayed by English ships leaving port, has Oxford-blue flowers but rather dowdy foliage in poorer soils.

A new group of hybrids of decided value comes from Alan Bloom of England: 'Barcarolle,' a deep rose; 'Pavane,' medium rose; and 'Minuet,' a soft pink. They are far superior to former offerings, and are very easily grown.

VERONICASTRUM **Culvers Root** **Scrophulariaceæ**

Closely related to the veronicas and sometimes listed with them, *Veronicastrum virginicum* is native in many of the eastern and central states. It grows to 4 feet and has white flowers, much like an extremely vigorous veronica. Completely hardy, of very simple culture, it forms bold clumps which can function as background plants in a border or as effective accents in naturalized plantings. Dense racemes to 10 inches long make a modest display from mid-July to mid-August. Occasional division will be needed to reduce the size of older plants.

VINCA **Periwinkle, Trailing Myrtle** **Apocynaceæ**

An ideal ground cover should be vigorous, hardy and fast growing, yet not rampant. It should be attractive in foliage and flower; if evergreen, it has an additional attribute. Finally, tolerance of various conditions and simple cultural needs are imperative for large-scale ventures. The periwinkle is commendable on all counts.

As a quickly established ground cover in partial shade, *V. minor* is widely grown. Where grass fails under trees or shrubs, on steep banks, in large rock gardens, or even in cascades from walls, in fact wherever a low trailing plant can be effectively used, this species immediately comes to mind. It will keep the surface of the soil shaded and cool, protecting the shallow surface roots of lilies, for example, but it is not a plant to be introduced into perennial borders. Mertensias, pulmonarias, and daffodils are often interplanted among patches of vinca. In the spring, and occasionally throughout the season, slate-blue flowers are an added attraction.

It has no special requirements, although in partial shade the foliage is glossier and richer. If the soil has adequate humus and moisture, vinca is satisfactory in the sun. Planting at 6- to 12-inch intervals is usually done in spring or early September. As growth increases, light shearing promotes bushier plants, while sterner treatment, when necessary, will hold plants in bounds.

'Bowles Variety' is vastly preferable to the species, since the leaves are larger and glossier, and the brilliant blue flowers often recur in autumn. This may well be the acme of ground covers.

The variety *alba* has white flowers and light green leaves but is less vigorous. Variety *multiplex* consists of rarely seen forms with double flowers in white, reddish, and blue tones. 'Alpina' is a reddish purple double or semidouble that is not particularly floriferous, and is best considered a novelty. Forms with yellow variegations on the foliage have never achieved great popularity in this country.

Plants are propagated by cuttings taken in summer. Trailing stems may be cut into several pieces for rooting. Division in spring is feasible, but it must be followed by heavy pruning and watering.

In view of the fact that vinca exceeds even pachysandra in popularity, and millions of plants are raised annually, it probably is sufficiently well known to preclude the necessity of further comment.

VIOLA — Violet — Violaceæ

Viola is a genus of about 300 species indigenous over much of the north and south temperate zones. Beyond a few that stand in great public favor, the majority are interesting mainly as wild flowers, even though they are sometimes transferred to cultivated areas.

Garden Value: Limited massing or specimen planting in rock gardens or borders is customary. Some cut flower virtue is evident, but stems are extremely short in most cases. The fragrance of some and the showy flowers of others create sentimental and often nostalgic associations.

Soil and Exposure: In general, soils should be fairly rich, with some organic matter incorporated; drainage must be good. Semi-shade is desirable.

Care: Spring-planting is recommended. Seed pods should be removed to encourage additional flowering. Watering is a necessity during dry periods, for red spiders and aphids may be problems in very hot, dry seasons. Leaf spot may be evidenced by brownish leaf blotches at times. An all-purpose spray containing insecticides and fungicides should control the troubles.

Propagation: Seeds give best results when sown in late summer. Cuttings are made by the trade for certain hardy violas. Division of many can be made in early spring or late summer if the long shoots are cut back halfway to lessen wilting.

Species

V. cornuta, Tufted Pansy, Horned Violet. Truly perennial, it increases by tufts from underground stolons. It tolerates summer heat well, as befits its Spanish and Pyrennean habitats, so is well constituted for American gardens. Plants less than a foot in height have basically violet flowers, to 1½ inches in size. They bloom all summer if seeds are not allowed to form. A prominent spur or "horn" is visible at the back of each flower.

Violettas, of moderate interest, are very tiny versions of this species. Much smaller leaves and flowers are evident, and distribution is limited mainly to the British Isles. They were named by Dr. Charles Stuart, in whose English garden a chance white miniature first appeared in 1887.

Because of its impressive hardiness, *V. cornuta* has been diligently hybridized with the common pansy, *V. tricolor* var. *hortensis*. The inevitable results were larger, definitely attractive, more colorful flowers, but also looser habit of growth and, in many cases, short life.

A class known commercially as bedding violas blooms longer than the pansies, but is best handled from seeds in the same manner. Most of these grow to 10 inches and are best in light shade. Selections include: 'Beauty of Laronne,' a large blue-flowered type; 'Apricot,' a rich apricot-bronze; 'Admiration,' a deep purple; 'Arkwright Ruby,' a terra cotta; 'Perfection,' a soft blue; and 'White Perfection,' a milky white.

In addition, there are several hybrids of relatively permanent character but of uncertain parentage. Light summer shearing encourages new shoots. Winter protection and division each second year may be necessary. Loosely known as hardy violas, they will not reproduce true to type from seeds.

Hardy Viola Cultivars

'Jersey Gem' was introduced by the late Thomas A. Weston in 1924 and it became a world-wide sensation. He raised it from a packet of English seeds. Answers to later inquiries suggested the parentage to be *V. cornuta* crossed with a white violetta. When true to name, it bears open-faced flowers of violet-blue all summer and is extremely hardy. However, many imposters have been grown from seeds so that genuine 'Jersey Gem' may no longer be available. Easily the finest hardy viola, it was quickly utilized for further breeding.

'Purple Heart' ('Jersey Gem' × 'Beauty of Laronne') produces large 2- to 3-inch flowers of rich purple, with wavy edges and yellow centers. The 12-inch stems make them especially desirable for cutting.

Other cultivars include: 'Catherine Sharp,' a compact, dark violet-purple, quite hardy; 'John Wallmark,' a long blooming gray-lavender, from Sweden; 'Yellow Vixen,' a soft yellow, hardy; 'Maggie Mott,' an excellent English favorite, but only for cool summers or partial shade, pale mauve with white eye; and 'Bluette,' a recent violet-blue introduction of prolific bloom if not stunned by the heat.

V. cucullata. Accustomed to wet spots from Newfoundland to Georgia, this species prefers moist shade in gardens, where it will

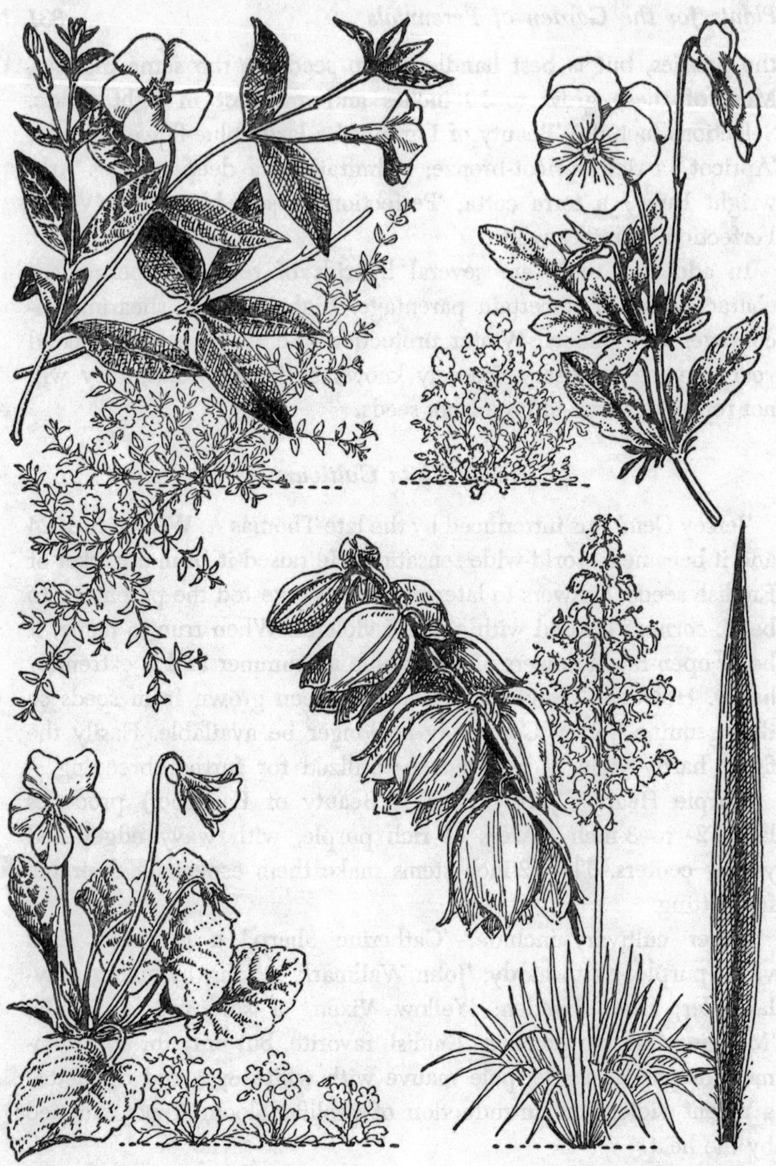

Vinca minor
Viola odorata

Viola cornuta
Yucca smalliana

quickly naturalize itself. Small bluish violet flowers with white and purple venation are found on 6-inch stems. There is also a carmine-red form.

V. odorata. This is the fragrant violet famed in florists' bouquets, poetry, and legend. Colors range from deep violet or white to the infrequently seen rose shades. There are also double forms, like the 'Parma' of greenhouse renown. In the early years of the century, there was considerable interest in greenhouse culture, and even today appreciable numbers are still raised for cutting purposes under glass and in frames. In gardens they flower from mid-April through May, although a type known as 'Semperflorens' is supposed to bloom later, into the summer.

Variety *rosina* is a 6-inch plant with many deep rose flowers of great fragrance in early spring. Seeding should be discouraged, for inferior purple mongrels may take over.

'Double Russian' is a small double purple, flowering in June, but some shade and moisture are imperative. 'Royal Robe' is dark purple, with 8-inch stems, and is very fragrant. 'White Wonder' ('The Czar') has faint blue and yellow streaks through chalky white petals.

V. pedata, Bird's Foot Violet. The pattern of the deeply cut basal foliage is the reason for the common name. Small flowers are violet on the upper petals and pale lilac on the lower ones. Many color variations occur. Poor, sandy, acid soil and full sun give best results.

Final Comment: A host of other species will surely interest the collector. With attention to cultural requirements, they may be of value in wild gardens.

YUCCA Spanish Bayonet, Adam's Needle Agavaceæ

Yucca smalliana (*Y. filamentosa*) is the only species of the genus that is reliably hardy and commonly grown throughout the country. It is satisfactory even in parts of Canada. This species is often used as a dominant accent plant in large borders or as specimens among shrubbery. The heavy basal leaves are long, spiny, and bayonet-shaped; clumps can be 2 feet tall, making an exotic effect which is even more pronounced when the plants are in flower. Branched scapes up to 5 feet in height bear white bell-like flowers from mid-July to mid-August.

Light sandy soil with good drainage and full sun should be provided. Plants are noted for their drought resistance. Propagation is by root cuttings or by division in spring. Digging the heavy root mass may be a chore; instead, rooted offsets may be severed from around the edges of the parent plant. Seeds, if well formed, germinate easily, but it takes two or three years for plants to reach flowering size.

Other species, such as *Y. gloriosa*, *Y. aloifolia*, and *Y. whipplei*, are encountered in nursery lists, but few gardeners can afford the space they require.

Part 3

SOME USEFUL LISTS

Plant Families Included, and Their Common Names

Common and Botanical Names of All Species Treated

Glossary

Outstanding Species, Their Characteristics, and Their Garden Uses

I Plant Families Included and Their Common Names

Acanthaceæ—Acanthus
Agavaceæ—Agave
Amaryllidaceæ—Amaryllis
Apocynaceæ—Dogbane
Aristolochiaceæ—Birthwort or Aristolochia
Asclepiadaceæ—Milkweed
Berberidaceæ—Barberry
Boraginaceæ—Borage
Buxaceæ—Box
Campanulaceæ—Bellflower
Caryophyllaceæ—Pink
Commelinaceæ—Spiderwort
Compositæ—Composite or Daisy
Crassulaceæ—Orpine
Cruciferæ—Mustard
Dipsacaceæ—Teasel
Euphorbiaceæ—Spurge
Fumariaceæ—Fumitory
Geraniaceæ—Geranium
Iridaceæ—Iris
Labiatæ—Mint
Leguminosæ—Pea
Liliaceæ—Lily
Linaceæ—Flax
Lobeliaceæ—Lobelia
Lythraceæ—Loosestrife
Malvaceæ—Mallow
Onagraceæ—Evening Primrose
Pæoniaceæ—Peony
Papaveraceæ—Poppy
Plumbaginaceæ—Plumbago or Leadwort
Polemoniaceæ—Phlox
Primulaceæ—Primrose
Ranunculaceæ—Crowfoot or Buttercup
Rosaceæ—Rose
Rubiaceæ—Madder
Rutaceæ—Rue
Saxifragaceæ—Saxifrage
Scrophulariaceæ—Figwort
Umbelliferæ—Parsley
Valerianaceæ—Valerian
Violaceæ—Violet

II Common and Botanical Names of All Species Treated of Plants Discussed

Common Name	*Botanical Name*
Aconite	*Aconitum* species
Adam's Needle	*Yucca* species, esp. *Y. smalliana*

Common Name	*Botanical Name*
Alkanet	*Anchusa* species
Alpine Aster	*Aster alpinus*
Alpine Pink	*Dianthus alpinus*
Alumroot	*Heuchera* species
Angels-hair	*Artemisia schmidtiana* var. *nana*
Asphodel	*Asphodeline lutea*
Avens	*Geum* species
Babys-breath	*Gypsophila* species
Balloon-flower	*Platycodon grandiflorum*
Barrenwort	*Epimedium* species
Basket-of-gold	*Alyssum saxatile*
Beach Wormwood	*Artemisia stelleriana*
Bearded Iris	*Iris germanica* types, usually
Beardtongue	*Penstemon* species
Bedstraw	*Galium* species
Beebalm	*Monarda didyma*
Bellflower	*Campanula* species
Bergamot	*Monarda fistulosa*
Bethlehem-sage	*Pulmonaria saccharata*
Betony	*Stachys* species
Blackberry-lily	*Belamcanda* species
Blanket-flower	*Gaillardia aristata*
Blazing Star	*Liatris* species
Bleeding Heart	*Dicentra* species, esp. *D. spectabilis*
Bloodflower	*Asclepias curassavica*
Bloodroot	*Sanguinaria canadensis*
Bluebell	*Campanula* species, *Mertensia* species
Bluebells of Scotland	*Campanula rotundifolia*
Bugbane	*Cimicifuga* species
Bugle, Bugleweed	*Ajuga* species
Bugloss	*Anchusa azurea*
Bunch-of-gold	*Doronicum pardalianches*
Burning Bush	*Dictamnus albus*
Bush-clover	*Lespedeza thunbergii*
Butterfly-weed	*Asclepias tuberosa*
Button Snakeroot	*Liatris* species
Campion	*Lychnis coronaria*
Candytuft	*Iberis* species
Canterbury Bells	*Campanula medium*
Cardinal-flower	*Lobelia cardinalis*
Carnation	*Dianthus caryophyllus*
Carpathian Harebell	*Campanula carpatica*
Catchfly	*Lychnis viscaria*

Common Name	*Botanical Name*
Catmint	*Nepeta* species
Catnip	*Nepeta cataria*
Chamomile	*Anthemis nobilis*
Cheddar Pink	*Dianthus gratianopolitanus*
Christmas-rose	*Helleborus niger*
Clary	*Salvia sclarea*
Clove Pink	*Dianthus caryophyllus, D. plumarius*
Columbine	*Aquilegia* species
Coneflower	*Rudbeckia* species
Coral Bells	*Heuchera* species
Cornflower	*Centaurea* species
Cornflower-aster	*Stokesia lævis*
Cottage Pink	*Dianthus plumarius*
Cowslip	*Primula veris*
Cranesbill	*Geranium* species
Creeping Jenny	*Lysimachia nummularia*
Creeping Myrtle	*Vinca minor*
Creeping Phlox	*Phlox stolonifera*
Crested Iris	*Iris cristata*
Culvers Root	*Veronicastrum virginicum*
Cupid's Dart	*Catananche cærulea*
Dalmatian Bellflower	*Campanula portenschlagiana*
Dames-rocket	*Hesperis matronalis*
Daylily	*Hemerocallis*
Dead Nettle	*Lamium maculatum*
Dittany	*Dictamnus albus*
Double Orange Daisy	*Erigeron aurantiacus*
Dropwort	*Filipendula hexapetala*
Dunesilver	*Artemisia stelleriana*
Dusty Meadowrue	*Thalictrum rugosum*
Dusty Miller	*Artemisia stelleriana, Lychnis coronaria,* and almost any other gray-leaved plant
Dutchman's Breeches	*Dicentra cucullaria*
English Daisy	*Bellis perennis*
Eryngo	*Eryngium* species
European Ginger	*Asarum europæum*
Evening-primrose	Some *Œnothera* species
False Babys-breath	*Galium aristatum*
False Dragonhead	*Physostegia virginiana*
False Indigo	*Baptisia* species
False Lupine	*Thermopsis* species
False Rock-cress	*Aubrieta deltoidea*

Common Name	*Botanical Name*
False Spirea	*Astilbe* species
False Starwort	*Boltonia* species
Fernleaf Peony	*Pæonia tenuifolia*
Feverfew	*Chrysanthemum parthenium*
Flax	*Linum* species
Fleabane	*Erigeron* species
Forget-me-not	*Myosotis* species
Foxglove	*Digitalis* species
Foxtail-lily	*Eremurus* species
Fraxinella	*Dictamnus albus*
Fumitory	*Corydalis* species
Funkia	*Hosta* species
Garden-heliotrope	*Valeriana officinalis*
Gas-plant	*Dictamnus albus*
Gayfeather	*Liatris* species
German Catchfly	*Lychnis viscaria*
Germander	*Teucrium chamædrys*
German Iris	*Iris germanica* types and hybrids
Ghost-plant	*Artemisia albula*
Giant Scabiosa	*Cephalaria tatarica*
Ginger	*Asarum* species
Globeflower	*Trollius* species
Globe-thistle	*Echinops*
Goatsbeard	*Aruncus sylvester*
Gold-banded Lily	*Lilium auratum*
Golden-aster	*Chrysopsis* species
Golden Eardrops	*Dicentra chrysantha*
Goldenglow	*Rudbeckia laciniata* var. *hortensis*
Golden Marguerite	*Anthemis tinctoria*
Goldenstar	*Chrysogonum virginianum*
Goldentuft	*Alyssum saxatile*
Gooseneck Loosestrife	*Lysimachia clethroides*
Grass Pink	*Dianthus plumarius*
Great Blue Lobelia	*Lobelia siphilitica*
Greek Valerian	*Polemonium cæruleum*
Ground Clematis	*Clematis recta*
Ground-pink	*Phlox subulata*
Hardy Ageratum	*Eupatorium cœlestinum*
Hardy Bachelor's Button	*Centaurea* species
Hardy Statice	*Limonium* species
Hardy Zinnia	*Heliopsis* species
Harebell	*Campanula rotundifolia*
Heath Aster	*Aster ericoides*
Hellebore	*Helleborus* species

Common Name	*Botanical Name*
Hemp-agrimony	*Eupatorium cannabinum 'Flore-pleno'*
Hen-and-chickens	*Sempervivum* species
Hollyhock	*Althæa rosea*
Horned Violet	*Viola cornuta*
Iceland Poppy	*Papaver nudicaule*
Italian Aster	*Aster amellus*
Jacob's Ladder	*Polemonium cæruleum*
Japanese Anemone	*Anemone hybrida*
Japanese Iris	*Iris kæmpferi*
Japanese Spurge	*Pachysandra terminalis*
Joe Pye-weed	*Eupatorium purpureum*
Jove's (Jupiter's) Beard	*Centranthus ruber*
Kamchatka Meadowsweet	*Filipendula camtschatica*
Lady's Mantle	*Alchemilla vulgaris*
Lambs-ear	*Stachys olympica*
Larkspur	*Delphinium* species
Lavender	*Lavandula officinalis*
Lavender Mist	*Thalictrum rochebrunianum*
Leadwort	*Ceratostigma plumbaginoides*
Lenten-rose	*Helleborus orientalis*
Leopardsbane	*Doronicum* species
Lily	*Lilium* species
Lily-of-the-valley	*Convallaria majalis*
Loosestrife	*Lysimachia* species and *Lythrum*
Lungwort	*Pulmonaria* species
Lupine	*Lupinus* species
Madonna Lily	*Lilium candidum*
Madwort	*Alyssum* species
Maiden Pink	*Dianthus deltoides*
Maltese Cross	*Lychnis chalcedonica*
Martha Washington Plume	*Filipendula rubra* var. *venusta*
Mary-and-Joseph	*Pulmonaria angustifolia*
Matricaria	*Chrysanthemum parthenium*
Meadow-rue	*Thalictrum* species
Meadowsweet	*Filipendula* species
Michaelmas Daisy	Usually *Aster novi-belgii* cultivars
Milfoil	*Achillea* species
Milkweed	*Asclepias* species
Mist-flower	*Eupatorium cœlestinum*
Moneywort	*Lysimachia nummularia*
Monkshood	*Aconitum* species
Moss Phlox, Moss-pink	*Phlox subulata*
Mountain-bluet	*Centaurea montana*

Common Name	*Botanical Name*
Mourning Bride	*Scabiosa* species
Mouse-ear Chickweed	*Cerastium* species
Mugwort	*Artemisia lactiflora*
Mullein	*Verbascum*
Mullein-pink	*Lychnis coronaria*
Mum	*Chrysanthemum morifolium* cultivars
Myrtle	*Vinca minor*
New England Aster	*Aster novæ-angliæ*
New York Aster	*Aster novi-belgii*
Nippon Daisy	*Chrysanthemum nipponicum*
Northern Bedstraw	*Galium boreale*
Obedient-plant	*Physostegia virginiana*
Old Woman	*Artemisia stelleriana*
Orange Sunflower	*Heliopsis* species
Oriental Poppy	*Papaver orientale*
Oswego Tea	*Monarda didyma*
Oxlip	*Primula elatior*
Painted Daisy	*Chrysanthemum coccineum*
Pansy	*Viola tricolor* var. *hortensis*
Pasque-flower	*Anemone pulsatilla*
Peachbells	*Campanula persicifolia*
Peony	*Pæonia* species and cultivars
Periwinkle	*Vinca* species
Peruvian Lily	*Alstrœmeria aurantiaca*
Pincushion Flower	*Scabiosa* species
Pinks	*Dianthus* species
Plantain-lily	*Hosta* species
Plume Bleeding Heart	*Dicentra eximia*
Plume-poppy	*Macleaya cordata*
Poppy	*Papaver* species
Poppy Mallow	*Callirhoë involucrata*
Prairie Mallow	*Sidalcea* species and hybrids
Prickly Comfrey	*Symphytum asperum*
Primrose	*Primula* species
Purple Bush-clover	*Lespedeza thunbergii*
Purple Coneflower	*Echinacea purpurea*
Purple Loosestrife	*Lythrum salicaria*
Pyrethrum	*Chrysanthemum coccineum*
Queen-of-the-meadow	*Filipendula ulmaria*
Queen-of-the-prairie	*Filipendula rubra*
Red-hot Poker	*Kniphofia* species
Red Valerian	*Centranthus* species
Regal Lily	*Lilium regale*

Common Name	*Botanical Name*
Rock-cress	*Arabis* species
Rock-jasmine	*Androsace* species
Rose Campion	*Lychnis coronaria*
Rose Mallow	*Hibiscus* species
Sage (general)	*Salvia* species
Sage (specific)	*Salvia officinalis*
Sand Pink	*Dianthus arenarius*
Sandwort	*Arenaria cæspitosa* var. *verna*
Saxifrage	*Saxifraga* species
Scarlet Turk's Cap	*Lilium pumilum*
Sea-holly	*Eryngium* species
Sea-lavender	*Limonium* species
Sea-pink	*Armeria* species
Shasta Daisy	*Chrysanthemum maximum*
Shooting Star	*Dodecatheon* (chiefly *D. meadia*)
Showy Aster	*Aster spectabilis*
Siberian Bugloss	*Brunnera macrophylla*
Siberian Iris	*Iris sibirica*
Silver King	*Artemisia albula*
Six-petaled Dropwort	*Filipendula hexapetala*
Snakeroot	*Cimicifuga* species
Sneezeweed	*Helenium autumnale*
Sneezewort	*Achillea ptarmica*
Snow-in-summer	*Cerastium tomentosum*
Snow Thoroughwort	*Eupatorium rugosum*
Soapwort	*Saponaria* species
Soldiers-and-sailors	*Pulmonaria angustifolia*
Solomon's Seal	*Polygonatum* species
Spanish Bayonet	*Yucca smalliana*
Speedwell	*Veronica* species
Spiderwort	*Tradescantia virginiana*
Spring Phlox	*Phlox divaricata*
Spurge	*Euphorbia* species and *Pachysandra*
Starry Grasswort	*Cerastium* species
Starwort	*Aster* species
Stokes Aster	*Stokesia lævis*
Stonecress	*Æthionema* species
Stonecrop	*Sedum* species
Summer Phlox	*Phlox paniculata*
Sundrops	Various *Œnothera* species
Sunflower	*Helianthus* species
Sweet William	*Dianthus barbatus*
Sweet Woodruff	*Asperula odorata*
Tarragon	*Artemisia dracunculus*

Common Name	*Botanical Name*
Thoroughwort	*Eupatorium* species
Thread-leaf Coreopsis	*Coreopsis verticillata*
Thrift	*Armeria* species
Thyme	*Thymus* species
Tickseed	*Coreopsis* species
Torch-lily	*Kniphofia* species
Trailing-myrtle	*Vinca minor*
Tree-celandine	*Macleaya cordata*
Tripmadam	*Sedum acre*
Tritoma	*Kniphofia* species
Tufted Pansy	*Viola cornuta*
Tunic-flower	*Tunica saxifraga*
Valerian	*Centranthus ruber, Valeriana officinalis*
Vesper Iris	*Iris dichotoma*
Violet	*Viola* species
Virginia Bluebells	*Mertensia virginica*
Waldmeister	*Asperula odorata*
Wall-cress	*Arabis* species
Wall-pepper	*Sedum acre*
Wand Loosestrife	*Lythrum virgatum*
Western Bleeding Heart	*Dicentra formosa*
White Snakeroot	*Eupatorium rugosum*
Wild Ginger	*Asarum canadense*
Wild Indigo	*Baptisia* species
Wild Senna	*Cassia* species
Wild Sweet William	*Phlox divaricata*
Willow Amsonia	*Amsonia tabernæmontana*
Windflower	*Anemone* species
Wind-primrose	*Œnothera speciosa*
Winter-aconite	*Eranthis hyemalis*
Wolfsbane	*Aconitum vulparia*
Woodruff	*Asperula* species
Wormwood	*Artemisia* species
Yarrow	*Achillea* species
Yellow Bedstraw	*Galium verum*
Yellow Scabiosa	*Cephalaria tatarica*
Yellowtuft	*Alyssum murale*
Yellow Wild Indigo	*Baptisia tinctoria*

Glossary

Acid. With respect to soils, having a pH below 7.0. Acid soils have, and require for their maintenance, a high proportion of nitrogen.

Alkaline. With respect to soils, having a pH above 7.0. Alkaline soils usually have a considerable lime content, as opposed to acid soils.

Annual. A plant that completes its life cycle from seed to maturity to death in one growing season.

Anther. Pollen-bearing portion of a stamen.

Asexual. In plant propagation, by means other than by seed.

Axil. The angle formed by a leaf-stalk and a stem at their point of junction.

Axis. A stem of a plant, upon which leaves or flowers are borne.

Biennial. A plant that normally requires two growing seasons to complete its life cycle from seed to maturity to death.

Binomial. Scientific name of a species, composed of two words in Latin or Latinized form.

Bract. Modified leaf, especially one of the leaves (usually small but sometimes large and petal-like) in a flower cluster or associated with individual flowers.

Bulb. Thickened, basal portion of some plants, made up chiefly of overlapping, fleshy scales.

Bulbel. Bulb coming from the mother bulb; also spelled *bulbil.*

Bulblet. Small bulb produced in a leaf axil or other unusual position.

Calyx. Outer circle of floral segments: the sepals collectively. When a flower has no corolla, calyx may be composed of petaloid sepals.

Capitate. Of flowers, in a head or compact cluster.

Cauline. Of or pertaining to a stem.

Chromosome. One of a given number of microscopic bodies in almost all living cells, arranged in a definite set for each given kind of plant or animal, and largely controlling development; transferred more or less intact by inheritance.

Compound. Composed of two or more similar parts in one organ; of a leaf, consisting of separate divisions, called leaflets, each separately attached to the midrib or one of its branches.

Cordate. Heart-shaped at the base.

Corolla. Inner circle of floral segments; the petals collectively.

Corymb. Flat-topped cluster of flowers whose stalks arise from different points on one axis. The outer flowers usually open first.

Crown. Region of union between the roots and above-ground portions of a plant; the part from which the stem arises.

Cultivar. Variety of a plant species distinguished by characteristics significant in cultivation.
Cyme. Broad, flat-topped flower cluster; usually much branched.
Digitate. Radiating like the fingers of a hand.
Disk. Usually an elevated, ring-shaped development of a receptacle about the pistil; sometimes the receptacle itself.
Family. Group of related genera; a family name usually ends in "-aceæ." (Some families consist of but a single genus which has no close relatives.)
Farina. Whitish, mealy powder which occurs on portions of certain plants.
Filament. The stalk of a stamen.
Floret. Individual flower of a dense inflorescence.
Genus. Group of related species. (Some genera consist of but a single species which has no close relatives.) The generic name is the first word of a scientific binomial, and is always capitalized when so used; also when it stands alone, unless it is being used as a common name.
Glabrous. Not hairy.
Glaucous. Covered with a whitish bloom.
Herbaceous. Having no persistent woody parts above ground.
Humus. Organic matter of soil, such as manure, leafmold, compost, peatmoss, formed by partial decomposition of animal or vegetable material.
Hybrid. Plant (or animal) resulting from crossing two parents classified in different groups (varieties, species, etc.).
Inflorescence. Group of flowers arranged in a definite manner, not including foliage leaves.
Lanceolate. Lance-shaped, much longer than broad, and tapering to the apex.
Node. Joint where a leaf is, or could be, borne.
Obovate. With the outline of an egg, the broadest portion away from the base or stalk.
Ovary. Basal part of a pistil, containing the rudimentary seeds.
Ovate. With the outline of an egg, the broadest portion near the base or stalk.
Palmate. Lobed or divided in the form of a hand, the segments radiating from a single point.
Panicle. A loose, much branched inflorescence.
Pedicel. Stem of a single flower in a flower cluster.
Peduncle. Stem of a flower cluster.
Perennial. A plant that lives three or more years.
Perianth. Calyx plus corolla: the sepals and petals collectively.
Petal. One of the inner floral segments, usually colored otherwise than leaf-green and often showy; the petals together compose the corolla.
Petaloid. Like a petal in color and form.

Petiole. Stalk of a leaf.

pH. An arbitrary symbol denoting the degree of acidity or alkalinity, for instance in soils. When the reaction is expressed as pH 7.0, the soil is neutral. Below 7.0 the soil is acid; above 7.0 it is alkaline. Figures below 5.6 and above 8.4 indicate extremes that are unfavorable to most plants.

Pinnate. Of leaves, in a feather-like formation, with leaflets of a compound leaf on both sides of a common midrib (rachis); also used of the veins.

Pistil. Female organ of a flower, usually composed of stigma, style, and ovary. The ovary contains the rudiments of the seeds.

Pubescent. Bearing hairs.

Raceme. Inflorescence composed of stalked flowers attached along a common axis.

Rachis. The axis of an inflorescence or the midrib of a compound leaf.

Ray. Straplike floret, often circumferential, of many composite flowers.

Receptacle. End of a stem on which the parts of one flower are borne; or, in the Compositæ, the structure on which the florets of a single flower head are borne.

Rhizome. Horizontally extended underground stem; distinguished from a root by the presence of nodes, buds, or scale-like leaves.

Rosette. Group of leaves radiating from a central crown, usually very close to the ground.

Scape. Flower stalk arising from the ground, bearing one or many flowers; it may have bracts, but no true leaves.

Selection. Special form of a plant chosen for certain characteristics.

Sepal. One segment of the calyx, usually green but sometimes otherwise colored, especially when a corolla is lacking.

Species. Group of plants, in rank between genus and variety, alike in several characteristics, most of which reappear in offspring. A species is named by a binomial (that is, with two words in Latin or Latinized form).

Spike. Spire-like inflorescence, usually unbranched, whose flowers have no stalks.

Stalk. The part of any organ by which it is attached, such as the petiole of a leaf or the peduncle of a flower cluster.

Stamen. Male, or pollen-bearing, organ of a flower, usually composed of filament and anther.

Stem. Leaf-bearing and flower-bearing axis of a plant.

Stigma. In the pistil of a flower, the portion that receives the pollen.

Stolon. Horizontal stem at the surface of the ground, giving rise to new aerial parts at its tip; similar stems (rhizomes) just beneath the surface are also loosely referred to as stolons.

Style. More or less elongated portion of the pistil between ovary and stigma.

Subshrub. A rather woody plant, or a very small shrub.

Subspecies. Group subordinate to a species, often typical of a given geographical region.
Taxonomic. Relating to laws governing classification.
Ternate. Appearing or divided in units of three.
Tomentose. Densely woolly.
Tuber. Enlarged subterranean part, usually of a stem, sometimes of a root.
Umbel. Inflorescence, often flat-topped, in which the pedicels (also the peduncles if it is compound) arise from a common point, like ribs of an umbrella.
Variant. Individual plant which differs from others of its kind or group in some of its characteristics.
Variety. Group of plants subordinate to species, known to occur in the wild, properly named by three words in Latin or Latinized form.
Whorl. Group of three or more leaves, flowers, or other parts arising from the same point, in a ring.

Outstanding Species, Their Characteristics, and Their Garden Uses

In using the following chart, which is based on plant performance in central New York State, it must be remembered that plants exhibit organic diversity. Average heights are given, but they depend on the particular cultivar, soil conditions, location, and climate. Cutting value and fragrance may indicate flowers or foliage or both. Foliage effect may refer to texture, color, or over-all effect. Sun, shade, dry, and moist are relative terms; these are amplified in the discussion of each genus.

Under period of bloom, each x represents approximately 10 days. In different parts of the country, where the season is earlier or later, dates will have to be moved forward or backward, but the sequence of bloom of the various plants will remain approximately the same.

Abbreviations:

Color: B Blue, L Lavender, O Orange, P Purple, Pn Pink, R Red, V Various, W White, Y Yellow

Situation: D Dry, M Moist, SU Sun, SH Shade

Special points: C Cut, FR Fragrance, FO Foliage effect

CHECK LIST OF OUTSTANDING SPECIES

SCIENTIFIC NAME	HEIGHT IN FEET	COLOR	SUN OR SHADE	DRY OR MOIST	CUT	FRA-GRANCE	FOLIAGE EFFECT	PERIOD OF BLOOM: MAR	APR	MAY	JUN	JUL	AUG	SEP
Achillea filipendulina	4	Y	SU	D	C		FO					xx	xxx	
Achillea tomentosa	¾	Y	SU	D			FO				xx	xxx		
Aconitum carmichaelii	3½	B	SH		C		FO							xxx
Aconitum napellus	4	P	SH		C		FO						xxx	x
Æthionema grandiflorum	1	Pn	SU	D			FO			x	xx			
Ajuga reptans	¾	B	SH							xx	xx			
Althaea rosea	6	V	SU									xx	xxx	
Alyssum saxatile	1	Y	SU				FO		x	xxx				
Amsonia tabernæmontana	3	B			C		FO			x	xx			
Anchusa azurea	5	B	SU								xxx	xxx	xx	
Anemone × hybrida	4	Pn W	SH		C		FO						xx	xxx
Anemone pulsatilla	1	P W Pn		D					xx	xx				
Anthemis tinctoria	3	Y	SU	D	C	FR	FO				x	xxx	xxx	
Aquilegia × hybrida	3	V			C		FO				xxx	xx		
Arabis caucasica	1	W	SU		C		FO		xx	xxx				
Armeria maritima	1	R Pn	SU	D	C		FO			xx	xxx			
Artemisia lactiflora	4	W	SU		C								xxx	xx
Artemisia schmidtiana var. *nana*	¾	—	SU	D			FO							
Asarum europæum	¾	—	SH	M			FO							
Asclepias tuberosa	3	O	SU	D	C							x	xxx	

Asperula odorata	¾	W	SH	M	C	FR	FO			x	xx			
Aster amellus	2	P R	SU										xx	xx
Aster novi-belgii	4	V	SU										x	xxx
Astilbe × arendsii	2½	R Pn W	SH	M	C		FO					xx	x	
Aubrieta deltoidea	½	P							x	xxx	xx			
Baptisia australis	4	B			C		FO				xxx			
Bergenia cordifolia	1½	Pn	SH	M	C		FO		x	xxx				
Brunnera macrophylla	1½	B	SH						xx	xxx	x			
Campanula carpatica	1	P B W					FO					xx	xxx	x
Campanula glomerata	2½	P	SH		C						xx	xx		
Campanula latifolia	3	P	SH								xx			
Campanula medium	2½	P B Pn W									x	xx		
Campanula persicifolia	3	B W	SH		C		FO				x	xxx		
Catananche cærulea	2	B W	SU	D	C							xxx	xxx	
Centaurea dealbata	2½	L			C		FO				xx	xxx		
Centaurea montana	2	B								x	xx		x	xx
Centranthus ruber	2½	R		D		FR						xx	xxx	x
Cephalaria tatarica	6	Y			C							xx	x	
Cerastium tomentosum	¾	W	SU	D			FO			x	xxx			
Ceratostigma plumbaginoides	1	B					FO						xx	xxx
Chrysanthemum coccineum	2½	R Pn W	SU		C		FO				xxx	x		
Chrysanthemum maximum	3	W			C						xxx	xxx	xx	

Check List of Outstanding Species (continued)

SCIENTIFIC NAME	HEIGHT IN FEET	COLOR	SUN OR SHADE	DRY OR MOIST	CUT	FRAGRANCE	FOLIAGE EFFECT	PERIOD OF BLOOM MAR	APR	MAY	JUN	JUL	AUG	SEP
Chrysanthemum morifolium	1–3½	V			C	FR							xx	xxx
Chrysanthemum parthenium	1½	W Y	SU		C							xxx	xx	
Cimicifuga racemosa	6	W	SH	M	C		FO					xxx	x	
Clematis integrifolia	2	B	SH								xxx	xx		
Convallaria majalis	1	W	SH		C	FR	FO			xx				
Coreopsis lanceolata	2½	Y	SU	D	C						x	xxx	xxx	xx
Coreopsis verticillata	3	Y	SU		C		FO				x	xxx	xx	
Corydalis lutea	1	Y	SH		C		FO			x	xxx	xxx	xxx	
Delphinium cheilanthum	4	B W			C						x	xxx		
Delphinium elatum	6	B P W			C						x	xxx		
Dianthus barbatus	½–2	V			C						xx	xxx		
Dianthus plumarius	1	R Pn W		D	C	FR	FO			x	xxx			
Dicentra eximia	1½	Pn	SH		C		FO			xxx	xxx	xxx	x	
Dicentra spectabilis	2¾	R W	SH		C					xx	xxx			
Dictamnus albus	3	W Pn			C	FR	FO				xxx			
Digitalis purpurea	5	L P W	SH		C						xx	xx		
Dodecatheon meadia	1¾	W Pn	SH							xxx	xx			
Doronicum pardalianches	3	Y			C					xxx	x			

Echinacea purpurea	4	P		D	C							x	xxx	x
Echinops 'Taplow Blue'	4	B		D	C		FO					xx	xxx	x
Epimedium species	1½	W Y R	SH		C		FO			xx	x			
Eranthis hyemalis	½	Y	SU					xx	xx					
Eupatorium cœlestinum	2	P			C								x	xxx
Euphorbia epithymoides	2	Y	SU	D			FO			xx	x			
Filipendula hexapetala	1½	W	SH				FO				xxx			
Filipendula rubra	4	R Pn	SH	M							x	xx		
Filipendula ulmaria	4	W	SH			FR						xxx		
Gaillardia aristata	3	Y R	SU	D	C						xxx	xxx	xxx	xx
Geranium grandiflorum	1¼	P								x	xxx	x		
Geranium sanguineum	1	R P	SH				FO			x	xxx	xxx	x	
Geum cultivars	2½	R O Y					FO			xx	xxx	x		
Gypsophila paniculata	3	W	SU	D	C							xxx	xxx	
Gypsophila repens	½	W Pn	SU	D						x	xxx	xxx	x	
Helenium autumnale	3	Y R	SU	M	C								xx	xxx
Heliopsis scabra	3	Y	SU		C							xxx	xxx	xxx
Helleborus niger	1¼	W Pn	SH		C		FO	November to March						
Helleborus orientalis	1¼	W Pn	SH		C		FO	xxx	xxx	xx				
Hemerocallis cultivars	2–4	Y O R	SH					late May to Sept according to cultivar						
Heuchera sanguinea	1½	R Pn W	SH		C		FO			x	xxx	xxx	xxx	x
Hibiscus hybrids	6	R W Pn	SH	M									xx	xx
Hosta fortunei	3	L W	SH		C		FO				x	xxx		
Hosta lancifolia	2	L	SH		C		FO						xxx	x

Check List of Outstanding Species (continued)

SCIENTIFIC NAME	HEIGHT IN FEET	COLOR	SUN OR SHADE	DRY OR MOIST	CUT	FRAGRANCE	FOLIAGE EFFECT	PERIOD OF BLOOM MAR	APR	MAY	JUN	JUL	AUG	SEP
Hosta plantaginea	2½	W	SH		C	FR	FO						xx	xxx
Hosta ventricosa	2½	B	SH		C		FO					xxx		
Iberis sempervirens	1	W					FO			xxx	x			
Iris, dwarf bearded	1½	V	SU						x	xxx				
Iris, tall bearded	3	V	SU			FR	FO			xx	xx			
Iris kaempferi	3	R P W	SH	M							xx	xxx		
Iris sibirica	3	R P W	SH		C		FO				xxx			
Kniphofia cultivars	2½	R Y O W	SU		C		FO					xx	xxx	x
Lamium maculatum	1	L W	SH				FO		x	xxx	xxx	xxx	xxx	x
Lavandula officinalis	2	L P		D	C	FR	FO				x	xxx	xxx	
Liatris species	2–4	L P W	SU		C							x	xxx	x
Limonium latifolium	2½	L	SU		C								xxx	x
Linum flavum	1¾	Y	SU	D							x	xxx	xx	
Linum perenne	2	B W	SU	D			FO			x	xxx	xxx	xx	
Lobelia cardinalis	4	R	SH	M	C							x	xxx	xx
Lupinus polyphyllus	4	V			C		FO				xxx	x		
Lychnis chalcedonica	3	R		D							x	xxx		
Lychnis coronaria	2	R P W		D			FO				x	xxx	x	
Lychnis viscaria	1¾	R Pn									xxx	x		
Lysimachia clethroides	3	W	SH	M	C							xx	xxx	
Lysimachia punctata	3	Y	SH	M							xx	xx		
Lythrum cultivars	4	R P	SH	M	C							xxx	xxx	

Macleaya cordata	6	W			C		FO					xx	x	
Mertensia virginica	2	B	SH	M					x	xxx				
Monarda didyma	3½	R Pn W	SH		C	FR						xxx	xxx	
Myosotis scorpioides	1	B	SH	M							xxx	xxx	xxx	
Nepeta × faassenii	1½	B				FR	FO				xxx	xxx	xxx	x
Œnothera tetragona	2	Y	SU								xx	xxx	x	
Pachysandra terminalis	¾	—	SH				FO							
Papaver orientale	3	R O W									xxx			
Pæonia lactiflora	3	W Pn R			C	FR	FO			xx	xxx			
Pæonia suffruticosa	6	R Pn W Y								xx	x			
Pæonia tenuifolia	2	R			C		FO			xx	x			
Penstemon torreyi	3	R		D	C						x	xxx		
Phlox carolina	3½	W P			C					x	xxx			
Phlox divaricata	1½	B W	SH			FR				xxx	x			
Phlox paniculata	3	V										xxx	xxx	x
Phlox subulata	½	V					FO			xxx	x			
Physostegia virginiana	3½	W Pn L			C							x	xxx	x
Platycodon grandiflorum	3	P W B		D								xx	xxx	x
Polemonium cæruleum	2	B W	SH				FO			x	xxx	x		
Primula denticulata	¾	L W	SH		C				x	xx				
Primula japonica	1¼	R W Pn	SH		C					x	xxx	x		
Primula × polyantha	¾	V	SH		C				xx	xxx				
Pulmonaria saccharata	1	B	SH				FO		xx	xxx				
Rudbeckia sullivantii	2½	Y	SU		C								xxx	x

Check List of Outstanding Species (continued)

SCIENTIFIC NAME	HEIGHT IN FEET	COLOR	SUN OR SHADE	DRY OR MOIST	CUT	FRAGRANCE	FOLIAGE EFFECT	PERIOD OF BLOOM MAR	APR	MAY	JUN	JUL	AUG	SEP
Salvia hæmatodes	3	B			C						xxx	x		
Salvia pratensis	2	P B W								x	xxx	x		
Salvia × superba	2½	P									x	xxx	xx	
Saponaria ocymoides	½	Pn	SU	D						x	xxx			
Scabiosa caucasica	2	B			C							xxx	x	
Sedum spectabile	1½	P R	SU				FO						xx	xx
Stachys olympica	1	Pn	SH				FO				xx	xx		
Stokesia lævis	1¾	B W										xx	xxx	
Teucrium chamædrys	1	—	SU				FO							
Thalictrum aquilegifolium	3	P L W	SH		C					x	xxx			
Thalictrum rochebrunianum	4	L	SH		C							x	xxx	x
Thalictrum rugosum	6	Y	SH		C		FO					xx	xx	
Thermopsis caroliniana	4	Y			C						xx	x		
Thymus serpyllum	⅓	P L R	SU			FR					xxx	xxx	x	
Tradescantia cultivars	1½–3	B W P	SH							x	xx		x	xx
Trollius europæus	2	Y	SH	M	C					xxx	x			
Trollius ledebouri	3	Y O	SH	M	C						xxx			
Tunica saxifraga	¾	Pn W	SU								xx	xxx		
Valeriana officinalis	4	W L	SH	M	C	FR						xxx	xx	

Veronica latifolia	2	B									xxx			
Veronica longifolia	2½	B W P			C							xx	xxx	
Veronica prostrata	½	P Pn B								xx	x			
Veronica spicata	1½	B Pn			C						x	xxx		
Vinca minor	½	B	SH				FO		x	xxx	x			
Viola cornuta	¾	V	SH		C					xx	xxx	xxx	xxx	xx
Viola odorata	¼	P W	SH		C	FR			x	xxx				
Yucca smalliana	5	W	SU	D	C		FO					xx	xx	

Index

Terms defined in the Glossary (pages 344–347) are not included.

For common names not listed here, see pages 336–343 where appropriate generic name is included.

Page numbers in **boldface** type indicate the major treatment of genus concerned. Illustrations are listed in *italic* type.